ROCK ALMANAC

CHARLIE GILLETT is co-producer for Oval Records in London, England. He is the author of two books on rock music, *The Sound of the City* and *Making Tracks*. He hosts "Honky Tonk" and "Single File" on BBC Radio London.

STEPHEN NUGENT is an American anthropologist currently living in Brazil.

ANCHOR BOOKS
ANCHOR PRESS/DOUBLEDAY
GARDEN CITY, NEW YORK
1978

ROCK ALMANAC

ROCK ALMANAC

**TOP TWENTY
AMERICAN AND BRITISH
SINGLES AND ALBUMS
OF THE
'50s, '60s, and '70s**

**edited by
STEPHEN NUGENT AND CHARLIE GILLETT**

ROCK ALMANAC

Library of Congress Cataloging in Publication Data
Gillett, Charlie.
Rock Almanac.

1. Rock Music—United States—Discography.
2. Rock Music—Great Britain—Discography.
I. Nugent, Stephen, joint author. II. Title.
ML156.4.P6G54   016.7899'12
ISBN: 0-385-11204-1
Library of Congress Catalog Card Number 75–32294

CONTENTS

CONTRIBUTORS

CHARLIE GILLETT is co-producer for Oval Records in London, England. He is the author of two books on rock, *The Sound of the City* and *Making Tracks*. He hosts "Honky Tonk" and "Single File" on BBC Radio London.

STEPHEN NUGENT is an American anthropologist currently living in Brazil.

PETE AND ANNIE FOWLER live in Macclesfield, England, where Pete teaches and records for Oval Records.

SIMON FRITH teaches sociology at the University of Warwick, England, and writes for *Let It Rock* and other publications. His book *The Sociology of Rock* is forthcoming.

PAUL GAMBACCINI is *Rolling Stone's* man in London, where he presents a weekly show on BBC's Radio One.

DAVID MARSH works for *Rolling Stone* in New York and contributes to *Creem,* the New York *Times,* and other publications.

MARK STEN plays in a band and collects records in Portland, Oregon.

CARL GAYLE is an editor of *Black Music* in London, where he is the leading writer on Jamaican music.

INTRODUCTION

Through a combination of fading memories, wishful thinking, and ignorance, all kinds of distortions affect the vernacular history of popular music as recalled in conversation and retold in the music press. The prime purpose of *Rock Almanac* is to re-establish what actually happened, and when. Here, in alphabetical order, are all the singers and musicians, comedians and narrators, film stars, footballers and animals who ever had a record make the top twenty in America or Britain.

Listed here are the records that were played most on the radio and jukeboxes, the albums that sold the most copies over the counters. If you never heard some of the hits listed here, or if you can't find some others that you're sure were really big hits, it could be because in the United States each radio station has its own countdown of the week's top records, and every list is different. So when *Billboard* makes a national chart, inevitably some big local hits get left out because not every region is playing them. Paul Gambaccini's article "American Radio Today," which follows, further explains this policy.

In Britain it's easier to compute a national chart, because of the pervasive influence of the nationally networked BBC Radio One and Radio Two (one pop, the other MOR). Not every record played by the BBC is inevitably a big seller, but it's hard to get into the national top twenty unless the BBC pop station plays it. In these pages Simon Frith reports on the peculiarities of the market in his piece "Playing Records in Britain." Frith illustrates the difficulty of trying to make any sort of generalization about taste in music as the industry perceives it. Far too many records are released each week for anyone to absorb. The various labels' rationales for what they put out are not consistent, and this further disrupts easy explanations of the process that follows means/ends formulas. Some singles are not intended to reach the charts in the first place; some are samples meant only to attract attention to albums by the same artists; others are wholly inexplicable. Among the points made in the article, it is noted that the success of a given record label may often hinge on the showing of no more than one or two performers. The costs of running such an industry are high, payment being gleefully extracted from performers and consumers.

Both those articles look behind the hits to see how they got there. In "The In-Between Years," Mark Sten takes the log of hits head on and sifts through the formulas and fads to see what ingenuity and originality, if any, can be found in what is widely considered to be the fallow period of the rock era, 1958–63. The creative spirit of rock 'n' roll had been sapped, and the surge of the Beatles had yet to come. Was there anything of interest in between? Mark leaves no stone unturned in his quest to find out. For devout collectors who want even more information than we've supplied here, Joel Whitburn may be the answer to your needs. He has compiled several privately published monographs listing every entry to *Billboard*'s Pop Hot 100, Rhythm and Blues, Country & Western, Album, and Easy Listening charts, which he supplies from P. O. Box 82, Menomonee Falls, Wisconsin 53051.

Carl Gayle, writing about Jamaican music, presents a signal opportunity for most readers—the chance to read about ska/blue beat/reggae/skank as it is understood by one who knows what he has been listening to and talking about. He shatters some illusions and looks at the real reggae thing. Of all the styles of music currently treated as possible successors to the frequently abandoned center-stage spotlight, Jamaican music has been the subject of more lame introductions than most, but Gayle sets out not only a history of the music's passage to England, but also a rendering of the milieu in which the music has thrived. Although until recently most American readers were introduced to Jamaican music through Johnny Nash (who isn't mentioned in Gayle's piece at all, and who, it should be noted, once helped perpetrate a song called "Teen Commandments") and the redoubtable Jimmy Cliff and equally formidable Desmond Dekker, most of the "real fans" twist their ears to a far more esoteric brand of the blues.

The only palpable reason for introducing Jamaican music to a broader audience is to debunk prevailing misconceptions and allow the progenitors the opportunity to pick up a little more than the spare change that now falls their way. There are substantial similarities between rock 'n' roll (pre-1960) and skank, and even now the process of commercializing the music has resulted in a noticeable disaffection of "real fans." The lyrics of much of the music will keep it off the radio, however, except in its most bowdlerized forms. What has passed for suggestiveness in American hits such as Hank Ballard's series of "Annie" records is bush-league pranksterism compared to skank poesy.

So here, we hope, is all you, the home researcher, need to do it yourself. What can be made of the statistic that more than two thirds of the artists who made the American top twenty never returned? Is the audience so fickle, or the star's ambition so easily satisfied, or the music business so rough?

Before leaving you to it, we're providing two recommended lists, one of one hundred singles, the other of one hundred albums, which we think represent the best and most enduring music of the era covered by these logs. Have fun.

CHARLIE GILLETT

STEPHEN NUGENT

ROCK ALMANAC

HOT ONE HUNDRED
SINGLES AND ALBUMS

Charlie Gillett
Simon Frith and Dave Marsh

Here's an attempt at the impossible, to condense the material of *Rock Almanac*'s logs down to two lists of one hundred records each. And if it is most unlikely that any reader will agree with every choice on our lists, at least we have sketched out the structure of a representative collection of records from the rock era.

The first list, of singles, was compiled in Britain by Charlie Gillett and Simon Frith, both of whom lived in the States for more than a year and so chose the records with both sides of the Atlantic in mind. Charlie and Simon also drew up a list of a hundred albums which they submitted to Dave Marsh for an American perspective. Accepting the over-all balance of their list, Dave substituted thirty different albums.

1: CHARLIE AND SIMON'S
HOT ONE HUNDRED SINGLES

This list is not necessarily the hundred *best* singles, but the hundred records that have had the most impact in the history of rock *as singles*. Despite the concerted attempts of the record business and its chroniclers to prove otherwise, rock music has advanced primarily through the medium of 45s, as heard on the radio, on jukeboxes, and in discothèques. So all the records listed here displayed their power through their sales either in America or Britain, most of them in both countries.

But while this is a list of hits, it is by no means a list of the best-selling records of all time. To be effective, a single must sell, but after that its significance depends on its particular musical qualities. These records not only caught public attention, they also seized the rock audience's collective consciousness, either by revealing new musical possibilities or by capturing the spirit of the time.

We have excluded nostalgia as a guide to choice (not always easy) and have appended dates to indicate rock's continuity. On the grounds that we could keep up the historian's *pretend* detachment about recent records, we have not included any made since 1972.

Beat Section.

A.   CLASSIC ROCKERS.

1.	Rock Around the Clock	Bill Haley and his Comets	1955
2.	Long Tall Sally	Little Richard	1956
3.	Blue Suede Shoes	Carl Perkins	1956
4.	Be Bop A Lula	Gene Vincent	1956
5.	Hound Dog	Elvis Presley	1956
6.	That'll Be the Day	Crickets	1957
7.	Great Balls of Fire	Jerry Lee Lewis	1957
8.	Johnny B Goode	Chuck Berry	1958

Notes: This includes all the main *popular* '50s rockers except Fats Domino (see smooch section below), with their most representative hits. Left out are the one-off hit groups such as Danny & the Juniors, whose "At the Hop" is a stand-by reserve (1958).

B. BRITISH BEAT.

9.	She Loves You	Beatles	1963/64
10.	I Wanna Hold Your Hand	Beatles	1963/64
11.	You Really Got Me	Kinks	1964
12.	Do Wah Diddy Diddy	Manfred Mann	1964
13.	Keep On Running	Spencer Davis Group	1965
14.	Wild Thing	Troggs	1966
15.	Honky Tonk Women	Rolling Stones	1969
16.	Whole Lotta Love	Led Zeppelin	1969
17.	All Right Now	Free	1970

Notes: No. 9 established the Beatles as an *unprecedented* phenomenon in Britain, 10 did the same in the States; the others show the evolution (from the crudest origins) of British R&B; 11 and 13 weren't American hits, 12 was despite being a cover. Obvious gaps are Cocker and Hendrix, who had hit singles but really made their mark as album/live artists. Reserves: "Hey Joe" by the Jimi Hendrix Experience (1967) and "With a Little Help from My Friends" by Joe Cocker (1968).

C. AMERICAN BEAT.

18.	Runaround Sue	Dion	1961
19.	Louie Louie	Kingsmen	1964
20.	Wooly Bully	Sam the Sham and the Pharaohs	1965
21.	Hang On Sloopy	McCoys	1965
22.	Light My Fire	Doors	1967
23.	The Letter	Box Tops	1967
24.	Proud Mary	Creedence Clearwater Revival	1969
25.	Spirit in the Sky	Norman Greenbaum	1970

Notes: No. 19 was not a British hit (though every British group of the time played it), and amazingly enough neither was 22, though somehow it is inside every British rock brain anyway.

26.	The Twist	Chubby Checker	1962
27.	The Locomotion	Little Eva	1962
28.	Dancing in the Street	Martha & the Vandellas	1964
29.	In the Midnight Hour	Wilson Pickett	1965
30.	River Deep, Mountain High	Ike & Tina Turner	1966
31.	Respect	Aretha Franklin	1967
32.	The Israelites	Desmond Dekker and the Aces	1969
33.	I Heard It Through the Grapevine	Marvin Gaye	1969
34.	Band of Gold	Freda Payne	1970
35.	I Want You Back	Jackson Five	1970
36.	Papa Was a Rolling Stone	Temptations	1972/73

Notes: No. 28 wasn't a hit in Britain until 1969, although it had been a disco anthem for seven years by then. No. 30 wasn't a hit in America for reasons that have more to do with Spector's business relations with American radio than with the record's undeniable classic status. Reserved here would probably be another Holland-Dozier-Holland production to go alongside Martha, "I Can't Help Myself" by the Four Tops.

E. BRUTAL BEAT.

| 37. | Get It On (U.S. title Bang a Gong) | T. Rex | 1971 |
| 38. | Mama Weer All Crazee Now | Slade | 1972 |

2. SMOOCH SECTION

A. CLASSIC BALLADS.

| 39. | The Great Pretender | Platters | 1955/56 |

40.	Heartbreak Hotel	Elvis Presley	1956
41.	Blueberry Hill	Fats Domino	1956
42.	Only the Lonely	Roy Orbison	1960
43.	I Can't Stop Loving You	Ray Charles	1962
44.	House of the Rising Sun	Animals	1964
45.	You've Lost That Lovin' Feeling	Righteous Brothers	1964/65
46.	When a Man Loves a Woman	Percy Sledge	1966
47.	Reach Out (I'll Be There)	Four Tops	1966
48.	You Don't Have to Say You Love Me	Dusty Springfield	1966
49.	Hey Jude	Beatles	1968
50.	Bridge over Troubled Water	Simon & Garfunkel	1970
51.	Maggie May	Rod Stewart	1971

3. POIGNANT SECTION

A. TEEN.

52.	Why Do Fools Fall in Love	Frankie Lymon & the Teenagers	1956
53.	Diana	Paul Anka	1957
54.	Wake Up Little Suzie	Everly Brothers	1957
55.	Peggy Sue	Buddy Holly	1957
56.	Yakety Yak	Coasters	1958
57.	Summertime Blues	Eddie Cochran	1958
58.	Teenager in Love	Dion and the Belmonts	1959
59.	Donna	Ritchie Valens	1959
60.	It's Late/Never Be Anyone Else but You	Ricky Nelson	1959
61.	Take Good Care of My Baby	Bobby Vee	1961

62.	Breaking Up Is Hard		
	to Do	Neil Sedaka	1962
63.	Runaway	Del Shannon	1962

Notes: Nos. 58 and 59 were British hits for Marty Wilde. Reserve: "Save the Last Dance for Me" by the Drifters (1960)

B. GIRL TALK.

64.	Will You Love Me		
	Tomorrow	Shirelles	1961
65.	Please Mr. Postman	Marvelettes	1962
66.	He's So Fine	Chiffons	1963
67.	Da Doo Ron Ron	Crystals	1963
68.	It's My Party	Lesley Gore	1963
69.	My Guy	Mary Wells	1964
70.	Where Did My Love		
	Go	Supremes	1964
71.	My Boy Lollipop	Millie Small	1964
72.	Leader of the Pack	Shangri-Las	1965
73.	Ode to Billie Joe	Bobbie Gentry	1967

Notes: No. 65 was not a hit in Britain, where it was covered as an LP track by the Beatles. Of Spector's girls, we favored the Crystals over the Ronettes, and we left out altogether such dream queens as Brenda Lee, Connie Francis, and Helen Shapiro.

C. ANGST.

74.	Satisfaction	Rolling Stones	1965
75.	Eve of Destruction	Barry McGuire	1965
76.	Like a Rolling Stone	Bob Dylan	1965
77.	My Generation	Who	1965
78.	For What It's Worth	Buffalo Springfield	1966
79.	A Whiter Shade of		
	Pale	Procol Harum	1967
80.	That You/Everybody	Sly & the Family	
	Is a Star	Stone	1970
81.	American Pie	Don McLean	1972

Notes: No. 77 was not a hit in the States, where they have been trying to make up for it ever since; 78 and 80 were not hits in Britain, whose reserve would be "She's Not There" by the Zombies (1965) or "Those Were the Days" by Mary Hopkins (1968).

4. JOYOUS SECTION

A. NOVELTIES.

82.	Little Darlin'	Diamonds	1957
83.	Blue Moon	Marcels	1961
84.	Duke of Earl	Gene Chandler	1962
85.	Sylvia's Mother	Dr. Hook and the Medicine Show	1972

Notes: No. 84 was not a hit with the British, on whose behalf we apologize to Gene Chandler.

B. INSTRUMENTALS.

86.	Rebel Rouser	Duane Eddy	1958
87.	Green Onions	Booker T & the MG'S	1962
88.	Albatross	Fleetwood Mac	1968

Notes: No. 87 wasn't a hit in Britain but has somehow been accepted as a radio oldie anyway.

C. SUMMER SONGS

89.	It Might As Well Rain Until September	Carole King	1962
90.	I Get Around	Beach Boys	1964
91.	Mr. Tambourine Man	Byrds	1965
92.	Summer in the City	Lovin' Spoonful	1966
93.	Good Vibrations	Beach Boys	1966
94.	California Dreamin	Mamas and Papas	1966
95.	Sunshine Superman	Donovan	1967

96.	Waterloo Sunset	Kinks	1967
97.	Groovin'	Rascals	1967
98.	Itchycoo Park	Small Faces	1967
99.	In the Summertime	Mungo Jerry	1970
100.	I Can See Clearly Now	Johnny Nash	1972

Notes: No. 94 was not a British hit and 96 was not an American hit, but each captured its own national spirit at the time. Reserves: for the idea, "Here Comes Summer" by Jerry Keller (1959); "Happy Together" by the Turtles (1967).

Conclusion: We don't know what they prove, but here are the year-by-year breakdowns, indicating the number of hits included in our top one hundred from 1955 to 1972.

1955–2	1958–4	1961–4	1964–10	1967–8	1970–7
1956–7	1959–3	1962–9	1965–10	1968–2	1971–2
1957–6	1960–1	1963–5	1966–10	1969–5	1972–5

If we are right, this leaves 1960 as the worst year of the era, and the period 1964–67 as the golden age. Seventy-five of the records are American, twenty-three British, and two Jamaican; fourteen were American hits that didn't score in Britain, and six British hits missed in America.

Now for the LPs.

ONE HUNDRED ESSENTIAL ROCK ALBUMS, DAVE MARSH

This is not a list of the hundred "best" albums, nor have we tried to give an order of preference. Rather, we imagined someone hearing rock for the first time in 1974–75, a Martian perhaps, or a well-intentioned but uninformed person wanting to bone up on rock's heritage. These are the hundred albums we think he or she would want to hear in order to understand where we're at.

There is no critical consensus about rock, but we have tried to weigh the impact of records in their own time and on other musicians. We excluded people who we considered never attracted more than a cult following, however vociferous and articulate, such as Captain Beefheart, Love, or the Stooges. Eliminated too are many of our own personal favorites, making way in some cases for records we actively dislike.

More than two thirds of the albums chosen are compilations of records that were originally released as singles. Albums made as albums have had to bear comparison with them, and we have ruthlessly excluded those that did not significantly vary ideas or sounds from one track to another.

We had to make some arbitrary and inevitably controversial definitions in order to restrict the list to one hundred. Because it is explicitly a list of *rock* records, we've left out parallel but separate streams such as country music, and in the roots section excluded such influential people as Robert Johnson, Woody Guthrie, and the Ink Spots, on the grounds that they are no longer easily accessible to the rock audience. We've also omitted pop and middle-of-the-road music, since by definition it is imitative rather than innovative.

Also missing are most of the many artists who exposed the full range of their talent on one side of a hit 45 and then repeated the formula until (and often long past) the public lost interest. We have collected a representative (though not definitive) sample of them by including a few various artists' compilations, but still found no room for the Four Seasons or Neil Sedaka, the Monkees or Status Quo. Before you shout in rage, look over the list to see who could be left out to make room for somebody else.

When assembling a list such as this—the definitive one hundred albums—the author quickly realizes this impossibility of the task. When Charlie Gillett and Simon Frith did their English original, they had each other to rely upon, to counterbalance their personal idiosyncrasies if nothing else. I have not had that advantage, and while I have tried to maintain something like the same standards, it is hard for me to include Iron Butterfly and leave out the Young Rascals. (Gillett and Frith may find the latter's art succinctly contained on one side of a hit single, but I have not been able to find the former.)

I have cheated outrageously, I think, only once. That was in the inclusion of Atlantic's eight-record History of Rhythm and Blues set as a single entry. However, I find it impossible to leave this collection out. It is, in my opinion—with the sixty-four Greatest Motown Hits compilation—the most important document (document, I said, not record) of the rock era. In any event, this list should give the listener and the reader an approximation of what still seems important in 1975. If nothing else, it is a starting point from which to argue.

ONE HUNDRED ESSENTIAL ALBUMS
1955–72

I. ROOTS: THE BIRTH AND GROWTH OF ROCK AND ROLL, 1955–62

1. Hank Williams, *24 Greatest Hits* (MGM, double)
2. Jerry Lee Lewis, *Greatest Hits, Vol. 1 and 2* (Sun)
3. Fats Domino, *Legendary Masters Series* (United Artists, double)
4. Little Richard, *17 Original Hits* (Specialty)
5. Elvis Presley, *A Legendary Performer* (RCA)
6. Elvis Presley, *For LP Fans Only* (RCA)
7. Chuck Berry, *Golden Decade, Vol. 1* (Chess, double)
8. The Coasters, *Their Greatest Recordings: The Early Years* (Atco)
9. The Everly Brothers, *History* (Barnaby)
10. Charlie Rich, *Greatest Hits* (Epic)
11. Various artists, *American Graffiti Sound Track* (MCA)
12. Buddy Holly, *A Rock and Roll Collection* (MCA)
13. Roy Orbison, *All Time Greatest Hits* (Monument)
14. Rick Nelson, *Legendary Masters Series* (United Artists)

These are the men who shaped the map the others have attempted to follow. It may not be true that more great rock was created in this era than in any of the others, but it is true that everything that has followed is based quite directly upon it. Presley, Berry, Williams, Domino, Richard, and Lewis did it directly. But singers such as Orbison and Nelson have made their kinds of legend (the loser, the teen idol) a mythic base, too. Outrageously, there is no available collection of Phil Spector's productions, but the Graffiti sound track enables us to catch up on many of the one-shot heroes of the period (a distinct problem with an album list is that it does not allow for these) while Charlie Rich reminds us, in the only historically skew entry, of what has become of most of these men.

II.   THE BLACK TRADITION: BLUES + GOSPEL = SOUL

15. Bo Diddley, Howlin' Wolf, Muddy Waters, and Chuck Berry, *Pop Origins* (Chess)
16. Ray Charles, *25 Years in Show Business* (ABC, double)
17. B. B. King, *Live at the Regal* (ABC)
18. Bobby Bland, *Best* (Duke)
19. Sam Cooke, *This Is* (RCA, double)
20. Otis Redding, *History of Otis Redding* (Atco, double)
21. Various artists, *Atlantic History of Rhythm and Blues,* Vol. 1–8 (Atlantic, eight volumes)
22. Aretha Franklin, *I Never Loved a Man* (Atlantic)
23. James Brown, *Soul Classics* (Polydor)
24. Various artists, *64 Greatest Motown Hits* (Motown/Cimco, 4 vols.)
25. The Impressions, *Big Sixteen* (ABC)
26. Jerry Butler, *Greatest Hits* (Mercury)
27. Little Willie John, *Free at Last* (King)

Basically, this list traces the blues as it moves to the city (15, 17), becomes electrified and turns into R&B (21, 23, 18), then merges with gospel (16, 19, 25, 27). Finally, the mélange absorbs (rather than is absorbed by, a singular feat) mainstream pop and becomes soul (20, 22, 26). Nos. 21 and 24 are representative of the two most important trends; especially in the volumes of the Atlantic set, the transition can be heard as it occurred.

III.   THE BRITISH INVASION, ITS TRANSFORMATION, AND ITS REIGN

28. The Beatles, *Second Album* (Apple)
29. The Beatles, *'65* (Apple)
30. The Beatles, *Rubber Soul* (Apple)
31. The Animals, *Greatest Hits* (ABKCO, double)
32. The Rolling Stones, *Now* (London)

33. John Mayall, *Bluesbreakers* featuring Eric Clapton (London)
34. The Kinks, *Greatest Hits* (Reprise)
35. The Yardbirds, *Greatest Hits* (Epic)
36. The Who, *Meaty, Beaty, Big and Bouncy* (MCA/Track)
37. Traffic, *Heavy Traffic* (United Artists)
38. Pink Floyd, *Ummagumma* (Capitol, double)
39. Jeff Beck, *Truth* (Epic)
40. The Beatles, *Sgt. Pepper's Lonely Hearts Club Band* (Apple)
41. Cream, *Heavy* (Polydor, double)
42. Procol Harum, *Shine On Brightly* (London)
43. Jethro Tull, *Stand Up* (Reprise)
44. Jimi Hendrix, *Smash Hits* (Reprise)
45. Rolling Stones, *Let It Bleed* (London)
46. Rolling Stones, *Get Your Ya Ya's Out* (London)
47. The Who, *Tommy* (MCA/Track, double)

This is where rock achieves its first crucial importance at the transparent level, but also where opinions begin to diverge. In some cases, and there are several, in which I was unable to make a judgment based on my own taste, I based my selection on the record that seemed to be most important to the group's fans. (Exception: 43, whose fans would argue for "Aqualung," but I figure I had to be able to sit all the way through every one of these at least once.) Much of the best of some British groups (Traffic, Cream) is deleted and we are left with the ragtag anthologies listed. On the other hand, we have here the greatest live album ever recorded (46), the birth of British blues (33) and the first major rock opera (47). Unfortunately, the amount of waste on the only two serious British pop anthologies (*History of British Rock,* Vol. 1 and 2, both Sire doubles) precludes the inclusion of such important Top 40 acts as the Hollies and Manfred Mann.

IV. AMERICA IN THE '60s: NEWPORT TO WOODSTOCK,
   VIA GREENWICH VILLAGE AND CALIFORNIA

48. Bob Dylan, *Freewheelin'* (Columbia)
49. Bob Dylan, *Highway 61 Revisited* (Columbia)

50. Bob Dylan, *Blonde on Blonde* (Columbia, double)

51. Bob Dylan, *The Basement Tapes* (Columbia, double)

52. Four Seasons, *Gold Vault of Hits* (Philips)

53. Beach Boys, *Endless Summer* (Capitol, double)

54. Byrds, *Mr. Tambourine Man* (Columbia)

55. The Doors, *The Doors* (Elektra)

56. Big Brother and the Holding Company, *Cheap Thrills* (Columbia)

57. Mothers of Invention, *We're Only in It for the Money* (MGM)

58. Grateful Dead, *Live/Dead* (Warner Bros., double)

59. Buffalo Springfield, *Buffalo Springfield* (Atlantic, double)

60. Moby Grape, *Great Grape* (Columbia)

61. Various artists, *Sound Track from "Woodstock"* (Cotillion, triple)

62. Flying Burrito Brothers, *Gilded Palace of Sin* (A&M)

63. The Rascals, *Time/Peace, Greatest Hits* (Atlantic)

The most difficult problem here is with the American record companies' disconcerting penchant for deletions. Such significant groups as the Lovin' Spoonful have either nothing at all or nothing respectable left to recommend, even in the way of anthologies, in their record companies' catalogues. On the other hand, such so-called "important" groups as Country Joe and the Fish, the Jefferson Airplane, and Santana, as well as such singers as Richie Havens and Joan Baez, are represented by the Woodstock anthology, where they belong.

V. AMERICA AT THE END OF THE '60S: THE SOUND OF THINGS TO COME

64. Bob Dylan, *John Wesley Harding* (Columbia)

65. James Taylor, *Mud Slide Slim* (Reprise)

66. The Band, *Second Album* (Capitol)

67. The Band, *Rock of Ages* (Capitol, double)

68. Crosby, Stills, Nash and Young, *So Far* (Atlantic)

69. Neil Young, *After the Gold Rush* (Reprise)

70. Simon and Garfunkel, *Bookends* (Columbia)

71. Creedence Clearwater Revival, *Green River* (Fantasy)
72. Van Morrison, *Moondance* (Warner Bros.)
73. Velvet Underground, *Loaded* (Cotillion)
74. Randy Newman, *Sail Away* (Reprise)

The rise of the singer-songwriter and the articulate rock band, both of them often obsessed with America, its politics and its history, produced a series of clear-cut album triumphs. Typically, Dylan led the way, but notice, please, that there is only one greatest-hits package here (68), and that made by—it has since become clear—the greatest one-shot band in history. There has probably been more good rock criticism written about these records than any other dozen; significantly, all but the last two were best-sellers as well.

VI. SOUNDS OF THE '70s

a) Black Music

75. Sly and the Family Stone, *Greatest Hits* (Epic)
76. Sly and the Family Stone, *There's a Riot Goin' On* (Epic)
77. Marvin Gaye, *What's Going On?* (Tamla)
78. Jackson Five, *Greatest Hits* (Motown)
79. Various artists, *Sound Track from "The Harder They Come"* (Island)
80. Al Green, *I'm Still in Love with You* (Hi)
81. Stevie Wonder, *Talking Book* (Tamla)
82. The Spinners, *The Spinners* (Atlantic)
83. Curtis Mayfield, *Superfly* (Curtom)

While classic soul (romance, sweet harmony, a dance beat) still flourished (see 75, 78, 80, 82, and parts of every one of these), something new (militance, a sense of doom) was in the air. Sly Stone kicked it off, moving in four years from the utter optimism of "Dance to the Music" to the utter despair of "Thank You for Talking to Me, Africa." Gaye, Wonder, and Mayfield keyed into it best but it was a little reggae movie, *The Harder They Come,* made to celebrate a musical genre which slammed the message home hardest. Was this a mere temporary flowering of reggae or something more substantial? Only Stevie Wonder has been consistently able to give us a hint. His answer? Maybe.

b) Britain

84. Led Zeppelin, *Fourth Album* (Runes) (Atlantic)
85. Bad Company, *Bad Company* (Swan Song)
86. Moody Blues, *In Search of the Lost Chord* (Deram)
87. Yes, *Fragile* (Atlantic)
88. Deep Purple, *Machine Head* (Reprise)
89. Rod Stewart, *Every Picture Tells a Story* (Mercury)
90. Roxy Music, *Stranded* (Atco)
91. Mott the Hoople, *Mott* (Columbia)
92. Rolling Stones, *Exiles on Main Street* (Rolling Stones/Atlantic)

Though it sometimes seemed as though our options were between being bludgeoned to death with guitars or tweaked to the outer limits of aural pain with synthesizers (84 and 85 versus 86 and 87), some kept the faith. Indeed, Roxy Music managed to make synthesizers a pleasure for the most hard-core Stones fan—something the Stones themselves, without any of Moog's encumbrances, only sometimes seemed to do. When they did, however, they (quite typically) made the best album of the decade. Meanwhile, sex got stranger and stranger, as Mott the Hoople revealed. For some, that is. Rod Stewart was bemoaning adolescent heart crushers all along; we love him for it.

c) America

93. Derek and the Dominoes, *Layla* (Polydor, double)
94. The Allman Brothers Band, *Live at the Fillmore* (Capricorn, double)
95. Alice Cooper, *Greatest Hits* (Warner Bros.)
96. Joni Mitchell, *Court and Spark* (Asylum)
97. John Lennon, *Plastic Ono Band* (Apple)
98. Paul Simon, *There Goes Rhymin' Simon* (Columbia)
99. Steely Dan, *Can't Buy a Thrill* (ABC)
100. Elton John, *Greatest Hits* (MCA)

Why are three British musicians on this list? Because Clapton (Derek), Lennon and Elton John were so obsessed that they made American albums—the first two literally so, the second one the most figurative celebration of America imaginable.

AMERICAN RADIO TODAY

Paul Gambaccini

"Nobody in town believes it!" stormed an infuriated Ken Shelton, music director WBZ-FM in Boston. "The fix *has* to be in somewhere. No one is getting requests for it, and we're not getting sales reports from the stores. Besides, *no* record jumps like that."

The leap of 23 to 5 on the *Billboard* singles chart achieved by Tony Orlando and Dawn's "He Don't Love You (Like I Love You)" in the third week of April, 1975, did indeed look suspicious, for no record had taken that big a jump since Wings' "Live and Let Die" shot from 21 to 3 in the summer of 1973. But whereas "Live and Let Die" peaked at number 2, as did "The Horse" by Cliff Nobles and Co., which took the extraordinary rise of 21 to 2 in 1968, "He Don't Love You (Like I Love You)" followed through to the number one position on May 3, 1975.

"It *was* a big jump," an Elektra official conceded the week of Dawn's unusual leap. "But it was selling nation-wide, and it was getting air play. After the big deal we did to get Tony

Orlando it was decided that if any single was going to be a hit this month, it would be his. The national promotion director made sure of that: he pushed that one personally."

The three weeks in the life of "He Don't Love You" had illustrated several aspects of how records are broken in the United States. Local radio stations rely largely on local sales and requests to determine their charts, while the trade magazines are heavily influenced by the local lists in compiling their surveys. Promotion is thus heavily focused on the local station and music directors like Ken Shelton, who in the course of one week may receive a phone call from Al Martino, a Wombles sweatshirt, and an invitation to a Foghat pie-throwing party at a local roller derby. When the national charts feature records not selling in several major markets, radio station personnel get suspicious, for good reasons or not. They tend to add a record doing very well on the national chart, and if it fails locally they feel burned.

Because the number of stations playing pop music is literally in the thousands, there are many ways by which a song may be broken. Unlike British promotion men, who spend half their lives pacing the halls of Broadcasting House hoping against hope to get their records programmed on the BBC and at least another quarter trying to get their soul titles played in discos, American promo men have any number of opportunities at hand to break a title. Local radio, syndicated programs, local television, and national late-night television concerts offer more outlets for rock than Britons have ever seen.

Sometimes a hit is broken without record company initiative at all. Rosalie Trombley, the programming genius of CKLW, serving Detroit from Windsor, Ontario, played "Bennie and the Jets" as an album cut from *Goodbye Yellow Brick Road*. She received great listener response, but so did a local soul station. The result was that MCA released "Bennie and the Jets" as an A-side single in America and promoted it in the soul market as well as in Elton John's traditional pop audience. The record went gold, entered the top twenty of the national soul charts, and proved to be the second-biggest record of John's American career.

Trombley has broken so many off-the-wall number-one hits, including Henry Mancini's "Love Theme from *Romeo and Juliet*," Bobby Goldsboro's "Honey," and Terry Jack's "Seasons in the Sun," that CKLW has acquired a reputation as a "barometer" station. If a pop record breaks in the heavily black Detroit market, it is considered a certain national smash by radio programmers, and many doubting stations add the record. When Roger Whittaker's "The Last Farewell" zoomed from 22 to 4 on CKLW, many music directors threw in the towel and added the unlikely hit to their rotation schedule. If a soul record reaches the top three of the CKLW chart, it has historically been a good bet that it will break nationally within three months.

Detroit is not the only barometer market in the United States. Boston, considered the most British city in America, appropriately breaks British singles, most recently Queen's "Killer Queen," Leo Sayer's "Long Tall Glasses," Ace's "How Long," and Pilot's "Magic." New York, for years notorious as the last market to go on a hit, has become the focal point of the Stateside disco craze, the result being that WABC, once the despair of America's promo men for its minuscule play list, is now the first major station on disco crossovers.

"I'm in the radio business, not the record business," WABC program director Rick Sklar has stated. He is interested not so much in breaking records as in maintaining the highest ratings possible. "We play middle-of-the-road music," he told a radio programming conference in 1974. "Middle-of-the-road is what people in our demographic range want to hear at the moment. There is no MOR sound, but there are MOR records."

Sklar thus added the Hues Corporation's "Rock the Boat" in the summer of 1974 after the record achieved fifteen thousand sales in New York City off discothèque play. Programming the single increased sales enough to put the record in *Billboard* chart, and once there the record was home. The exact same sequence has been followed in cases of several records since, including George McCrae's "Rock Your Baby," Shirley & Co's "Shame Shame Shame," Eddie Harris' "Hijack," and Consumer Rapport's "Ease on Down the Road."

The last record had another factor in its favor. It was the catchiest tune from the all-black Broadway version of *The Wizard of Oz, The Wiz.* When the play won the hearts of New Yorkers, eventually winning the Antoinette Perry Award for the best musical of the year, the single version of the song started to sell and pick up disco play. Songs from entertainment productions traditionally do better in America than Britain. If an entertainment reaches the level of mass-market acceptance, the popularity of the theme tune is assured, unless the song is absolutely diabolical. Barbra Streisand's "The Way We Were" and Marvin Hamlisch's "The Entertainer" both went to number one, and even Mike Oldfield's "Tubular Bells" became a gold single in an edition he didn't authorize, when billed as "Theme from *The Exorcist.*"

Stations across the country are anxious to find out what the barometer stations are breaking and what their fellow stations are playing, and a small industry has blossomed to fill that need. Each trade magazine carries a play-list column, while several prominent tip sheets inform broadcasters what records are getting key plays.

The trade magazine play-list pioneer was Kal Rudman, who wrote an r&b column in *Music Business* in the mid-sixties. After *Music Business* died with the top-forty British invasion, Rudman resurfaced writing pop and r&b columns for *Record World.* These weekly pieces became industry legends, asserting in strong language that certain unlikely records were going to become hits. They almost always became so, rendering the suggestion that Rudman was receiving gifts from record companies almost redundant. Although it is true that he championed many unusual Columbia releases, such as Clint Holmes's "Playground in My Mind," Dr. Hook's "Cover of Rolling Stone," and Loudon Wainwright's "Dead Skunk," it is also true that these records became major American hits. "I only write about a record I believe in," Rudman asserted when asked if his consultancy fees hurt his judgment. In 1974 he discontinued the *Record World* column, saying, "I was only competing with myself, wasn't I?" and concentrating his full efforts on his tip sheet and radio programming conference.

The winner and still champion of the tip-sheet sweepstakes is the long-lived *Bill Gavin Report.* The veteran California broadcaster/publisher is read coast to coast for his air-play reports, weighted air-play charts, and personal opinions. He is one of the few tipsters whose *personal* opinion is given much value, and it was his praise of Paul Anka's "(You're) Having My Baby" as tasteful as well as commercial that helped get the record away.

When Rudman left *Record World,* the magazine recognized it had lost one of its most popular features. The editors launched a section called "AM Airplay Report," which quickly paled into insignificance compared to other innovative trade services. The "Radio Active" chart in *Cashbox* lists singles in rank order of percentage of stations adding them during the week, and thus a quick reference is available for programmers making local play-list additions. *Billboard*'s "Singles Report" has turned out to be the most informative of the lot. The editors divide the country into regions, pick key stations in each to supply weekly play-list additions and chart jumpers, and print these with a summary of what records are moving in each region.

These trade-magazine features allow programmers to see what they should be adding far less expensively than if they subscribed to the tip sheets. The high cost of the sheets is a direct result of their low, specialized circulation.

A perfect example of what one can discover from the trade play-list features is that "Shaving Cream" could go from the twenties to number one in medium-sized metropolitan areas. This novelty disc, recorded by Benny Bell with vocalist Paul Wynn in 1946, was ignored when originally released, presumably because its repetitious play on the unspoken word "shit" is rather risqué and because it has no melodic virtues. The record broke in 1975 in a most unusual fashion. Dr. Demento, the Los Angeles-based disc jockey whose weekly program of bizarre pop singles is syndicated across America, featured "Shaving Cream" on his chart of strange listener favorites. WNBC in New York, which runs Dr. Demento, promoted him by featuring "Shaving Cream" in a trailer that ran during the Bruce Morrow show. Morrow, long New York's most popular evening disc jockey, received numerous requests to play the novelty in its entirety. He did, and the song debuted at number 24 on the WNBC chart. Vanguard Records dug out the master, re-released the number as a single, and saw it go into the national Hot Hundred off New York sales. Several stations went onto the record on that basis, and two reported to the *Billboard* "Singles Report" that the record had leaped from the twenties to number one in their town. This kind of report helps spread a record onto stations whose programmers follow the trades.

Record companies themselves try to clue radio stations in on their prime pushes by circulating weekly news sheets. The main goal here, other than to get records onto play lists, is to mask the hype with enough humor or information to get programmers interested in reading the bleeding things. Warner Brothers' *Circular* seems to win this competition hands down, featuring both instructive articles and witty contests. Atlantic's mail-out is generally a catalogue of chart positions, tour dates, and release schedules. Buddah and Elektra have mail-outs to their promotion men and women which deserve mention, Buddah's for its unmasked desperation and Elektra/Asylum's for the prose.

Sometimes a record breaks without radio entirely. Television proved it had surprising power in breaking singles when two dirges featured as theme tunes of teleplays about dying women went to number one in 1973. John Denver's "Sunshine on My Shoulder" and Jim Croce's "Time in a Bottle" went to number one after being the signature songs of *Sunshine* and *She Lives,* respectively.

It had long been known that a series could sell records, from Ricky Nelson to the Monkees and the Archies. Lately the merchandising emphasis has been placed on hosting variety series, such as Tony Orlando, Mac Davis, and Cher. Mac Davis sang his then current American hit "Rock and Roll (I Gave You the Best Years of My Life)" three times on his short-lived program.

TV appearances coupled with concentrated promotion can increase sales significantly. When Chicago had an hour-long special of their own in 1974, all their LPs reappeared on the *Billboard* chart. Half the battle of selling a record is getting it into the shops, and with an investment of in-store promotional aids tying Chicago's back catalog to their TV special, Columbia was able to restock the stores with all of the group's albums.

But it is always difficult to tell whether the albums listed as making gains in the bottom section of the industry album charts are actually selling, since these numbers are awarded in fickle fashion. The personal preferences of the chart compilers, opinions as to what dealers should stock as catalogue material, and judgments as to which albums are likely to move in the weeks ahead have as much effect on the listings as actual sales. Industry insiders are always trying to figure out which of the three major trade charts is most accurate at any given time.

The subjectiveness of the charts occasionally reflects itself in spectacularly disparate listings. Uriah Heep's *Sweet Freedom* was number ten on the *Cashbox* album chart when it wasn't even in *Billboard*'s top thirty. David Essex's "Rock On" was number one in *Cashbox* during a week when it wasn't in the *Billboard* top ten.

Billboard itself had some astonishing chart trends from mid-1974 to mid-1975. During one six-week stretch, every number-one single became number twelve the next week, a statistical near impossibility. During the first four months of 1975, only two records in the number one position retained that slot the next week, both Elton John singles; the number-two singles otherwise automatically ascended to number one.

The chart listings are vitally important to most AM programmers, but there still remain a few FM stations that dare to program without the express guidance of *Billboard* and its ilk. WBCN-FM in Boston, for example, maintains a library of literally thousands of albums and singles in the studio itself, enabling the disc jockey to exercise one of the widest selections in commercial radio. It is true that some singles and albums are set aside into recommended categories, but the deejay can still decide when these records are to be featured.

In contrast are the tight structures of WBZ and WRKO, the two AM giants in Boston. (Although WHDH is mostly music and occasionally number one in the city, it plays fewer current discs.) At WBZ, where this writer worked for several months as executive producer and sat in on weekly music meetings, a majority vote of a "music meeting" panel is required to approve the addition of a record to the play list, which is not set at a specific number but tends to be on the shy side of thirty. The general manager, program director, music director, executive producer, and a disc jockey usually sit in. Since at least two of these figures do not come from distinctly musical backgrounds, a record is judged on its sound as much as on any artistic merit.

In the weeks this writer voted, many hits were rejected for air play on the basis that they were not suitable for 25–49-year-old housewives, considered the bulk of the daytime audience. Elton John's "The Bitch Is Back" was banned by the Westinghouse network for the use of the word "bitch," but it wouldn't have been played anyway because of its freneticism. "Fire" by the Ohio Players, an American number one, was dismissed out of hand as being "too raucous," which the music director, a black, often sadly equated with "too black." William DeVaughn's "Be Thankful for What You Got" was considered too soul-oriented, while Paul McCartney's "Junior's Farm" was flipped in favor of "Sally G," the easier side.

On the other hand, many easy-listening records that were not actual big sellers were passed, including several Charlie Rich singles and everything released by Helen Reddy. WBZ's programming decisions are typical of American stations that see themselves as being contemporary middle-of-the-road, and it is for these stations that *Billboard* publishes its Easy Listening Chart, based primarily on air play. This approach is in conflict with Rick Sklar's philosophy: "There is no MOR sound, but there are MOR records."

WRKO tends to dance to the tune piped by RKO headquarters in

California. The local music director, a young woman, can make some decisions and recommendations on the local level, particularly in light of sales returns, but final decisions often come from chain headquarters in California. She was mortified when she had to go on Telly Savalas' "If," a colossal stiff in America that failed to make the top hundred and was the object of gleeful jibes from other Boston programmers for weeks.

WRKO has another unusual feature in that its records are all played at the wrong speed. "I play them all between 45½ and 47½ [rpm]," WRKO programming consultant Paul Drew revealed in November 1974. "Sometimes I have to adjust. For example, I have to call KHJ [Los Angeles HQ] tomorrow and tell them to slow down 'Please Mr. Postman,' it sounds too fast now. I once had 'Bridge over Troubled Water' on too fast, and it sounded like Mickey Mouse." One WRKO employee revealed that when a commercial for the Jackson Five's *Dancing Machine* was played, several people ran into the studio, fearing the cartridge was defective. It was actually being played at its correct speed, but they had heard the single played at the wrong speed for so long they mistook WRKO-real for real-real.

Drew and other major AM programmers tend to discriminate against length in general. American radio philosophy is that if a record lasts only three minutes instead of three fifteen, there is far less chance of the listener tuning out, and for the sake of ratings tuneout must be avoided at all costs. The general manager of CKLW recently announced that singles over three thirty had virtually no chance on his station, unless they were by Elton John or were "Hey Jude." The increased speed, shortened length, and restricted play list all help give AM radio an essentially manic flavor that keeps listeners tuned through the commercials.

An occasional record by a local hero can help. Aerosmith's "Dream On" was Boston's number-one hit of 1973, although it never entered the *Billboard* top thirty. "La Grange" by Z. Z. Top spent nearly half a year on *Billboard*'s Hot Hundred, mainly on sales from the Southwest. Sometimes a local hit breaks nationally to thrill the rock historian. "In the Year 2525" went to number one in Nebraska before reaching the national charts in 1969. "The Mouse" by local television star Soupy Sales hit number three on New York's WMCA in 1965, placing the record on the national chart, where it eventually peaked in the fifties.

But most records follow the tried-but-true road of Broadway plays. They are tried out in middle markets, and if successful there are added on the major stations. It sounds boring, but with thousands of stations the variations are nearly infinite. Besides, there is always the incentive of recognition that goes to a programming pioneer. "Last year we got gold records for breaking 'Hooked on a Feeling' and 'Just You and Me,'" Ken Shelton enthused. "I'm hoping 'Magic' and 'Killer Queen' go gold, because if they do, we get gold records for breaking them."

ARE YOU READY
FOR RUDE AND ROUGH REGGAE?

Carl Gayle

The Real Thing

Chris Blackwell, the white Jamaican boss of Island Records said recently that he would like to get rid of the name "reggae." It was all right at first but now everyone uses it, including people who neither care for nor understand the music but think that anything with a repetitive Jamaican rhythm is reggae.

"Reggae" was really the name of the dance that replaced "rock steady," just as the latter had replaced "ska," or "blue beat." As a dance became popular, Jamaican musicians capitalized on it by making records to suit the dance fans. Thus with "reggae" came such records as "Bangerang" and "No More Heartaches," which were real reggae records—some times, indeed, the lyrics of such songs simply contained the word reggae used over and over again, as in "Do the Reggae" by the Maytals, a great favorite at the time. In the normal course of events, as a dance's popularity decreased its name became less frequently used in records, and this is what should have happened to the term "reggae."

By this time, however, records such as "Israelites," "Return of Django," "Liquidator" and "Long Shot Kick the Bucket" were making the English national charts because they were also being bought by skinheads, who at that time identified with the music and with some of its musicians, people like Desmond Dekker and the Pioneers. Out of this trend another developed, whereby records such as "Reggae in Your Jeggae," "Moon Hop," and "Skinhead Moon Stomp" were specially made for the skinheads, who in turn found new favorites like Dandy and Derek Morgan.

By then the name "reggae" was hardly used by the real fans but it remained popular with the skinheads, who continued to buy things like "Elizabethan Reggae," even in early 1970. It was this type of skinhead music which eventually gained the greater exposure (via the charts, etc.) as opposed to the music genuinely in the same vein as "Long Shot Kick the Bucket" (such as "Alidina" by the Maytals or "Too Proud to Beg" by the Uniques) which was not made for skinheads but typified the music that the real reggae fans were enjoying. The two types of record were separable but were conveniently heaped together as "reggae" by the people who were more interested in the financial rewards than the music itself. The result was that when the skinhead trend ended, in 1970, so did reggae chart success.

The next trend was for the musicians to aim for a wider market by commercializing their sound. At first this was done by adding strings and background vocals and by using a less ethnic approach in the singing (e.g., "Wonderful World, Beautiful People" and "You Can Get It If You Really Want It"); later on, "reggae" versions of other well-known songs appeared (e.g. "Young, Gifted and Black"). This commercial trend further widened the gap between what was widely known as "reggae" and what the real fans were digging.

When someone is looking for a reggae party to go to on a Saturday night he might ask, "Where is the blues?" but he won't use the word "reggae," not if he's a real fan. To him, "reggae" now refers to the stuff (like "Suzanne Beware of the Devil") that gets into the charts, and not to his music, which gets very little air play and never makes the charts. Such groups as Greyhound and the Pioneers are dismissed as "commercial" (compare the latter's "Long Shot Kick the Bucket" to their "Let Your Yeah Be Yeah"), and by using the term "blues" the real fan is subconsciously affirming his music's affinity, in feel and intensity, with blues music.

Real reggae tunes must be danceable (witness "Breakfast in Bed" by Lorna Bennett or "Jimmy Brown" by Ken Parker); there must be a continuous, repetitive riff to provide the dance beat. In "rock steady" the bass sound was even more important, now that you danced to it alone. People who criticize reggae music by saying that it all sounds the same are usually referring to the repetitive rhythm and fail to understand that repetition is inherent in the music's quality.

None the less, the lyrics are always equally important, even in the spoken comments over a background tune that are the trademark of someone like U. Roy. If the words are incomprehensible they still form a vital part of the total effect or "feel," as in the blues; they are never surreal, as in much pop or progressive music.

The singing is very important, too. Again as in blues, the ethnic voice, its mannerisms, its tone and, most important, its Jamaican accent, contribute much to the final sound. Eric Donaldson, one of the most popular singers on the scene, is a good example. He has a falsetto voice I disliked at first but which provides a very ethnic quality. This, more than any other factor, has been responsible for his quick success. "Cherry Oh Baby," his first hit, won 1971's Jamaican Song Festival, and "Blue Boot" is even better.

When I hear DJs call Paul Simon's "Mother and Child Reunion" a good reggae record I have to disagree. It can't be considered a reggae record just because the backing was done by reggae musicians, and like many white blues copyists, Simon falls down because of his voice. Even things like "Black and White" by Greyhound and "Suzanne Beware of the Devil" by Dandy Livingstone, which are good pop songs, are not good reggae records. Such musicians no longer retain the "feel" which was evident in their music at the outset.

The real enthusiasts are fed up with this type of commercial reggae which is popular and gets exposure on the radio. Hearing a few good tunes on Radio London's "Reggae Time" is not nearly enough to relieve the frustration of having to wait a week or of being disappointed by a group like Greyhound on "Top of the Pops."

The interest taken in reggae by soul and progressive musicians will help to break down all types of barriers between music fans and to popularize the real stuff, but the imitators (such as Paul Simon) should be ready to admit that they are *imitators* and that they can't achieve a true sound, or at least not yet. They should be credited with taking the music to a new and wider audience but they should not pretend that they are originators. The new audience will inevitably discover the real stuff (people like Prince Buster, Laurel Aitken, the Maytals, et al.), and these artists should, in turn, receive the acclaim they deserve not only from their new audience but also from the musicians—just as Muddy Waters, B. B. King, and others were acclaimed by their imitators. Such white musicians as Paul McCartney have already found new scope in Jamaican music but are, so far, wrongly attempting to duplicate it instead of using it to add something to their own type of music.

But before reggae music can become more acceptable in its ethnic form it must be promoted so that people outside the circles can gain a better understanding—you can't like something you don't understand. This is why the sound-systems fans who completely dismiss commercial reggae are not helping the situation. Even if it is a commercial dilution, at least some reggae does get into the charts, and people like Jimmy Cliff can't be expected to limit their scope by sticking solely to ethnic reggae. It is only someone like Cliff who can take the music to another audience, as he has done, in part, through the movie *The Harder They Come.*

Meanwhile "outsiders" should look into the sound systems, since they are where the best ethnic music is played. All the big systems (Sir Coxsone, Count Shelley, et al.) have a large following who expect (and get) the very latest sounds. If the people who understand the music and recognize the importance of the sound systems would communicate their knowledge in the press, then rock fans would gain a much better understanding of reggae music. To whet your appetite, these LP's are recommended:

"Tighten Up, Vol. 4" (TBL 163); "Reggae Chartbusters, Vol. 1" (TBL 105), "Vol. 2" (TBL 147); "Club Reggae, Vol. 4" (TBL 188); "The Harder They Come" (Island ILPS 9202); "Jimmy Cliff" (TRLS 16); "Eric Donaldson" (JAG 5401); "Monkey Man" by the Maytals; "Trojan's Greatest Hits, Vol. 2"; "Sixteen Dynamic Hits" (TBL 191). All of the above are on the Trojan label.

Watch This Sound

The biggest, most competitive sound systems (the forerunners of the present mobile discos) have been around since the early sixties. They have always been able to provide the very latest sounds and a few "specials" which they own exclusively (through arrangements with Jamaican producers and artists). In a 1971 sound-systems contest between Sir Coxsone and Duke Reid, both produced their own specials, drawing wild cheers from their respective supporters.

An important trend among the DJs operating the systems developed out of the "ska" era, and influenced, or led to, later styles. The fast-tempo ska records were especially popular with young dancers, who shuffled their feet fast but stylishly in time to the jerky bass riffs typical of such records as "Confucius" by Don Drummond, "Al Capone" by Prince Buster and "Broadway Jungle" by the Maytals. The DJs developed a habit of egging on the dancers, making scat noises, and interjecting comments into their amplified microphones like those on the traditional ska number "Lawless Street." There was a time when a sound system's reputation was dependent on its DJ's ability on the mike, and though the styles and the music have changed the practice is still widespread.

In 1967 the Ram Jam club in Brixton became the most popular among Jamaicans because the new "rock steady" sounds, such as "Ba Baa Boom" by the Jamaicans, "Rock Steady" by Alton Ellis, "Get Ready, Rock Steady" by the Soul Agents, and "Train to Skaville" by the Ethiopians were well featured. It was here that the English kids who came along were exposed to the Jamaican music, probably for the first time. Records like "Everybody Rude Now" by Keith McCarthy, "Tougher than Tough" and "Court Dismiss" by Derrick Morgan, "Judge Dread" by Prince Buster (hence his successful tour that year) and "007" by Desmond Dekker, which reflected the "rude boy" problem currently of prime concern in Jamaica, were very well received, particularly as they were such good dance records. English kids soon discovered that they could hear other goodies, such as "Sir Collins' Special" by Lester Sterling (one of the first DJ talk-over tunes), "Fatty Fatty" by the Heptones and "Kill Me Dead" by Derrick Morgan (two suggestive records), and the Hamlins' "Soul and Inspiration" (a very good sentimental record), only on sound systems.

By 1968, the resident systems, like Sir Coxsone at the Ram Jam, the Go Go at the Oval, Count Shelly at the 007 in Dalston, Sir Fanso at the Sunset in Islington, Neville at the Ska Bar, Woolwich, and later, Duke Reid at the Blue Ribbon in Peckham, drew consistently large audiences. The majority of the records that they were playing were not released as singles for weeks, sometimes never at all. Nevertheless, records such as "Gimme Little Loving" by the Pioneers, or "The Upsetter" and "People Funny Boy" by Lee Perry, sold in good quantities at "pre-release" prices. These records typified a new, harder sound and contrasted with and outsold old sounds like the rock-steady style "Do the Beng Beng" (Derrick Morgan). The new, heavier, more intense sounds could especially be appreciated when listening to Neville's system. He had a style of playing records, with the treble control turned right up, that later became popular among other systems. The effect of it was to produce a sharper, tighter sound, particularly noticeable in the rhythm guitar, which seemed to cut across the rest of the instruments. "Seeing Is Knowing" by Stranger Cole and Glady and "Woman a Grumble" by Derrick Morgan (in his new style) were two favorites that amply demonstrated this.

A notable aspect of the young whites was that the majority preferred such records as "Fire in Your Wire" (Laurel Aitken), "Bang Bang Lulu" (Lloyd Terrell), and "Rough Rider" (Prince Buster), because of their "rude" content. "54–56 That's My Number" by the Maytals, which was for me as good as Desmond Dekker's hit "Ah It Mek," was a hit only among ethnic fans.

The sound systems helped to create the boom that Jamaican music enjoyed in 1969. More English kids were being attracted by the sounds the systems were playing uniquely, records such as "Too Proud to Beg" by the Uniques and "Decimal Money" by the Maytals, which were as acceptable to them as songs like the Pioneers' "Long Shot," which they had, in turn, helped to reach the charts. They were also attracted by faster-tempo records such as "Work It" by the Voiceroys and "Mama Look Deh" by the Pioneers, records that led to the making of "reggae" (faster than rock steady). Another very popular record, "Tighten Up" by the Untouchables, also brought with it a new dance and (later on) an LP of the same name containing other, similar-sounding tunes, such as "John Jones" by Rudy Mills and "Watch This Sound" by the Uniques (a retitled version of Steve Stills's "For What It's Worth").

Meanwhile, Alton Ellis, who did a version of Tyrone Davis' "Change My Mind" retitled "Change of Plans," John Holt singing "Tonight," Pat Kelly with "How Long Will It Take," and Slim Smith with "Everyone Needs Love" paved the way for the smoother, sentimental vocalist. Together with such good instrumentals as Clancy Eccles and the Dynamites and Lee Perry and the Upsetters were consistently making, these smoother sounds offered a relief from the heavier stuff that the systems were playing.

Another development was the talk-over. Just as King Stitt with "Fire Corner," "The Ugly One," and "Vigorton Two" in 1968 and Sir Collins in 1967 had successfully *recorded* in the ska-influenced DJ style, so (in late 1970) did U. Roy, who was himself a sound-system operator. It brought him quick recognition just because the style was already so commonplace among the systems. U. Roy's records "Wear You to the Ball," "Wake the Town" and "Rule the Nation" occupied the first three positions in the Jamaican charts for several weeks, created a new excitement and were well featured by all the other DJs. Everyone wanted to hear the latest U. Roy tune, and his style was soon imitated by other recording artists.

The type of music that the sound systems are playing today has not changed much since 1969, though in 1971 there was a revival of a type of record that reflected life back home. When records like "Johnny Too Bad" by the Slickers, "Let the Power Fall" by Max Romeo and "Rivers of Babylon" by the Melodians were played loud they evoked a real feeling of spiritual togetherness in the audience. But they never displaced such happier tunes as "One-eye Enos" (The Maytals) and "Flashing My Whip" (U. Roy) or sentimental ones like "Stick by Me" (John Holt) and "Stand by Your Man" (Merlene Webber), and the systems still offer a complete range of Jamaican music.

Even when some of their supporters were consistently causing trouble, the sound systems always found somewhere to play. And whether it was in a pub, a bath hall, or a cold basement, there has always been an enthusiastic audience. If you go to the Roaring Twenties club in Carnaby Street, where Sir Coxsone is the resident DJ, you won't hear any commercial "reggae" and you might be disappointed with the records that you do hear, but you will notice the complete involvement of the audience, which, encouraged by the sound systems and their records, is *the* market for the real ethnic music.

Dub Wise Skank: Talk-over

Jamaica's four biggest talk-over artists are Dennis Al Capone, Big Youth, I. Roy and U. Roy. Most others who have recorded in this style are once-only, "have a go" opportunists, who would not have got into a studio, let alone made a record, but for U. Roy, who made the style popular and demanded "Do not imitate, because I originate." But a few of these opportunists have made very good records (Prince Jazzbo's "Mr. Harry Skank" (TE 921), "Vampire Rock" (GR 3034) by Jah Fish), and I hope we'll be hearing more from them, since the records are still party favorites.

The decline of U. Roy, the emergence of Big Youth and I. Roy, and the chart consistency of Dennis Al Capone (even when he was a little overshadowed by the other two's arrival), are all good talking points on the Jamaican music scene. Most agree that U. Roy's sharpest imitators have captured the feel for this type of music much better than the man himself, who seems to have lost it for the moment.

U. Roy's arrival, late in 1970, was a time of rejuvenation and excitement on the scene. Not that the music was at a low ebb then; it wasn't. It's just that U. Roy's sounds (which on close examination were definitely a ripoff from King Stitt, 1969's DJ hero, and only a continuation of the ska DJ's style in the mold of the present music) were so different from everything else and so immediately infectious. Maybe it was because whatever U. Roy was he always created the energy that only the best records have, making you happy or sad, making you want to dance and shout. Maybe he did create. King Stitt was never quite like this; he only hinted at it. U. Roy was intense from start to finish, shouting, singing, and screaming from a self-induced excitement that was possible only when he felt the rhythm. He was revealing his musical soul. It wouldn't have worked any other way: people weren't going to listen to a guy shouting over a microphone unless they were *involved*. He was one of us; he just cut discs directly for us to play.

So U. Roy made the records and we always bought them, because they were and are the best sounds around ("You'll Never Get Away," (DR 2514), "Tom Drunk" (DR 2517), "Flashing My Whip" (DR 2519), "Love I Tender" (DU 105), etc., etc., etc.). He made "specials" expressly for the big sound systems, and when he came to England hundreds went, anxious and curious, to see and hear him, raved with him, and came away very satisfied. And now these same people have put him down with the usual "He's gone commercial." Well, maybe they're right. His records are just not as good as they used to be; there are too many and they are not as urgent or intense as they should be. Maybe the people who put him on "Reggae Time" have something to do with it all.

"Ripe Cherry" (DYN 422), one of Dennis Al Capone's first hits, used the music to "Cherry Oh Baby," Eric Donaldson's festival winner. Before they became so popular, the annoying thing about these recordings was that they spoiled the original song. Now that we're used to them they are accepted as records in their own right and we wonder why we ever used to quibble. Al Capone was the first imitator and although he was good I suspected that he was "created" to cash in, like the Monkees. But Capone has his stern supporters, his phrases are unique, and he has made some very good records: "Teacher Teacher," "It Must Come," "Master Key," "Out of This World," "Musical Alphabet," etc. Even as I write, he tops the charts with "Cassius Clay" (JP 808), a fine record (with the greatest catch phrase: *chi wa wa chi woo*) that celebrates the master's win over Bugner. But his popularity or anyone else's for that matter has so far never matched U. Roy's at its height.

The two most fashionable musical hosts of the moment are Big Youth and I. Roy. Their styles are distinctive, although I. Roy has the more easily recognizable voice: more piercing than King Stitt's and usually accompanied by heavy echo effects. Big Youth's and I. Roy's popularity might easily be because they are the latest imitators, but the more likely reason is that their voices integrate more readily with the currently prevalent "skank" sounds. The other two, particularly U. Roy, are falling behind because the backing music of their best records comes from the late rock-steady and mid-reggae periods.

It's not easy to pin down just why Big Youth is the most popular right now, but his records do catch the attention quicker than most. His voice is heavy and outlandish and his phrases are usually more controlled and sensible than U. Roy's or Al Capone's. Maybe it's because Big Youth was the one to come up with "Ace 90 Skank" (DT 492). The record introduced this dance to the floors of Jamaica, and since the term *skank* had been used repeatedly in records since 1970 (when it was used in a record called "El Paso") and the dance was popular, it's only natural that the name should stick and eventually come to describe the actual music, which hasn't changed much apart from losing a little pace and leaning too much on bass and drums. Whether skank replaces reggae or not doesn't really matter; what is more important is that new musical styles and new dances emerge almost every week.

Again, Big Youth's emergence might be connected with his two very ethnic recordings "Foreman v. Frazier" (GR 3040) and

"George Foreman." These two records really captured the feel and excitement of what it meant to Jamaicans at the time of the fight. The event was a showdown, and George Foreman was the people's hero because he'd beat Joe Frazier, so Big Youth became the people's hero because we could relive the excitement through his music.

I. Roy has made the fewest records of the four, and much of his stuff is owned by sound-systems and pre-release addicts only. On his latest record, "Black Man Time" (DT 503), his voice nails you, then the melodic bass line grabs you, makes you move to it. The vocal isn't as piercing as it can be on this, but as the record builds, those nonsensical phrases rip out and suddenly at the chorus he almost sings (would you believe it!), and of course you catch the verse and almost sing too. And although what he is singing or shouting is made up on the spot and many of the words are not grammatically correct (they're sound effects, really) it is effective, it is original and it's a respected skill.

Rude Reggae

How do you make a hit without really trying? Simple. Just overdub some half-sung, half-spoken, suggestive nursery-rhyme lyrics onto a reggae-backing track (preferably an old instrumental). Judge Dread's "Big Six" (Big Shot B1608) was a poor effort by any standard, yet it has sold over three hundred thousand copies. "Big Seven" (B 1613) was an even bigger seller, and the only change was a slightly better backing track.

Judge Dread (real name Alex Hughes) seems to like the Jamaican sound, which I can understand, but the one-time debt collector, bouncer, DJ, etc., isn't helping the music's already misunderstood reputation (or his own) with these substandard rude reggae records. Maybe it's a good thing that the lyrics prevent radio exposure: outsiders would be misled even further. The Judge's records would certainly not have sold so well if it hadn't been for the "suggestive" lyrics, but surely he can do better than:

> Mary had a little pig
> She couldn't stop it grunting
> She took it up the garden path
> And kicked its little rump in.

This kind of thing only comes across as pathetic to true reggae fans.

OK! So where's the real stuff, then? Well, try this for a start: "Pussy Price" (Nu Beat NB 046), issued by Laurel Aitken in 1968. This is one of the most directly offensive rude records ever, more offensive even than his others—"Fire in Your Wire" and "The Rise and Fall of Laurel Aitken"—and as influential on rude reggae as Prince Buster's 1967 "Rough Rider." Aitken's gruff voice is well suited to his subject, which is quickly made clear.

When I started to play Aitken's record to refresh my memory, the lady of the house (not my mother) complained: "Don't play that record again! Whatever you do, don't play that record." I didn't argue—it's not as if the lyrics are easily forgotten anyway. Aitken makes no attempt at subtlety, the music is as crude as the lyrics, hard, direct, and apt. And it's so effective that it used to make the grownups leave the room at parties. The youngsters just laughed, of course: if it was so offensive, why did it sell so well?

Other records had the same effect. Lloyd Terrel's "Birth Control" (Pama PM 710) is an example of this. Prince Buster's "Big Five" (Buster label) was another. He took a reggae version of "Rainy Night in Georgia" and changed the lyrics to produce the most influential rude reggae record yet.

Prince Buster's records usually have a boastful quality, this one had an additional abrasiveness:

> Today I smoked an ounce of weed
> Tonight I'm gonna plant a seed
> In her womb all right, . . .

and in "Wreck a Pum Pum" (Pama—deleted) the singer reveals his frustration with similar aggression.

Rude reggae can be outrageous and amusing simultaneously, as "Trial of Pama Dice" (Sioux S1022) by Lloyd Dice and Mum proved. Pama Dice comes up for trial on a rape charge (for which he subsequently gets one thousand years) before a Judge Dread-type magistrate (Prince Buster's character) who completely dominates the proceedings, being judge, prosecution, and jury. Pama Dice is denied the chance to speak and has to listen to his accuser's (Mum's) story, which might not be as innocent as it seems:

> It was last Thursday night and I was going home and
> he came up to me and he said "Hello," so I said "Hello."
> (When are we going to get to the point?) And he said

can I kiss you? So I said "No." So he said "Oh!" Then
he pushed me and hit me and he started to, you know,
wreck the pum pum.

"Fatty Fatty" (Studio One S02014) is both flirty and dirty. It's a
very melodic tune, sung in a typically laid-back "rock-steady," almost hypnotic, style—the Heptones haven't had a record since. The
bouncy, bubbling, guitar intro (is it a bass?) is the very same one
that Jackie Mittoo used in his organ-based instrumental "Ram Jam."
The call-and-response method, using a male chorus, works well:

> I need a fat a very fat girl (fat for tonight), I'm in
> the mood (I'm in the mood), I'm feeling rude, girl
> (I'm feeling rude).

The bracketed words are sung by the chorus and create the atmos-
phere: "I say now, when you feel it girl you're gonna say it is (so
nice)." The bass and lead guitars duet in the same fashion, making
the song as memorable as the experience: so nice!
Derrick Morgan's "Kill Me Dead" (Pyramid—deleted) proved
that you didn't have to be crude to be rude. A smooth horn warning
gets it off: look out, here I come! Then the catch line is sung,
achingly: "Mind you kill me dead"—and repeated three more times
to get it home. The whole thing just slides along till: "I said the pres-
sure is hot—take your hand from me neck—hold me round the waist
—wind me wind me line—rub and squeeze now." All this time a girl
duet, sexy voices, reply to each line "old lady!" (or is it "oh
Lloydy!"?) or an occasional "Rub it up, push it up!" The lyrical climax is as good as any I've heard: "The river comes down—old
lady!" The musical experience is as satisfying; who said repetition is
boring?
The most successful rude reggae records were "Bang Bang Lulu"
(Lloyd Terrell, Pama PM710) and "Wet Dream" (Max Romeo,
Unity UN503), which both captured the attention of young white
reggae listeners, using double-meaning (if obvious) lyrics and easily
memorable tunes and chorus:

> Bang Bang Lulu's gone away
> Who is gonna bang bang bang when Lulu's gone away

and

> Every night me go to sleep me have wet dream
> Lie down gal, make me push it up push it up lie down.

In the former song their imagination didn't have to be stretched to discover the omitted word as the singer dramatically built the story behind the song:

> Lulu had a boyfriend
> His name was Tommy Tucker
> He took her down the alley
> To see if he could. . . .

And you would have to be very naïve to believe Max Romeo's claims that the words "push it up" in "Wet Dream" refer to his attempts to prop something up into his leaking ceiling when it rained. Besides, what about the second verse? "Look how you big and fat, like a big shot, give the crumpet to big foot Joe, give the fanny to me!"

More recently, one of the biggest-selling rude records among ethnic fans has been "Big Seven" (also known as "Punanni") by Charlie Ace and Fay (Pama PM853). The guy is in a hurry: "Take it off no!" "Wait no," comes the reply. "Just because you know I can make eight eighty eighty." (Work that one out!) The chick then phones up the "sex station" DJ, who proceeds to play his tune and provide an accompaniment for the couple "doing their thing" (judging by the amount of oohs, aahs, moans, and groans). "Do it the same way," she moans. "If I scream do it the same way." An ingenious record.

Let me finish with one of the first rude records, by Justin Hines: "Penny Reel O." The record was extremely popular, maybe because it illustrated an ideal way of settling debts:

> Gal you owe me a little
> money—Penny reel O
> And you have it back fi
> gimme—Penny reel O
> I beg you shub your cushu
> gimme—Penny reel O
> And let me rub out me
> money—Penny reel O.

For those of you whose curiosity has been whetted, check out the following LPs. Prince Buster's "Big Five" (Melodisc MLP 12-157) and Lloydie and the Lowbites' "Censored" (Lowbite 001) are the most offensive and the best musically, the latter containing very good cover versions of the most well-known reggae tunes, Prince Buster taking the rhythms of other popular reggae tunes and adding his own rude lyrics. Another good value is "Birth Control," an anthology on Economy (SEC 032), and Max Romeo's "A Dream" (Pama PMLPP4). The former LP includes the title track plus "Pussy Price" and "Ben Wood Dick" by Laurel Aitken, and others in the same vein from Max Romeo, the Ethiopians and others. "Wet Dream" is on "A Dream," with tracks like "The Horn," "Winc Her Goosie," etc. The LP "Bang Bang Lulu" (Pama PMLPP4) contains non-rude items (e.g. by Derrick Morgan and Lynn Taitt and the Jets) as well as the title track, "Wet Dream" again and other not so well-known rude material.

We all need humor, whatever our musical tastes, and it's fair to say that "rude reggae" satisfies both the commercial and the ethnic audiences, its common appeal being its sexual suggestiveness, which is so basic that it makes you laugh (or blush!). There's a lesson to be learned from this: Rock musicians, for instance, are too hung up on their "image." What little humor there is left in rock comes wrapped up in irony and cynicism, which doesn't help make rock accessible to the fans of other music. What we need is music we can all identify with. Long live rude reggae!

PLAYING RECORDS IN BRITAIN

Simon Frith

Introduction

More and more I think of the pop marketplace as a battlefield—the record buyer straggling just quirkily enough to frustrate the record companies' attempts to control his tastes and their sales.

The outcome is less certain than it is in other consumer battles because the means of persuasion that record companies control most directly (advertising) is their least effective one. Telling people to listen to a record isn't the same as making them hear it, and one complete spin on BBC Radio One is worth any number of full-page ads in *New Musical Express* or critical raves from a reviewer, or thirty-second spots on such stations as Capital or ITV. Even weeny idols must be heard as well as seen; the increasingly beseeching pictures of Ricky Wilde in *Jackie* don't compensate for the BBC's lukewarm shoulder, and the only other direct promotion a company can use is live performance, which increasingly means a gathering of an already mutual admiration society. Shows can *confirm* star status (which guarantees sales to the next record) but, at least in the singles market, they rarely cause it—sell-out concerts *follow* sell-out records, and in 1973–74 only Cockney Rebel could have claimed otherwise.

To sell a single, record companies have got to get a *sound* to the public, and they can do this only indirectly, through a middle man, the disc jockey. The DJ's position in the record-sales struggle is ambiguous not because of the legal restraints (payola, in all its various forms, represents the record companies' attempt to win the battle unfairly, by controlling the DJ) but because of the nature of his job—to please the public. He can't *simply* be on the record sellers' side (whether innocently or not), because if he doesn't play what his public wants to hear, he'll be out of work himself (this was the defense made by several American DJs in the payola scandals of the fifties). But neither can he *simply* be on the record buyers' side (not even John Peel), because, like it or not, his position is one of control (over what his public will hear) and his effect is on sales (a DJ who never moved anyone to buy anything would be a failure even by his own standards). Whose side is a disc jockey on? He sits and hopes that the records he plays will sell not because that will benefit him directly, but because if his taste is thus confirmed then his audience will continue to tune their trannies (transistor radios) to hear him.

The DJ's role is important but ambiguous, and it has been made more important (and more ambiguous) by the development since the sixties of *two* stages on which to perform it—the discothèque as well as the radio. Clubs with records as their only means of entertainment came to Britain (from France, I suppose) in the early sixties. Before then DJs and records had been used in ballrooms (e.g. Jimmy Saville's Teen and Twenty Club in Manchester), but not as alternatives to live music—imagine what would have happened to the Beatles had the Cavern been a disco and had its kids preferred original records to live covers. Initially discothèques served two sorts of in crowd: rock aristocrats seeking exclusion, and soul freaks; but by the late sixties, as live rock became increasingly undanceable, expensive, and in the wrong places (colleges and concert halls), discos took on pop (rather than cult) significance as places where a lot of record buyers were hearing a lot of records. Record companies were slow to realize the implications, but finally began to notice inexplicably high sales for records they had inadvertently neglected to delete from their catalogues. Backtracking through their sales departments to the source of demand, they discovered: the Northern Scene.

ROCK ALMANAC

* * * * * * *

The Northern Discos by Tony Cummings*

The northern soul scene is an inheritance from Britain's mod era of the early and mid-sixties.

The mods were the first to discover soul (or R and B as it was still called), and soon the music of new-wave black artists like The Miracles, Marvelettes, and Impressions was blasting from the all-night discothèques that began to spring up all over London's Soho. It was a heady time, when short hair was hip, clothes and dances changed literally from week to week, and energy was sustained on pills and scotch-and-Coca-Cola.

British bands began to copy the music, just as they had copied the rougher sounds of Chuck, Bo, Muddy and Wolf a few years earlier. Soon clubs all over Britain were playing soul. The music of Detroit and Memphis began to hit the charts. It was the dance music of the time. A golden age.

It didn't last long. Too much success, too much exposure, was killing the soul goose. By 1968 the psychedelic era had arrived and, with it, new tastes in clothes, drugs, and music. Many kids—including many former mods—preferred the heavier, more daring sounds of rock to the "gotta-gotta" predictability that much of soul had fallen into.

Within months UK clubs that had featured a soul discothèque (boosted with the occasional visit of an Edwin Starr or a Geno Washington) had been swayed by the "soul-is-idiot-dancing-music" bile that was streaming forth from the followers of the new music. Each month saw more clubs close or move over to a progressive-rock policy. By '68 London was a soul-less wilderness save for a few clubs playing James Brown or reggae for a black/white integrated audience. The bulk of the kids who went to the clubs in the South of England wanted head-blasting rock. To southern disco dwellers, soul was passé. Their northern cousins didn't agree.

When the "soul boom" got under way in Britain, the kids from Manchester, Stoke, Leicester, and other points north who wanted a blast of the sounds at first journeyed down to such clubs as the "Smoke." But soon they were forming their own little clubs, the

* from *Black Music;* used with permission

PLAYING RECORDS IN BRITAIN

Oodly Boodly (later the Night Owl) in Leicester, the Mojo in Sheffield, the Dungeon in Nottingham, and the Twisted Wheel in Manchester. And it was the latter which became the place that legends are made of. It was *the* club, it played the best records, had the best DJs and attracted the biggest crowds.

By 1968 the decline in the South of England soul scene was complete. Nobody told the Wheelites. A kid who journeyed there from Crewe remembered:

> Yeah, the Wheel scene was fantastic. There was an atmosphere about the place that was really electric. The all nighters were packed. Girls and fellows came from all over the North. In the early days they played all the big Motown things but bit by bit it kind of changed. They started playing more and more rare sounds. Not only records that hadn't been released in the States but sounds that hadn't sold at all here either.

The change in the record play list was significant, though it's difficult to identify the exact reasons for obscure discs (like Chuck Woods's "Seven Day Too Long" or Larry Williams and Johnny Watson's "A Quitter Never Wins") becoming such popular sounds. One reason may have been that it had become more and more apparent that the black American music scene had splintered into several diverse schools. Areas like psychedelic soul or hard James Brown-style funk were selling more and more, and the careering dance beats of the old-style Motown were no longer the staple diet of the U.S. soul charts. The lack of appropriately stomping hits necessitated the DJs' digging deeper and deeper into the morass of discs that never made it.

Another factor must have been the kind of kids who went to the northern clubs and the kind of dancing they did. A fan explained:

> A lot of the kids who used to go to soul discos in London and then went on to rock, heavy music like, were middle class, white-collar workers and such. But in the North it was, still is, very much a working-class scene. We didn't want anything to do with progressive music so we stayed with soul. And the kind of soul we wanted was fast dance things. We work hard, bloody hard, and we want to work hard on the dance floor. The faster the better.

Fast dancing wasn't the only kind of speed on the northern scene. With a proliferation of all nighters there was a parallel increase in the amount of dope taken by the minority. Said a fan at Leeds:

The scene has always been a pill scene. It's all uppers to make things go that much faster. It's all a part of the soul thing.

For some it undoubtedly was. Bit by bit the police started clamping down, and by 1970 drug raids produced a considerable trove of hapless victims.

In 1970 the Twisted Wheel, after a couple of busts, was forced to close. A fan who'd been dedicated to the northern club scene for a decade reminisced:

Something changed when the Wheel closed. You know there was never quite the same everything-for-the-good-of-the-music scene. We used to go to clubs like the Mojo (Sheffield), The Lantern (Market Harborough), Up the Junction (Crewe). The Blue Orchid (Derby) but the police stopped the all nighters there too. The pill heads were making it tough for the kids who just wanted to hear sounds. Then the Torch (Hanley, near Stoke) became the No. 1 scene.

As the clubs became more scattered, the music got more obscure. As far back as 1969, DJs like Les Cockell and Tony Jebb were playing rarities to the exclusion of hits. A record had to contain a fast, percussive dance beat but it *had* to be totally unknown. DJ Ian Levine explained:

Each area of the North and the Midlands has, or had, one club which kids would travel long distances to come to. A club couldn't be filled just by the kids in the immediate vicinity, there weren't that many soul fans. So the disc jockeys took to playing rare records, records nobody else had. If the kids wanted to hear them, they'd have to come to the club, that was the only way.

Unfortunately it wasn't. The scourge of the bootleggers was about to see to that. But certainly club disc jockeys were taking on the role of product hunters (the first DJs relied on super-hip record collectors to discover their obscurities but now several of the top disc jockeys find their own rarities) and promotion men (acting as the initial means of exposure for obscure records). In 1970 Tami Lynn's "I'm Gonna Run Away from You," a years-old forgotten dancer from Atlantic's archives, became *the* northern record. Polydor's Mojo label picked up on it and the record made the Top Ten—the first of many such northern revivals to break into the pop charts.

* * * * * * *

Pop Discos

Northern discos have become (over the past five years) a way of launching singles, but it is important to stress that their use is indirect: what northern success may do is convince a watchful record company that a single is worth trying nationally, but it is the pop discos that will then make or break it—the Coventry Mecca is more important than the Blackpool Mecca for the commercial exploitation of discothèques that can create a *chart* hit.

The disco hit of 1974 was R. Dean Taylor's "There's a Ghost in My House," and its road to the top was long and winding. A staff producer and writer at Motown, Taylor made occasional records as a singer in the late sixties and had two hits in England ("Gotta See Jane" and "Indiana Wants Me"). But he eventually decided that he wasn't getting as much attention from the company as his black colleagues, and he left in 1972 to try his luck on another label. Meanwhile the English Motown organization had discovered the potency of their sixties sound in the North and had responded in two ways: first, they began to issue a series of album anthologies of "disco classics"—old tracks that were good enough to dance to and obscure enough to satisfy northern cultishness; second, they employed a string of "reporters" in the biggest discos, to return a card each week indicating which Motown records (old or new) were proving particularly popular. Early in 1974 Taylor's "Ghost" was issued on a budget compilation of his Motown recordings, and the cards began to come in reporting its special popularity. Motown decided to risk it on a wider audience and issued it as a single.

The point of Motown's subsequent promotion was to break "Ghost" as a national dancing record, and they concentrated their efforts on discos—not just the northern ones which were playing the record already, but the major dance halls around the country (mostly the Mecca chain), sending the DJs the record, telling them that it was already a northern smash. The only radio station to get the full hype treatment was Manchester's Radio Piccadilly (on which Andy Peebles has an influential and broad-minded soul show for three hours on Friday evenings), and when the record first arrived on the national charts most BBC producers had not even heard of it. Their immediate response was to call up the British Market Research Bureau (who supply the chart) to check that everything was, uh, in order—was this unknown record for real? Were its sales *genuine?* The BMRB had triple checked already, equally taken by surprise— their sampling method (a careful geographical distribution of the shops whose sales figures they use) makes it virtually impossible for a local hit (even if the locality is as big as "the North") to show on the BBC chart. But "Ghost" had been selling nationally, and by the time the BBC belatedly finished giving it *their* treatment (Noel Edmonds' record of the week, etc.) it was in the top ten.

"Ghost" reached the public through three sorts of disc jockey: the northern soul men revealed its sales potential; the BBC jocks confirmed and enhanced its success; but it was the journeymen in the middle, the hundreds of commercial DJs with their mobiles and resident clubs up and down the country, who really brought the sound to the people who bought it. Chris Bond, for example, one of Coventry's most successful DJs, plays records to a thousand people seven nights a week and must, in the course of this, reach a good proportion of Cov's singles buyers: he covers teen-agers at the Locarno, their elder brothers and sisters in Mr. George's, and the young execs of the Villa Country Club.

Chris started playing records as a sixteen-year-old in 1968, saving up to buy some cheap, secondhand equipment, playing the current and immediate-past Top Twenty to whatever youth clubs would give him a couple of quid. This is the apprenticeship all DJs must go through, not just learning a mike manner but, more importantly, discovering disco taste—what to leave out of the Top Twenty, which oldies go down well, which new releases will be appreciated, how to balance the obscure and the familiar. By 1971 Chris had learned enough to be employed professionally by an agency, holding down spots around the West Midlands—Stratford on Friday, Smethwick on Saturday, Warwick on Sunday. . . . Stage Two of the DJ career and the lesson to be learned now was how to match an evening to an audience, how to vary a choice of records to suit different places and ages and styles. Chris extended his range even further by spending a year on the Continent (where DJs don't speak but English ones are in demand, as they are chic) and learning the disco possibilities of heavy metal (Led Zeppelin makes music the Swiss like to dance to) and non-pop soul.

By August 1973 he was a full-time professional DJ, with residencies seven evenings a week, a wide range of experience and an expandingly comprehensive record collection. What most impressed record companies though (and guaranteed Chris a place on most of their mailing lists) was the *number* of people he played to, his selling power. (Bell, ever efficient, sends down spies to check he's still got the audience he claims.) This is not quite how Chris sees himself. He is an entertainer putting on a show, and it's for the show that his records are selected. His audience wants to dance (and sometimes smooch), they want to be surprised (by something new) and confirmed (by traditional favorites), they want to remember the past (oldies), and bask in the present (current hits); a DJ must put on a *balanced* show, and the balance means different records for different audiences. Chris listens open-eared to every single he's sent but he'll play it only if it's right for *his* show.

Discos are vital for selling disco records (whether Gary Glitter or the Philly Sound) but they can't make any difference to the wrong sort of sound. The importance of a DJ like Chris Bond is that he's better able than most record-company people to judge what is a "disco record" (his livelihood depends on this), and intelligent promo departments treat him with respect and care (Phonogram, for example, regularly use their DJ letter to knock their own company's non-disco product—promising one week a Don Covay LP as a reward for breaking a single and threatening a Lena Zavoroni LP as a punishment for failure).

Compared with the Luxemburg DJs in the fifties or the Pirate/ Radio One DJs in the sixties, a seventies disco DJ is knowledgeable about music and genuinely enthusiastic. His special concern is soul music, the source of most of the best dancing records. So another Conventry DJ, Pete Waterman, runs an excellent soul record shop, where he and Chris Bond keep a permanently sharp ear open for soul album tracks or American imports with which to spice their acts. George McCrae's "Rock Your Baby," for example, was a regular sound in the Coventry Locarno (and probably elsewhere) as soon as it was released in America and weeks before it was released in England. He won't play anything "obscure" though, Chris Bond.

Monday night at the Coventry Locarno is teen-age night, and an aging voyeur is made to feel clumsy. Dancing for these cool kids is in lines and there are precisely choreographed steps for each different record. A lot of sweet-talking is going on but not much pairing off, and the clothes are slightly pre-rock 'n' roll (pony tails are almost back). For a night like this Chris doesn't use more than thirty records, all played at maximum volume, highest energy. On the radio there's not much in common between the fake exuberance of the Rubettes and the elegant beat of the O'Jays; but here they are equal in their mastery of and mastery by dancing feet. The few oldies played are disco classics—"Jimmy Mack" and "Jungle Boogie" and "Funky Nassau"—and there's a smattering of reggae for the smattering of West Indian kids doing splits (is *that* doing reggae in your jeggae?). There were two records I hadn't heard before: the Peppers' "Pepperbox" and Al Brown's very fine "Here I Am"—and the evening's newie was the Chi-Lites' "I've Got Sunshine," at that time a track off an American LP. The evening's biggest surprise was discovering how much sense Grand Funk's lumbering "Locomotion" made on the dance floor.

Except for some of the black records, though, the evening's music at the Mecca wasn't that much different from what you hear on Radio One—just confined to a dancing beat. The difference between Chris Bond's show and, say, Dave Lee Travis' is less one of tastes or values than of purpose—a disco has a different use from a tranny. Chris wouldn't want to work on a radio station, because he values his independence, but he doesn't see that such a change would make a huge musical difference, and certainly, from the other side, BBC DJs do a lot of work in discos. DLT and Stuart Henry are on the road more often than in the studio; the Rosko show is simply a broadcast of his live spectacular (only the go-go girls are missing); Noel Edmonds has a franchised mobile disco. Only the old men of the Beeb, Tony Blackburn and David Hamilton, confine their public appearances to supermarkets and pantomimes. There is a difference in what radio DJs do with records, but this reflects not so much their own interests as the peculiar institution within which they are confined.

The BBC

The basic constraint on the BBC is, paradoxically, the sheer size of its potential audience. There's hardly anyone in Britain who can't listen to the radio, and as a public service the BBC is obliged to consider the needs and interests of all this population. (And so the Beeb's audience-research department calculates audiences as percentages of possible listeners—everyone in transmitter range except the under-fives and over-eighties!) Since 1967, Radio One has been confined to providing a pop service; but even that is aimed at a vast and varied market, and this affects what comes out in two ways: first, the BBC is obsessed with audience size and shape and satisfaction, and carries out endless research to discover who is listening to what and when and why. Secondly, the corporation can't escape consciousness of its *responsibilities*—its programs are the product of an elaborate and cautious bureaucracy; there must be no scandal or uncertainty or offense. Underlying Radio One's use of records is an old slogan: Give the public what it wants.

The public is divided into three parts—weekday daytime, weekday evening, and weekend—and the most important of these is the weekday daytime. The daily shows (Noel Edmonds, Tony Blackburn, Johnny Walker, and David Hamilton) are the core of the BBC radio presentation of pop. Originally it was the responsibility of the producer of each show to put together an appropriate program. There were constraints (needle time,* the disapproval of the next man up the BBC hierarchy), but basically a producer could choose his own music. This system had to be dropped when it was discovered that some popular (i.e., best-selling) records were never getting chosen. The charts are one of the best indicators of what the pop public do want, and if Radio One was ignoring them then clearly the BBC was not fulfilling its obligations. Hence the play list.

Play-list broadcasting originated on commercial AM radio in the States; the station manager would draw up a list of records, and all the DJs would be required to play only records on the list. In 1973 the BBC began to organize Radio One in the same way. Each week, the four producers of the daily strip shows meet to put together a list of fifty-six records—a play list for them all. Add one oldie of the week (to be played in every program every day) and a record of the week for each DJ, and you get the sixty-one singles that take up about two thirds of the fifty hours a week of daytime Radio One.

The remaining time is taken up with album tracks, oldies, and new releases. The album tracks and oldies are still chosen by the

* ". . . a limit set by the British Musicians Union on the weekly amount of records allowed to be played on the radio, other music to be performed live or specially recorded for radio broadcasts."

producers individually and are mostly used for audience participation—the various DJs all have spots for requests. New releases are used as a way of extending needle time. Playing a record for review purposes (which means both commenting on it and giving listeners the details of its catalogue number) exempts it from the needle-time statistics, and at one time Radio One had a daily hour of "What's New." This was unsatisfactory for both the BBC (who were stuck with a program that was frequently lifeless) and the record companies (who didn't enjoy hearing their records being slagged off), and a new deal was made. The hour of new records would be spread through the strip shows in the form of new spins, and the DJs wouldn't comment on them though they would still name their labels. There are now four or five new spins in every show and one of the four daily producers is responsible for selecting and placing all of them.

The needle-time agreement obliges the BBC to broadcast a proportion of its music in the form of specially recorded tapes, but this makes hardly any difference to the play-list policy. For a start, the tapes are used unevenly. Audience research shows that Radio One has its biggest audience at breakfast time and slowly loses listeners all day. Tapes are deployed accordingly: Noel Edmonds plays only records; David Hamilton plays hardly any apart from new spins. Virtually all the tapes are of groups and records that are on the play-list anyway and, as the BBC's studio facilities have improved, mostly you don't know you're not listening to the record. The only drawbacks of the tape system are that it benefits British groups at the expense of American ones (though visitors get very favorable treatment) and that it involves the use of a tape five days running, which limits the extent David Hamilton's show can vary from day to day.

The most startling thing about the way Radio One works is the insignificance of the DJs. They have nothing to do with the play list and not much to do with the album tracks, oldies, or even records of the week—the producers don't think they are of much help: "Except for Johnny Walker, they're too busy opening shops and judging models to know anything about pop trends or tastes." The BBC DJ's role is independent of the music he plays; he must have an appealing and individual personality and sell *that* to the listener. The format of all the strip shows is the same: in each half-hour unit there are two chart records and two others from the play list, a new spin, an oldie, and an album track. What varies is the packaging: the DJ's spots and quirks. The idea is that Tony Blackburn and David Hamilton could play exactly the same records in exactly the same order and still have different shows.

For Radio One, as for disco DJs, playing records is just a means to the end of entertaining the public, and both claim that it's their respective publics (which for Radio One vary from school kids to housewives to workers according to the time of day) who determine which records are played. But whereas a disco DJ has a clear idea of what his audiences want (to dance) and is in direct communication with them, can watch their reactions to his choices, the producers who compile the Radio One play list are working with an imprecise notion of what pop radio is for, and know their audience and its reactions only secondhand.

Their surest measure is the charts, and these are the basis of the play list. Every Saturday the chosen dealers return their week's sales figures to BMRB; on Monday these are fed into a computer and on Tuesday morning the chart arrives at the BBC. The producers' meeting is right away—by Tuesday evening they have compiled the play list that will determine their programs from the following Monday (i.e. almost two weeks after the popularity of the records it includes was demonstrated). Their first rule of thumb is that every climber on the chart (they work with the Top Fifty) will be on the list, and that every record that has dropped out of the Top Twenty won't be. Falling records in the Top Twenty are treated on their merits: How fast are they falling? How long have they been on the play list? Gutted this way, the charts yield thirty to thirty-five of the records on the play list, and there'll also be five or six new releases a week which are chart certainties—new records from big stars, follow-ups to big hits.

This leaves fifteen to twenty records on the play list with uncertain popularity: the producers have to use other criteria of "good program material." These are rarely explicit; producers talk mysteriously of "other indicators of public taste besides sales," and claim obligations to both record makers and listeners. They listen to every new single they get, and treat them sympathetically: four or five of each week's risk records are new releases, and once on the play list a record is usually given a chance to prove itself, being played for anything up to seven weeks even if not a hit. But at the same time, the play list won't include records that it's thought the public doesn't want ("we can't really play that to housewives"), and this judgment

ROCK ALMANAC

tends to be narrow and patronizing; only in the evenings and on weekends will the BBC admit to an "up market" for pop. Demographically they may be right, the bulk of the daily audience is housewives and children rather than students or rock fans; what's offensive is the contemptuous certainty with which this audience is satisfied.

The BBC can be so certain only because their argument is circular. A record on the play list has a good chance of being a hit, a single not on it has hardly a hope. These results appear to confirm the producers' judgments, but they are equally a consequence of them. BBC people refer to a record that gets TV's "Top of the Pops" exposure but doesn't make the Top Fifty as a "dog record": it must be exceptionally unappealing, to gain nothing from the industry's best promotional spot; but it's just as unusual for a record to get full Radio One treatment and flop and even more unusual for a record to get no Radio One play and make it. There are some alternative means of national promotion—films (*The Entertainer*), TV ("She"), the astute use of discos ("There's a Ghost in My House")—but these are so rare that Radio One is basically indispensable. Commercial stations are restricted to their local areas so that, for example, while the BBC admit that Capital Radio was responsible for Prelude's "After the Goldrush" being released as a single, they're still sure it became a hit only after Radio One started playing it.

Radio One knows its importance for the record business and doesn't wear its responsibilities lightly. One reason for its elaborate organization is to minimize the possibilities of payola, and while the BBC has "good relations" with record companies (they're all part of the show-biz family), the business' *direct* salesmen, the pluggers, don't get much joy. The BBC isn't Luxemburg; there's no money to be made from playing a record or seeing it sell. But though the BBC's honor is intact, its account of its role in pop—as a sort of honest broker, benevolently selecting from the mass of weekly releases just those records its audience wants to hear—is disingenuous.

The Radio One DJs and producers may not be there to be bought, but they are involved in selling, and record companies know it. The BBC molds as well as responds to public taste, and record companies respond to as well as mold the play list. Either way, the effect on English pop is deadening. The no-risk policy, the firm control of every sound, means that the listener is rarely stimulated and that record companies can work out what is a "BBC record." The latter effect is the more dire. Given the pop that's available, the BBC doesn't do a bad job with Radio One (at least in terms of record selection—presentation is something else). The problem is its influence on what pop is available; the more cautious the BBC, the more predictable is the average British pop song, as record companies try to ensure their best access to the public. It was for this reason that the pirate radio stations, despite their own problems, were necessary for the creativity of British pop in 1964–67. Can commercial radio, the new rival to the BBC, make a similar impact?

Capital Radio

Capital Radio is the most significant alternative to Radio One because of its audience size (much greater than for its fellows in Birmingham, Manchester, and Glasgow), its impact on the pop world (which is almost entirely based in London), and its function as a music station (the rest of local radio, BBC and commercial, has to provide the whole range of broadcasting in a single station). It is worth studying Capital, then, as an example of how non-BBC pop radio can be organized.

Some of its attitudes are just the same (Aidan Day, the musical director, is an ex-BBC producer: the audience is similarly divided into weekday, evening, and weekend parts; needle time (nine hours a day out of twenty-four) is concentrated on the daytime shows, tapes are used only in the early evening; programs are adjusted as the day progresses: housewives come into their own at 9 A.M., students at 6:30 P.M.; there is a play list. This is put together by Day alone, who selects forty records a week, six climbers (new releases), and a few instrumentals and album tracks for occasional variation. The justification for the smallness of the list is that few people listen to the radio continuously; they mostly listen in a series of segments —while making the beds, driving to work, having a tea break. Day programs his play list accordingly, using the American AM "carousel system" to arrange the records in a repeated but varied pattern from 6:30 A.M. to 6:30 P.M. Nicky Horne (coming on at 6:30 P.M.) chooses his own tracks, but Day keeps an eye on his plans and may advise him against too way-out music too early in the evening.

The object of the play list is to achieve the "over-all sound" that Day believes will appeal to his audience. It is not clear how he comes to this belief. The Capital chart is no help; it is compiled by Day not on the basis of London's sales figures but as the chart that "feels" right, that the audience "seems to want." Capital doesn't have to be comprehensive; it is confined to London listeners and can concentrate on the "sophisticated pop audience of 15–40" as a potentially attractive market for advertisers. What this audience wants is not just guessed; Capital have done their research. So the music is adjusted to suit the different audiences that are dominant at different times of day; and when, after a few months on the air, it was discovered that the audience hadn't grown as planned, there was "a slight redirection" in music policy: Day decided he'd been too sophisticated too soon, had tried to change radio habits too suddenly. Previously sneered-at pop hits were slipped into the schedules.

In musical terms Capital has two special characteristics: first, by having a small play list it does avoid the more mindless and middle-of-the-road chart sounds: Capital housewives aren't as musically moronic as BBC housewives—but this defiance of chart values depends on good audience figures; Capital's policy has changed once and it could change again. But Capital's play list is also much quicker on the ball than the BBC's—playing eventual hits much earlier. Aidan Day sees this as an indication of Capital's power to break records, arguing that 40 per cent of singles sales are in London and that, at the least, Capital gives the BBC an idea of what to play. But I think that what Day's play list really reveals is his flexibility: he's not confined by a chart that's already more than a week out of date, he can back his hunches immediately (no committee to argue with), his pursuit of the sophisticated audience is an incentive to risk-taking. The only direct influence on Day's decisions comes from the DJs—they have an open meeting weekly—and there is no evidence that record companies have any more power there than in Broadcasting House. Capital music is kept carefully separate from record commercials, and Day treats pluggers in his best BBC manner: they are useful messengers but should be neither seen nor heard by program planners.

In short snatches Capital is a more enjoyable pop station than Radio One. The commercials are less irritating than the banalities of Blackburn et al., and the music's better—less rubbish, more oddities. For longer or repeated listening, though, the short play list is wearing: Top Forty radio makes sense only if you've got lots of buttons to push. On the other hand, Capital has established a distinctive feel.

Maria Muldaur's "Midnight at the Oasis" and Lynsey de Paul's "Ooh Ooh Baby" were played on both Capital and Radio One, but Maria's is a Capital record, Lynsey's a BBC one. It is this difference that could prove important for British pop; what matters is not that one station is better than the other but that they provide space for different sorts of music. *How* records reach the public isn't going to change much, but the range of choice might.

THE IN-BETWEEN YEARS
(1958–63)

Mark Sten

The decline in 1959 of classical rock 'n' roll has been attributed to such external factors as the payola scandal and the sudden retirement of most major rock idols (Presley, Little Richard, Jerry Lee, Buddy Holly, and Chuck Berry). But a more general dynamic led up to the events of 1959 and the eclipse of the buoyant, boogie-derived rock 'n' roll of the rockabilly singers and crossover blacks like Berry and Little Richard. The end had actually come in the spring of 1958 with a sudden decadent implosion, which was followed by a resurgence of non-rock idioms and the birth of a new style of rock music, the teen ballad, a melancholy form best suited to expressions of loss and pain.

A review of the ⌗1 records for 1958 illustrates the disintegration of rock 'n' roll and the ascendance of the teen ballad. The first two songs are fast boppers, but the rest of the year is entirely given over to (I) rock 'n' roll novelty, (II) teen ballads, and (III) non-rock songs.

	At the Hop	Danny & the Juniors	6 weeks at #1
	Get a Job	Silhouettes	2
II	Don't	Elvis Presley	1
I	Tequila	Champs	5
III	Twilight Time	Platters	1
I	Witch Doctor	David Seville	3
II	All I Have to Do Is Dream	Everly Brothers	4
I	Purple People Eater	Sheb Wooley	5
I	Yakety Yak	Coasters	1
III	Patricia	Perez Prado	1
II	Poor Little Fool	Ricky Nelson	2
III	Volare	Domenico Modugno	5
II	Little Star	Elegants	1
III	It's All in the Game	Tommy Edwards	6
II	It's Only Make Believe	Conway Twitty	2
III	Tom Dooley	Kingston Trio	1
II	To Know Him Is to Love Him	Teddy Bears	3
III	The Chipmunk Song	Chipmunks	1

So rock 'n' roll died at mid-year in a spasm of humor, abandoning the charts to the new ballad genre and to a wave of pre-rock material which took over in 1959, filling the #1 spot for forty-one of fifty-two weeks with songs that had nothing to do with rock: "The Chipmunk Song," "Smoke Gets in Your Eyes," "Venus," "The Three Bells," "The Ballad of New Orleans," "Come Softly," and "Mr. Blue," "Lonely Boy," "Heartaches by the Number," and "Mack the Knife," the biggest record of the year.

Other indicators also point to early and middle 1958 as pivotal. The year's up-tempo hits had begun to deal with strangely miscellaneous topics, as if rock 'n' roll had somehow lost focus. "Don't Let Go" (Roy Hamilton, 3:1),* "The Walk" (Jimmy McCracklin, 7:2), and "Do You Wanna Dance" (Bobby Freeman, 5:5) were straightforward, but the others . . . "Short Shorts" (Royalteens,

* Notation explained: The numbers in parentheses refer to the highest ranking reached on the *Billboard* weekly Top 100 survey, and to the month and year the record first entered the Top 100; thus, (5:7/62) means that the record entered the charts in July of 1962 and went to a top rating of #5.

3:1), "Endless Sleep" (Jody Reynolds, 5:6), "Willie and the Hand Jive" (Johnny Otis, 9:6), "Rockin Robin" (Bobby Day, 2:8), "Chantilly Lace" (Big Bopper, 6:8) and "All American Boy" (Bill Parsons, 2:12) . . . these aren't exactly novelty numbers like "Purple People Eater" or "Yakety Yak," but they do indicate that the rock 'n' roll thrust was fragmenting. By 1959 the pop consciousness was wandering aimlessly over the culture-scape, scarfing down odd bits of history, items of dress, cartoon characters, and spewing them back as "Tom Dooley," "Tall Paul" (Annette, 7:1), "Tan Shoes and Pink Shoelaces" (Dodie Stevens, 3:2), "Kookie Lend Me Your Comb" (Ed Byrnes, 4:4), "Waterloo" (Stonewall Jackson, 4:5), "Battle of New Orleans" (Johnny Horton, 1:5), "Running Bear" (Johnny Preston, 1:10), "El Paso" (Marty Robbins, 1:11), "Yellow Polka Dot Bikini" (Brian Hyland, 1:7/60), and ultimately "Alley Oop" (Hollywood Argyles, 1:6/60), a terrific song, but really.

The year 1958 was also bad for the King: from his first RCA single ("Heartbreak Hotel," 1:2/56) through "Don't" (1:1/58) Elvis had seven ※1's out of nine releases, but from early 1958 through late 1959 he put out four singles in a row that failed to reach the top, before he finally scored again with "Stuck on You" and "A Big Hunk o' Love," throwbacks from the rockabilly mold of "All Shook Up" and "Don't Be Cruel." But rock 'n' roll had expired by then, and Colonel Parker was to chart a new course for Elvis, steering him into the post-1950s mainstream with the Ankoid "It's Now or Never," Wagnerian pop melodrama, and with his next two ※1's, "Are You Lonesome Tonight" and "Surrender."

Few rock artists launched careers in 1958; probably the biggest was Jack Scott (Jack who?), who came in with a double-sided hit. The rock 'n' roll side, "Leroy," entered the Top 100 first (apparently released as the A side) and reached ※25, but it was overshadowed by the ballad on the flip side, "My True Love," which entered three weeks later and oozed up to ※3 before ebbing. And in mid-1958 Ricky Nelson and the Everly Brothers each peaked with ※1 ballads that marked turning points in their own careers and in the general development of rock.

Ricky and the Everlys had both started in mid-1957, singing rock 'n' roll, the Everlys with "Bye Bye Love" and "Wake Up Little Susie," Ricky with "I'm Walkin," "Be Bop Baby," "Stood Up" and "Believe What You Say." Then each made a dramatic shift to heartbreak ballads ("Poor Little Fool" and "All I Have to Do Is Dream"), a type of song that proved better suited to their soft, smooth voices and to the ultimate roots of their romantic appeal as tender-headed losers at life and love. Each then more or less abandoned bop rock in favor of ballad-oriented careers. Of the Everlys' eleven Top 20 singles that followed "All I Have to Do Is Dream," only "Bird Dog" resembles their earlier rock 'n' roll material. Some of the rest had a certain strength, especially "When Will I Be Loved" and "Cathy's Clown," but it was a forlorn fortitude in the context of downers like "So Sad," "Ebony Eyes," "Crying in the Rain" and the rest. Ricky's story was essentially the same; his twelve Top 20 follow-ups to "Poor Little Fool" usually featured a ballad side and a rock side, and the ballad side always was placed higher. His ballad lyrics weren't invariably laments (as they were with the Everlys, the Neil Youngs of their day); "Travelin Man," for example, had its carefree superstar stud theme, but the music and the melody were so despondent that the record seems oddly schizoid. For contrast, check in eight months later on Dion's snarling "Wanderer," in which the same theme is sung and played with real guts, highlighting the fundamental gentleness of Ricky's trip.

Like rock 'n' roll, the teen ballad represents a fusion of black and country idioms, but the ballad drew from the mellower, less raucous aspects of the doo-wop vocal group heritage, and emphasized the harmonic sweetness and melodic strength of its country, western, and folk sources. Country precursors of the teen ballad appeared in 1956 and 1957—for example, "Dreamy Nights" by Dicky Lee (Patches, 62). Johnny Cash was a major link between upbeat mid-'50s rockabilly and the ballads of 1958–60, drawing as he did on non-blues song forms and on a country tradition of harmonic simplicity, a reliance on the unadorned triadic chording that characterized most future country-rock ballads, distinguishing the genre from corresponding black ballad forms in which accidentals and blue notes appeared much more frequently (the split goes on). The teen ballad was also foreshadowed by "Young Love" (Sonny James, 2:12/56, and Tab Hunter, 1:1/57), which showed a country singer embracing pop themes closer to the hearts of a mass teen audience than to the folks back home. This was repeated by Marty Robbins ("White Sport Coat," 3:4/57) and Johnny Cash ("Ballad of a Teenage Queen," 16:1/58).

One element used in countless mid-'50s doo-wop tunes and then absorbed wholesale in 1958 by the teen ballad was the minor-sixth-turnaround chord pattern (I-mVI-IV-V, i.e., C-Am-F-G), the chord sequence of "Poor Little Fool," "Little Darlin," "Angel Baby," "Bristol Stomp," "Happiness Is a Warm Gun," and so on. The racially integrated Dell-Vikings ("Come Go with Me," 5:2/57 and "Whispering Bells," 9:6/57) achieved the first hit synthesis of white rock 'n' roll with black doo-wop, establishing a new musical style where previous white vocal groups like the Crew Cuts and the Diamonds had simply mimicked black models. The Dell-Vikings paved the way for acts like Danny and the Juniors, the Monotones ("Book of Love," 5:3/58), the Kalin Twins ("When" 5:6/58) and ultimately Dion and the Belmonts. Hits in this style combined the minor-sixth turnaround with an ebullient rock 'n' roll feel, conveying an exuberance that is absent from the maudlin turnaround ballets that followed.

Paul Anka's turnaround-based debut, "Diana" (2:7/57), is both buoyant and maudlin. I'm not sure Anka really belongs in rock; he seems to hark back to some earlier strain, perhaps operatic, definitely Italian. It's never clear whether he's going for Presley's belt or Sinatra's, a confusion he shares with Andy Williams, Steve Lawrence, Pat Boone, and others who began with rock 'n' roll in 1955, '56, and '57, but who reconverted to crooning during rock's lean period.

One of the most interesting offshoots of the minor-sixth-turnaround ballad was crystallized in late 1958 by Phil Spector's "To Know Him Is to Love Him" (Teddy Bears, 1:9/58), and reached its apotheosis two years later with "Angel Baby" (Rosie and the Originals, 5:12/60). This soft-heavy subgenre was defined by three common elements: a steady, medium-slow 6/8 rhythm with a pronounced backbeat (a gravid, rocking waltz tempo); a muffled band sound in which guitar, bass, and piano melt together into a single pulse; and an intimate female voice of vaguely juvenile character.

Spector's model was "You" (21:4/58) by the Aquatones, a startling song that had already developed the major ingredients reworked by Spector in "To Know Him": the 6/8 beat, the instrumental track, the emphasis on unadorned chord changes, the male chorus, and above all the tenor of the lead vocalist's pleading lament. The Aquatones' lead singer effectively communicated heartbreak and vulnerability not through the phrasings and mannerisms of an expressive singer, but with a virtual monotone; moving evenly from note to note and never varying the uniformity of her attack, she relied on pure tone itself for emotional impact. The Teddy Bears' female lead captured some of this same essence in "To Know Him," but her whine was less pronounced and lacked a certain shrill intensity of feeling. The performance was a strong one nevertheless, cutting through the muted, echo-ridden backing track. The hymnlike quality implicit in the rock-ballad idiom came to full realization in "To Know Him," which is suffused with a religious ambience that rises to a climax with the break and its inspired chain of devotional chords.

The soft sound reached an apogee of sorts in 1959 wth the arrival of the Fleetwoods and "Come Softly to Me," quiet at the loudest volumes, a song so soft you could bruise it with marshmallows; I hear no drums. The subgenre yielded no further monsters for over a year, but other minor-sixth ballads from 1959 displayed influences in common with "To Know Him" and its successors. The 6/8 beat caught on and appeared in "It's Only Make Believe" (Conway Twitty, 1:9/58), "Donna" (Richie Valens, 2:11/58), "Need You" (Donnie Owens, 25:10/58), "Tragedy" (Thomas Wayne, 5:2/59), and "Sleepwalk" (Santo and Johnny, 1:8/59). The echoing muffle characteristic of the soft-heavy instrumental sound was used on "Donna," "Tragedy," "Sleepwalk," "Susie Darlin" (Robin Luke, 5:8/58), and "Sea of Love" (Phil Phillips, 2:7/59). (The country-flavored ballads favored a crisper, twangy sound more reminiscent of James Burton's Sun-styled guitar on "Poor Little Fool"; these included "It's Only Make Believe," "Need You," "Sandy" (Larry Hall, 15:11/59), "Tell Him No" (Travis and Bob, 8:3/59), and "Robbin the Cradle" (Tony Bellus, 25:5/59).

Connie Stevens' "16 Reasons" (3:2/60) combined the standard soft-heavy elements with a vocal style new to rock, a breathy, cloying suggestive eagerness pioneered by another actress, Debbie Reynolds, on "Tammy" (1:7/57) and carried to extremes by Phil Spector and the Paris Sisters in 1961 and by Jane Birkin in the '70s. But the culmination of the soft-heavy offshoot came at the end of 1960, with "1000 Stars" (Kathy Young and the Innocents, 3:10/60) and "Angel Baby" (Rosie and the Originals, 5:12/60). The sharp, high clarity of the leads in "You" and "To Know Him" was further exaggerated by Kathy and Rosie, whose voices shared a nasal, prepubescent timbre that rendered their appeal more childlike than adolescent. "Angel Baby," the more radical of the two, reduced the instrumental track to the ultimate minimum: the piano/bass/guitar meld simply repeated the minor-sixth turnaround for the length of the song, generating a robot mantra devoid of embellishment or variation, the perfect underpinning for Rosie's piercing, disembodied-siren vocal.

With "Angel Baby," rock had regressed as far as it could, some nameless dread loosed within the collective Top 40 mind had run its course and spent itself in a lost mournful wail. "Angel Baby" was the final moonlit flowering of rock's medieval phase, paean to a purity and innocence no longer possible in the real world. The decline and fall of rock in 1958, the loss of vigor and the swift evaporation of musical energy, had faded into a deep melancholia that found musical reflection in the wistful ballads of late 1958 and '59. And as the survivors of Rome's collapse drew solace from religious doctrines of escape and otherworldliness, so the heartbroken pop consciousness turned to Christianity's musical equivalent. Angel Baby indeed—sexuality transmuted into a dual promise of heaven and childhood, set to music completely steeped in the tragic sensibility of the ballad era. "Angel Baby" marked the close of that era; pure form now actualized. Nothing remained but to move on.

Just the sort of two-bit metaphysical hyperbole these pointy-headed bastards are always palming off as insight on an unwitting public that never heard of Cathy Jean and the Roommates, or if they did they're in no shape to remember. Her "Please Love Me Forever" (12:3/61) has to be some forty-six-year-old producer's idea of a cash-in, an assembly-line model with all the features: 6/8 time, heavy backbeat, male chorus, shrill female lead, white sidewalls, factory air . . . The song's MOR origins are betrayed by the professionally sterilized sound engineering, a couple of high-society chord changes that snuck past the label's youth experts, and Cathy Jean's obvious discomfort at being coerced into singing through her nose like an eight-year-old.

And then there are the Paris Sisters.

The degeneration of rock 'n' roll in the late '50s led not only to the rock ballad and the re-emergence of non-rock forms, but also to two more-extreme reactions, opposing pop branches that developed as radical rejections of mainstream trends. The impact of instrumental rock and popularized folk music survived their passing after 1963, and the polarity they represent is central to the music of the late '60s and early '70s.

The success of instrumentals in 1958 and especially in 1959 amounted to a retreat from the directions vocal rock had taken: the ballad and the formula rock 'n' roll that sprang into being in 1959 centered around Fabian, Bobby Rydell, Frankie Avalon, and other photogenic youths with unpleasant voices. With the exception of "Sleepwalk" (a minor-sixth-turnaround ballad), the important instrumentals of this period retain the hard, simplistic drive of mid-'50s rock. The year 1958 saw a few rockabilly instrumentals: "Raunchy" (Ernie Freeman, 3:11/57), "Tequila," "Rebel Rouser" (Duane Eddy, 6:6/58), "Mexican Hat Rock," (the Applejacks, 16:9) and "Rumble" (Link Wray, 16:4, the first recorded heavy metal in history)—but the real boom came in 1959, with "Guitar Boogie Shuffle" (the Virtues, 5:3), "Happy Organ" (Dave Baby Cortez, 1:3), "Bongo Rock" (Preston Epps, 14:5), "Sleepwalk," "Red River Rock" (Johnny and the Hurricanes, 5:8), "Teen Beat" (Sandy Nelson, 4:9), "Woo Hoo" (the Royal Tones, 16:10), and honorable mentions to "Rockin Crickets" (the Hot Toddys, 57:4), and "Tall Cool One" (the Wailers, 36:5). The number fell off in 1960, with only "Beatnik Fly" (Johnny and the Hurricanes, 15:2), "Because They're Young" (Duane Eddy, 5:4), and "Walk Don't Run" (the Ventures, 2:7), but in 1961 another surge welled up, opening with four piano songs all based on classical riffs: "Asia Minor" (Kokomo, 8:2), "On the Rebound" (Floyd Cramer, 4:3), "Bumble Boogie" (B. Bumble and the Stingers, 21:4), and "Like Longhair" (Paul Revere and the Raiders, 38:4). Other instrumentals of 1961 included "Wheels" (the Stringalongs, 3:1), "Apache" (Jorgen Ingmann, 2:1), "Quite a Party" (the Fireballs, 27:7), "Last Night" (the Mar-Keys, 3:7), "Let There Be Drums" (Sandy Nelson, 7:11), and the first surfing hit, "Let's Go Trippin" (Dick Dale, 60:12). But the surf wave took another year to crest: 1962's big instrumentals were "Rinky-Dink" (Dave Baby Cortez, 10:7), "Green Onions" (Booker T and the MGs, 3:8), "Wiggle Wobble" (Les Cooper, 22:10), and a slug of surf songs at the end of the year: "Let's Go" (the Routers, 19:11), "Telstar" (the Tornadoes, 1:11), "Wild Weekend" (the Rockin Rebels, formerly Hot Toddys, 8:12), and "Surfer's Stomp" (the Marketts, 31:1/62). Nineteen sixty-three produced "Pipeline" (the Chantays, 4:3), "Wipeout" (the Surfaris, 2:6), "Bust-Out" (the Busters, 25:9), "Outer Limits" (the Marketts, 3:12), "Penetration" (the Pyramids, 18:2/64), and just one non-surfing Top 20 rock instrumental, Lonnie Mack's "Memphis" (5:6/63).

The lack of vocals obliged these bands to experiment with tonal innovation and led them away from the acoustic guitars of the rockabilly period into electric variations on the rock 'n' roll theme. By contrast, the Kingston Trio and their descendants in the early '60s de-emphasized the instrumental component by eliminating the rhythm section and falling back on a standardized acoustic-guitar sound, relying for commercial appeal on cleverness of lyric, on message. The voice itself was stripped of its more interesting properties, the shrieks and growls of rock 'n' roll in its heyday.

The folk acts and the instrumental groups shared one important characteristic: both were small, self-contained bands, not backup musicians behind a name singer but genuinely egalitarian musical units, a form then new to pop which would become predominant with the Beatles. In this respect, and in their opposing emphases (the exploration of exotic electric sounds versus acoustic uniformity and the primacy of message) these two wings prefigured changes in rock that followed the advent of the Beatles in 1964.

The early '60s also saw several other developments that had important long-range effects: the spread of rock beyond its natural cultural boundaries into the adult world, the transcendence by songwriters like Roy Orbison, Goffin-King, and Crewe-Gaudio of the narrow horizons of '50s rock 'n' roll and the rock ballad, the widening range of sound possibilities available to producers oriented like Phil Spector to the recording studio, and the appearance of the rock band in its modern form. These trends lie at the heart of the rock revolution of the mid and late '60s, a revolution that first took shape in the three years prior to the arrival of the Beatles, 1961–63. The early '60s are often seen as an extension of the late '50s, the whole stretch supposedly a single barren interregnum between Chuck Berry and the Beatles. We offer a revisionist interpretation of 1961–63, stressing the distinction between this period and the late '50s and emphasizing the growth of a new dynamism from 1961 on. This dynamism can be measured statistically by comparing the number of songs to enter the Top 20 in different years.

1958–135 new songs
1959–147
1960–147
1961–176
1962–178
1963–177

Please note the quantum leap that occurs in 1961. In 1964, the year of the Beatles, the figure stays at 175, but by 1966 another jump has occurred, with 196 new songs placing in the Top 20. In 1968 the number had dropped back to 161, 10 per cent *below* the average for 1961–63.

So much for progressive rock.

Rock 'n' roll's emphasis on rhythm naturally led to a lot of dancing, and the ubiquity of bop lyrics in the '50s reflects this. In 1960, rock dancing was transformed by the twist; partners dancing apart was the crucial terpsichorean innovation of the past few decades, and it brought on a new pop cycle, the dance era of the early '60s. The era began with Hank Ballard's re-emergence in mid-1960, following years of relative obscurity after the "Work with Me Annie" series in 1955. Beginning with "Finger-Poppin' Time" (7:5/60), Ballard and the Midnighters put out seven consecutive Top 40 hits in fourteen months, all songs about dances ("Twist," "Hootchie Cootchie Coo," "Continental Walk," and "Switcharoo") or dance parties ("Finger-Poppin' Time," "Let's Go Let's Go Let's Go," and "Let's Go again"). His "Twist" might have gone higher than ⋕28 if Chubby Checker hadn't covered it with the version that reached ⋕1. The twist was happening, and various has-beens made leaps at the bandwagon as it passed: Danny and the Juniors ("Twistin USA," 27:9/60), Santo and Johnny ("Twistin Bells," 49:12/60), Bill Doggett ("Let's Do the Hully Gully Twist," 66:1/61), Fabian ("Kissin and Twistin," 91:11/60). But most impressed by the success of the twist was Chubby himself, whose next thirteen singles were all dance records, all but two making the Top 20.

Nineteen sixty-one saw the introduction of some historic new steps, by Chubby ("Pony Time," 1:1/61), by the Vibrations ("Watusi," 25:2/61), and by the Dovells ("Bristol Stomp," 2:9/61), as well as some less viable ones: "The Fish" (Bobby Rydell, 25:7), "The Fly" (Chub, 7:10), and "The Majestic" (Dion, 36:12). The hully gully took another bow, as "Peanut Butter" (Marathons a k a Vibrations, 26:4). Two hot party records came out at mid-year: "Quarter to Three" (Gary "U.S." Bonds, 1:5) and Chris Kenner's "I Like It Like That" (2:6). But the big news was the return of the twist itself, both Chubby's original version (1:11) and Joey Dee's "Peppermint Twist" (1:11). Seems that a crowd of Manhattan socialites out slumming had stumbled upon these raw, vital dance dens in the darkest heart of the teen jungle, and those who returned lost no time alerting the adult world. The twist went on to achieve a popularity and acceptance among the middle-aged that rock had never before enjoyed, for whatever that's worth.

The twist craze ran until mid-1962 and attracted both talent and scavengers. (Strictly from hunger: Count Basie, "The Basie Twist" (94:1/62), Rod McKuen, "The Oliver Twist" (76:1), the Champs, "Tequila Twist" (99:2), the Chipmunks, "The Alvin Twist" (40:3), Perez Prado, "The Patricia Twist" (65:4), Frank Sinatra, "Everybody's Twistin" (75:4). Pingading ding.) The dance careerists keep cranking it out to meet the demand: Chubby, the Dovells, Joey Dee, and "U.S." Bonds all enjoyed further Top 10 hits in the first months of 1962. Two instrumentals clicked: "Percolator Twist" (10:1/62), Billy Joe's impersonation of a coffee pot; and "Soul Twist" (17:2), King Curtis' first chart entry. Sam Cooke had his biggest hit since "Chain Gang" (2:8/60) with "Twistin the Night Away" (9:2/62), and the Isley Brothers came on late with "Twist and Shout" (17:6/62), *their* biggest hit until 1966.

The dance idiom as a whole stayed healthy until the end of 1962. The stomp survived "Bongo Stomp" (Little Joey and the Flips, 33:6/62) mutating into the "Surfer's Stomp" (Marketts, 31:1/62). The Watusi came back as "Wah Watusi" (Orlons, 2:6/62). The year 1962 also saw several new dances: "Mashed Potatoes" (DeeDee Sharp, 2:3/62), "Hitch Hike" (Chubby Checker, 10:9/62, and Marvin Gaye, 30:1/63), the "Bird" (Rivingtons 48:8/62), and the "Locomotion" (Little Eva, 1:6/62).

The dance fad also led to several party records in 1962. "Let Me In" (Sensations, 4:1/62) and "Party Lights" (Claudine Clark, 5:6/62), the year's two big girl-group party songs, shared a common theme of frustration, both vocalists pleading for access to the fun in progress. I haven't quite determined the full meaning of this, one of rock's more obscure coincidences, but I'm working on it. Other dance hits for the year include "Shout Shout Knock Yourself Out" (6:3/62) for Dion's songwriter, Ernie Maresca, "Let's Dance" (Chris Montez, 4:8/62), and "Do You Love Me" (Contours, 3:8/62). August also saw the release of a great little disc by Bunker Hill, arguably the most deranged screamer since Little Richard himself. I'll take it on faith there's a rhythm guitar somewhere on "Hide and Go Seek" (33:8/62), but all I can hear is bass, drums, yelling, and energy. Lee Hazlewood managed to turn dance awareness to Duane Eddy's advantage, putting a female chorus behind him (in front of him, actually) on "Dance with the Guitar Man" (12:10/62), a cut that displays the well-programmed lack of spontaneity characteristic of a declining trend. Like classical rock 'n' roll in 1958, the dance boom closed with a decisive burst of decadence, the second major fusion of rock with the Hollywood Gothic sensibility, the "Monster Mash" (Bobby Boris Pickett, 1:9/62). Like its predecessor, "Dinner with Drac" (Zacherle, 6:3/58), "Monster Mash" set a ghoulish spoken recitation over a snappy, hypnotic band track. The genre was too mortified to go on, and late 1962 and 1963 trailed off into leavings: Johnny Thunder's limpid "Loop de Loop" (4:12/62), "Cinnamon Cinder" (Pastel Six, 25:12/62), "El Watusi" (Ray Barretto, 17:4/63), "Martian Hop" (Randells, 16:8/63), and "Surfin Bird" (4:12/63) by the Trashmen, a subterranean crusher of stark power and raw, uh, simplicity. Sounds like Captain Beefheart while he was still a corporal.

Party records outlived dance records by several months, well into 1963. "South Street" (Orlons, 3:2/63) and "Down at Papa Joe's" (Dixie Belles, 9:9/63) were the year's hard-core good-time hits, but the party motif also figured in Leslie Gore's debut, "It's My Party" (1:5/63), Stevie Wonder's debut, "Fingertips" (1:6/63), and Jackie Wilson's "Baby Workout" (5:3/63). With "Papa Joe's" in autumn of 1963, the curtain fell on the dance era of the early '60s, although new dances appeared each year for a while (1963, monkey; 1964, swim; 1965, jerk), and dance mania continued as an integral part of rock through the go-go period of the mid-'60s, until 1967 or whenever it was everybody got high and stopped moving. I mean, why be uncool when you can lie on your back, you know, pass out or something?

If the dance cycle was one distinctive hallmark of the early '60s, the girl-group phenomenon was the other. The early '60s were easily the richest period for female singers in all rock history; the flood of girl-group hits began in 1961 and lasted into 1965, and at its crest, in 1963, women and mixed-sex vocal groups rivaled men for quantitative domination of the charts, actually placing a majority of the year's #1 records.

Year	No. of Top 20 by female or mixed vocal group	Per cent of Top 20 by male vocal group	Total #1's
1959	21	14	15
1960	24	16	20
1961	34	20	21
1962	42	24	20
1963	51	29	20
1964	34	19	23

Year	Total #1's by female or mixed vocal group	Total #1's by black female or m. v. group	Percent of female Top 20 by black artists
1959	3	0	29
1960	4	0	13
1961	3	3	35
1962	5	3	50
1963	11	3	57
1964	6	5	65

Some notes on the data:

All female #1's in 1959 were by the Fleetwoods and the Browns, and all female #1's in 1960 were by Connie Francis and Brenda Lee.

Five of the six Top 20 black female songs in 1959 were by Della Reese, Nina Simone, Sarah Vaughan, and Dinah Washington, riding the tail end of that year's pre-rock resurgence.

Eight of 1960's twenty #1's reached #1 during the last quarter of the year; thus, the rate of turnover for most of 1960 is essentially as slow as during 1959.

The figures for 1961 count "Hit the Road Jack" (Ray Charles, 1:9/61) as a mixed vocal group.

In 1964, four of the female #1's were on Motown (three by the Supremes), and two were on Red Bird. Six of the male #1's were by the Beatles.

The Shirelles were the first Top 40 girl group of the decade, arriving with "Will You Still Love Me Tomorrow" (1:11/60). Arranged by Carole King and co-written with her husband, Gerry Goffin, this medium-tempo ballad featured sprightly, excessive strings similar to the backings on Atlantic's Drifters tracks of 1959 and 1960. The flip was an R&B rocker, "Boys," written and arranged by Luther Dixon, who produced the rest of their hits. The Shirelles gravitated toward orchestras and soft material, but songs like "Baby It's You" and "Soldier Boy" were unique, landmarks that surpassed the conventional ballads of the day. And lead Shirley Alston delivered good hard rock on occasion: "Tonight's the Night," "Big John," and "Mama Said." The combination of superior material, inspired arrangements, and vocal sex appeal made the Shirelles the most successful early-'60s girl group until the breakthrough of the Supremes in 1964.

Motown's first female hit was "Bye Bye Baby," Mary Wells' debut (45:2/61), written by her and produced by Berry Gordy. The Motown assembly line was beginning to roll; Gordy had started in the late '50s by producing Jackie Wilson for Brunswick, Marv Johnson for U.A., and the Miracles for Chess, and then Barrett Strong's "Money" (23:2/59) on Gordy's sister's Anna label. Wilson had several hits for Gordy in 1957–58, and Johnson peaked with "You Got What It Takes" (10:11/59), but "Shop Around" (Miracles, 2:12/60), Motown's first million seller, was on Tamla, the first major Motown family label. "Bye Bye Baby" followed shortly; rugged and crude compared to later Motown products, it explored a set of musical ideas that came to fruition with "Please Mr. Postman" (Marvelettes, 1:9/61), the most significant girl-group record of the year, with its twist beat, rinky piano, thudding production, and scratchy vocals. Most girl-group dance hits of 1962 amount to variations on "Please Mr. Postman."

The year 1961 saw a heavy resurgence of '50s-styled doo-wop material, with dozens of such songs entering the Top 40 and three reaching ⚡1 between late 1960 and early 1962: "Stay" (Maurice Williams and the Zodiacs), "Blue Moon" (Marcels), and "Duke of Earl" (Gene Chandler). Interestingly, women played no part in this final hour of the vocal groups; the doo-wop sensibility infused three major female hits of 1961, but each represents a step forward into the '60s. "Look in My Eyes" (14:9/61) was the last big one for the Chantels, the only late-'50s girl group of any consequence. Their '50s hits ("Maybe," "The Plea," etc.) had been rooted in the doo-wop ballad tradition, but "Look in My Eyes" came off as pop rather than vocal R&B, with a silky ethereality that reappears at the end of 1963 in hits by the Jaynettes, Murmaids, Sapphires, and

Caravelles. "All in My Mind" (Maxine Brown, 19:1/61) and "Gee Whiz" (Carla Thomas, 10:2/61) were both 6/8 ballads, but Maxine and Carla were essentially soul singers, moving away from the integrated vocal harmonies of the '50s toward a more liberated, personalized, self-expressive style, which distinguishes black soul pop of the '60s from black vocal-group pop of the '50s.

Nineteen sixty-one was a good year for tough songs, with "Mama Said," "Hit the Road Jack," and "Bye Bye Baby," but the toughest of them all was "I Know It's Gonna Work Out Fine" by Ike and Tina Turner (14:8/61).

Meanwhile, the white folks were off on a new tack of their own. Rosie was still warm in her grave when Linda Scott's "I've Told Every Little Star" emerged, skipping rope, chewing gum, singsonging nonsense words, the music moving forward in time again, growing older into vigor and hope. By extrapolating from the alternating expansion and contraction of the physical universe to a larger peristaltic view of reality, we can see that rock had filtered down from the maturity of black blues and R&B, growing younger to become the adolescence that was rock 'n' roll, and then younger still through the pubescent idols of 1959 into the troubled, shadowy, narcissistic childhood of "Angel Baby," until breaching the moment of birth (or conception?) and reversing course. Oh yeah. With Linda Scott, then, the pop mood had turned fresh, an optimism reborn which would mature and carry through the early Beatles into '65 or '66, when things started getting vicious.

The other white female hits of 1961 were also pretty up. "Triangle" (Janie Grant, 29:4/61) was a close reflection of "I've Told Every Little Star," with a very similar drum pattern and an equivalent use of nonsense syllables; "Let's Get Together" (Hayley Mills, 8:9/61) was Disney Rock, Anglo Annette, good clean fun, more sincere but less effective than "Norman"; Sue Thompson sings as if she knows better but it doesn't bother her, both on "Norman" (3:12/60) and on "Sad Movies" (5:9/61).

I still don't know what to make of "The Mountain's High" (2:8/61). Dick and DeeDee did normal songs for the rest of their career, but this one was just weird. Elliptically apocalyptic. Doom-filled echo chambers and an incessant, bone-rattling snare drill created a tense, ominous backdrop for the agitated, cryptic wailing of the two lovers. High drama. Some of the same drama showed up in the Shirelles' "Baby It's You" (8:12/61), which shared none of "Mountain's High"'s anarchy but struck a similar reverberating minor-sixth eeriness. "Baby It's You" initiated the Shirelles' first comeback, which peaked with their next release, "Soldier Boy" (1:3/62). Social themes also figured in "Uptown" by the Crystals (13:3/62), a florid reworking by Phil Spector of Latinisms from his own "Spanish Harlem" (Ben E. King, 10:1/61). "There's No Other Like My Baby" (20:11/61) and "Uptown" were Spector's first hits on his new label, Philles Records, one of the best things that happened to the early '60s. The Philles records turned the prevailing teen ethos into art, and stand as some of rock's finest recordings. The Crystals' next song, "He Hit me (and It Felt Like a Kiss)," came out in mid-'62 and received a favorable initial response from DJs and listeners, but the subject matter overstepped most AM limits and the record died fast, a victim of its own SM undertones, failing even to enter the Top 100. The next one got to #1. He called it the Crystals but it was actually Darlene Love singing lead on "He's a Rebel" (1:9/62), the first teen-culture classic of the girl-group era. Phil put a lot of effort into Darlene, first as lead for Bob B Soxx and the Blue Jeans and then as a solo, but with the exception of "He's a Rebel" he fared better commercially with his other female leads, LaLa Brooks of the Crystals and his wife, Veronica, of the Ronettes. Darlene's only other Top 20 hit came next, as a Blue Jean with Bob B Soxx on "Zip-a-Dee-Doo-Dah" (8:11/62), fuzz guitar and all, the wracked resurrection of an ancient chestnut which inspired another stoned soul excursion down memory lane, "Mockingbird" (7:6/63) by Inez and Charlie Foxx. (Also "How Much Is That Doggie in the Window" by Baby Jane, also "Good Ship Lollipop" by Donna Loren, also "Yes Sir That's My Baby" by the Date with Soul, also . . . enough.)

For most of 1962, Spector was still getting his bearings, working with different writers (Goffin-King, Mann-Weil, even Gene Pitney on "He's a Rebel") and experimenting with sound and arrangements. His early releases were eclipsed on the charts by a very homogeneous bloc of girl-group twist songs derived from "Please Mr. Postman," songs that rose with and fueled the dance fad: "Let Me In" (Sensations, 4:1/62), "I Sold My Heart to the Junkman" (Patty LaBelle and the BlueBelles, 15:4/62), "Playboy" (Marvelettes, 7:5/62), "Party Lights" (Claudine Clark, 5:6/62), "Tell Him" (the Exciters, 4:12/62) and the Cameo-Parkway hits by DeeDee Sharp ("Mashed Potato Time" (2:3/62), "Gravy" (9:6/62), "Ride" (5:10/62), "Do the Bird" (10:3/63) and the Orlons ("Wah Watusi" (2:6/62),

"Don't Hang Up" (4:10/62), "South Street" (3:2/63). After 1962, the "Please Mr. Postman" style more or less vanished, except perhaps for the Essex hits in 1963 ("Easier Said Than Done" (1:6/63) and "Walking Miracle" (12:8/63). The most blatant replications of the Marvelettes' milestone were the debuts of the Orlons ("Wah Watusi") and DeeDee Sharp ("Mashed Potato Time") on Cameo-Parkway, already established as the premier dance label with Chubby Checker and the Dovells. As their career faded, the Orlons gradually worked free of dance lyrics into a richer repertoire ("Not Me," "Bon Doo Wah," "Knock Knock," "Come On Down Baby Baby"), but DeeDee rode the fad for the rest of her life on the charts. Too bad. Carole King and Gerry Goffin's Dimension label got off the ground with a dance hit, "Locomotion" by Little Eva (1:6/62), but unlike their counterparts at Cameo-Parkway, the Dimension moguls moved easily to more general themes; the Cookies' songs in fact are the most straightforward, unashamed exploitations of teen romance in the entire early '60s: "Chains" (17:11/62), "Don't Say Nothing Bad About My Baby" (7:3/63), and "Girls Grow Up Faster than Boys" (33:11/63), plus Little Eva's "Keep Your Hands off My Baby" (12:11/62)—truly this was slut rock at its finest. Pure high school. Compare also "Johnny Get Angry" (Joannie Sommers, 7:5/62); this nascent hit syndrome came into its own with crunching finality in "My Boyfriend's Back" (Angels, 1:8/63), some kind of peak experience in rock's early-'60s adolescence.

Young love was explored from other angles as well in 1962–63. The soothing saccharinity of "Johnny Angel" (Shelley Fabares, 1:3/62) and "Hey Paula" (Paul and Paula, 1:12/62) contrasted with the strident insecurity of "Bobby's Girl" (Marcy Blane, 3:10/62) and "I Will Follow Him" (Little Peggy March, 1:3/63), but the huge success of all these songs points up the essentially juvenile character of the age; statements of maturity fared poorly by comparison. In 1962 these consist of maybe one white number, "Silver Threads and Golden Needles" (20:8/62) by the Springfields (with Dusty); the rest were black: "I'm Blue" (Ikettes, 19:1/62), "Love Letters" (Ketty Lester, 5:2), "You'll Lose a Good Thing" (Barbara Lynn, 8:6), "Release Me" (Esther Phillips, 8:10), "Don't Make Me Over" (Dionne Warwick, 21:12), and three by Mary Wells on Motown: "The One Who Really Loves You" (8:3), "You Beat Me to the Punch" (9:8), and "Two Lovers" (7:12). These three had a great impact on the neosophisticated soul girl-group music of the next months; several hits in early 1963 bore an unmistakable Mary Wells imprint: "Mama Didn't Lie" (Jan Bradley, 14:1/63), "Our Day Will Come" (Ruby and the Romantics, 1:2/63), "Hello Stranger" (Barbara Lewis, 3:5/63), and, tangentially, "That's How Heartaches Are Made" (Baby Washington, 40:3/63) and "The Love of My Man" (Theola Kilgore, 21:4/63). The over-all tone of these performances was cool and breathy, laid-back, almost jazz-like in its lack of surface energy—these records are hard to twist to. The Chiffons ("He's So Fine," 1:2/63, and "One Fine Day," 5:6/63) were the only important black girl group running counter to this trend for most of 1963. Passion began to return with "Just One Look" (Doris Troy, 10:6/63). The band was still quite relaxed, but the new urgency of Doris' vocal performance prefigured the hard-edged soul that surfaced in late 1963: "Heat Wave" (Martha and the Vandellas, 4:8/63), "Cry to Me" (Betty Harris, 23:9/63), "You're No Good" (Betty Everett, 5:11/63), "Nitty Gritty" (Shirley Ellis, 8:11/63), and the Supremes' first Top 40 hit, "When the Lovelight Starts Shining Through His Eyes" (23:11/63). The mellow feel of the earlier songs was extended in some pop productions at the end of 1963, but the sultry ethereality of Mary Wells and the others had become more spaced out than funky on "Sally Go Round the Roses" (Jaynettes, 2:8/63), "Popsicles Icicles" (Murmaids, 3:11/63), "You Don't Have to Be a Baby to Cry" (Caravelles, 3:11/63), and "Who Do You Love" (Sapphires, 25:1/64).

Spector's Philles label did well in 1963, first with the Crystals and then with the Ronettes. The Crystals' follow-up to "He's a Rebel," "He's Sure the Boy I Love" (11:12/62) established a rhythm style that scored hard with their next release, "Da Doo Ron Ron" (3:4/63). The pounding, flat-out pulse was widely imitated on some fabulous girl-group records of late 1963–64, most of which unfortunately failed to enter the charts. Some that did place included "Not Too Young To Get Married" (Bob B Soxx and the Blue Jeans, 63:6/63), "He's Mine" (Alice Wonderland, 62:9/63), "When the Boy's Happy" (Four Pennies, 95:11/63), and "Jimmy Boy" (Girlfriends, 49:12/63). Some that didn't place included "He's My Dream Boy" (Marie Antoinette), "Baby Baby I Still Love You" (Cinderellas), "Ya Gotta Take a Chance" (Bonnetts), "Summertime USA" (Pixies Three), "Usher Boy" (Merry Clayton), and "Wishing Well" (Shangri-Las). Buy these records.

Personally, I think "Da Doo Ron Ron" was Spector's peak; the Ronettes' work that followed lacks the incredible energy propelling both the band and the singer on "Da Doo Ron Ron." The Veronica vocals are as torrid and suggestive as Darlene's or the Crystals' (albeit slightly more tongue-in-cheek), but the songs, the arrangements, the band performances . . . all seem smoothed out, less inspired and less interesting than the "Da Doo Ron Ron"/"Not Too Young"/ "He's Sure the Boy I Love" nexus and some of the earlier, less conscious, and less cautious experiments: "He's a Rebel," "Uptown," "Zip-a-Dee-Doo-Dah." The increasing enervation of Spector's later product may explain the failure of any Philles records to break into the Top 20 between the fall of 1963 (the Ronettes' debut, "Be My Baby," (2:8/63) and the beginning of 1965, when "You've Lost That Lovin' Feeling" (Righteous Brothers) yawned its way to ⧣1. I dunno, folks, that one put me to sleep then and it puts me to sleep now.

The girl-group wave had been created in 1963, ebbing in '64 and '65, until by 1966 only the Motown girl groups were left on the Top 20. The year 1964 saw the last girl-group hits done in an early-'60s style, and most of these were white efforts: "Navy Blue" (Diane Renay, 6:1/64), "Party Girl" (Bernadette Carroll, 47:5/64), a strong song that would have done much better a year earlier, and the Red Bird releases; the only retrogressive black numbers were "I'm into Something Good" (Earl-Jean, 3:6/64) and the "Shoop Shoop Song (It's in His Kiss)" by Betty Everett (6:2/64). Red Bird Records met with considerable success in 1964, but the smell of decay hung over this spiritual successor to the Philles and Dimension labels of 1962–63. "Going to the Chapel" (Dixie Cups, 1:5/64) was an engaging, well-produced piece of fluff, as were "I Wanna Love Him So Bad" (Jelly Beans, 9:6/64) and the less successful "Goodnight Baby" (Butterflys, 51:9/64), but the Shangri-Las, Red Bird's main act, carried the teen ethos of the Cookies and the Crystals into its terminal phase, and beyond. It's kind of sad the Shangri-Las got so camp so fast, because their first record ("Remember" 5:8/64) was a killer, futuristic in its leaden, chorded heaviness, with one of the best climaxes on wax. She really was an excellent singer, the best blonde in the business, gifted with a powerful, expressive delivery and one of the half dozen most distinctive voices of the whole girl-group period. Besides, she's dead.

Flo Ballard was on welfare two years before she died.

Conventional rock wisdom has held that the Beatles revitalized the moribund pop scene, restoring vigor to a music that had fallen lame in 1959 and never recovered. In fact, rock's health had been improving steadily since late 1960, and the success of the Beatles served to focus momentum that was already building.

Evolution proceeds through the rise and decline of prototypes, basic models and forms within which a range of variation occurs, but which remain distinguishable from other basic models. Some recent prototypes of biological evolution include fish, amphibians, reptiles, birds, and mammals. Sinatra symbolizes a musical prototype: the '40s crooner. Presley symbolizes the '50s rock 'n' roll singer; less viable forms include Carl Perkins, Bill Haley, Gene Vincent, et al. The Shirelles symbolize the early-'60s girl group, as do the Chiffons, the Crystals, the Ronettes and others. The Beatles embodied a protoype that would dominate the rest of the '60s, the rock band. Yet this prototype would have developed in their absence; in fact, it had already emerged by the time they appeared, at the beginning of 1964.

The rock band represents autonomy—the idea of a small, self-contained, self-sufficient co-operative musical unit separate from and independent of the outside world. When the '60s got out of hand and generational warfare broke out, the band proved an ideal vehicle for wresting artistic (if not financial) control from industry executives, who tended to take a dim view of the gathering madness championed by so many of their acts. The prototypical rock band displays three primary characteristics: it plays its own instruments, it writes its own music, and it projects the image of a group. These characteristics first appeared with the Four Seasons and then with the Beach Boys in 1962–63. The careers of these two seminal bands flourished through the British invasion of 1964, as did those of some late-blooming girl groups, the Motown stable, and some early-'60s heavies: Mary Wells, the Righteous Brothers, and Roy Orbison; the invasion did not in fact cut down American artists still capable of growth.

The Beach Boys continued on a trajectory that had been rising since mid-1962, peaking with "I Get Around" (1:5/64) and again with "Help Me Rhonda" (1:4/65), and placing thirteen consecutive

Top 20 singles between 1964 and late 1967. The Four Seasons had peaked at their onset in 1962, with "Sherry" (1:8/62), "Big Girls Don't Cry" (1:10/62), and "Walk Like a Man" (1:1/63), but they enjoyed a comeback with "Rag Doll" (1:6/64), and they too put thirteen singles into the Top 20 between 1964 and late 1967. But for all their talent and significance, it wasn't the Beach Boys or the Four Seasons who touched off the hysteria, it was the Beatles. The two American bands projected very explicit images at the American rock audience, images loaded with readily identifiable cultural connotations. Each group was hopelessly typecast, each was obviously the musical extension of a particular set of sociocultural values, and each fell afoul of divisions within the American teen scene that the Beatles straddled effortlessly.

A nascent counterculture existed in the United States by the early 1960s: budding freaks and a dawning youth movement focused then, as later, around political radicalism, a permissive life-style, and drugs. By and large, rock was poorly received by this vanguard, which gravitated instead to the acoustic message music of the period. Rock was insufficiently thoughtful, it lacked seriousness, it wasn't committed: Spector women never sang about important stuff like civil rights and nuclear disarmament. Certain social divisions, since blurred, were new then, more intense and sharply felt, and the Four Seasons with their greasy Italian pompadours, greasy showbiz grins, and greasy adenoidal love songs must have looked like one more sick permutation of mainstream American values to the folkies, already caught up in a developing ethos of rebellion. And the Beach Boys, with their enthusiastic celebration of a politically unconscious youth culture . . . hot rods and surfing were one thing, but with "Be True to Your School" the Klean Kut Kar Krazy Kalifornia Kwintet finally came out and said it, embracing the high school status quo and generally coming off as mindless hedonistic reactionaries.

Well, shit, it mattered to me.

But the Beatles were outsiders, nobody recognized them, they aroused no preconditioned hostilities among the young. The Beatles greatly stimulated the long-range process that saw a succession of new audiences attracted to rock, audiences whose influences would in turn expand rock's musical scope. The first and most important of these new audiences was the folk crowd and its musicians, who would start turning up in 1965 playing in electric bands like the

Byrds and the Lovin' Spoonful, but mainly Bob Dylan. With Dylan converted, the rest of the world fell in line, the mind and body of youth culture were fused, the engine of rock 'n' roll was harnessed to the ideology of folk culture, and social revolt shifted into overdrive.

PREFACE TO THE LOG
OF AMERICAN AND BRITISH
TOP TWENTY SINGLES

The American material was compiled by Stephen Nugent from *Billboard,* January 1955 through December 1973. The British material was compiled by Pete and Annie Fowler from the *New Musical Express* (January 1955 to December 1958), *Record Mirror* (January 1959 to December 1968), and *Music Week* (January 1969 to December 1973). British entries are always in *italics.*

Billboard's chart from January to November 1955 was based purely on retail sales; since then, the chart has been assessed on both retail reports and on sample polls of disc jockeys and jukebox operators.

The British charts are all based on sales reports from retailers. A print strike prevented *Record Mirror* from going to press from July 4 to August 9, 1959; the *New Musical Express* chart was used for this period. Because no chart is compiled in Britain during Christmas week, every record that was in the previous week's chart has been credited with an extra week at the same position.

A discrepancy occurs in some artists' entries because of the different attitude to "B" sides in America and Britain. Because *Billboard's* chart is based partly on radio play, "B" sides are often listed separately, whereas in Britain a record is listed as one item even if both sides receive radio play. In several cases, the American system has inflated the number of apparent hits compared to the British figures for the same artist. The roll call of hit makers is based on the number of separate titles logged by each artist and unavoidably favors those artists whose "B" sides received heavy American air play.

Many thanks to the editors of *Billboard, Music Week, New Musical Express,* and *Record Mirror* for giving permission and facilities for the research.

Where both sides of a single record were logged separately, we have annotated one side b/w* (backed with*) and asterisked the other (*). In artist entries where this happened more than once, successive records each have individual annotation, with their own multiples of asterisks, daggers, circles, and diamonds.

THE LOG
OF AMERICAN AND BRITISH
TOP TWENTY SINGLES
1955–73

LABEL	DATE OF CHART ENTRY	HIGHEST POSITION REACHED	NUMBER OF WEEKS IN CHARTS
ACE, JOHNNY			
Pledging My Love			
(US) Duke	3 12 55	17	3
ACKLIN, BARBARA			
Love Makes a Woman			
(US) Brunswick	8 24 68	15	3
AD LIBS			
The Boy from New York City			
(US) Blue Cat	2 13 65	8	5
ADDERLY, JULIAN "CANNONBALL"			
Mercy Mercy Mercy			
(US) Capitol	2 18 67	11	4
AKENS, JEWEL			
The Birds and the Bees			
(US) Era	2 27 65	3	8
ALFIE AND HARRY			
The Trouble with Harry			
(UK) London	3 23 56	15	3
ALICE COOPER			
School's Out			
(US) Warner Brothers	7 8 72	7	7
(UK) Warner Brothers	7 22 72	1	9
Elected			
(UK) Warner Brothers	10 14 72	4	7
Hello Hurray			
(UK) Warner Brothers	2 17 73	6	8
No More, Mr. Nice Guy			
(UK) Warner Brothers	5 5 73	10	4
ALIVE AND KICKING			
Tighter Tighter			
(US) Roulette	7 4 70	7	4
ALLEN, REX			
Don't Go Near the Indians			
(US) Mercury	10 20 62	17	1
ALLISONS			
Are You Sure?			
(UK) Fontana	2 12 61	1	12
ALLMAN BROTHERS BAND			
Ramblin' Man			
(US) Capricorn	9 22 73	2	9
ALL STAR HIT PARADE (various artists)			
All Star Hit Parade (Vol. 1)			
(UK) Decca EP	6 29 56	2	8
All Star Hit Parade (Vol. 2)			
(UK) Decca EP	8 9 57	15	2
ALPERT, HERB (*AND THE TIJUANA BRASS)			
Lonely Bull*			
(US) A&M	11 17 62	6	9

LABEL	DATE OF CHART ENTRY	HIGHEST POSITION REACHED	NUMBER OF WEEKS IN CHARTS
Taste of Honey*			
(US) A&M	10 30 65	7	8
Spanish Flea			
(UK) Pye International	*1 15 66*	*3*	*12*
Zorba the Greek*			
(US) A&M	2 5 66	11	4
Work Song*			
(US) A&M	7 23 66	18	3
Mame*			
(US) A&M	12 17 66	19	2
This Guy's in Love with You			
(US) A&M	6 1 68	1	11
(UK) A&M	*7 20 68*	*2*	*11*
AMBOY DUKES			
Journey to the Center of the Earth			
(US) Mainstream	8 3 68	16	6
AMEN CORNER			
Gin House			
(UK) Deram	*9 2 67*	*12*	*5*
Bend Me, Shape Me			
(UK) Deram	*1 27 68*	*3*	*9*
High in the Sky			
(UK) Deram	*8 17 68*	*6*	*9*
Half As Nice			
(UK) Immediate	*2 8 69*	*1*	*7*
Hello Susie			
(UK) Immediate	*7 5 69*	*4*	*6*
AMERICA			
Horse with No Name			
(UK) Warner Brothers	*1 15 72*	*3*	*7*
(US) Warner Brothers	3 4 72	1	12
I Need You			
(US) Warner Brothers	6 17 72	9	5
Ventura Highway			
(US) Warner Brothers	11 18 72	8	6
AMERICAN BREED			
Bend Me, Shape Me			
(US) Acta	12 23 67	5	8
AMES, ED			
My Cup Runneth Over			
(US) RCA	2 25 67	8	6
Who Will Answer			
(US) RCA	1 13 68	19	2
AMES BROTHERS			
Naughty Lady of Shady Lane			
(US) Victor	1 1 55	3	9
(UK) HMV	*2 4 55*	*6*	*6*
My Bonnie Lassie			
(US) Coral	10 15 55	11	7

	DATE OF CHART ENTRY	HIGHEST POSITION REACHED	NUMBER OF WEEKS IN CHARTS
LABEL			
It Only Hurts a Little While			
(US) Victor	6 9 56	15	13
Melodie d'Amour			
(US) Victor	10 28 57	12	10
Pussy Cat			
(US) RCA	10 27 58	17	3
ANDERSON, BILL			
Still			
(US) Decca	5 25 63	8	7
ANDERSON, LYNN			
Rose Garden			
(US) Columbia	1 2 71	3	10
(UK) CBS	*3 6 71*	*3*	*10*
ANDREWS, CHRIS			
Yesterday Man			
(UK) Decca	*10 21 65*	*3*	*11*
To Whom It May Concern			
(UK) Decca	*12 18 65*	*13*	*5*
ANDREWS, EAMONN			
Shifting, Whispering Sands			
(UK) Parlophone	*1 20 56*	*18*	*3*
ANDREWS, LEE AND THE HEARTS			
Teardrops			
(US) Chess	12 30 57	20	1
ANDY, BOB; AND GRIFFITHS, MARCIA			
Young, Gifted and Black			
(UK) Harry J.	*3 21 70*	*5*	*8*
Pied Piper			
(UK) Trojan	*7 3 71*	*11*	*5*
ANGELS			
'Til			
(US) Caprice	12 25 61	14	2
My Boyfriend's Back			
(US) Smash	8 17 63	1	10
ANIMALS			
The House of the Rising Sun			
(UK) Columbia	*7 4 64*	*1*	*7*
(US) MGM	8 15 64	1	9
I'm Crying			
(UK) Columbia	*9 26 64*	*8*	*6*
(US) MGM	11 7 64	19	1
Don't Let Me Be Misunderstood			
(UK) Columbia	*2 13 65*	*3*	*7*
(US) MGM	3 27 65	15	2
Bring It On Home to Me			
(UK) Columbia	*4 17 65*	*7*	*8*
We've Gotta Get out of This Place			

LABEL	DATE OF CHART ENTRY	HIGHEST POSITION REACHED	NUMBER OF WEEKS IN CHARTS
(UK) Columbia	7 24 65	2	8
(US) MGM	9 18 65	13	4
It's My Life			
(UK) Columbia	11 6 65	7	6
Inside Looking Out			
(UK) Decca	2 26 66	12	4
Don't Bring Me Down			
(UK) Decca	6 4 66	6	6
(US) MGM	6 18 66	12	5

[See also: **ERIC BURDON AND THE ANIMALS; ERIC BURDON AND WAR**]

ANKA, PAUL

Diana			
(US) ABC-Paramount	8 12 57	2	16
(UK) Columbia	8 16 57	1	23
I Love You Baby			
(UK) Columbia	11 8 57	3	13
You Are My Destiny			
(UK) Columbia	1 31 58	6	10
(US) ABC-Paramount	2 10 58	7	5
Crazy Love			
(US) ABC-Paramount	5 5 58	19	1
All of a Sudden My Heart Sings			
(US) ABC-Paramount	1 26 59	15	5
(UK) Columbia	1 31 59	10	9
Lonely Boy			
(US) ABC-Paramount	6 8 59	1	12
(UK) Columbia	8 9 59	3	12
Put Your Head on My Shoulder			
(US) ABC-Paramount	9 21 59	2	12
(UK) Columbia	10 31 59	7	8
It's Time to Cry			
(US) ABC-Paramount	12 7 59	4	9
Puppy Love			
(US) ABC-Paramount	3 7 60	2	9
My Home Town			
(US) ABC-Paramount	6 13 60	8	7
Summer's Gone			
(US) ABC-Paramount	10 24 60	11	3
Story of My Love			
(US) ABC-Paramount	2 13 61	16	2
Tonight My Love, Tonight			
(US) ABC-Paramount	4 17 61	13	4
Dance On, Little Girl			
(US) ABC-Paramount	6 19 61	10	5
Love Me Warm and Tender			
(US) RCA	3 31 62	12	5
(UK) RCA	4 7 62	19	2
Steel Guitar, Glass of Wine and You			
(US) RCA	6 16 62	13	4

LABEL	DATE OF CHART ENTRY	HIGHEST POSITION REACHED	NUMBER OF WEEKS IN CHARTS
Eso Beso			
(US) RCA	12 8 62	19	1
ANNETTE			
Tall Paul			
(US) Disneyland	2 2 59	7	8
First Name Initial			
(US) Vista	1 11 60	20	1
O, Dio Mio			
(US) Vista	3 14 60	10	5
Pineapple Princess			
(US) Vista	9 19 60	11	5
ANN-MARGRET			
I Just Don't Understand			
(US) RCA	9 4 61	17	2
ANTHONY, BILLY			
This Ole House			
(UK) Columbia	*1 7 55*	*12*	*4*
ANTHONY, RAY			
Peter Gunn Theme			
(US) Capitol	2 2 59	8	9
ANTHONY, RICHARD			
If I Loved You			
(UK) Columbia	*5 9 64*	*18*	*3*
APOLLO 100			
Joy			
(US) Mega	1 29 72	6	8
APPLEJACKS			
Mexican Hat Rack			
(US) Cameo	10 20 58	16	5
APPLEJACKS			
Tell Me When			
(UK) Decca	*3 21 64*	*7*	*8*
Like Dreamers Do			
(UK) Decca	*7 4 64*	*20*	*1*
APPLEWHITE, CHARLIE			
Blue Star			
(UK) Brunswick	*9 23 55*	*20*	*1*
ARBORS			
The Letter			
(US) Date	4 5 69	20	2
ARCHIES			
Sugar Sugar			
(US) Calendar	8 23 69	1	15
(UK) RCA	*10 18 69*	*1*	*17*
Jingle Jangle			
(US) Kirshner	1 3 70	10	7

LABEL	DATE OF CHART ENTRY	HIGHEST POSITION REACHED	NUMBER OF WEEKS IN CHARTS
ARDEN, TONI			
Padre			
(US) Decca	6 30 58	18	2
ARGENT			
Hold Your Head Up			
(*UK*) *Epic*	*4 1 72*	*5*	*6*
(US) Epic	8 5 72	5	6
God Gave Rock and Roll to You			
(*UK*) *Epic*	*4 21 73*	*18*	*1*
ARMSTRONG, LOUIS			
Theme from "Threepenny Opera"			
(US) Columbia	3 17 56	20	1
(*UK*) *Philips*	*4 20 56*	*8*	*7*
Hello Dolly			
(US) Kapp	3 14 64	1	16
(*UK*) *London*	*6 13 64*	*4*	*8*
Wonderful World			
(*UK*) *Stateside*	*3 16 68*	*1*	*16*
ARMY GAME (cast from the TV show)			
The Army Game			
(*UK*) *HMV*	*6 6 58*	*5*	*6*
ARNOLD, EDDY			
Make the World Go Away			
(US) RCA	11 27 65	6	7
(*UK*) *RCA*	*3 5 66*	*8*	*10*
ARRIVAL			
Friends			
(*UK*) *Decca*	*1 17 70*	*8*	*5*
I Will Survive			
(*UK*) *Decca*	*6 20 70*	*16*	*4*
ARSENAL FC			
Good Old Arsenal			
(*UK*) *Pye*	*5 22 71*	*16*	*1*
ASHTON, GARDNER AND DYKE			
Resurrection Shuffle			
(*UK*) *Capitol*	*1 30 71*	*3*	*8*
ASSEMBLED MULTITUDE			
Overture from "Tommy"			
(US) Atlantic	8 15 70	16	4
ASSOCIATION			
Along Comes Mary			
(US) Valiant	7 2 66	7	4
Cherish			
(US) Valiant	9 10 66	1	8
Windy			
(US) Warner Brothers	6 10 67	1	11
Never My Love			
(US) Warner Brothers	9 16 67	2	10

LABEL	DATE OF CHART ENTRY	HIGHEST POSITION REACHED	NUMBER OF WEEKS IN CHARTS
Everything That Touches You (US) Warner Brothers	2 24 68	10	5
ATOMIC ROOSTER			
Tomorrow Night (*UK*) *B&C*	*3 6 71*	*11*	5
Devils Answer (*UK*) *B&C*	*7 24 71*	*4*	6
ARNOLD, P. P.			
First Cut Is the Deepest (*UK*) *Immediate*	*6 10 67*	*18*	*3*
ATTWELL, WINIFRED			
Let's Have Another Party (medley) (*UK*) *Philips*	*1 7 55*	*2*	*2*
Let's Have Another Ding Dong (medley) (*UK*) *Decca*	*11 4 55*	*3*	*10*
Poor People of Paris (*UK*) *Decca*	*3 16 56*	*1*	*15*
Port Au Prince (*UK*) *Decca*	*5 18 56*	*18*	*6*
Left Bank (*UK*) *Decca*	*7 20 56*	*14*	*4*
Make It a Party (medley) (*UK*) *Decca*	*11 2 56*	*7*	*10*
Let's Have a Ball (medley) (*UK*) *Decca*	*12 6 57*	*8*	*5*
Piano Party (medley) (*UK*) *Decca*	*12 5 59*	*15*	*4*
AUSTIN, SIL			
Slow Walk (US) Mercury	12 8 56	19	1
AVALON, FRANKIE			
Dede Dinah (US) Chancellor	2 10 58	7	5
Ginger Bread (US) Chancellor	7 28 58	9	8
I'll Wait for You (US) Chancellor	11 17 58	15	2
Venus (US) Chancellor	3 2 59	1	11
Bobby Sox to Stockings (US) Chancellor	6 15 59	8	7
Boy Without a Girl (US) Chancellor	6 29 59	10	5
Just Ask Your Heart (US) Chancellor	9 21 59	7	8
Why (US) Chancellor	12 14 59	1	10
(*UK*) *HMV*	*1 16 60*	*15*	*3*

LABEL	DATE OF CHART ENTRY	HIGHEST POSITION REACHED	NUMBER OF WEEKS IN CHARTS
AVONS			
Seven Little Girls			
(UK) Columbia	11 21 59	4	9
BACHARACH, BURT			
Trains and Boats and Planes			
(UK) London	5 29 65	4	7
BACHELORS			
Charmaine			
(UK) Decca	3 2 63	6	9
Whispering			
(UK) Decca	9 21 63	18	1
Diane			
(UK) Decca	2 8 64	1	11
(US) London	5 30 64	10	5
I Believe			
(UK) Decca	3 28 64	2	11
Ramona			
(UK) Decca	6 13 64	4	8
I Wouldn't Trade You for the World			
(UK) Decca	8 29 64	5	11
No Arms Could Ever Hold You			
(UK) Decca	12 12 64	7	7
Marie			
(UK) Decca	5 29 65	9	6
(US) London	7 24 65	15	2
Sound of Silence			
(UK) Decca	3 26 66	3	8
Marta			
(UK) Decca	7 22 67	20	1
BADFINGER			
Come and Get It			
(UK) Apple	1 17 70	4	7
(US) Apple	3 28 70	7	7
No Matter What			
(US) Apple	12 5 70	8	5
(UK) Apple	1 23 71	5	8
Day After Day			
(US) Apple	1 1 72	4	9
(UK) Apple	2 12 72	10	5
Baby Blue			
(US) Apple	4 15 72	14	4
BAEZ, JOAN			
There but for Fortune			
(UK) Fontana	7 17 65	8	7
The Night They Drove Old Dixie Down			
(US) Vanguard	9 4 71	3	11
(UK) Vanguard	10 23 71	6	7
BAKER, LAVERN			
I Cried a Tear			
(US) Atlantic	2 2 59	6	9

88

LABEL	DATE OF CHART ENTRY	HIGHEST POSITION REACHED	NUMBER OF WEEKS IN CHARTS
BALDRY, LONG JOHN			
Let the Heartaches Begin			
(UK) Pye	11 18 67	1	9
Mexico			
(UK) Pye	11 9 68	15	4
BALL, KENNY			
Samantha			
(UK) Pye	2 19 61	7	8
I Still Love You All			
(UK) Pye	5 21 61	18	2
Midnight in Moscow			
(UK) Pye	11 11 61	4	14
(US) Kapp	2 24 62	2	9
March of the Siamese Children			
(UK) Pye	2 24 62	3	8
Green Leaves of Summer			
(UK) Pye	6 2 62	7	8
So Do I			
(UK) Pye	9 1 62	14	4
Suki Yaki			
(UK) Pye	2 3 63	10	7
BALLARD, HANK, and the MIDNIGHTERS			
Finger-Poppin' Time			
(US) King	7 25 60	7	10
Let's Go Let's Go Let's Go			
(US) King	10 31 60	6	7
THE BAND			
Rag Mama Rag			
(UK) Capitol	4 25 70	16	4
BANDWAGON			
Breaking Down the Walls of Heartache			
(UK) Direction	11 2 68	4	11
[See also: **JOHNNY JOHNSON AND THE BANDWAGON**]			
BARBER, CHRIS			
Petite Fleur			
(UK) Pye-Nixa	2 14 59	4	18
(US) Laurie	2 16 59	5	6
BARE, BOBBY			
Detroit City			
(US) RCA	7 27 63	16	3
500 Miles from Home			
(US) RCA	11 9 63	10	4
BAR-KAYS			
Soul Finger			
(US) Volt	7 22 67	17	4
BARRETTO, RAY			
El Watusi			
(US) Tico	6 1 63	17	2

LABEL	DATE OF CHART ENTRY	HIGHEST POSITION REACHED	NUMBER OF WEEKS IN CHARTS
BARRON KNIGHTS			
Call Up the Groups			
(UK) Columbia	7 18 64	3	9
Pop! Go the Workers			
(UK) Columbia	4 10 65	5	8
Merrie Gentle Pops			
(UK) Columbia	12 25 65	9	5
Under New Management			
(UK) Columbia	12 24 66	15	4
BARRY, JOHN, ORCHESTRA			
Hit and Miss			
(UK) Parlophone	2 27 60	12	8
Walk Don't Run			
(UK) Parlophone	9 18 60	7	9
Black Stockings			
(UK) Parlophone	1 1 61	13	2
James Bond Theme			
(UK) Columbia	11 24 62	13	4
Theme from "The Persuaders"			
(UK) CBS	1 15 72	13	4
BARRY LEN			
1—2—3			
(US) Decca	10 23 65	2	9
(UK) Brunswick	11 13 65	3	11
Like a Baby			
(UK) Brunswick	2 5 66	10	4
BASS, FONTELLA			
Rescue Me			
(US) Checker	10 30 65	4	8
(UK) Chess	12 11 65	11	7
BASSEY, SHIRLEY			
Banana Boat Song			
(UK) Philips	3 8 57	8	6
Kiss Me Honey Honey Kiss Me			
(UK) Philips	1 3 59	4	13
As I Love You			
(UK) Philips	1 17 59	2	15
As Long As He Needs Me			
(UK) Columbia	7 31 60	2	17
You'll Never Know			
(UK) Columbia	5 7 61	3	8
Reach for the Stars			
(UK) Columbia	7 29 61	3	10
I'll Get By			
(UK) Columbia	11 18 61	9	5
What Now My Love?			
(UK) Columbia	9 22 62	5	10
I (Who Have Nothing)			
(UK) Columbia	10 12 63	6	10

LABEL	DATE OF CHART ENTRY	HIGHEST POSITION REACHED	NUMBER OF WEEKS IN CHARTS
Goldfinger			
(US) United Artists	3 6 65	8	6
Something			
(UK) United Artists	*7 4 70*	*4*	*12*
For All We Know			
(UK) United Artists	*9 18 71*	*6*	*11*
Never Never Never			
(UK) United Artists	*3 17 73*	*8*	*8*
BAXTER, LES			
Unchained Melody			
(US) Capitol	4 9 55	2	20
(UK) Capitol	*5 13 55*	*10*	*9*
Wake the Town and Tell the People			
(US) Capitol	8 20 55	10	11
Poor People of Paris			
(US) Capitol	2 25 56	1	17
BAY CITY ROLLERS			
Keep On Dancing			
(UK) Bell	*10 16 71*	*9*	*5*
B. BUMBLE and the STINGERS			
Nut Rocker			
(UK) Top Rank	*4 28 62*	*1*	*11*
(UK) Stateside (reissue)	*7 7 72*	*19*	*2*
BEACH BOYS			
Surfin' Safari			
(US) Capitol	10 6 62	14	3
Surfin' USA			
(US) Capitol	4 27 63	3	10
Surfer Girl			
(US) Capitol b/w*	8 24 63	7	9
Little Deuce Coupe*			
(US) Capitol	9 28 63	15	2
Be True to Your School			
(US) Capitol	11 23 63	6	7
Fun Fun Fun			
(US) Capitol	2 29 64	5	7
I Get Around			
(US) Capitol	6 6 64	1	12
(UK) Capitol	*7 25 64*	*7*	*8*
When I Grow Up to Be a Man			
(US) Capitol	10 3 64	9	5
Dance Dance Dance			
(US) Capitol	11 28 64	8	5
Do You Wanna Dance?			
(US) Capitol	3 20 65	12	4
Help Me Rhonda			
(US) Capitol	5 15 65	1	8
California Girls			
(US) Capitol	8 14 65	3	7

LABEL	DATE OF CHART ENTRY	HIGHEST POSITION REACHED	NUMBER OF WEEKS IN CHARTS
Little Girl I Once Knew			
(US) Capitol	1 1 66	20	1
Barbara Ann			
(US) Capitol	1 21 66	2	6
(UK) Capitol	*2 26 66*	*3*	*8*
Sloop John B			
(US) Capitol	4 16 66	3	7
(UK) Capitol	*4 30 66*	*2*	*11*
God Only Knows			
(UK) Capitol b/w**	*8 6 66*	*2*	*9*
Wouldn't It Be Nice**			
(US) Capitol	8 27 66	8	5
Good Vibrations			
(US) Capitol	11 5 66	1	11
(UK) Capitol	*11 5 66*	*1*	*11*
Then I Kissed Her			
(UK) Capitol	*5 13 67*	*4*	*8*
Heroes and Villains			
(US) Capitol	8 19 67	12	3
(UK) Capitol	*9 2 67*	*8*	*5*
Darlin'			
(US) Capitol	2 3 68	19	2
(UK) Capitol	*2 3 68*	*11*	*9*
Do It Again			
(UK) Capitol	*8 10 68*	*1*	*10*
(US) Capitol	9 14 68	20	2
I Can Hear Music			
(UK) Capitol	*3 22 69*	*11*	*7*
Break Away			
(UK) Capitol	*6 28 69*	*6*	*6*
Cottonfields			
(UK) Capitol	*5 30 70*	*5*	*12*
BEATLES			
Love Me Do			
(UK) Parlophone	*12 15 62*	*17*	*2*
(US) Tollie (reissue) b/w*	5 9 64	1	9
Please Please Me			
(UK) Parlophone	*2 3 63*	*2*	*11*
(US) Vee Jay (reissue)	2 29 64	3	8
From Me to You			
(UK) Parlophone	*4 27 63*	*1*	*16*
She Loves You			
(UK) Parlophone	*8 31 63*	*1*	*24*
(US) Swan (reissue)	2 8 64	1	12
I Want to Hold Your Hand			
(UK) Parlophone	*12 7 63*	*1*	*13*
(US) Capitol b/w**	1 25 64	1	13
I Saw Her Standing There			
(US) Capitol**	3 7 64	14	3
Twist and Shout			
(US) Tollie (reissue)	3 21 64	2	9

LABEL	DATE OF CHART ENTRY	HIGHEST POSITION REACHED	NUMBER OF WEEKS IN CHARTS
Can't Buy Me Love			
(*UK*) Parlophone	*3 28 64*	*1*	*9*
(US) Capitol	4 4 64	1	7
Do You Want to Know a Secret			
(US) Vee Jay (reissue)	4 11 64	2	8
P.S. I Love You			
(US) Tollie (reissue)*	5 23 64	10	4
Hard Day's Night			
(*UK*) Parlophone	*7 18 64*	*1*	*11*
(US) Capitol	7 25 64	1	10
And I Love Her			
(US) Capitol	8 22 64	12	4
Ain't She Sweet			
(US) Atco (reissue)	8 22 64	19	1
Matchbox			
(US) Capitol	10 3 64	17	3
I Feel Fine			
(*UK*) Parlophone	*12 5 64*	*1*	*10*
(US) Capitol b/w***	12 12 64	1	8
She's a Woman* **			
(US) Capitol	12 19 64	4	6
Eight Days a Week			
(US) Capitol	2 27 65	1	8
Ticket to Ride			
(*UK*) Parlophone	*4 17 65*	*1*	*9*
(US) Capitol	5 1 65	1	9
Help			
(*UK*) Parlophone	*7 31 65*	*1*	*10*
(US) Capitol	8 14 65	1	9
Yesterday			
(US) Capitol	10 2 65	1	8
Day Tripper			
(*UK*) Parlophone } b†	*12 11 65*	*1*	*10*
(US) Capitol	1 1 66	5	5
We Can Work It Out†			
(US) Capitol	12 25 65	1	9
Nowhere Man			
(US) Capitol	3 12 66	3	7
Paperback Writer			
(*UK*) Parlophone	*6 18 66*	*1*	*7*
(US) Capitol	6 18 66	1	8
Eleanor Rigby			
(*UK*) Parlophone } b/w††	*8 13 66*	*1*	*9*
(US) Capitol	9 17 66	11	3
Yellow Submarine††			
(US) Capitol	8 27 66	2	7
Penny Lane			
(*UK*) Parlophone } b/w†††	*2 27 67*	*2*	*8*
(US) Capitol	3 11 67	1	6
Strawberry Fields†††			
(US) Capitol	3 11 67	8	5

LABEL	DATE OF CHART ENTRY	HIGHEST POSITION REACHED	NUMBER OF WEEKS IN CHARTS
All You Need Is Love			
(*UK*) *Parlophone*	7 15 67	*1*	*10*
(US) Capitol	8 5 67	1	7
Hello Goodbye			
(*UK*) *Parlophone*	12 2 67	*1*	*10*
(US) Capitol	12 9 67	1	9
Magical Mystery Tour			
(*UK*) *Parlophone EP*	12 16 67	*2*	*9*
Lady Madonna			
(*UK*) *Parlophone*	3 23 68	*1*	*6*
(US) Capitol	3 30 68	4	8
Hey Jude			
(*UK*) *Apple*	9 14 68	*1*	*10*
(US) Apple	9 14 68	1	16
Revolution			
(US) Apple	9 21 68	12	9
Get Back			
(*UK*) *Apple*	4 26 69	*1*	*10*
(US) Apple	5 10 69	1	11
Ballad of John and Yoko			
(*UK*) *Apple*	6 7 69	*1*	*8*
(US) Apple	6 28 69	8	6
Something/Come Together			
(US) Apple	10 18 69	1	14
(*UK*) *Apple*	11 5 69	*4*	*7*
Let It Be			
(*UK*) *Apple*	3 14 70	*2*	*6*
(US) Apple	3 21 70	1	11
Long and Winding Road/For You Blue			
(US) Apple	5 30 70	1	8
BEAU BRUMMELS			
Laugh Laugh			
(US) Autumn	2 13 65	15	4
Just a Little			
(US) Autumn	5 22 65	8	6
BECK, JEFF			
Hi Ho Silver Lining			
(*UK*) *Columbia*	5 6 67	*14*	*5*
(*UK*) *RAK (reissue)*	11 18 72	*17*	*4*
BEDROCKS			
Ob-La-Di-Ob-La-Da			
(*UK*) *Columbia*	1 4 69	*20*	*1*
BEE GEES			
New York Mining Disaster 1941			
(*UK*) *Polydor*	5 13 67	*12*	*5*
(US) Atco	6 17 67	14	3
To Love Somebody			
(US) Atco	8 19 67	17	2
Massachusetts			

LABEL	DATE OF CHART ENTRY	HIGHEST POSITION REACHED	NUMBER OF WEEKS IN CHARTS
(UK) Polydor	*9 30 67*	*1*	*10*
(US) Atco	12 2 67	11	4
Holiday			
(US) Atco	11 11 67	16	2
Words			
(UK) Polydor	*12 2 67*	*8*	*7*
(US) Atco	2 24 68	15	4
World			
(UK) Polydor	*2 10 68*	*9*	*10*
I've Gotta Get a Message to You			
(UK) Polydor	*8 17 68*	*1*	*11*
(US) Atco	9 21 68	8	7
I Started a Joke			
(US) Atco	1 11 69	6	7
First of May			
(UK) Polydor	*3 8 69*	*6*	*6*
Don't Forget to Remember			
(UK) Polydor	*8 23 69*	*3*	*11*
Lonely Days			
(US) Atco	1 9 71	3	7
How Can You Mend a Broken Heart			
(US) Atco	7 10 71	1	12
My World			
(UK) Polydor	*12 2 72*	*16*	*5*
(US) Atco	2 26 72	16	2
Run to Me			
(UK) Polydor	*8 12 72*	*11*	*5*
(US) Atco	9 9 72	16	4
BEGINNING OF THE END			
Funky Nassau			
(US) Alston	6 26 71	15	4
BELAFONTE, HARRY			
Mary's Boy Child			
(US) Victor	1 5 57	15	1
(UK) RCA	*11 15 57*	*1*	*9*
Jamaica Farewell			
(US) Victor	1 12 57	17	5
Banana Boat Song			
(US) Victor	1 19 57	5	13
(UK) HMV	*3 1 57*	*2*	*14*
Mama Look-A-Booboo			
(US) Victor	4 13 57	13	6
Island in the Sun			
(UK) RCA	*6 21 57*	*3*	*22*
Scarlet Ribbons			
(UK) HMV	*9 20 57*	*18*	*2*
Little Bernadette			
(UK) RCA	*8 22 58*	*16*	*4*
Mary's Boy Child			
(UK) RCA (re-entry)	*12 5 58*	*10*	*5*

LABEL	DATE OF CHART ENTRY	HIGHEST POSITION REACHED	NUMBER OF WEEKS IN CHARTS
The Son of Mary			
(UK) RCA	12 19 58	18	2
BELL, ARCHIE, AND THE DRELLS			
Tighten Up			
(US) Atlantic	4 27 68	1	9
I Can't Stop Dancing			
(US) Atlantic	8 17 68	9	5
Here I Go Again			
(UK) Atlantic	11 11 72	11	3
BELL, FREDDIE, AND THE BELL BOYS			
Giddy Up a Ding Dong			
(UK) Mercury	9 28 56	4	8
BELL, WILLIAM. See **JUDY CLAY**			
BELL NOTES			
I've Had It			
(US) Time	2 23 59	6	8
BELLS			
Stay Awhile			
(US) Polydor	4 24 71	7	6
BELMONTS			
Tell Me Why			
(US) Sabrina	6 26 61	18	4
[see also: **DION**]			
BENNETT, BOYD			
Seventeen			
(US) King	7 23 55	5	13
(UK) Parlophone	12 23 55	16	1
BENNETT, CLIFF, AND THE REBEL ROUSERS			
One Way Love			
(UK) Parlophone	10 24 64	9	4
Got to Get You into My Life			
(UK) Parlophone	9 10 66	6	4
BENNETT, JOE, AND THE SPARKLETONES			
Black Slacks			
(US) ABC-Paramount	10 9 57	17	3
BENNETT, TONY			
Stranger in Paradise			
(UK) Philips	4 15 55	1	16
Close Your Eyes			
(UK) Philips	9 16 55	18	1
Can You Find It in Your Heart			
(US) Columbia	6 2 56	19	1
In the Middle of an Island			
(US) Columbia	9 9 57	9	8
Firefly			
(US) Columbia	10 13 58	20	1
I Left My Heart in San Francisco			
(US) Columbia	10 20 62	19	1

LABEL	DATE OF CHART ENTRY	HIGHEST POSITION REACHED	NUMBER OF WEEKS IN CHARTS
I Wanna Be Around			
(US) Columbia	3 23 63	14	3
Good Life			
(US) Columbia	6 15 63	18	2
BENTON, BROOK			
It's Just a Matter of Time			
(US) Mercury	3 2 59	3	9
Endlessly			
(US) Mercury	5 18 59	12	5
Thank You Pretty Baby			
(US) Mercury	8 17 59	16	5
So Many Ways			
(US) Mercury	11 2 59	6	9
Baby (with **DINAH WASHINGTON**)			
(US) Mercury	2 15 60	5	10
Rockin' Good Way (with **DINAH WASHINGTON**)			
(US) Mercury	6 13 60	7	7
Kiddio			
(US) Mercury b/w*	9 5 60	7	8
Same One			
(US) Mercury*	9 12 60	16	5
Think Twice			
(US) Mercury	3 13 61	11	5
Boll Weevil Song			
(US) Mercury	6 12 61	2	10
Frankie and Johnny			
(US) Mercury	9 11 61	20	2
Revenge			
(US) Mercury	1 6 62	15	2
Shadrack			
(US) Mercury	2 17 62	19	1
Lie to Me			
(US) Mercury	9 29 62	13	3
Hotel Happiness			
(US) Mercury	12 15 62	3	7
Rainy Night in Georgia			
(US) Cotillion	2 14 70	4	9
BERNARD, ROD			
This Should Go On Forever			
(US) Argo	4 13 59	20	1
BERNSTEIN, ELMER			
The "Johnny Staccato" Theme			
(UK) Capitol	12 19 59	5	8
BERRY, CHUCK			
Maybelline			
(US) Chess	8 20 55	5	10
School Days			
(US) Chess	4 29 57	5	10
Rock and Roll Music			
(US) Chess	11 25 57	8	9

LABEL	DATE OF CHART ENTRY	HIGHEST POSITION REACHED	NUMBER OF WEEKS IN CHARTS
Sweet Little Sixteen			
(US) Chess	2 24 58	2	9
(UK) London	*5 9 58*	*16*	*3*
Johnny B. Goode			
(US) Chess	5 5 58	8	9
Carol			
(US) Chess	9 29 58	18	2
Let It Rock/Memphis, Tennessee			
(UK) Pye (reissue)	*10 26 63*	*6*	*7*
No Particular Place to Go			
(UK) Pye	*5 23 64*	*3*	*7*
(US) Chess	6 27 64	10	4
You Never Can Tell			
(US) Chess	8 29 64	14	3
My Ding-a-Ling (live recording)			
(US) Chess	9 23 72	1	9
(UK) Chess	*11 11 72*	*1*	*10*
Reelin' and Rockin' (live recording)			
(UK) Chess	*2 24 73*	*18*	*2*
DAVE BERRY AND THE CRUISERS			
Memphis, Tennessee			
(UK) Decca	*11 9 63*	*19*	*1*
The Crying Game			
(UK) Decca	*8 22 64*	*5*	*7*
Little Things			
(UK) Decca	*4 10 65*	*6*	*6*
Mama			
(UK) Decca	*7 23 66*	*5*	*10*
BERRY, MIKE			
Tribute to Buddy Holly			
(UK) HMV	*10 28 61*	*18*	*1*
Don't You Think It's Time			
(UK) HMV	*1 20 63*	*6*	*7*
BEVERLY SISTERS			
Little Drummer Boy			
(UK) Decca	*2 14 59*	*9*	*11*
Little Donkey			
(UK) Decca	*11 28 59*	*16*	*2*
BIG BEN BANJO BAND			
Let's Get Together Again			
(UK) Columbia	*12 9 55*	*15*	*4*
BIG BOPPER			
Chantilly Lace			
(US) Mercury	9 29 58	6	11
(UK) Mercury	*1 17 59*	*14*	*6*
BIG BROTHER AND THE HOLDING COMPANY			
Piece of My Heart			
(US) Columbia	10 12 68	12	5

LABEL	DATE OF CHART ENTRY	HIGHEST POSITION REACHED	NUMBER OF WEEKS IN CHARTS
BILK, ACKER			
Summer Set			
(*UK*) *Columbia*	1 16 60	10	11
Buona Sera			
(*UK*) *Columbia*	12 25 60	9	8
That's My Home			
(*UK*) *Columbia*	7 22 61	11	8
Creole Jazz			
(*UK*) *Columbia*	11 4 61	17	1
Stranger on the Shore			
(*UK*) *Columbia*	11 25 61	1	39
(US) Atco	4 14 62	1	13
Frankie and Johnny			
(*UK*) *Columbia*	3 10 62	19	2
Lonely			
(*UK*) *Columbia*	10 13 62	14	4
A Taste of Honey			
(*UK*) *Columbia*	2 10 63	16	3
BILLIE AND LILLIE			
La Dee Dah			
(US) Swan	1 20 58	9	7
Lucky Ladybug			
(US) Swan	1 26 59	14	1
BILLY JOE AND THE CHECKMATES			
Percolator (Twist)			
(US) Dore	2 24 62	10	5
BIRKIN, JANE; and GAINSBOURG, SERGE			
Je 'Aime Moi Non Plus			
(*UK*) *Fontana*	8 23 69	2	7
(*UK*) *Major Minor* (*relicense*)	10 4 69	1	7
BILL BLACK'S COMBO			
Smokie (Pt. 2)			
(US) Hi	1 4 60	17	3
White Silver Sands			
(US) Hi	3 28 60	9	9
Josephine			
(US) Hi	7 18 60	18	2
Don't Be Cruel			
(US) Hi	10 10 60	11	7
Blue Tango			
(US) Hi	12 19 60	16	1
Hearts of Stone			
(US) Hi	3 20 61	20	1
BLACK, CILLA			
Anyone Who Had a Heart			
(*UK*) *Parlophone*	2 15 64	1	11
You're My World			
(*UK*) *Parlophone*	5 16 64	1	10

LABEL	DATE OF CHART ENTRY	HIGHEST POSITION REACHED	NUMBER OF WEEKS IN CHARTS
It's for You			
(UK) Parlophone	8 15 64	7	6
You've Lost That Lovin' Feeling			
(UK) Parlophone	1 23 65	2	5
I've Been Wrong Before			
(UK) Parlophone	5 15 65	17	2
Love's Just a Broken Heart			
(UK) Parlophone	1 29 66	5	6
Alfie			
(UK) Parlophone	4 9 66	9	7
Don't Answer Me			
(UK) Parlophone	6 18 66	6	6
A Fool Am I			
(UK) Parlophone	11 5 66	13	4
Step Inside Love			
(UK) Parlophone	3 30 68	8	5
Surround Yourself with Sorrow			
(UK) Parlophone	2 22 69	3	9
Conversations			
(UK) Parlophone	7 26 69	7	6
If I Thought You'd Ever Change Your Mind			
(UK) Parlophone	1 10 70	20	1
Something Tells Me (Something's Gonna Happen Tonight)			
(UK) Parlophone	12 4 71	6	8
BLACK, JEANNE			
He'll Have to Stay			
(US) Capitol	5 16 60	4	7
BLACKFOOT SUE			
Standing in the Road			
(UK) DJM	8 26 72	4	6
BLACK SABBATH			
Paranoid			
(UK) Vertigo	9 26 70	4	8
BLAND, BILLY			
Let the Little Girl Dance			
(US) Old Town	4 18 60	7	8
(UK) London	5 8 60	18	2
BLAND, BOBBY			
Ain't Nothing You Can Do			
(US) Duke	4 11 64	20	2
BLANE, MARCIE			
Bobby's Girl			
(US) Seville	11 10 62	3	11
BLOODSTONE			
Natural High			
(US) London	6 23 73	10	6
BLOOD, SWEAT AND TEARS			
You've Made Me So Very Happy			
(US) Columbia	3 29 69	2	8

LABEL	DATE OF CHART ENTRY	HIGHEST POSITION REACHED	NUMBER OF WEEKS IN CHARTS
Spinning Wheel			
(US) Columbia	6 14 69	2	10
And When I Die			
(US) Columbia	11 1 69	2	10
Hi-De-Ho			
(US) Columbia	8 29 70	14	3
BLOOM, BOBBY			
Montego Bay			
(*UK*) *Polydor*	*9 12 70*	*3*	*8*
(US) MGM	11 7 70	8	6
BLUE, BARRY			
Dancing on a Saturday Night			
(*UK*) *Bell*	*8 11 73*	*2*	*9*
Do You Wanna Dance			
(*UK*) *Bell*	*11 10 73*	*7*	*6*
BLUE BELLES			
I Sold My Heart to the Junkman			
(US) Newtown	5 26 62	15	3
BLUE CHEER			
Summertime Blues			
(US) Philips	4 13 68	14	6
BLUE MINK			
Melting Pot			
(*UK*) *Philips*	*11 29 69*	*3*	*10*
Good Morning Freedom			
(*UK*) *Philips*	*4 18 70*	*10*	*4*
Our World			
(*UK*) *Philips*	*10 10 70*	*17*	*2*
Banner Man			
(*UK*) *Regal Zonophone*	*6 5 71*	*3*	*9*
Stay with Me			
(*UK*) *Regal Zonophone*	*12 2 72*	*11*	*4*
Randy			
(*UK*) *EMI*	*7 14 73*	*9*	*5*
BLUE RIDGE RANGERS			
Jambalaya			
(US) Fantasy	2 17 73	16	4
BLUES IMAGE			
Ride Captain Ride			
(US) Atco	6 6 70	4	9
BLUES MAGOOS			
(We Ain't Got) Nothin Yet			
(US) Mercury	1 21 67	5	7
BLUE STARS			
Lullaby of Birdland			
(US) Mercury	2 25 56	20	1
BLUNSTONE, COLIN			
Say You Don't Mind			
(*UK*) *Epic*	*3 4 72*	*15*	*3*

LABEL	DATE OF CHART ENTRY	HIGHEST POSITION REACHED	NUMBER OF WEEKS IN CHARTS
BOB AND EARL			
Harlem Shuffle			
(*UK*) *Island* (*reissue*)	*4 19 69*	*7*	*6*
BOB B SOXX AND THE BLUE JEANS			
Zip-A-Dee-Doo-Dah			
(US) Philles	12 22 62	8	6
BOBETTES			
Mr. Lee			
(US) Atlantic	9 2 57	6	11
BO DIDDLEY			
Say Man			
(US) Checker	10 26 59	20	1
BONDS, GARY "U.S."			
New Orleans			
(US) LeGrand	11 7 60	6	8
(*UK*) *Top Rank*	*2 12 61*	*20*	*1*
Quarter to Three			
(US) LeGrand	6 12 61	1	10
(*UK*) *Top Rank*	*7 22 61*	*11*	*8*
School Is Out			
(US) LeGrand	8 7 61	5	6
Dear Lady Twist			
(US) LeGrand	1 27 62	9	8
Twist, Twist Señora			
(US) LeGrand	4 14 62	9	6
BONNEY, GRAHAM			
Supergirl			
(*UK*) *Columbia*	*4 30 66*	*19*	*1*
BONZO DOG DOO DAH BAND			
I'm the Urban Spaceman			
(*UK*) *Liberty*	*11 30 68*	*5*	*10*
BOOKER T and the MG's			
Green Onions			
(US) Stax	9 15 62	3	8
Soul Limbo			
(US) Stax	8 17 68	17	4
Hang 'Em High			
(US) Stax	1 25 69	9	6
Time Is Tight			
(US) Stax	4 26 69	6	6
(*UK*) *Stax*	*5 31 69*	*4*	*10*
BOONE, DANIEL			
Daddy Don't You Walk So Fast			
(*UK*) *Penny Farthing*	*9 25 71*	*17*	*4*
Beautiful Sunday			
(US) Mercury	9 2 72	15	5

LABEL	DATE OF CHART ENTRY	HIGHEST POSITION REACHED	NUMBER OF WEEKS IN CHARTS
BOONE, PAT			
Two Hearts			
(US) Dot	4 16 55	16	6
Ain't It a Shame			
(US) Dot	7 9 55	2	18
(UK) London	*11 18 55*	*7*	*9*
At My Front Door/No Arms Can Ever Hold You			
(US) Dot	10 29 55	7	9
I'll Be Home			
(US) Dot b/w*	2 18 56	5	17
(UK) London	*4 27 56*	*1*	*23*
Tutti Frutti			
(US) Dot*	2 18 56	12	5
Long Tall Sally			
(US) Dot	5 12 56	18	2
(UK) London	*8 24 56*	*18*	*2*
I Almost Lost My Mind			
(US) Dot	6 16 56	1	17
(UK) London	*8 17 56*	*14*	*6*
Friendly Persuasion			
(US) Dot b/w**	10 6 56	1	12
(UK) London	*12 21 56*	*3*	*17*
Chains of Love			
(US) Dot**	10 6 56	20	1
Don't Forbid Me			
(US) Dot	1 5 57	1	15
(UK) London	*2 8 57*	*2*	*14*
Why Baby Why			
(US) Dot	3 30 57	6	10
(UK) London	*5 10 57*	*17*	*1*
Love Letters in the Sand			
(US) Dot	5 20 57	1	19
(UK) London	*7 5 57*	*2*	*21*
Remember You're Mine			
(UK) London	*10 4 57*	*5*	*13*
(US) Dot	10 21 57	20	1
April Love			
(US) Dot	11 11 57	1	16
(UK) London	*12 20 57*	*7*	*18*
It's Too Soon to Know			
(US) Dot } b/w***	2 24 58	13	5
(UK) London	*4 11 58*	*7*	*8*
A Wonderful Time Up There***			
(US) Dot	3 10 58	10	9
(UK) London	*4 4 58*	*2*	*14*
Sugar Moon			
(US) Dot	5 19 58	11	8
(UK) London	*6 27 58*	*6*	*10*
If Dreams Came True			

LABEL	DATE OF CHART ENTRY	HIGHEST POSITION REACHED	NUMBER OF WEEKS IN CHARTS
(US) Dot	7 28 58	12	5
(UK) London	*9 19 58*	*16*	*5*
I'll Remember Tonight			
(UK) London	*1 31 59*	*17*	*3*
'Twixt Twelve and Twenty			
(US) Dot	7 13 59	17	3
(UK) London	*8 9 59*	*16*	*3*
For a Penny			
(UK) London	*7 18 59*	*19*	*1*
(Welcome) New Lovers			
(US) Dot	3 21 60	18	2
Moody River			
(US) Dot	5 29 61	1	9
(UK) London	*7 2 61*	*16*	*3*
Big Cold Wind			
(US) Dot	9 18 61	19	2
Johnny Will			
(UK) London	*12 2 61*	*3*	*8*
I'll See You in My Dreams			
(UK) London	*3 10 62*	*19*	*2*
Speedy Gonzales			
(US) Dot	7 14 62	6	8
(UK) London	*7 21 62*	*2*	*13*
The Main Attraction			
(UK) London	*12 1 62*	*12*	*7*
BOSWELL, EVE			
Pickin' a Chicken			
(UK) Parlophone	*1 6 56*	*9*	*10*
BOWEN, JIMMY			
I'm Sticking with You			
(US) Roulette	4 22 57	14	3
BOWIE, DAVID			
Space Oddity			
(UK) Philips	*10 4 69*	*5*	*8*
(US) RCA (reissue)	3 24 73	15	4
Starman			
(UK) RCA	*7 15 72*	*10*	*6*
John I'm Only Dancing			
(UK) RCA	*10 7 72*	*12*	*5*
The Jean Genie			
(UK) RCA	*12 23 72*	*2*	*8*
Drive-In Saturday			
(UK) RCA	*4 14 73*	*3*	*7*
Life on Mars			
(UK) RCA	*7 7 73*	*3*	*8*
Laughing Gnome			
(UK) Deram	*9 29 73*	*6*	*6*
Sorrow			
(UK) RCA	*10 20 73*	*3*	*8*

LABEL	DATE OF CHART ENTRY	HIGHEST POSITION REACHED	NUMBER OF WEEKS IN CHARTS
BOX TOPS			
The Letter			
(US) Mala	9 2 67	1	10
(UK) Stateside	*9 30 67*	*5*	*8*
Cry Like a Baby			
(US) Mala	3 23 68	2	10
(UK) Bell	*4 20 68*	*15*	*5*
Soul Deep			
(US) Mala	8 30 69	8	2
BOYCE, TOMMY; AND HART, BOBBY			
I Wonder What She's Doing Tonight			
(US) A&M	2 3 68	8	7
BRADLEY, JAN			
Mama Didn't Lie			
(US) Chess	2 16 63	14	6
BREAD			
Make It with You			
(US) Elektra	7 11 70	1	12
(UK) Elektra	*8 29 70*	*5*	*7*
It Don't Matter to Me			
(US) Elektra	10 31 70	10	5
If			
(US) Elektra	4 17 71	4	8
Baby I'm-a Want You			
(US) Elektra	11 13 71	3	7
(UK) Elektra	*1 29 72*	*14*	*4*
Everything I Own			
(US) Elektra	2 19 72	5	8
Diary			
(US) Elektra	5 27 72	15	5
Guitar Man			
(US) Elektra	8 19 72	11	5
(UK) Elektra	*10 28 72*	*16*	*2*
Sweet Surrender			
(US) Elektra	12 2 72	15	6
Aubrey			
(US) Elektra	3 17 73	15	3
BREMERS, BEVERLY			
Don't Say You Don't Remember			
(US) Scepter	2 19 72	15	5
BRENDA and the TABULATIONS			
Dry Your Eyes			
(US) Dionn	4 15 67	20	2
BRENNAN, WALTER			
Old Rivers			
(US) Liberty	5 5 62	5	6
BRENT, TONY			
Cindy Oh Cindy			
(UK) Columbia	*12 14 56*	*16*	*3*

LABEL	DATE OF CHART ENTRY	HIGHEST POSITION REACHED	NUMBER OF WEEKS IN CHARTS
Dark Moon			
(UK) *Columbia*	7 19 57	17	5
The Clouds Will Soon Roll By			
(UK) *Columbia*	9 5 58	16	5
BRESSLAW, BERNARD			
Mad Passionate Love			
(UK) *HMV*	9 12 58	6	9
BREWER, TERESA			
Let Me Go Lover			
(US) *Coral*	1 1 55	8	7
(UK) *Vogue-Coral*	2 4 55	9	3
A Tear Fell			
(US) *Coral* b/w*	3 10 56	7	14
(UK) *Vogue-Coral*	4 13 56	2	15
Bo Weevil			
(US) *Coral**	4 7 56	17	3
Sweet Old Fashioned Girl			
(US) *Coral*	7 7 56	9	11
(UK) *Vogue-Coral*	7 13 56	3	13
Empty Arms			
(US) *Coral*	5 6 57	18	4
BREWER AND SHIPLEY			
One Toke over the Line			
(US) *Buddah*	4 3 71	10	6
BRIGHTER SIDE OF DARKNESS			
Love Jones			
(US) *20th Century*	1 20 73	16	5
BROOK BROTHERS			
Please Help Me, I'm Falling			
(UK) *Pye*	8 14 60	16	1
Warpaint			
(UK) *Pye*	3 5 61	6	10
Ain't Gonna Wash for a Week			
(UK) *Pye*	8 19 61	8	6
Married			
(UK) *Pye*	11 11 61	17	3
BROOKLYN BRIDGE			
Worst That Could Happen			
(US) *Buddah*	1 18 69	3	7
BROOKS, DONNIE			
Mission Bell			
(US) *Era*	7 25 60	7	9
BROTHERHOOD OF MAN			
United We Stand			
(UK) *Deram*	2 21 70	10	6
(US) *Deram*	6 20 70	13	4
BROTHERS FOUR			
Greenfields			

LABEL	DATE OF CHART ENTRY	HIGHEST POSITION REACHED	NUMBER OF WEEKS IN CHARTS
(US) Columbia	4 4 60	2	11
(UK) Philips	*5 1 60*	*19*	*1*

BROWN, ARTHUR, CRAZY WORLD OF
Fire

(UK) Track	*7 13 68*	*1*	*10*
(US) Atlantic	9 21 68	2	10

BROWN, JAMES (*and the FAMOUS FLAMES)
Prisoner of Love

(US) King	6 15 63	18	2

Papa's Got a Brand New Bag*

(US) King	8 14 65	8	6

I Got You (I Feel Good)*

(US) King	11 20 65	3	9

It's a Man's Man's Man's World*

(US) King	5 21 66	8	5
(UK) Pye International	*7 9 66*	*13*	*2*

Cold Sweat*

(US) King	8 12 67	7	6

I Got the Feelin*

(US) King	3 30 68	6	9

Licking Stick*

(US) King	6 15 68	14	4

Say It Loud (I'm Black and I'm Proud)

(US) King	10 5 68	10	6

Give It Up or Turn It Loose

(US) King	2 15 69	15	5

I Don't Want Nobody to Give Me Nothing

(US) King	5 10 69	20	1

Mother Popcorn (pt. 1)

(US) King	6 28 69	11	8

Get Up I Feel Like Being a Sex Machine (pt. 1 & pt. 2)

(US) King	8 8 70	15	2

Super Bad (pt. 1 & pt. 2)

(US) King	10 31 70	13	5

Hot Pants (pt. 1)

(US) People	7 24 71	15	5

Good Foot (pt. 1)

(US) Polydor	10 7 72	18	3

BROWN, JOE
Picture of You

(UK) Piccadilly	*6 2 62*	*2*	*14*

It Only Took a Minute

(UK) Piccadilly	*12 1 62*	*6*	*8*

That's What Love Will Do

(UK) Piccadilly	*2 24 63*	*3*	*8*

BROWN, MAXINE
All in My Mind

(US) Nomar	2 13 61	19	3

LABEL	DATE OF CHART ENTRY	HIGHEST POSITION REACHED	NUMBER OF WEEKS IN CHARTS
BROWNE, JACKSON			
Doctor My Eyes			
(US) Asylum	4 15 72	8	6
BROWNS			
Three Bells			
(US) RCA	8 10 59	1	12
(UK) RCA	*9 12 59*	*5*	*11*
Scarlet Ribbons			
(US) RCA	12 9 59	13	5
Old Lamplighter			
(US) RCA	4 11 60	5	8
BROWNSVILLE STATION			
Smokin' in the Boys' Room			
(US) Big Tree	12 22 73	3	8
BRUBECK, DAVE			
Take Five			
(UK) Fontana	*10 21 61*	*6*	*12*
Unsquare Dance			
(UK) CBS	*6 9 62*	*14*	*4*
BRUCE, TOMMY			
Ain't Misbehavin'			
(UK) Columbia	*6 5 60*	*4*	*10*
BRYANT, ANITA			
Paper Roses			
(US) Carlton	5 16 60	5	9
In My Little Corner of the World			
(US) Carlton	8 15 60	10	6
Wonderland by Night			
(US) Carlton	12 31 60	18	3
BUBBLE PUPPY			
Hot Smoke and Sassafras			
(US) International Artists	3 29 69	14	3
BUCHANAN AND GOODMAN			
Flying Saucers			
(US) Luniverse	8 18 56	7	10
Flying Saucer the Second			
(US) Luniverse	8 12 57	19	2
BUCKINGHAMS			
Kind of a Drag			
(US) U.S.A.	1 21 67	1	9
Don't You Care			
(US) Columbia	4 22 67	6	6
Mercy Mercy Mercy			
(US) Columbia	7 15 67	5	6
Hey Baby (They're Playing Our Song)			
(US) Columbia	10 7 67	12	5
Susan			
(US) Columbia	1 13 68	11	6

ROCK ALMANAC

LABEL	DATE OF CHART ENTRY	HIGHEST POSITION REACHED	NUMBER OF WEEKS IN CHARTS
BUFFALO SPRINGFIELD			
For What It's Worth			
(US) Atco	3　4　67	7	8
BUOYS			
Timothy			
(US) Scepter	5　1　71	17	4
BURDON, ERIC, AND THE ANIMALS			
See See Rider			
(US) MGM	10　8　66	10	5
Help Me Girl			
(UK) Decca	*11　12　66*	*14*	*4*
When I Was Young			
(US) MGM	5　6　67	15	3
San Franciscan Nights			
(US) MGM	9　9　67	9	3
(UK) MGM	*11　4　67*	*7*	*5*
Good Times			
(UK) MGM	*10　7　67*	*20*	*1*
Monterey			
(US) MGM	1　13　68	15	2
Sky Pilot			
(US) MGM	7　20　68	14	3
[see also: **ANIMALS; ERIC BURDON AND WAR**]			
BURDON, ERIC, AND WAR			
Spill the Wine			
(US) MGM	7　25　70	3	9
BURNETTE, JOHNNY			
Dreamin'			
(US) Liberty	8　22　60	11	7
(UK) London	*10　7　60*	*6*	*10*
You're Sixteen			
(US) Liberty	12　5　60	8	5
(UK) London	*1　8　61*	*5*	*7*
Little Boy Sad			
(US) Liberty	3　13　61	7	3
(UK) London	*4　9　61*	*13*	*6*
God, Country and My Baby			
(US) Liberty	11　20　61	18	1
BURNS, RAY			
Mobile			
(UK) Columbia	*12　11　55*	*4*	*13*
That's How a Love Song Was Born			
(UK) Columbia	*8　26　55*	*14*	*6*
BUSCH, LOU			
Zambesi			
(UK) Capitol	*1　27　56*	*2*	*15*
BUTLER, JERRY			
For Your Precious Love (and the **IMPRESSIONS**)			
(US) Abner	7　7　58	11	5

LABEL	DATE OF CHART ENTRY	HIGHEST POSITION REACHED	NUMBER OF WEEKS IN CHARTS
He Will Break Your Heart			
(US) Vee Jay	11 21 60	7	9
Moon River			
(US) Vee Jay	11 27 61	11	5
Make It Easy on Yourself			
(US) Vee Jay	9 1 62	20	1
Let It Be Me (with **BETTY EVERETT**)			
(US) Vee Jay	10 10 64	5	7
Never Give You Up			
(US) Mercury	7 20 68	20	1
Hey, Western Union Man			
(US) Mercury	10 19 68	16	5
Only the Strong Survive			
(US) Mercury	3 29 69	4	8
What's the Use of Breaking Up			
(US) Mercury	10 11 69	20	1
BUTTERSCOTCH			
Don't You Know			
(UK) RCA	*5 30 70*	*17*	*4*
BYGRAVES, MAX			
Mr. Sandman			
(UK) HMV	*1 21 55*	*16*	*1*
Meet Me on the Corner			
(UK) HMV	*11 18 55*	*2*	*11*
Davy Crockett			
(UK) HMV	*2 17 56*	*20*	*1*
Out of Town			
(UK) HMV	*6 15 56*	*18*	*2*
Heart			
(UK) Decca	*4 5 57*	*14*	*7*
You Need Hands/Tulips from Amsterdam			
(UK) Decca	*5 16 58*	*3*	*21*
My Ukulele			
(UK) Decca	*1 10 59*	*16*	*2*
Jingle Bell Rock			
(UK) Decca	*12 26 59*	*11*	*1*
Fings Ain't What They Used to Be			
(UK) Decca	*3 13 60*	*6*	*8*
Deck of Cards			
(UK) Pye	*10 27 73*	*13*	*5*
BYRD, CHARLIE. See **GETZ, STAN**			
BYRDS			
Mr. Tambourine Man			
(US) Columbia	6 5 65	1	9
(UK) CBS	*7 3 65*	*1*	*9*
All I Really Want to Do			
(UK) CBS	*8 21 65*	*9*	*1*
Turn Turn Turn			
(US) Columbia	11 13 65	1	10

LABEL	DATE OF CHART ENTRY	HIGHEST POSITION REACHED	NUMBER OF WEEKS IN CHARTS
Eight Miles High			
(US) Columbia	5 7 66	14	3
Chestnut Mare			
(UK) CBS	2 27 71	19	1
BYRNES, ED, AND STEVENS, CONNIE			
Kookie, Kookie (Lend Me Your Comb)			
(US) Warner Brothers	5 4 59	4	8
(UK) Warner Brothers	5 1 60	20	1
C. ROY			
Shotgun Wedding			
(UK) Island	5 7 66	6	6
(UK) UK (reissue)	12 9 72	8	7
CADETS			
Stranded in the Jungle			
(US) Modern	7 28 55	18	2
CAIOLA, AL			
Bonanza			
(US) United Artists	5 15 61	19	2
CALVERT, EDDIE			
Cherry Pink			
(UK) Columbia	4 8 55	1	21
Stranger in Paradise			
(UK) Columbia	3 13 55	14	4
John and Julie			
(UK) Columbia	7 29 55	6	11
Zambesi			
(UK) Columbia	3 9 56	13	5
Mandy			
(UK) Columbia	2 21 58	9	11
CAMPBELL, GLEN			
Wichita Lineman			
(US) Capitol	11 23 68	3	11
(UK) Ember	2 22 69	7	8
Galveston			
(US) Capitol	3 15 69	4	9
(UK) Ember	5 24 69	14	5
All I Have to Do Is Dream (with **BOBBIE GENTRY**)			
(UK) Capitol	12 13 69	3	10
Honey Come Back			
(US) Capitol	2 21 70	19	2
(UK) Capitol	5 23 70	4	10
It's Only Make Believe			
(US) Capitol	10 17 70	10	4
(UK) Capitol	11 28 70	4	11
CAMPBELL, JUNIOR			
Hallelujah Freedom			
(UK) Deram	10 28 72	10	5

LABEL	DATE OF CHART ENTRY	HIGHEST POSITION REACHED	NUMBER OF WEEKS IN CHARTS
Sweet Illusion			
(UK) Deram	6 16 73	15	4
CANNED HEAT			
On the Road Again			
(UK) Liberty	8 24 68	8	7
(US) Liberty	9 21 68	16	2
Going up the Country			
(US) Liberty	12 28 68	11	7
(UK) Liberty	2 15 69	19	1
Let's Work Together			
(UK) Liberty	2 7 70	2	9
CANNON, ACE			
Tuff			
(US) Hi	2 24 62	17	4
CANNON, FREDDIE			
Tallahassie Lassie			
(US) Swan	6 1 59	6	8
(UK) Top Rank	8 22 59	15	2
Way Down Yonder in New Orleans			
(US) Swan	12 14 59	3	9
(UK) Top Rank	1 3 60	4	10
California Here I Come			
(UK) Top Rank	2 27 60	19	2
The Urge			
(UK) Top Rank	5 22 60	18	2
Palisades Park			
(US) Swan	6 2 62	3	9
(UK) Stateside	7 14 62	20	1
Abigail Beecher			
(US) Warner Brothers	2 29 64	16	2
Action			
(US) Warner Brothers	9 11 65	13	3
CAPITOLS			
Cool Jerk			
(US) Karen	5 28 66	7	8
CAPRIS			
There's a Moon Out Tonight			
(US) Old Town	2 6 61	3	7
CARAVELLES			
You Don't Have to Be a Baby to Cry			
(UK) Decca	8 17 63	6	8
(US) Smash	11 30 63	3	7
CAROSONE, RENATE			
Torero			
(US) Capitol	6 9 58	19	2
CARPENTERS			
Close to You			
(US) A&M	7 4 70	1	13
(UK) A&M	9 26 70	6	8

LABEL	DATE OF CHART ENTRY	HIGHEST POSITION REACHED	NUMBER OF WEEKS IN CHARTS
We've Only Just Begun			
(US) A&M	10 3 70	2	13
For All We Know			
(US) A&M	2 27 71	3	9
Rainy Days and Mondays			
(US) A&M	5 22 71	2	10
Superstar			
(US) A&M (b/w Bless the Beasts and Children)			
	9 11 71	2	11
(UK) A&M (b/w For All We Know)			
	11 6 71	*18*	*3*
Hurting Each Other			
(US) A&M	1 29 72	2	8
It's Going to Take Some Time			
(US) A&M	5 27 72	12	4
Goodbye to Love			
(US) A&M	8 12 72	7	5
(UK) A&M	*10 21 72*	*9*	*6*
Sing			
(US) A&M	3 17 73	3	9
Yesterday Once More			
(US) A&M	6 23 73	2	9
(UK) A&M	*7 28 73*	*2*	*8*
Top of the World			
(UK) A&M	*10 27 73*	*5*	*8*
(US) A&M	11 3 73	1	9
CARR, CATHY			
Ivory Tower			
(US) Fraternity	4 28 56	6	13
CARR, JOE "FINGERS"			
Portuguese Washer Women			
(UK) Capitol	*7 6 56*	*20*	*1*
CARR, PEARL; AND JOHNSON, TEDDY			
Sing Little Birdy			
(UK) Columbia	*3 21 59*	*12*	*5*
CARR, VIKKI			
It Must Be Him			
(UK) Liberty	*7 1 67*	*2*	*10*
(US) Liberty	10 21 67	3	6
CARROLL, DON			
Melody of Love			
(US) Mercury	1 29 55	9	11
CARROLL, RONNIE			
Walk Hand in Hand			
(UK) Philips	*7 25 56*	*13*	*6*
Wisdom of a Fool			
(UK) Philips	*3 29 57*	*20*	*1*
Roses Are Red			
(UK) Philips	*8 18 62*	*3*	*11*

LABEL	DATE OF CHART ENTRY	HIGHEST POSITION REACHED	NUMBER OF WEEKS IN CHARTS
Say Wonderful Things			
(UK) *Philips*	3 23 63	6	8
CARSON, JOHNNY			
You Talk Too Much			
(UK) *Fontana*	12 11 60	18	1
CARSON, KIT			
Band of Gold			
(US) Capitol	2 18 56	17	1
CARSON, MINDY			
Wake the Town and Tell the People			
(US) Columbia	9 3 55	20	2
CARTER, CLARENCE			
Slip Away			
(US) Atlantic	9 7 68	6	7
Too Weak to Fight			
(US) Atlantic	1 4 69	13	1
Patches			
(US) Atlantic	8 15 70	4	9
(UK) *Atlantic*	10 17 70	2	8
CARTER, MEL			
Hold Me, Thrill Me, Kiss Me			
(US) Imperial	8 7 65	8	7
CASCADES			
Rhythm of the Rain			
(US) Valiant	2 2 63	3	11
(UK) *Warner Brothers*	3 16 63	5	11
CASH, ALVIN, AND THE CRAWLERS			
Twine Time			
(US) Mar-V-Lus	2 6 65	14	5
CASH, JOHNNY			
I Walk the Line			
(US) Sun	11 10 56	19	3
Ballad of a Teenage Queen			
(US) Sun	3 3 58	16	4
Guess Things Happen That Way			
(US) Sun	7 14 58	11	3
Ring of Fire			
(US) Columbia	7 20 63	17	3
A Boy Named Sue			
(US) Columbia	8 2 69	2	10
(UK) *CBS*	9 20 69	2	9
What Is Truth			
(US) Columbia	5 9 70	19	3
A Thing Called Love			
(UK) *CBS*	4 29 72	4	7
CASINOS			
Then You Can Tell Me Goodbye			
(US) Fraternity	2 11 67	6	7

114　　　　　　　　　　　　　　　　　　　ROCK ALMANAC

LABEL	DATE OF CHART ENTRY	HIGHEST POSITION REACHED	NUMBER OF WEEKS IN CHARTS
CASS, MAMA			
Dream a Little Dream of Me			
(US) Dunhill	8 3 68	12	4
(UK) RCA	*8 31 68*	*11*	*7*
It's Getting Better			
(UK) Stateside	*9 20 69*	*8*	*7*
CASSIDY, DAVID			
Cherish			
(US) Bell	11 27 71	9	8
Could It Be Forever?			
(UK) Bell	*4 22 72*	*2*	*9*
How Can I Be Sure?			
(UK) Bell	*9 16 72*	*1*	*8*
Rock Me Baby			
(UK) Bell	*12 2 72*	*11*	*4*
I'm a Clown/Some Kind of a Summer			
(UK) Bell	*3 31 73*	*3*	*8*
Daydreamer/Puppy Song			
(UK) Bell	*10 13 73*	*1*	*8*
[see also: **PARTRIDGE FAMILY**]			
CASTAWAYS			
Liar, Liar			
(US) Soma	10 2 65	12	6
CASTELLS			
Sacred			
(US) Era	7 24 61	20	2
CASTOR, JIMMY, BUNCH			
Troglodyte (Cave Man)			
(US) RCA	6 3 72	6	7
CASUALS			
Jesamine			
(UK) Decca	*9 14 68*	*2*	*11*
CATES, GEORGE			
Theme from "Picnic"/"Moonglow"			
(US) Coral	5 5 56	4	15
CATHY JEAN AND THE ROOMMATES			
Please Love Me Forever			
(US) Valmor	4 3 61	12	5
CCS			
Whole Lotta Love			
(UK) RAK	*11 14 70*	*13*	*5*
Walking			
(UK) RAK	*3 27 71*	*7*	*7*
Tap Turns on the Water			
(UK) RAK	*9 18 71*	*5*	*7*
CHACKSFIELD, FRANK			
In Old Lisbon			
(UK) Decca	*2 24 56*	*15*	*4*

LABEL	DATE OF CHART ENTRY	HIGHEST POSITION REACHED	NUMBER OF WEEKS IN CHARTS
CHAD AND JEREMY			
Summer Song			
(US) World Artists	9 26 64	7	6
Willow Weep for Me			
(US) World Artists	1 2 65	15	4
Before and After			
(US) Columbia	6 19 65	17	3
CHAIRMEN OF THE BOARD			
Give Me Just a Little More Time			
(US) Invictus	2 21 70	3	9
(UK) Invictus	*8 29 70*	*3*	*8*
You've Got Me Dangling on a String			
(UK) Invictus	*11 21 70*	*5*	*10*
Pay to the Piper			
(US) Invictus	1 2 71	13	3
Everything's Tuesday			
(UK) Invictus	*2 27 71*	*12*	*5*
Working on the Building of Love			
(UK) Invictus	*8 19 72*	*20*	*1*
CHAKACHAS			
Jungle Fever			
(US) Polydor	3 4 72	8	7
CHAMBERLAIN, RICHARD			
Theme from "Dr. Kildare"			
(UK) MGM	*6 23 62*	*12*	*3*
(US) MGM	6 30 62	10	7
Love Me Tender			
(UK) MGM	*11 24 62*	*15*	*5*
Hi-Lili-Hi-Lo			
(UK) MGM	*3 9 63*	*20*	*1*
All I Have to Do Is Dream			
(US) MGM	3 23 63	14	4
CHAMBERS BROTHERS			
Time Has Come Today			
(US) Columbia	9 21 68	11	5
CHAMPS			
Tequila			
(US) Challenge	3 10 58	1	20
(UK) London	*4 4 58*	*5*	*7*
CHANDLER, GENE			
Duke of Earl			
(US) Vee Jay	1 27 62	1	11
Just Be True			
(US) Constellation	8 15 64	19	3
Nothing Can Stop Me			
(US) Constellation	6 19 65	18	1
Groovy Situation			
(US) Mercury	9 12 70	12	4

LABEL	DATE OF CHART ENTRY	HIGHEST POSITION REACHED	NUMBER OF WEEKS IN CHARTS
CHANNEL, BRUCE			
Hey! Baby			
(US) Smash	2 17 62	1	10
(*UK*) *Mercury*	*3 31 62*	*2*	*9*
Keep On			
(*UK*) *Bell*	*8 3 68*	*11*	*6*
CHANTAYS			
Pipeline			
(US) Dot	4 13 63	4	8
(*UK*) *London*	*5 25 63*	*16*	*4*
CHANTELS			
Maybe			
(US) End	2 10 58	15	4
Look in My Eyes			
(US) Carlton	10 9 61	14	4
CHARLES, JIMMY			
A Million to One			
(US) Promo	9 5 60	5	9
CHARLES, RAY			
What'd I Say			
(US) Atlantic	8 3 59	6	7
Georgia on My Mind			
(US) ABC-Paramount	10 17 60	1	8
One Mint Julep			
(US) Impulse	4 10 61	8	6
Hit the Road Jack			
(US) ABC-Paramount	9 25 61	1	9
(*UK*) *HMV*	*10 21 61*	*5*	*7*
Unchain My Heart			
(US) ABC-Paramount	12 18 61	9	6
Hide nor Hair			
(US) ABC-Paramount	5 5 62	20	1
I Can't Stop Loving You			
(US) ABC-Paramount	5 26 62	1	12
(*UK*) *HMV*	*6 23 62*	*1*	*13*
You Don't Know Me			
(US) ABC-Paramount	8 11 62	2	6
(*UK*) *HMV*	*9 29 62*	*9*	*8*
You Are My Sunshine			
(US) ABC-Paramount	12 15 62	7	5
Your Cheating Heart			
(*UK*) *HMV*	*12 29 62*	*13*	*4*
Don't Set Me Free			
(US) ABC-Paramount	3 30 63	20	1
Take These Chains from My Heart			
(US) ABC-Paramount	5 4 63	8	6
(*UK*) *HMV*	*6 1 63*	*5*	*13*

LABEL	DATE OF CHART ENTRY	HIGHEST POSITION REACHED	NUMBER OF WEEKS IN CHARTS
Busted			
(US) ABC-Paramount	9 28 63	4	8
That Lucky Old Sun			
(US) ABC-Paramount	1 18 64	20	2
Crying Time			
(US) ABC-Paramount	1 29 66	6	6
Together Again			
(US) ABC-Paramount	4 30 66	19	1
Here We Go Again			
(US) ABC	7 8 67	15	4
CHARLES, RAY, SINGERS			
Love Me with All Your Heart			
(US) Command	5 16 64	3	8
CHARLES, SONNY, AND THE CHECKMATES			
Black Pearl			
(US) A&M	6 14 69	13	7
CHARMS			
Hearts of Stone			
(US) Deluxe	1 1 55	15	4
CHECKER, CHUBBY			
Twist			
(US) Parkway	8 8 60	1	13
Hucklebuck			
(US) Parkway	11 14 60	14	4
Pony Time			
(US) Parkway	2 6 61	1	11
(UK) Columbia	*3 26 61*	*19*	*1*
Let's Twist Again			
(US) Parkway	7 17 61	8	7
(UK) Columbia	*1 20 62*	*2*	*16*
Fly			
(US) Parkway	10 16 61	7	8
Twist (reissue)			
(US) Parkway	11 27 61	1	15
(UK) Columbia	*1 13 62*	*12*	*5*
Slow Twistin'			
(US) Parkway	3 17 62	3	10
Dancing Party			
(US) Parkway	7 14 62	12	4
(UK) Columbia	*8 25 62*	*19*	*2*
Popeye (Hitchhiker)			
(US) Parkway	10 20 62	10	5
Limbo Rock			
(US) Parkway	10 27 62	2	14
Let's Limbo Some More			
(US) Parkway	3 16 63	20	1
20 Miles			
(US) Parkway	4 13 63	15	2

LABEL	DATE OF CHART ENTRY	HIGHEST POSITION REACHED	NUMBER OF WEEKS IN CHARTS
Birdland			
(US) Parkway	6 15 63	12	3
Loddy Lo			
(US) Parkway	12 7 63	12	4
Hooka Tooka			
(US) Parkway	2 1 64	17	4
CHEECH AND CHONG			
Basketball Jones (featuring **TYRONE SHOELACES**)			
(US) Ode	10 6 73	15	4
CHEERS			
Black Denim Trousers (and Motorcycle Boots)			
(US) Capitol	10 1 55	6	9
CHELSEA FC			
Blue Is the Color			
(UK) Penny Farthing	2 26 72	5	7
CHER			
All I Really Want to Do			
(US) Imperial	8 14 65	15	4
(UK) Liberty	9 4 65	9	5
Bang Bang			
(US) Imperial	3 26 66	2	8
(UK) Liberty	4 9 66	3	8
You Better Sit Down Kids			
(US) Imperial	11 25 67	9	7
Gypsies Tramps and Thieves			
(US) Kapp	10 16 71	1	11
(UK) MCA	11 13 71	4	9
Way of Love			
(US) Kapp	2 26 72	7	7
Half-Breed			
(US) MCA	9 15 73	1	11
[see also: **SONNY AND CHER**]			
CHERRY, DON			
Band of Gold			
(US) Columbia	12 24 55	5	16
(UK) Philips	2 10 56	6	11
CHESTER, PETE, AND THE CHESTERNUTS			
Ten Swinging Bottles			
(UK) Pye International	12 18 60	14	2
CHICAGO			
I'm a Man			
(UK) Columbia	1 24 70	8	5
Make Me Smile			
(US) Columbia	5 16 70	9	7
25 or 6 to 4			
(US) Columbia	8 15 70	4	8
(UK) Columbia	8 15 70	7	7

LABEL	DATE OF CHART ENTRY	HIGHEST POSITION REACHED	NUMBER OF WEEKS IN CHARTS
Does Anybody Really Know What Time It Is?			
(US) Columbia	11 28 70	7	9
Free			
(US) Columbia	4 3 71	20	1
Beginnings/Color My World			
(US) Columbia	7 24 71	7	8
Saturday in the Park			
(US) Columbia	8 26 72	3	7
Feelin' Stronger Every Day			
(US) Columbia	7 21 73	10	9
Just You 'n' Me			
(US) Columbia	11 3 73	4	9
CHICKEN SHACK			
I'd Rather Go Blind			
(UK) *Blue Horizon*	6 7 69	14	5
CHICORY TIP			
Son of My Father			
(UK) *CBS*	2 5 72	1	10
What's Your Name			
(UK) *CBS*	6 17 72	13	1
Good Grief Christina			
(UK) *CBS*	5 5 73	17	2
CHIFFONS			
He's So Fine			
(US) Laurie	3 9 63	1	11
(UK) *Stateside*	5 4 63	16	6
One Fine Day			
(US) Laurie	6 15 63	5	6
Sweet Talkin Guy			
(US) Laurie	5 28 66	10	6
(UK) *London* (reissue)	4 1 72	4	7
CHI-LITES			
Have You Seen Her?			
(US) Brunswick	11 6 71	3	10
(UK) *MCA*	1 29 72	3	7
Oh Girl			
(US) Brunswick	4 22 72	1	11
(UK) *MCA*	6 24 72	14	3
CHIMES			
Once in a While			
(US) Tag	1 23 61	11	4
CHIPMUNKS [see **DAVID SEVILLE**]			
CHORDETTES			
Mr. Sandman			
(US) Cadence	1 1 55	1	11
(UK) *Columbia*	1 7 55	11	5
Eddie My Love			
(US) Cadence	3 31 56	18	3

LABEL	DATE OF CHART ENTRY	HIGHEST POSITION REACHED	NUMBER OF WEEKS IN CHARTS
Born to Be with You			
(US) Cadence	6 16 56	5	13
(UK) London	*8 31 56*	*8*	*8*
Lay Down Your Arms			
(US) Cadence	11 17 56	16	2
Just Between You and Me			
(US) Cadence	10 21 57	19	1
Lollipop			
(US) Cadence	3 17 58	2	10
(UK) London	*4 25 58*	*6*	*5*
Zorro			
(US) Cadence	6 16 58	17	2
Never on Sunday			
(US) Cadence	7 17 61	13	6
CHRISTIE			
Yellow River			
(UK) CBS	*5 16 70*	*1*	*11*
San Bernardino			
(UK) CBS	*11 7 70*	*7*	*6*
CHRISTIE, LOU			
Two Faces Have I			
(US) Roulette	5 11 63	6	7
Lightnin' Strikes			
(US) MGM	1 29 66	1	8
(UK) MGM	*3 5 66*	*11*	*5*
Rhapsody in the Rain			
(US) MGM	4 30 66	16	1
I'm Gonna Make You Mine			
(US) Buddah	10 4 69	10	5
(UK) Buddah	*10 4 69*	*2*	*8*
CHRISTIE, TONY			
I Did What I Did for Maria			
(UK) MCA	*5 29 71*	*2*	*9*
Is This the Way to Amarillo?			
(UK) MCA	*12 18 71*	*18*	*4*
CINQUETTI, GIGLIOLA			
Non Ho l'Età			
(UK) Decca	*5 30 64*	*17*	*4*
CLANTON, JIMMY			
Just a Dream			
(US) Ace	8 4 58	4	12
Go Jimmy Go			
(US) Ace	12 28 59	5	8
Venus in Blue Jeans			
(US) Ace	9 15 62	7	7
CLAPTON, ERIC			
After Midnight			
(US) Atco	12 12 70	18	2

[see also: **CREAM; DELANEY AND BONNIE; DEREK AND THE DOMINOS**]

LABEL	DATE OF CHART ENTRY	HIGHEST POSITION REACHED	NUMBER OF WEEKS IN CHARTS
CLARK, CLAUDINE			
Party Lights			
(US) Chancellor	8 11 62	5	6
CLARK, DAVE, FIVE			
Glad All Over			
(UK) Columbia	*11 30 63*	*1*	*14*
(US) Epic	3 14 64	6	9
Bits and Pieces			
(US) Epic	4 18 64	4	7
(UK) Columbia	*4 22 64*	*2*	*9*
Do You Love Me			
(US) Epic	5 23 64	11	4
Can't You See That She's Mine			
(UK) Columbia	*6 13 64*	*10*	*6*
(US) Epic	6 27 64	4	7
Because			
(US) Epic	8 15 64	3	7
Everybody Knows			
(US) Epic	10 31 64	15	2
(UK) Columbia (*reissue*)	11 18 67	2	8
Any Way You Want It			
(US) Epic	12 19 64	14	6
Come Home			
(US) Epic	3 13 65	14	3
(UK) Columbia	*6 19 65*	*16*	*3*
I Like It Like That			
(US) Epic	7 24 65	7	4
Catch Us If You Can			
(UK) Columbia	*7 31 65*	*5*	*6*
(US) Epic	9 11 65	4	7
Over and Over			
(US) Epic	11 27 65	1	8
At the Scene			
(US) Epic	3 5 66	18	2
Try Too Hard			
(US) Epic	4 30 66	12	2
You Got What It Takes			
(US) Epic	4 22 67	7	6
Red Balloon			
(UK) Columbia	*9 28 68*	*7*	*6*
Good Old Rock and Roll			
(UK) Columbia	*12 20 69*	*7*	*8*
Everybody Get Together			
(UK) Columbia	*3 14 70*	*8*	*5*
CLARK, DEE			
Just Keep It Up			
(US) Abner	6 8 59	18	2
(UK) London	*9 12 59*	*19*	*1*
Hey Little Girl			
(US) Abner	9 21 59	20	1

LABEL	DATE OF CHART ENTRY	HIGHEST POSITION REACHED	NUMBER OF WEEKS IN CHARTS
Raindrops			
(US) Vee Jay	5 29 61	2	10
CLARK, PETULA			
Majorca			
(*UK*) *Polygon*	2 18 55	13	5
Suddenly There's a Valley			
(*UK*) *Nixa*	11 25 55	8	10
With All My Heart			
(*UK*) *Nixa*	8 2 57	4	16
Alone			
(*UK*) *Pye Nixa*	11 22 57	8	9
Baby Lover			
(*UK*) *Pye Nixa*	3 14 58	12	4
Sailor			
(*UK*) *Pye*	1 15 61	2	10
Romeo			
(*UK*) *Pye*	7 2 61	4	11
My Friend the Sea			
(*UK*) *Pye*	11 18 61	10	6
Ya Ya Twist			
(*UK*) *Pye*	7 21 62	14	4
Downtown			
(*UK*) *Pye*	11 21 64	2	12
(US) Warner Brothers	1 2 65	1	11
I Know a Place			
(*UK*) *Pye*	3 27 65	17	2
(US) Warner Brothers	4 10 65	3	7
My Love			
(US) Warner Brothers	1 22 65	1	8
(*UK*) *Pye*	2 19 66	4	6
Sign of the Times			
(US) Warner Brothers	4 16 66	11	3
I Couldn't Live Without Your Love			
(*UK*) *Pye*	7 16 66	6	7
(US) Warner Brothers	8 6 66	9	5
Color My World			
(US) Warner Brothers	1 21 67	16	3
This Is My Song			
(*UK*) *Pye*	2 11 67	1	10
(US) Warner Brothers	3 25 67	3	7
Don't Sleep in the Subway			
(*UK*) *Pye*	6 24 67	12	4
(US) Warner Brothers	6 24 67	5	5
The Other Man's Grass			
(*UK*) *Pye*	1 13 68	20	1
Kiss Me Goodbye			
(US) Warner Brothers	3 23 68	15	4
CLARK, ROY			
Yesterday, When I was Young			
(US) Dot	8 2 69	19	1

LABEL	DATE OF CHART ENTRY	HIGHEST POSITION REACHED	NUMBER OF WEEKS IN CHARTS
CLARK, SANFORD			
Fool			
(US) Dot	8 25 56	9	10
CLASSICS IV			
Spooky			
(US) Imperial	1 20 68	3	9
Stormy			
(US) Imperial	11 23 68	5	9
Traces			
(US) Imperial	3 1 69	2	9
Every Day with You Girl			
(US) Imperial	6 14 69	19	2
CLAY, JUDY; and BELL, WILLIAM			
Private Number			
(UK) Stax	*12 21 68*	*8*	*9*
CLAY, TOM			
What the World Needs Now Is Love/Abraham, Martin and John			
(US) Mowest	7 31 71	8	5
CLEFTONES			
Heart and Soul			
(US) Gee	6 19 61	18	1
CLIFF, JIMMY			
Wonderful World, Beautiful People			
(UK) Trojan	*11 1 69*	*6*	*8*
Wild World			
(UK) Island	*9 5 70*	*8*	*5*
CLIFFORD, BUZZ			
Baby Sittin' Boogie			
(US) Columbia	2 13 61	6	7
(UK) Philips	*2 19 61*	*16*	*10*
CLIFFORD, MIKE			
Close to Cathy			
(US) United Artists	10 27 62	12	5
CLIMAX			
Precious Few			
(US) Rocky Road	1 29 72	3	10
CLINE, PATSY			
Walkin' After Midnight			
(US) Decca	3 23 57	17	3
I Fall to Pieces			
(US) Decca	8 21 61	12	3
Crazy			
(US) Decca	11 13 61	9	5
She's Got You			
(US) Decca	3 10 62	14	5
CLOONEY, ROSEMARY			
This Old House			

LABEL	DATE OF CHART ENTRY	HIGHEST POSITION REACHED	NUMBER OF WEEKS IN CHARTS
(US) Columbia	1 1 55	4	5
(UK) Philips	1 7 55	10	5
Mambo Italiano			
(US) Columbia	1 1 55	17	1
(UK) Philips	1 7 55	3	13
Where Will the Dimple Be?			
(UK) Philips	5 20 55	6	13
Hey There			
(UK) Philips	9 30 55	4	11
Mangos			
(UK) Philips	5 24 57	17	1

COASTERS

Young Blood			
(US) Atco (b/w*)	5 27 57	18	4
Searchin'*			
(US) Atco	5 27 57	5	14
Yakety Yak			
(US) Atco	6 16 58	1	10
(UK) London	8 15 58	12	7
Charlie Brown			
(US) Atco	2 16 59	2	10
(UK) London	3 28 59	5	10
Along Came Jones			
(US) Atco	6 8 59	9	6
Poison Ivy			
(US) Atlantic	9 14 59	7	9
(UK) London	11 21 59	15	2

COCHRAN, EDDIE

Sittin' in the Balcony			
(US) Liberty	4 20 57	18	2
Summertime Blues			
(US) Liberty	9 1 58	8	7
(UK) London	11 28 58	18	2
C'Mon Everybody			
(UK) London	3 21 59	8	10
Three Steps to Heaven			
(UK) London	5 8 60	3	12
Lonely/Sweetie Pie			
(UK) London	9 30 60	19	1
Weekend			
(UK) London	6 11 61	15	8

COCKER, JOE

With a Little Help from My Friends			
(UK) Regal Zonophone	10 19 68	1	8
Delta Lady			
(UK) Regal Zonophone	10 25 69	10	5
The Letter			
(US) A&M	5 23 70	7	6

	DATE OF CHART ENTRY	HIGHEST POSITION REACHED	NUMBER OF WEEKS IN CHARTS
Cry Me a River			
(US) A&M	10 31 70	11	5
COCKEREL CHORUS			
Nice One Cyril			
(*UK*) *Young Blood*	3 10 73	14	5
COFFEY, DENNIS, AND THE DETROIT GUITAR BAND			
Scorpio			
(US) Sussex	12 4 71	6	11
Taurus			
(US) Sussex	4 8 72	18	3
COGAN, ALMA			
Can't Tell a Waltz from a Tango			
(*UK*) *HMV*	1 7 55	6	6
Dreamboat			
(*UK*) *HMV*	5 27 55	1	16
Banjo's Back in Town			
(*UK*) *HMV*	9 23 55	17	1
Go On By			
(*UK*) *HMV*	10 14 55	16	4
Never Do a Tango with an Eskimo			
(*UK*) *HMV*	12 23 55	6	5
Twenty Tiny Fingers			
(*UK*) *HMV*	12 16 55	17	1
Willie Can			
(*UK*) *HMV*	3 30 56	13	7
Middle of the House			
(*UK*) *HMV*	11 23 56	20	2
You Me and Us			
(*UK*) *HMV*	1 18 57	18	3
Sugartime			
(*UK*) *HMV*	2 28 58	16	3
COLE, COZY			
Topsy II			
(US) Love	10 13 58	3	11
COLE, NAT "KING"			
A Blossom Fell			
(*UK*) *Capitol*	2 25 55	3	10
(US) Capitol	5 14 55	2	18
Darling (Je Vous Aime Beaucoup)			
(US) Capitol	3 5 55	10	13
My One Sin			
(*UK*) *Capitol*	8 26 55	17	2
Someone You Love/Forgive My Heart			
(US) Capitol	10 22 55	16	3
Dreams Can Tell a Lie			
(*UK*) *Capitol*	1 27 56	10	9
Too Young to Go Steady			
(*UK*) *Capitol*	5 18 56	11	10

LABEL	DATE OF CHART ENTRY	HIGHEST POSITION REACHED	NUMBER OF WEEKS IN CHARTS
That's All There Is to That			
(US) Capitol	7 28 56	18	4
Love Me as Though There Were No Tomorrow			
(UK) Capitol	*10 26 56*	*11*	*7*
Night Light			
(US) Capitol	12 1 56	16	4
When I Fall in Love			
(UK) Capitol	*4 19 57*	*2*	*19*
Send for Me			
(US) Capitol	7 15 57	7	12
Looking Back			
(US) Capitol	5 5 58	5	11
That's You			
(UK) Capitol	*5 22 60*	*17*	*5*
Let Your True Love Begin			
(UK) Capitol	*12 2 61*	*19*	*1*
Let There Be Love (with **GEORGE SHEARING**)			
(UK) Capitol	*8 4 62*	*11*	*7*
Ramblin' Rose			
(US) Capitol	9 1 62	2	10
(UK) Capitol	*10 6 62*	*5*	*9*
Dear Lonely Hearts			
(US) Capitol	12 15 62	13	4
Those Lazy-Hazy-Crazy Days of Summer			
(US) Capitol	6 1 63	6	7
That Sunday, That Summer			
(US) Capitol	10 12 63	12	5
COLLINS, DAVE AND ANSELL			
Double Barrel			
(UK) Technique	*4 10 71*	*1*	*8*
Monkey Spanner			
(UK) Technique	*7 3 71*	*7*	*8*
COLLINS, JUDY			
Both Sides Now			
(US) Elektra	11 23 68	8	6
(UK) Elektra	*2 21 70*	*14*	*3*
Amazing Grace			
(UK) Elektra	*1 16 71*	*5*	*13*
(US) Elektra	2 6 71	15	5
(UK) Elektra (re-entry)	*5 20 71*	*20*	*1*
COLTRANE, CHI			
Thunder and Lightning			
(US) Columbia	11 4 72	17	3
COMMANDER CODY AND HIS LOST PLANET AIRMEN			
Hot Rod Lincoln			
(US) Paramount	4 29 72	9	7
COMO, PERRY			
Papa Loves Mambo			
(US) Victor	1 1 55	9	4

LABEL	DATE OF CHART ENTRY	HIGHEST POSITION REACHED	NUMBER OF WEEKS IN CHARTS
Home for the Holidays			
(US) Victor	1 1 55	18	2
Ko Ko Mo			
(US) Victor	2 5 55	4	12
Tina Marie			
(US) Victor	8 27 55	6	14
Juke Box Baby			
(US) Victor	3 17 56	10	7
Hot Diggity			
(US) Victor	3 24 56	2	14
(UK) HMV	5 25 56	4	12
More			
(US) Victor	6 30 56	9	11
(UK) HMV	10 5 56	10	8
Glendora			
(US) Victor	6 30 56	14	7
(UK) HMV	10 19 56	18	2
Round and Round			
(US) Victor	3 9 57	2	16
Girl with the Golden Braids			
(US) Victor	6 24 57	15	1
Just Born			
(US) Victor	11 18 57	19	2
Magic Moments			
(UK) RCA (b/w*)	2 7 58	1	15
Catch a Falling Star			
(US) Victor	2 10 58	9	12
(UK) RCA*	3 14 58	9	7
Kewpie Doll			
(US) Victor	4 28 58	12	7
(UK) RCA	5 16 58	9	5
I May Never Pass This Way Again			
(UK) RCA	6 6 58	15	4
Moontalk			
(UK) RCA	10 3 58	17	4
Love Makes the World Go Round			
(UK) RCA	11 7 58	7	8
Mandolins in the Moonlight			
(UK) RCA	11 28 58	15	5
Tomboy			
(UK) RCA	2 28 59	12	10
I Know			
(UK) RCA	7 18 59	11	7
Delaware			
(UK) RCA	2 20 60	3	8
It's Impossible			
(US) RCA	12 5 70	10	10
(UK) RCA	2 13 71	4	11
I Think of You			
(UK) RCA	5 29 71	14	5

LABEL	DATE OF CHART ENTRY	HIGHEST POSITION REACHED	NUMBER OF WEEKS IN CHARTS
And I Love Her So			
(UK) RCA	5 5 73	3	12
For the Good Times			
(UK) RCA	9 22 73	7	10
CONGREGATION			
Softly Whispering I Love You			
(UK) Columbia	12 11 71	4	8
CONLEY, ARTHUR			
Sweet Soul Music			
(US) Atco	4 8 67	2	9
(UK) Stax	5 20 67	7	9
Funky Street			
(US) Atco	5 11 68	14	3
CONNIFF, RAY, SINGERS			
Somewhere My Love			
(US) Columbia	7 23 66	9	5
CONTOURS			
Do You Love Me			
(US) Gordy	9 29 62	3	8
CONWAY, RUSS			
More Party Pops (medley)			
(UK) Columbia	12 19 58	10	4
Side Saddle			
(UK) Columbia	2 28 59	1	23
Roulette			
(UK) Columbia	5 23 59	1	16
China Tea			
(UK) Columbia	8 22 59	4	10
Snow Coach			
(UK) Columbia	11 14 59	6	8
More and More Party Pops (medley)			
(UK) Columbia	11 28 59	9	6
Royal Event			
(UK) Columbia	2 20 60	14	4
Lucky Five			
(UK) Columbia	5 22 60	9	7
Even More Party Pops (medley)			
(UK) Columbia	12 18 60	15	1
Pepe			
(UK) Columbia	1 8 61	14	3
Toy Balloons			
(UK) Columbia	12 2 61	7	8
Lesson No. 1			
(UK) Columbia	2 24 62	12	4
COOK, PETER; AND MOORE, DUDLEY			
Goodbye			
(UK) Decca	7 17 65	18	3

LABEL	DATE OF CHART ENTRY	HIGHEST POSITION REACHED	NUMBER OF WEEKS IN CHARTS
COOKE, SAM			
You Send Me/Summertime			
(US) Keen	10 28 57	1	15
Only Sixteen			
(UK) HMV	*8 15 59*	*13*	*3*
Wonderful World			
(US) Keen	6 6 60	12	7
Chain Gang			
(US) RCA	9 12 60	2	10
(UK) RCA	*9 23 60*	*9*	*7*
Cupid			
(US) RCA	7 24 61	17	3
(UK) RCA	*8 5 61*	*9*	*8*
Twisting the Night Away			
(US) RCA	3 17 62	9	7
(UK) RCA	*3 17 62*	*6*	*10*
Having a Party			
(US) RCA	7 14 62	17	2
Bring It On Home to Me			
(US) RCA	8 25 62	13	1
Nothing Can Change This Love			
(US) RCA	11 10 62	12	3
Send Me Some Lovin'			
(US) RCA	2 16 63	13	5
Another Saturday Night			
(US) RCA	5 18 63	10	5
Frankie and Johnny			
(US) RCA	8 31 63	14	4
Little Red Rooster			
(US) RCA	11 23 63	11	5
Good News			
(US) RCA	2 29 64	11	4
Good Times			
(US) RCA	7 4 64	11	5
Shake			
(US) RCA	1 30 65	7	5
COOKIES			
Chains			
(US) Dimension	12 22 62	17	3
Don't Say Nothing Bad About My Baby			
(US) Dimension	4 13 63	7	5
COPELAND, KEN			
Pledge of Love			
(US) Imperial	5 20 57	17	1
CORDET, LOUISE			
I'm Just a Baby			
(UK) Decca	*8 11 62*	*13*	*5*
COREY, JILL			
Love Me to Pieces			
(US) Columbia	8 19 57	18	4

LABEL	DATE OF CHART ENTRY	HIGHEST POSITION REACHED	NUMBER OF WEEKS IN CHARTS
CORNELIUS BROTHERS AND SISTER ROSE			
Treat Her Like a Lady			
(US) United Artists	5 29 71	3	10
Too Late to Turn Back Now			
(US) United Artists	6 24 72	2	9
CORNELL, DON			
Hold My Hand			
(UK) *Vogue-Coral*	7 1 55	7	3
Stranger in Paradise			
(UK) *Vogue-Coral*	4 22 55	19	2
Most of All			
(US) Coral	5 28 55	20	1
Bible Tells Me So			
(US) Coral	9 10 55	7	9
CORNELL, LYN			
Never on Sunday			
(UK) *Decca*	10 14 60	18	2
CORONETS			
Twenty Tiny Fingers			
(UK) *Columbia*	11 25 55	20	1
CORSAIRS			
Smoky Places			
(US) Tuff	3 10 62	12	3
CORTEZ, DAVE "BABY"			
Happy Organ			
(US) Clock	4 13 59	1	10
Rinky Dink			
(US) Chess	9 1 62	10	4
COSBY, BILL			
Little Ole Man (Uptight—Everythin's All Right)			
(US) Warner Brothers	9 23 67	4	6
COSTA, DON			
Never on Sunday			
(US) United Artists	10 24 60	19	1
COUNT FIVE			
Psychotic Reaction			
(US) Double Shot	10 1 66	5	5
COWBOY CHURCH SUNDAY SCHOOL			
Open Up Your Heart			
(US) Decca	1 8 55	8	16
COWSILLS			
The Rain, the Park and Other Things			
(US) MGM	10 28 67	2	11
Indian Lake			
(US) MGM	6 29 68	10	5
Hair			
(US) MGM	4 5 69	2	10

COX, MICHAEL
Angela Jones

(*UK*) *Triumph*	6 12 60	8	7

Along Came Caroline

(*UK*) *HMV*	9 30 60	20	2

CRAMER, FLOYD
Last Date

(US) RCA	11 7 60	2	13

On the Rebound

(US) RCA	3 20 61	4	9
(*UK*) *RCA*	4 16 61	5	8

San Antonio Rose

(US) RCA	6 26 61	8	7

CRANE, LES
Desiderata

(US) Warner Brothers	11 13 71	8	5
(*UK*) *Warner Brothers*	3 18 72	7	7

CRAWFORD, JIMMY
I Love How You Love Me

(*UK*) *Columbia*	12 16 61	17	1

CRAWFORD, JOHNNY
Cindy's Birthday

(US) Del Fi	6 16 62	8	4

Your Nose Is Gonna Grow

(US) Del Fi	9 1 62	14	2

Rumors

(US) Del Fi	12 1 62	12	4

CRAZY ELEPHANT
Gimme Gimme Good Lovin'

(US) Bell	4 19 69	12	5
(*UK*) *Major Minor*	6 28 69	12	5

CRAZY OTTO
Glad Rag Doll

(US) Decca	3 5 55	19	2

CREAM
I Feel Free

(*UK*) *Reaction*	1 21 67	11	4

Strange Brew

(*UK*) *Reaction*	7 1 67	17	4

Sunshine of Your Love

(US) Atco	7 27 68	5	8

White Room

(US) Atco	10 26 68	6	7

Badge

(*UK*) *Polydor*	4 26 69	18	3

CREEDENCE CLEARWATER REVIVAL
Suzie Q

(US) Fantasy	10 12 68	11	6

Proud Mary

LABEL	DATE OF CHART ENTRY	HIGHEST POSITION REACHED	NUMBER OF WEEKS IN CHARTS
(US) Fantasy	2 22 69	2	9
(UK) Liberty	*6 21 69*	*8*	*6*
Bad Moon Rising			
(US) Fantasy	5 24 69	2	10
(UK) Liberty	*8 23 69*	*1*	*11*
Green River			
(US) Fantasy	8 16 69	2	10
(UK) Liberty	*12 27 69*	*19*	*2*
Fortunate Son/Down on the Corner			
(US) Fantasy	11 15 69	3	10
Travelin' Band/Who'll Stop the Rain?			
(US) Fantasy	2 7 70	2	8
(UK) Liberty	*4 18 70*	*8*	*7*
Up Around the Bend/Run Through the Jungle			
(US) Fantasy	5 9 70	4	8
(UK) Liberty	*6 27 70*	*3*	*7*
Long As I Can See the Light/Looking out My Back Door			
(US) Fantasy	8 22 70	2	10
(UK) Liberty	*9 26 70*	*20*	*1*
Have You Ever Seen the Rain/Hey Tonight			
(US) Fantasy	2 20 71	8	6
Sweet Hitch-Hiker			
(US) Fantasy	8 7 71	6	5

CRESCENDOS
Oh, Julie

(US) Nasco	2 17 58	5	8

CRESTS
16 Candles

(US) Coed	1 5 59	2	11
Step By Step			
(US) Coed	4 11 60	14	6
Trouble in Paradise			
(US) Coed	8 1 60	20	2

CREW CUTS
Earth Angel

(US) Mercury	2 5 55	8	11
(UK) Mercury	*4 15 55*	*4*	*20*
Koko Mo			
(US) Mercury	2 12 55	8	8
Don't Be Angry			
(US) Mercury	5 7 55	14	7
Story Untold			
(US) Mercury	7 9 55	16	4
Gum Drop			
(US) Mercury	8 27 55	10	7
Angels in the Sky			
(US) Mercury	1 14 56	13	9
Seven Days			
(US) Mercury	3 3 56	20	1

LABEL	DATE OF CHART ENTRY	HIGHEST POSITION REACHED	NUMBER OF WEEKS IN CHARTS
CREWE, BOB, GENERATION			
Music to Watch Girls By			
(US) Dyno Voice	2 4 67	15	3
CRIBBENS, BERNARD			
Hole in the Ground			
(UK) Parlophone	2 24 62	9	10
Right Said Fred			
(UK) Parlophone	7 21 62	10	4
CRICKETS			
That'll Be the Day			
(US) Brunswick	8 26 57	3	11
(UK) Vogue-Coral	9 27 57	1	12
Oh! Boy			
(US) Brunswick	12 30 57	10	6
(UK) Coral	1 10 58	3	12
Maybe Baby			
(UK) Coral	3 21 58	4	8
(US) Brunswick	3 31 58	18	2
Think It Over			
(UK) Coral	8 1 58	11	5
Don't Ever Change			
(UK) Liberty	7 7 62	5	9
My Little Girl			
(UK) Liberty	2 10 63	17	3
CRITTERS			
Mr. Dieingly Said			
(US) Kapp	9 24 66	17	4
CROCE, JIM			
You Don't Mess Around with Jim			
(US) ABC	8 12 72	8	5
Operator (That's Not the Way It Feels)			
(US) ABC	11 25 72	17	3
Bad, Bad Leroy Brown			
(US) ABC	6 9 73	1	12
I Got a Name			
(US) ABC	10 27 73	10	6
Time in a Bottle			
(US) ABC	12 1 73	1	5
CROSBY, BING			
Count Your Blessings			
(UK) Brunswick	1 7 55	11	3
Stranger in Paradise			
(UK) Brunswick	4 29 55	17	2
White Christmas			
(US) Decca (re-entry)	1 7 56	18	1
True Love (with **GRACE KELLY**)			
(US) Capitol	10 20 56	4	18
(UK) Capitol	11 23 56	4	23
Around the World			
(UK) Brunswick	5 24 57	5	14

LABEL	DATE OF CHART ENTRY	HIGHEST POSITION REACHED	NUMBER OF WEEKS IN CHARTS
White Christmas			
(US) Decca (re-entry)	12 25 61	12	2
CROSBY, STILLS AND NASH			
Marrakesh Express			
(UK) Atlantic	*9 13 69*	*17*	*2*
CROSBY, STILLS, NASH AND YOUNG			
Woodstock			
(US) Atlantic	4 18 70	11	7
Teach Your Children			
(US) Atlantic	7 25 70	16	2
Ohio			
(US) Atlantic	7 25 70	14	3
CROW			
Evil Woman Don't Play Your Games with Me			
(US) Ameret	1 10 70	19	2
CRYSTALS			
There's No Other (Like My Baby)			
(US) Philles	1 6 62	20	1
Uptown			
(US) Philles	5 12 62	13	5
He's a Rebel			
(US) Philles	10 13 62	1	10
(UK) London	*1 13 63*	*19*	*1*
He's Sure the Boy I Love			
(US) Philles	2 9 63	11	4
Da Doo Ron Ron			
(US) Philles	5 18 63	3	8
(UK) London	*6 29 63*	*5*	*12*
Then He Kissed Me			
(US) Philles	8 31 63	6	8
(UK) London	*9 28 63*	*2*	*10*
CUFF LINKS			
Tracy			
(US) Decca	10 11 69	9	6
(UK) MCA	*12 13 69*	*4*	*9*
When Julie Comes Around			
(UK) MCA	*4 11 70*	*10*	*6*
CURVED AIR			
Back Street Luv			
(UK) Warner Brothers	*9 4 71*	*4*	*6*
CYMARRON			
Rings			
(US) Entrance	8 7 71	17	2
CYMBAL, JOHNNY			
Mr. Bass Man			
(US) Kapp	4 6 63	16	3
CYRKLE			
Red Rubber Ball			
(US) Columbia	6 11 66	2	8

LABEL	DATE OF CHART ENTRY	HIGHEST POSITION REACHED	NUMBER OF WEEKS IN CHARTS
Turn Down Day			
(US) Columbia	9 10 66	16	2
DADDY DEWDROP			
Chick-A-Boom			
(US) Sunflower	4 24 71	9	8
DAKOTAS			
Cruel Sea			
(UK) Parlophone	*8 10 63*	*18*	*4*
[see also: **BILLY J. KRAMER**]			
DALE, ALAN			
Sweet and Gentle			
(US) Coral	7 2 55	12	7
DALE, JIM			
Be My Girl			
(UK) Parlophone	*10 25 57*	*2*	*12*
DALE AND GRACE			
I'm Leaving It Up to You			
(US) Montel-Michele	10 26 63	1	10
Stop and Think It Over			
(US) Montel-Michele	2 15 64	8	5
DALTREY, ROGER			
Giving It All Away			
(UK) Track	*4 28 73*	*5*	*6*
I'm Free (with **THE LONDON SYMPHONY ORCHESTRA**)			
(UK) Ode	*8 25 73*	*13*	*4*
[see also: **WHO**]			
DAMITA JO			
I'll Be There			
(US) Mercury	2 31 61	12	4
DAMONE, VIC			
On the Street Where You Live			
(US) Columbia	6 16 56	8	12
(UK) Philips	*5 16 58*	*1*	*15*
DANA			
All Kinds of Everything			
(UK) Rex	*4 4 70*	*1*	*8*
Who Put the Lights Out			
(UK) Rex	*3 13 71*	*14*	*3*
DANA, VIC			
Red Roses for a Blue Lady			
(US) Dolton	3 20 65	10	5
DANIELS, CHARLIE			
Uneasy Rider			
(US) Kama Sutra	8 4 73	9	5
DANKWORTH, JOHNNY			
Experiments with Mice			
(UK) Parlophone	*4 29 56*	*7*	*8*

LABEL	DATE OF CHART ENTRY	HIGHEST POSITION REACHED	NUMBER OF WEEKS IN CHARTS
African Waltz			
(*UK*) *Parlophone*	3 19 61	11	9
DANLEERS			
One Summer Night			
(US) Mercury	7 28 58	16	3
DANNY AND THE JUNIORS			
At the Hop			
(US) ABC-Paramount	12 16 57	1	14
(*UK*) *HMV*	1 17 58	3	13
Rock and Roll Is Here to Stay			
(US) ABC-Paramount	3 17 58	19	2
DANTE AND THE EVERGREENS			
Alley-Oop			
(US) Madison	6 20 60	15	5
DARIN, BOBBY			
Splish Splash			
(US) Atco	6 30 58	3	10
(*UK*) *London*	8 29 58	20	1
Queen of the Hop			
(US) Atco	3 11 58	9	10
Dream Lover			
(US) Atco	5 11 59	2	11
(*UK*) *London*	6 6 59	1	15
Mack the Knife			
(US) Atco	9 14 59	1	19
(*UK*) *London*	10 3 59	2	12
Beyond the Sea			
(*UK*) *London*	1 30 60	8	6
(US) Atco	2 8 60	6	8
Clementine			
(*UK*) *London*	3 27 60	13	5
(Won't You Come Home) Bill Bailey			
(US) Atco	7 4 60	19	1
Artificial Flowers			
(US) Atco	10 31 60	20	1
Lazy River			
(*UK*) *London*	3 5 61	4	10
(US) Atco	3 20 61	14	2
You Must Have Been a Beautiful Baby			
(US) Atco	9 25 61	5	6
(*UK*) *London*	10 14 61	18	2
Multiplication			
(*UK*) *London* (*b/w**)	1 6 62	3	8
Irresistible You*			
(US) Atco	2 3 62	15	3
Things			
(US) Atco	8 4 62	3	6
(*UK*) *London*	8 4 62	2	12

LABEL	DATE OF CHART ENTRY	HIGHEST POSITION REACHED	NUMBER OF WEEKS IN CHARTS
You're the Reason I'm Leaving			
(US) Capitol	2 9 63	3	10
18 Yellow Roses			
(US) Capitol	6 8 63	10	4
If I Were a Carpenter			
(US) Atlantic	10 15 66	8	7
(UK) Atlantic	10 29 66	9	7
DARRELL, GUY			
I've Been Hurt			
(UK) Santa Posa (reissue)	9 15 73	12	5
DARREN, JAMES			
Goodbye Cruel World			
(US) Colpix	11 13 61	3	10
(UK) Pye	1 6 62	15	3
Her Royal Majesty			
(US) Colpix	3 3 62	6	5
Conscience			
(US) Colpix	5 12 62	11	5
DARTELLS			
Hot Pastrami			
(US) Dot	5 11 63	11	6
DAVID, ANN MARIE			
Wonderful Dream			
(UK) Epic	5 12 73	13	4
DAVID AND JONATHAN			
Michelle			
(UK) Columbia	1 29 66	11	4
(US) Capitol	2 12 66	18	2
Lovers of the World Unite			
(UK) Columbia	8 20 66	7	7
DAVIES, DAVE			
Death of a Clown			
(UK) Pye	7 29 67	3	7
DAVIS, BILLIE			
Tell Him			
(UK) Decca	3 9 63	10	5
DAVIS, MAC			
Baby Don't Get Hooked on Me			
(US) Columbia	8 19 72	1	10
DAVIS, JR., SAMMY			
Something's Gotta Give			
(US) Decca } b/w*	6 4 55	9	11
(UK) Brunswick	7 29 55	11	7
Love Me or Leave Me*			
(US) Decca	6 4 55	9	11
(UK) Brunswick	9 9 55	8	8
That Old Black Magic			

LABEL	DATE OF CHART ENTRY	HIGHEST POSITION REACHED	NUMBER OF WEEKS IN CHARTS
(US) Decca	7 9 55	16	2
(UK) Brunswick	9 30 55	16	1
Hey There			
(UK) Brunswick	10 7 55	19	1
What Kind of Fool Am I			
(US) Reprise	10 20 62	17	3
The Shelter of Your Arms			
(US) Reprise	3 7 64	17	2
I've Gotta Be Me			
(US) Reprise	2 8 69	11	7
Candy Man			
(US) MGM	5 20 72	1	9
DAVIS, SKEETER			
End of the World			
(US) RCA	3 2 63	2	9
(UK) RCA	4 13 63	18	4
I Can't Stay Mad at You			
(US) RCA	10 12 63	7	6
DAVIS, SPENCER, GROUP			
Keep On Running			
(UK) Fontana	12 25 65	1	10
Somebody Help Me			
(UK) Fontana	4 2 66	1	7
When I Come Home			
(UK) Fontana	9 17 66	12	4
Gimme Some Lovin			
(UK) Fontana	11 12 66	2	7
(US) United Artists	2 11 67	7	6
I'm a Man			
(UK) Fontana	2 4 67	9	3
(US) United Artists	4 22 67	10	4
DAVIS, TYRONE			
Can I Change My Mind			
(US) Dakar	1 25 69	5	7
Turn Back the Hands of Time			
(US) Dakar	4 18 70	3	8
DAWN (featuring **TONY ORLANDO**)			
Candida			
(US) Bell	9 5 70	3	11
(UK) Bell	1 30 71	9	6
Knock Three Times			
(US) Bell	12 12 70	1	13
(UK) Bell	4 17 71	1	13
What Are You Doing Sunday?			
(UK) Bell	8 14 71	3	7
Tie a Yellow Ribbon Round the Old Oak Tree			
(US) Bell	3 24 73	1	14
(UK) Bell	3 24 73	1	17

LABEL	DATE OF CHART ENTRY	HIGHEST POSITION REACHED	NUMBER OF WEEKS IN CHARTS
Say, Has Anybody Seen My Sweet Gypsy Rose?			
(US) Bell	8 11 73	3	9
(UK) Bell	*9 1 73*	*12*	*5*
DAY, BOBBY			
Rockin' Robin/Over and Over			
(US) Class	9 1 58	2	13
DAY, DORIS			
Ready Willing and Able			
(UK) Philips	*4 8 55*	*7*	*9*
I'll Never Stop Loving You			
(US) Capitol	7 30 55	15	4
(UK) Philips	*10 21 55*	*17*	*3*
Love Me or Leave Me			
(UK) Philips	*9 9 55*	*20*	*1*
Whatever Will Be Will Be (Que Será Será)			
(UK) Philips	*6 29 56*	*1*	*19*
(US) Columbia	7 14 56	2	19
A Very Precious Love			
(UK) Philips	*7 4 58*	*16*	*5*
Everybody Loves a Lover			
(US) Columbia	8 4 58	14	8
Move Over Darling			
(UK) CBS	*4 11 64*	*8*	*8*
DEAN, JIMMY			
Big Bad John			
(US) Columbia	10 9 61	1	12
(UK) Philips	*10 21 61*	*2*	*9*
PT 109			
(US) Columbia	4 28 62	8	6
DE CASTRO SISTERS			
Teach Me Tonight			
(US) Abbott	1 1 55	5	6
(UK) London	*2 11 55*	*20*	*1*
DEE, DAVE, DOZY, BEAKY, MICK AND TITCH			
Hold Tight			
(UK) Fontana	*3 26 66*	*4*	*10*
Hideaway			
(UK) Fontana	*6 25 66*	*10*	*6*
Bend It			
(UK) Fontana	*9 24 66*	*2*	*9*
Save Me			
(UK) Fontana	*12 17 66*	*3*	*7*
Touch Me Touch Me			
(UK) Fontana	*4 15 67*	*8*	*5*
Okay			
(UK) Fontana	*6 10 67*	*4*	*6*
Zabadak			
(UK) Fontana	*10 21 67*	*3*	*8*

LABEL	DATE OF CHART ENTRY	HIGHEST POSITION REACHED	NUMBER OF WEEKS IN CHARTS
Legend of Xanadu			
(UK) Fontana	2 24 68	1	8
Last Night in Soho			
(UK) Fontana	7 27 68	8	6
Wreck of the Antoinette			
(UK) Fontana	10 12 68	14	5
DEE, JOEY, AND THE STARLITERS			
Peppermint Twist			
(US) Roulette	12 11 61	1	13
(UK) Columbia	1 13 62	13	6
Hey Let's Twist			
(US) Roulette	3 17 62	20	1
Shout			
(US) Roulette	4 14 62	6	7
What Kind of Love Is This			
(US) Roulette	10 6 62	18	2
DEE, KIKI			
Amoureuse			
(UK) Rocket	12 8 73	13	5
DEE, TOMMY			
Three Stars			
(US) Crest	4 20 59	11	4
DEEP PURPLE			
Hush			
(US) Tetragrammaton	8 31 68	4	7
Black Night			
(UK) Harvest	9 19 70	2	10
Strange Kind of Woman			
(UK) Harvest	3 20 71	8	6
Fireball			
(UK) Harvest	12 11 71	15	6
Smoke on the Water			
(US) Warner Brothers	6 23 73	4	9
DE FRANCO FAMILY			
Heartbeat It's a Lovebeat			
(US) 20th Century	10 13 73	3	9
DE JOHN SISTERS			
No More			
(US) Epic	1 1 55	8	9
DEKKER, DESMOND, AND THE ACES			
007			
(UK) Pyramid	7 29 67	14	4
The Israelites			
(UK) Pyramid	4 5 69	1	8
(US) Uni	6 7 69	12	6
It Mek			
(UK) Pyramid	7 12 69	7	5

LABEL	DATE OF CHART ENTRY	HIGHEST POSITION REACHED	NUMBER OF WEEKS IN CHARTS
You Can Get It If You Really Want It			
(UK) Trojan	9 5 70	2	10
DELANEY AND BONNIE AND FRIENDS			
Comin' Home (with **ERIC CLAPTON)**			
(UK) Atlantic	1 10 70	16	2
Never Ending Song of Love			
(US) Atco	7 17 71	13	6
Only You Know and I Know			
(US) Atco	11 6 71	20	2
DELEGATES			
Convention '72			
(US) Mainstream	11 11 72	8	3
DELFONICS			
La-La Means I Love You			
(US) Philly Groove	3 2 68	4	9
(UK) Bell (reissue)	8 7 71	19	2
Didn't I (Blow Your Mind This Time)			
(US) Philly Grove	2 21 70	10	6
DELIVERANCE [see **ERIC WEISSBERG**]			
DELLS			
There Is			
(US) Cadet	2 17 68	20	3
Stay in My Corner			
(US) Cadet	8 3 68	10	7
Always Together			
(US) Cadet	11 16 68	18	2
Love Is Blue/I Can Sing a Rainbow			
(UK) Chess	8 9 69	15	3
Oh, What a Night			
(US) Cadet	9 13 69	10	6
DE LOS RIOS, WALDO			
Mozart Symphony No. 40			
(UK) A&M	4 17 71	5	10
DEL VIKINGS			
Come Go with Me			
(US) Dot	4 6 57	5	15
Whispering Bells			
(US) Dot	7 29 57	9	9
DEMENSIONS			
Over the Rainbow			
(US) Mohawk	8 22 60	16	4
DENE, TERRY			
White Sports Coat			
(UK) Decca	6 21 57	18	2
Start Movin'			
(UK) Decca	8 16 57	15	2
Stairway of Love			
(UK) Decca	5 23 58	16	2

LABEL	DATE OF CHART ENTRY	HIGHEST POSITION REACHED	NUMBER OF WEEKS IN CHARTS
DENNIS, JACKIE			
La Dee Dah			
(*UK*) *Decca*	3 28 58	4	7
DENNY, MARTIN			
Quiet Village			
(US) Liberty	5 11 59	4	9
DENVER, JOHN			
Take Me Home Country Roads (with **FAT CITY**)			
(US) RCA	7 10 71	2	11
Rocky Mountain High			
(US) RCA	2 3 73	9	7
DENVER, KARL			
Marcheta			
(*UK*) *Decca*	6 18 61	16	8
Mexicali Rose			
(*UK*) *Decca*	10 14 61	7	7
Wimoweh			
(*UK*) *Decca*	2 3 62	5	12
Never Goodbye			
(*UK*) *Decca*	4 7 62	9	8
A Little Love a Little Kiss			
(*UK*) *Decca*	6 16 62	19	3
Still			
(*UK*) *Decca*	9 7 63	13	10
DEODATO			
Also Sprach Zarathustra			
(US) CTI	2 24 73	2	8
(*UK*) *CTI*	5 12 73	7	5
DE PAUL, LYNSEY			
Sugar Me			
(*UK*) *MAM*	8 26 72	5	6
Getting a Drag			
(*UK*) *MAM*	12 23 72	18	3
Won't Somebody Dance with Me			
(*UK*) *MAM*	11 3 73	14	5
DEREK			
Cinnamon			
(US) Bang	12 14 68	11	7
DEREK AND THE DOMINOS			
Layla			
(US) Atco (reissue)	7 1 72	10	7
(*UK*) *Polydor* (*reissue*)	8 19 72	7	5
DE SHANNON, JACKIE			
What the World Needs Now Is Love			
(US) Imperial	6 26 65	7	7
Put a Little Love in Your Heart			
(US) Imperial	8 9 69	4	7

LABEL	DATE OF CHART ENTRY	HIGHEST POSITION REACHED	NUMBER OF WEEKS IN CHARTS
DESMOND, JOHNNY			
Play the Hearts and Flowers			
(US) Coral	4 2 55	16	5
Yellow Rose of Texas			
(US) Coral	8 13 55	6	15
DETERGENTS			
Leader of the Laundromat			
(US) Roulette	1 9 65	19	1
DETROIT EMERALDS			
Feel the Need in Me			
(UK) Janus	3 3 73	4	7
You Want It, I Got It			
(UK) Westbound	6 2 73	12	3
DETRIOT SPINNERS [see **SPINNERS**]			
DIAMOND, NEIL			
Cherry, Cherry			
(US) Bang	9 24 66	6	6
I Got the Feeling (Oh No No)			
(US) Bang	12 3 66	16	4
You Got to Me			
(US) Bang	3 4 67	18	1
Girl, You'll Be a Woman Soon			
(US) Bang	5 13 67	10	4
Thank the Lord for the Night Time			
(US) Bang	8 12 67	13	5
Sweet Caroline			
(US) UNI	7 26 69	4	9
(UK) UNI (reissue)	2 27 71	8	7
Holly Holy			
(US) UNI	11 29 69	6	9
Cracklin' Rosie			
(US) UNI	9 19 70	1	10
(UK) UNI	11 21 70	3	13
He Ain't Heavy, He's My Brother			
(US) UNI	12 19 70	20	2
I Am . . . I Said			
(US) UNI	4 10 71	4	7
(UK) UNI	5 22 71	4	8
Stones/Crunchy Granola Suite			
(US) UNI	12 4 71	14	3
Song Sung Blue			
(US) UNI	5 27 72	1	9
(UK) UNI	6 17 72	14	4
Play Me			
(US) UNI	9 16 72	11	5
Walk on Water			
(US) UNI	12 30 72	17	2

LABEL	DATE OF CHART ENTRY	HIGHEST POSITION REACHED	NUMBER OF WEEKS IN CHARTS
DIAMONDS			
Why Do Fools Fall in Love			
(US) Mercury	3 31 56	17	3
Church Bells May Ring			
(US) Mercury	6 2 56	20	1
Little Darlin'			
(US) Mercury	3 30 57	2	17
(UK) Mercury	*6 7 57*	*3*	*15*
The Stroll			
(US) Mercury	1 20 58	5	9
She Say (Oom Dooby Doom)			
(US) Mercury	3 9 59	18	3
DICK AND DEEDEE			
Mountain's High			
(US) Liberty	9 11 61	2	6
Young and in Love			
(US) Warner Brothers	4 20 63	17	3
Thou Shalt Not Steal			
(US) Warner Brothers	1 16 65	13	3
DICKENS, LITTLE JIMMY			
May the Bird of Paradise Fly up Your Nose			
(US) Columbia	11 20 65	15	3
DI MUCCI, DION [see **DION**]			
DINNING, MARK			
Teen Angel			
(US) MGM	1 11 60	1	11
DINO, DESI AND BILLY			
I'm a Fool			
(US) Reprise	8 14 65	17	2
DION (*and the **BELMONTS**) (†**DION DI MUCCI**)			
Teenager in Love*			
(US) Laurie	5 4 59	5	10
Where or When*			
(US) Laurie	1 18 60	3	9
Lonely Teenager			
(US) Laurie	12 12 60	12	6
Runaround Sue			
(US) Laurie	10 9 61	1	11
(UK) Top Rank	*11 4 61*	*12*	*4*
Wanderer			
(US) Laurie	1 13 62	2	11
(UK) HMV	*2 24 62*	*10*	*8*
Lovers Who Wander			
(US) Laurie	5 12 62	3	7
Little Diane			
(US) Laurie	8 4 62	8	5
Love Came to Me			
(US) Laurie	12 8 62	10	4

LABEL	DATE OF CHART ENTRY	HIGHEST POSITION REACHED	NUMBER OF WEEKS IN CHARTS
Ruby Baby			
(US) Columbia	2 2 63	2	8
Donna the Prima Donna†			
(US) Columbia	10 5 63	6	7
Drip Drop†			
(US) Columbia	12 7 63	6	6
Abraham, Martin and John			
(US) Laurie	11 9 68	4	10
DISTEL, SACHA			
Raindrops Keep Falling on My Head			
(*UK*) *Warner Brothers*	2 28 70	10	5
DIXIEBELLS			
(Down at) Papa Joe's			
(US) Soundstage	11 9 63	9	5
Southtown USA			
(US) Soundstage	2 15 64	15	2
DIXIE CUPS			
Chapel of Love			
(US) Red Bird	5 16 64	1	9
People Say			
(US) Red Bird	8 8 64	12	5
Iko Iko			
(US) Red Bird	5 22 65	20	2
DOBKINS, CARL, JR.			
My Heart Is an Open Book			
(US) Decca	6 29 59	3	11
DR. HOOK AND THE MEDICINE SHOW			
Sylvia's Mother			
(US) Columbia	5 13 72	5	8
(*UK*) *CBS*	7 8 72	2	8
Cover of Rolling Stone			
(US) Columbia	2 17 73	6	7
DR. JOHN			
Right Place, Wrong Time			
(US) Atco	6 2 73	9	8
DODD, KEN			
Love Is Like a Violin			
(*UK*) *Columbia*	7 17 60	12	8
Tears			
(*UK*) *Columbia*	9 11 65	1	21
The River			
(*UK*) *Columbia*	11 27 65	3	11
Promises			
(*UK*) *Columbia*	5 21 66	6	8
More Than Love			
(*UK*) *Columbia*	8 20 66	14	4
Let Me Cry on Your Shoulder			
(*UK*) *Columbia*	2 4 67	11	3
Brokenhearted			
(*UK*) *Columbia*	12 19 70	15	6

LABEL	DATE OF CHART ENTRY	HIGHEST POSITION REACHED	NUMBER OF WEEKS IN CHARTS
When Love Comes Around Again			
(*UK*) *Columbia*	*9 18 71*	*19*	*1*
DOGGETT, BILL			
Honky Tonk (pt. 2)			
(US) King	9 15 56	2	16
DOLAN, JOE			
Make Me an Island			
(*UK*) *Pye*	*7 19 69*	*3*	*10*
Teresa			
(*UK*) *Pye*	*11 22 69*	*20*	*1*
You're Such a Good-Looking Woman			
(*UK*) *Pye*	*3 28 70*	*17*	*5*
DOMINO, FATS			
Ain't It a Shame			
(US) Imperial	7 16 55	16	4
I'm in Love Again			
(US) Imperial	5 18 56	5	13
(*UK*) *London*	*8 24 56*	*12*	*5*
Blueberry Hill			
(US) Imperial	10 20 56	4	19
(*UK*) *London*	*1 11 57*	*6*	*10*
Blue Monday			
(US) Imperial	1 19 57	9	10
I'm Walkin'			
(US) Imperial	3 23 57	5	11
(*UK*) *London*	*4 19 57*	*19*	*1*
Valley of Tears			
(US) Imperial	6 24 57	13	4
The Big Beat			
(*UK*) *London*	*4 11 58*	*20*	*1*
Whole Lotta Lovin'			
(US) Imperial	12 8 58	6	9
Margie			
(*UK*) *London*	*5 30 59*	*16*	*2*
I'm Ready			
(US) Imperial	6 1 59	16	4
I Want to Walk You Home			
(US) Imperial (b/w*)	8 24 59	8	7
(*UK*) *London*	*11 7 59*	*19*	*2*
I'm Gonna Be a Wheel Someday			
(US) Imperial*	9 7 59	17	2
Be My Guest			
(US) Imperial	11 16 59	8	5
(*UK*) *London*	*12 19 59*	*12*	*8*
Country Boy			
(*UK*) *London*	*4 3 60*	*18*	*1*
Walkin' to New Orleans			
(US) Imperial	7 18 60	6	7
Three Nights a Week			
(US) Imperial	10 10 60	15	3

LABEL	DATE OF CHART ENTRY	HIGHEST POSITION REACHED	NUMBER OF WEEKS IN CHARTS
My Girl Josephine			
(US) Imperial	12 5 60	14	3
Let the Four Winds Blow			
(US) Imperial	8 14 61	15	3
DON AND JUAN			
What's Your Name			
(US) Big Top	3 3 62	7	7
DONEGAN, LONNIE			
Rock Island Line			
(UK) Decca	1 6 56	8	17
(US) London	4 14 56	10	7
Lost John			
(UK) Nixa	4 27 56	2	14
Skiffle Session EP			
(UK) Nixa	7 6 56	20	1
Bring a Little Water, Sylvie			
(UK) Pye Nixa	9 14 56	7	8
Don't You Rock Me Daddy-O			
(UK) Pye Nixa	1 18 57	4	15
Cumberland Gap			
(UK) Pye Nixa	4 5 57	1	11
Puttin' On the Style/Gambling Man			
(UK) Pye Nixa	6 7 57	1	18
Dixie Darling			
(UK) Pye Nixa	10 11 57	10	8
Jack O'Diamonds			
(UK) Pye Nixa	12 20 57	14	6
Grand Coulee Dam			
(UK) Pye Nixa	4 25 58	6	9
Sally Don't You Grieve/Betty Betty Betty			
(UK) Pye Nixa	7 11 58	11	6
Tom Dooley			
(UK) Pye Nixa	11 21 58	3	12
Skiffle Party			
(UK) Pye Nixa EP	1 3 59	18	1
Does Your Chewing Gum Lose Its Flavor on the Bedpost Overnight?			
(UK) Pye Nixa	2 7 59	3	10
(US) Dot	8 28 61	5	6
Fort Worth Jail			
(UK) Pye Nixa	5 9 59	12	4
Battle of New Orleans			
(UK) Pye	6 20 59	2	14
Sal's Got a Sugar Lip			
(UK) Pye	9 19 59	16	3
My Old Man's a Dustman			
(UK) Pye	3 20 60	1	9
I Wanna Go Home			
(UK) Pye	5 22 60	5	9
Lorelei			
(UK) Pye	8 21 60	11	3

LABEL	DATE OF CHART ENTRY	HIGHEST POSITION REACHED	NUMBER OF WEEKS IN CHARTS
Lively			
(UK) Pye	11 20 60	10	4
Have a Drink on Me			
(UK) Pye	4 30 61	7	9
Michael/Lumbered			
(UK) Pye	9 2 61	6	7
The Commancheros			
(UK) Pye	1 27 62	17	3
The Party's Over			
(UK) Pye	4 28 62	9	7
Pick a Bale of Cotton			
(UK) Pye	9 1 62	11	5
DONNER, RAL			
Girl of My Best Friend			
(US) Gone	5 29 61	19	2
You Don't Know What You've Got (Until You Lose It)			
(US) Gone	8 7 61	4	7
(UK) Parlophone	10 28 61	16	2
She's Everything			
(US) Gone	2 10 62	18	2
DONOVAN			
Catch the Wind			
(UK) Pye	4 3 65	4	8
Colours			
(UK) Pye	6 19 65	4	6
Sunshine Superman			
(US) Epic	8 13 66	1	9
(UK) Pye	12 17 66	2	7
Mellow Yellow			
(US) Epic	11 26 66	2	8
(UK) Pye	2 18 67	8	5
Epistle to Dippy			
(US) Epic	3 11 67	19	2
There Is a Mountain			
(US) Epic	9 9 67	11	4
(UK) Pye	11 4 67	8	5
Jennifer Juniper			
(UK) Pye	3 2 68	5	6
Hurdy Gurdy Man			
(UK) Pye	6 8 68	4	7
(US) Epic	7 13 68	5	7
Atlantis			
(US) Epic	5 3 69	7	8
Babarabbajagal (with **JEFF BECK**)			
(UK) Pye	7 26 69	12	4
DOOBIE BROTHERS			
Listen to the Music			
(US) Warner Brothers	10 21 72	11	5
Long Train Running			
(US) Warner Brothers	6 9 73	8	7

LABEL	DATE OF CHART ENTRY	HIGHEST POSITION REACHED	NUMBER OF WEEKS IN CHARTS
China Grove			
(US) Warner Brothers	9 29 73	15	4
DOONICAN, VAL			
Walk Tall			
(UK) Decca	11 28 64	3	10
The Special Years			
(UK) Decca	2 6 65	7	8
Elusive Butterfly			
(UK) Decca	3 26 66	5	7
What Would I Be?			
(UK) Decca	11 19 66	2	11
Memories Are Made of This			
(UK) Decca	3 18 67	11	5
If the Whole World Stopped Loving			
(UK) Pye	11 4 67	3	13
If I Knew Then What I Know Now			
(UK) Pye	11 23 68	14	3
Morning			
(UK) Philips	12 18 71	12	6
DOORS			
Light My Fire			
(US) Elektra	7 1 67	1	12
People Are Strange			
(US) Elektra	10 21 67	12	4
Hello, I Love You			
(US) Elektra	7 20 68	1	9
(UK) Elektra	9 21 68	15	6
Touch Me			
(US) Elektra	1 11 69	3	10
Love Her Madly			
(US) Elektra	5 1 71	11	6
Riders on the Storm			
(US) Elektra	8 14 71	14	4
DORSEY, JIMMY			
So Rare			
(US) Fraternity	4 27 57	2	22
DORSEY, LEE			
Ya Ya			
(US) Fury	10 2 61	7	7
Working in a Coal Mine			
(US) Amy	8 20 66	8	5
(UK) Stateside	9 3 66	8	6
Holy Cow			
(UK) Stateside	11 12 66	6	7
DORSEY, TOMMY, ORCHESTRA			
Tea for Two Cha-Cha			
(US) Decca	9 29 58	7	9
(UK) Brunswick	11 7 58	4	13

LABEL	DATE OF CHART ENTRY	HIGHEST POSITION REACHED	NUMBER OF WEEKS IN CHARTS
DOUGLAS, CRAIG			
Teenager in Love			
(UK) Top Rank	6 13 59	14	7
Only Sixteen			
(UK) Top Rank	8 15 59	1	13
Pretty Blue Eyes			
(UK) Top Rank	1 23 60	5	9
Heart of a Teenage Girl			
(UK) Top Rank	4 17 60	10	8
A Hundred Pounds of Clay			
(UK) Top Rank	4 2 61	8	7
Time			
(UK) Top Rank	6 25 61	9	10
When My Little Girl Is Smiling			
(UK) Top Rank	4 7 62	9	7
Our Favorite Melodies			
(UK) Decca	7 14 62	9	5
Oh Lonesome Me			
(UK) Decca	11 10 62	15	4
DOUGLAS, MIKE			
The Men in My Little Girl's Life			
(US) Epic	1 15 66	6	5
DOVE, RONNIE			
Right or Wrong			
(US) Diamond	11 28 64	14	3
One Kiss for Old Times' Sake			
(US) Diamond	4 24 65	14	4
Little Bit of Heaven			
(US) Diamond	7 3 65	16	5
When Liking Turns to Loving			
(US) Diamond	2 26 66	18	3
Let's Start Over Again			
(US) Diamond	5 21 66	20	1
Cry			
(US) Diamond	12 24 66	18	3
DOVELLS			
Bristol Stomp			
(US) Parkway	9 25 61	2	11
You Can't Sit Down			
(US) Parkway	5 18 63	3	9
DOWELL, JOE			
Wooden Heart			
(US) Smash	7 24 61	1	9
DRAKE, CHARLIE			
Splish Splash			
(UK) Parlophone	8 15 58	7	9
Mr. Custer			
(UK) Parlophone	10 30 60	14	4
My Boomerang Won't Come Back			
(UK) Parlophone	10 7 61	10	5

LABEL	DATE OF CHART ENTRY	HIGHEST POSITION REACHED	NUMBER OF WEEKS IN CHARTS
DRAMATICS			
Whatcha See Is Whatcha Get			
(US) Volt	8 21 71	9	7
In the Rain			
(US) Volt	3 18 72	5	8
DRAPER, RUSTY			
Seventeen			
(US) Mercury	8 27 55	18	1
Shifting Whispering Sands			
(US) Mercury	10 8 55	6	12
Are You Satisfied			
(US) Mercury	1 14 56	12	5
In the Middle of the House			
(US) Mercury	10 13 56	20	1
Freight Train			
(US) Mercury	6 3 57	11	3
DREAMLOVERS			
When We Get Married			
(US) Heritage	9 11 61	10	3
DREAM WEAVERS			
It's Almost Tomorrow			
(US) Decca	12 3 55	8	16
(UK) Brunswick	*2 10 56*	*1*	*16*
DRIFTERS			
There Goes My Baby			
(US) Atlantic	7 13 59	2	10
Dance with Me			
(US) Atlantic	11 16 59	15	13
(UK) London	*1 16 60*	*18*	*2*
This Magic Moment			
(US) Atlantic	3 21 60	16	2
Save the Last Dance for Me			
(US) Atlantic	9 19 60	1	12
(UK) London	*10 21 60*	*2*	*13*
I Count the Tears			
(US) Atlantic	1 30 61	17	2
Please Stay			
(US) Atlantic	7 10 61	14	4
Sweets for My Sweet			
(US) Atlantic	10 16 61	16	3
Up on the Roof			
(US) Atlantic	1 12 63	5	7
On Broadway			
(US) Atlantic	4 20 63	9	4
Under the Boardwalk			
(US) Atlantic	7 18 64	4	9
Saturday Night at the Movies			
(US) Atlantic	12 12 64	18	3
(UK) Atlantic (reissue, b/w At the Club)			
	5 6 72	*3*	*9*

LABEL	DATE OF CHART ENTRY	HIGHEST POSITION REACHED	NUMBER OF WEEKS IN CHARTS
Come Over to My Place			
(UK) *Atlantic (reissue)*	9 16 72	9	6
Like Sister and Brother			
(UK) *Bell*	8 18 73	7	6
DRISCOLL, JULIE (with the **BRIAN AUGER TRINITY**)			
This Wheel's on Fire			
(UK) *Marmalade*	5 25 68	5	8
D'RONE, FRANK			
Strawberry Blonde			
(UK) *Capitol*	12 18 60	13	2
DUBLINERS			
Seven Drunken Nights			
(UK) *Major Minor*	4 22 67	7	9
Black Velvet Band			
(UK) *Major Minor*	9 23 67	18	5
DUKE, PATTY			
Don't Just Stand There			
(US) *United Artists*	7 31 65	8	5
DUNCAN, JOHNNY, & HIS BLUEGRASS BOYS			
Last Train to San Fernando			
(UK) *Columbia*	7 26 57	2	16
DUNN, CLIVE			
Grandad			
(UK) *Columbia*	12 12 70	1	14
DUPREE, SIMON, & THE BIG SOUND			
Kites			
(UK) *Columbia*	12 9 67	9	8
DUPREES			
You Belong to Me			
(US) *Coed*	9 1 62	7	6
My Own True Love			
(US) *Coed*	11 24 62	13	3
Have You Heard			
(US) *Coed*	12 14 63	18	2
DUSTY, SLIM			
A Pub with No Beer			
(UK) *Columbia*	2 14 59	3	11
DYLAN, BOB			
The Times They Are A'Changin'			
(UK) *CBS*	4 3 65	7	7
Subterranean Homesick Blues			
(UK) *CBS*	5 8 65	9	6
Like a Rolling Stone			
(US) *Columbia*	8 21 65	2	7
(UK) *CBS*	8 28 65	4	8
Positively 4th Street			
(US) *Columbia*	10 16 65	7	5
(UK) *CBS*	11 6 65	8	9

LABEL	DATE OF CHART ENTRY	HIGHEST POSITION REACHED	NUMBER OF WEEKS IN CHARTS
Can You Please Crawl out Your Window			
(UK) CBS	1 29 66	17	1
Rainy Day Women ∦12 & ∦35			
(US) Columbia	4 30 66	2	7
(UK) CBS	5 21 66	7	5
I Want You			
(US) Columbia	7 30 66	20	2
(UK) CBS	8 6 66	16	4
Lay Lady Lay			
(US) Columbia	8 9 69	7	8
(UK) CBS	9 27 69	5	7
Knockin' on Heaven's Door			
(US) Columbia	10 13 73	12	6
(UK) CBS	10 20 73	14	4
DYSON, RONNIE			
(If You Let Me Make Love to You Then) Why Can't I Touch You			
(US) Columbia	8 8 70	8	5
EAGLES			
Take It Easy			
(US) Asylum	7 1 72	12	6
Witchy Woman			
(US) Asylum	10 28 72	9	5
EARL, ROBERT			
I May Never Pass This Way Again			
(UK) Philips	5 2 58	14	9
EAST OF EDEN			
Jig-A-Jig			
(UK) Deram	5 8 71	7	6
EASYBEATS			
Friday on My Mind			
(UK) United Artists	11 19 66	6	9
(US) United Artists	5 6 67	16	5
Hello How Are You			
(UK) United Artists	4 27 68	20	1
ECHOES			
Baby Blue			
(US) Segway	4 3 61	14	6
ECKSTINE, BILLY			
No One but You			
(UK) MGM	1 7 55	3	9
Gigi			
(UK) Mercury	2 21 59	11	10
[see also: **SARAH VAUGHAN**]			
EDDY, DUANE			
Rebel Rouser			
(US) Jamie	7 7 58	6	10
(UK) London	9 12 58	19	5

LABEL	DATE OF CHART ENTRY	HIGHEST POSITION REACHED	NUMBER OF WEEKS IN CHARTS
Cannon Ball			
(US) Jamie	11 24 58	15	5
(UK) London	1 3 59	14	4
The Lonely One			
(UK) London	4 20 59	20	1
Peter Gunn/Yep			
(UK) London	6 20 59	6	8
40 Miles of Bad Road			
(US) Jamie	7 13 59	9	7
(UK) London	9 5 59	6	8
Some Kinda Earthquake			
(UK) London	12 12 59	7	6
Bonnie Came Back			
(UK) London	2 13 60	9	4
Shazam			
(UK) London	4 24 60	3	10
Because They're Young			
(US) Jamie	6 13 60	4	9
(UK) London	7 17 60	2	13
Kommotion			
(UK) London	11 6 60	10	3
Pepe			
(UK) London	1 1 61	3	8
(US) Jamie	1 30 61	18	8
Theme from "Dixie"			
(UK) London	4 9 61	6	6
Ring of Fire			
(UK) London	6 11 61	13	5
Drivin' Home			
(UK) London	9 2 61	18	2
Deep in the Heart of Texas			
(UK) RCA	6 23 62	19	1
Ballad of Paladin			
(UK) RCA	9 1 62	10	5
(Dance with the) Guitar Man			
(UK) RCA	11 17 62	4	12
(US) RCA	12 1 62	12	3
EDISON LIGHTHOUSE			
Love Grows (Where My Rosemary Goes)			
(UK) Bell	1 24 70	1	10
(US) Bell	3 7 70	5	9
EDMUNDS, DAVE			
I Hear You Knocking			
(UK) MAM	11 21 70	1	12
(US) MAM	1 23 71	4	7
Baby I Love You			
(UK) Rockfield	2 17 73	8	6
Born to Be with You			
(UK) Rockfield	6 23 73	5	7

LABEL	DATE OF CHART ENTRY	HIGHEST POSITION REACHED	NUMBER OF WEEKS IN CHARTS
EDWARD BEAR			
Last Song			
(US) Capitol	2 10 73	3	9
EDWARDS, BOBBY			
You're the Reason			
(US) Crest	10 30 61	11	5
EDWARDS, JONATHAN			
Sunshine			
(US) Capricorn	12 18 71	4	10
EDWARDS, TOMMY			
It's All in the Game			
(US) MGM	9 8 58	1	14
(*UK*) *MGM*	*10 10 58*	*1*	*15*
Love Is All We Need			
(US) MGM	12 1 58	15	5
Please Mr. Sun			
(US) MGM	3 23 59	11	3
I Really Don't Want to Know			
(US) MGM	7 4 60	18	1
8th DAY			
She's Not Just Another Woman			
(US) Invictus	6 19 71	11	6
ELBERT, DONNIE			
Where Did Our Love Go			
(US) All Platinum	12 11 71	15	3
(*UK*) *London*	*1 22 72*	*8*	*5*
I Can't Help Myself			
(*UK*) *Avco*	*3 4 72*	*11*	*5*
ELECTRIC INDIAN			
Keem-O-Sabe			
(US) United Artists	9 27 69	16	2
ELECTRIC LIGHT ORCHESTRA			
10538 Overture			
(*UK*) *Harvest*	*8 5 72*	*9*	*6*
Roll Over Beethoven			
(*UK*) *Harvest*	*2 3 73*	*6*	*5*
Showdown			
(*UK*) *Harvest*	*10 20 73*	*12*	*5*
ELECTRIC PRUNES			
I Had Too Much to Dream Last Night			
(US) Reprise	1 28 67	11	6
ELEGANTS			
Little Star			
(US) Apt	7 28 58	1	14
ELGINS			
Heaven Must Have Sent You			
(*UK*) *Tamla Motown* (*reissue*)	*5 15 71*	*3*	*9*

LABEL	DATE OF CHART ENTRY	HIGHEST POSITION REACHED	NUMBER OF WEEKS IN CHARTS
ELIAS AND HIS ZIG ZAG JIVE FLUTES			
Tom Hark			
(UK) *Columbia*	5 2 58	2	12
ELLIOTT, BERN, AND THE FENMEN			
Money (That's What I Want)			
(UK) *Decca*	12 14 63	14	4
ELLIS, SHIRLEY			
Nitty Gritty			
(US) Congress	12 28 63	8	5
Name Game			
(US) Congress	1 16 65	3	8
(UK) *London*	5 22 65	6	8
Clapping Song			
(US) Congress	4 10 65	8	5
ENGLAND WORLD CUP SQUAD			
Back Home			
(UK) *Pye*	5 2 70	1	9
ENGLISH, SCOTT			
Brandy			
(UK) *Horse*	10 30 71	12	5
EPPS, PRESTON			
Bongo Rock			
(US) Original	6 22 59	14	4
EQUALS			
Baby Come Back			
(UK) *President*	6 25 68	1	12
Viva Bobby Joe			
(UK) *President*	8 16 69	6	8
Blackskin Blue-Eyed Boys			
(UK) *President*	1 9 71	9	6
ERNIE			
Rubber Duckie			
(US) Columbia	9 12 70	16	3
ESQUIRES			
Get On Up			
(US) Bunky	10 7 67	11	6
ESSEX			
Easier Said than Done			
(US) Roulette	6 22 63	1	9
Walkin' Miracle			
(US) Roulette	9 21 63	12	3
ESSEX, DAVID			
Rock On			
(UK) *CBS*	9 1 73	3	7
Lamplight			
(UK) *CBS*	11 24 73	7	11
EVANS, MAUREEN			
Like I Do			
(UK) *Oriole*	12 22 62	3	12

LABEL	DATE OF CHART ENTRY	HIGHEST POSITION REACHED	NUMBER OF WEEKS IN CHARTS
EVANS, PAUL, AND THE CURLS			
Seven Little Girls			
(US) Guaranteed	10 26 59	9	7
(UK) London	*11 28 59*	*16*	*3*
Midnight Special			
(US) Guaranteed	2 22 60	16	4
Happy-Go-Lucky			
(US) Guaranteed	6 6 60	10	6
EVERETT, BETTY			
Shoop Shoop Song (It's in His Kiss)			
(US) Vee Jay	3 28 64	6	7
[see also: **JERRY BUTLER**]			
EVERLY BROTHERS			
Bye Bye Love			
(US) Cadence	6 3 57	2	20
(UK) London	*7 12 57*	*6*	*13*
Wake Up Little Susie			
(US) Cadence	10 7 57	1	16
(UK) London	*11 15 57*	*2*	*12*
All I Have to Do Is Dream			
(US) Cadence	4 28 58	1	13
(UK) London (b/w Claudette)	*5 30 58*	*1*	*19*
Bird Dog			
(US) Cadence ⎱ (b/w*)	8 18 58	2	13
(UK) London ⎰	*9 12 58*	*2*	*16*
Devoted to You*			
(US) Cadence	8 25 58	10	5
Problems			
(US) Cadence	11 24 58	2	9
(UK) London	*1 24 59*	*5*	*8*
Take a Message to Mary			
(US) Cadence	5 4 59	16	5
(UK) London (b/w Poor Jenny)	*5 30 59*	*11*	*7*
('Til) I Kissed You			
(US) Cadence	8 31 59	4	11
(UK) London	*9 12 59*	*2*	*14*
Let It Be Me			
(US) Cadence	2 1 60	7	8
Cathy's Clown			
(UK) Warner Brothers	*4 10 60*	*1*	*15*
(US) Warner Brothers	5 2 60	1	12
When Will I Be Loved/Be-Bop-A-Lula			
(US) Cadence	7 4 60	8	5
(UK) London	*7 10 60*	*4*	*12*
So Sad			
(US) Warner Brothers	9 12 60	7	8
(UK) Warner Brothers (b/w Lucille)	*9 18 60*	*4*	*8*
Like Strangers			
(UK) Warner Brothers	*12 25 60*	*12*	*3*
Walk Right Back			

158

LABEL	DATE OF CHART ENTRY	HIGHEST POSITION REACHED	NUMBER OF WEEKS IN CHARTS
(UK) Warner Brothers ⎫ (b/w**)	*1 29 61*	*1*	*13*
(US) Warner Brothers ⎭	3 6 61	7	6
Ebony Eyes**			
(US) Warner Brothers	2 24 61	8	5
Temptation			
(UK) Warner Brothers	*6 4 61*	*1*	*12*
Muskrat			
*(UK) Warner Brothers (b/w***)*	*9 30 61*	*16*	*1*
Don't Blame Me***			
(US) Warner Brothers	10 16 61	20	1
Crying in the Rain			
(US) Warner Brothers	1 27 61	8	10
(UK) Warner Brothers	*2 3 62*	*6*	*8*
How Can I Meet Her?			
(UK) Warner Brothers (b/w†)	*6 2 62*	*12*	*5*
That's Old Fashioned†			
(US) Warner Brothers	6 16 62	9	3
No One Can Make My Sunshine Smile			
(UK) Warner Brothers	*11 3 62*	*11*	*7*
Price of Love			
(UK) Warner Brothers	*5 29 65*	*2*	*10*
Love Is Strange			
(UK) Warner Brothers	*11 6 65*	*11*	*4*
EVERY MOTHER'S SON			
Come On Down to My Boat			
(US) MGM	6 10 67	6	8
EXCITERS			
Tell Him			
(US) United Artists	12 29 62	4	7
FABARES, SHELLEY			
Johnny Angel			
(US) Colpix	3 24 62	1	10
FABIAN			
Turn Me Loose			
(US) Chancellor	4 13 59	9	8
Tiger			
(US) Chancellor	6 29 59	3	8
Hound Dog Man			
(US) Chancellor	12 14 59	9	7
Friendly World			
(US) Chancellor	12 21 59	12	3
FABRIC, BENT			
Alley Cat			
(US) Atco	9 8 62	7	8
FACES			
Stay with Me			
(UK) Warner Brothers	*1 15 72*	*6*	*5*
(US) Warner Brothers	2 5 72	17	4

LABEL	DATE OF CHART ENTRY	HIGHEST POSITION REACHED	NUMBER OF WEEKS IN CHARTS
Cindy Incidentally			
(*UK*) *Warner Brothers*	2 17 73	2	7
Poolhall Richard/I Wish It Would Rain			
(*UK*) *Warner Brothers*	12 22 73	8	7
FAIRWEATHER			
Natural Sinner			
(*UK*) *RCA*	8 8 70	6	6
[see also: **AMEN CORNER**]			
FAITH, ADAM			
What Do You Want?			
(*UK*) *Parlophone*	11 21 59	1	13
Poor Me			
(*UK*) *Parlophone*	1 30 60	1	10
Someone Else's Baby			
(*UK*) *Parlophone*	4 10 60	2	9
Made You			
(*UK*) *Parlophone*	6 19 60	3	8
How About That			
(*UK*) *Parlophone*	9 11 60	2	10
Lonely Pup			
(*UK*) *Parlophone*	12 4 60	5	5
Who Am I/This Is It			
(*UK*) *Parlophone*	1 29 61	6	7
Easy Going Me			
(*UK*) *Parlophone*	4 23 61	9	5
Don't You Know It?			
(*UK*) *Parlophone*	7 22 61	10	5
The Time Has Come			
(*UK*) *Parlophone*	10 21 61	5	9
Lonesome			
(*UK*) *Parlophone*	2 3 62	12	3
As You Like It			
(*UK*) *Parlophone*	5 19 62	5	9
Don't That Beat All			
(*UK*) *Parlophone*	9 8 62	8	8
The First Time			
(*UK*) *Parlophone*	10 5 63	5	8
We Are in Love			
(*UK*) *Parlophone*	1 4 64	11	6
Message to Martha			
(*UK*) *Parlophone*	12 12 64	12	6
FAITH, HORACE			
Black Pearl			
(*UK*) *Trojan*	10 3 70	13	4
FAITH, PERCY			
Theme from "A Summer Place"			
(US) Columbia	2 1 60	1	15
(*UK*) *Philips*	2 27 60	4	12

LABEL	DATE OF CHART ENTRY	HIGHEST POSITION REACHED	NUMBER OF WEEKS IN CHARTS
FAITHFULL, MARIANNE			
As Years Go By			
(*UK*) *Decca*	8 22 64	9	10
Come and Stay with Me			
(*UK*) *Decca*	2 27 65	4	7
This Little Bird			
(*UK*) *Decca*	5 15 65	6	7
Summer Night			
(*UK*) *Decca*	8 7 65	10	5
FALCONS			
You're So Fine			
(US) Unart	7 6 59	17	3
FAME, GEORGIE			
Yeh, Yeh			
(*UK*) *Columbia*	12 26 64	1	8
Get Away			
(*UK*) *Columbia*	7 2 66	1	7
Sunny			
(*UK*) *Columbia*	10 8 66	13	4
Sittin' in the Park			
(*UK*) *Columbia*	12 31 66	12	7
Because I Love You			
(*UK*) *CBS*	4 15 67	15	2
Ballad of Bonnie and Clyde			
(*UK*) *CBS*	12 30 67	1	8
(US) Epic	3 16 68	7	9
Peaceful			
(*UK*) *CBS*	8 9 69	16	1
[see also: **FAME AND PRICE**]			
FAME AND PRICE			
Rosetta			
(*UK*) *CBS*	4 24 71	11	5
FAMILY			
Strange Band			
(*UK*) *Reprise*	9 19 70	11	5
In My Own Time			
(*UK*) *Reprise*	8 7 71	4	8
Burlesque			
(*UK*) *Reprise*	10 21 72	13	4
FAMILY DOGG			
Way of Life			
(*UK*) *Bell*	6 21 69	6	8
FANTASTIC JOHNNY C.			
Boogaloo Down Broadway			
(US) Phil-L.A. of Soul	11 25 67	7	9
FANTASTICS			
Something Old, Something New			
(*UK*) *Bell*	4 24 71	9	3

LABEL	DATE OF CHART ENTRY	HIGHEST POSITION REACHED	NUMBER OF WEEKS IN CHARTS
FARDON, DON			
Indian Reservation			
(US) GNP Crescendo	10 5 68	20	2
(*UK*) *Young Blood (reissue)*	*10 31 70*	*3*	*11*
FARGO, DONNA			
Happiest Girl in the Whole USA			
(US) Dot	7 29 72	11	5
Funny Face			
(US) Dot	12 2 72	5	9
FARLOWE, CHRIS			
Out of Time			
(*UK*) *Immediate*	*7 9 66*	*1*	*9*
FELICIANO, JOSE			
Light My Fire			
(US) RCA	8 10 68	3	9
(*UK*) *RCA*	*10 12 68*	*6*	*8*
FELIX, JULIE			
If I Could			
(*UK*) *RAK*	*5 23 70*	*19*	*1*
FENDERMEN			
Mule Skinner Blues			
(US) Soma	6 27 60	5	9
FENTON, SHANE AND THE FENTONES			
I'm a Moody Guy			
(*UK*) *HMV*	*8 4 62*	*19*	*1*
[see also: **ALVIN STARDUST**]			
FERKO STRING BAND			
Alabama Jubilee			
(US) Media	7 2 55	18	2
(*UK*) *London*	*8 12 55*	*20*	*1*
FERRANTE AND TEICHER			
Theme from "The Apartment"			
(US) United Artists	8 29 60	10	11
Exodus			
(US) United Artists	12 12 60	2	14
(*UK*) *United Artists*	*2 26 61*	*6*	*10*
Tonight			
(US) United Artists	11 20 61	8	6
Midnight Cowboy			
(US) United Artists	12 20 69	10	7
FERRY, BRYAN			
A Hard Rain's A-Gonna Fall			
(*UK*) *Island*	*10 13 73*	*10*	*5*
[see also: **ROXY MUSIC**]			
FIELDS, ERNIE			
In the Mood			
(US) Rendezvous	10 26 59	4	10
(*UK*) *London*	*1 9 60*	*18*	*1*

LABEL	DATE OF CHART ENTRY	HIGHEST POSITION REACHED	NUMBER OF WEEKS IN CHARTS
FIELDS, GRACIE			
Around the World			
(UK) Columbia	*5 31 57*	*8*	*6*
FIESTAS			
So Fine			
(US) Old Town	5 25 59	11	5
FIFTH DIMENSION			
Go Where You Wanna Go			
(US) Soul City	2 25 67	16	2
Up, Up and Away			
(US) Soul City	7 1 67	7	6
Stoned Soul Picnic			
(US) Soul City	6 29 68	3	9
Sweet Blindness			
(US) Soul City	11 9 68	13	2
Aquarius/Let the Sun Shine In			
(US) Soul City	3 22 69	1	14
(UK) Liberty	*5 24 69*	*11*	*4*
Workin' on a Groovy Thing			
(US) Soul City	8 23 69	20	2
Wedding Bell Blues			
(US) Soul City	10 18 69	1	10
(UK) Liberty	*2 14 70*	*16*	*1*
One Less Bell to Answer			
(US) Bell	12 5 70	2	12
Love's Lines, Angles and Rhymes			
(US) Bell	4 17 71	19	1
Never My Love			
(US) Bell	10 23 71	12	5
(Last Night) I Didn't Get to Sleep at All			
(US) Bell	5 20 72	8	7
If I Could Reach You			
(US) Bell	10 28 72	10	6
FIFTH ESTATE			
Ding Dong the Witch is Dead			
(US) Jubilee	6 17 67	11	4
FINNEGAN, LARRY			
Dear One			
(US) Old Town	4 14 62	11	4
FIREBALLS			
Quite a Party			
(UK) Pye	*8 5 61*	*20*	*1*
Bottle of Wine			
(US) Atco	2 10 68	9	6
[see also: **JIMMY GILMER**]			
FIRST CHOICE			
Armed and Extremely Dangerous			
(UK) Bell	*6 9 73*	*16*	*3*
Smarty Pants			
(UK) Bell	*8 18 73*	*9*	*5*

LABEL	DATE OF CHART ENTRY	HIGHEST POSITION REACHED	NUMBER OF WEEKS IN CHARTS

FIRST EDITION
Just Dropped In (to See What Condition My Condition Was In)

(US) Reprise	3 2 68	5	6

But You Know I Love You

(US) Reprise	3 8 69	19	1

[see also: **KENNY ROGERS AND THE FIRST EDITION**]

FISHER, EDDIE
I Need You Now

(US) Victor	1 1 55	4	5
(UK) HMV	1 21 55	1	19

Wedding Bells

(UK) HMV	3 18 55	5	11

Count Your Blessings

(US) Victor	1 1 55	5	5

Heart

(US) Victor	6 4 55	15	7

Song of the Dreamer

(US) Victor	9 3 55	16	5

Dungaree Doll

(US) Victor	12 31 55	7	11

Cindy, Oh Cindy

(US) Victor	11 3 56	10	12
(UK) HMV	11 23 56	5	13

FISHER, TONI
Big Hurt

(US) Signet	11 30 59	3	12

FITZGERALD, ELLA
Swinging Shepherd Blues

(UK) HMV	5 23 58	15	3

Mack the Knife

(UK) HMV	5 1 60	20	1

FIVE AMERICANS
Western Union

(US) Abnak	4 1 67	5	6

FIVE MAN ELECTRICAL BAND
Signs

(US) Lionel	7 31 71	3	8

FIVE STAIRSTEPS
O-Oh Child

(US) Buddah	7 4 70	8	8

FLACK, ROBERTA
First Time Ever I Saw Your Face

(US) Atlantic	3 25 72	1	14
(UK) Atlantic	6 24 72	14	4

Where Is the Love (with **DONNY HATHAWAY**)

(US) Atlantic	7 8 72	5	8

Killing Me Softly with His Song

(US) Atlantic	2 10 73	1	12
(UK) Atlantic	3 3 73	6	8

LABEL	DATE OF CHART ENTRY	HIGHEST POSITION REACHED	NUMBER OF WEEKS IN CHARTS
FLAMINGOS			
I Only Have Eyes for You			
(US) End	6 22 59	11	7
FLEETWOOD MAC			
Albatross			
(US) Blue Horizon	12 14 68	1	13
Man of the World			
(UK) Immediate	4 19 69	2	9
Oh Well			
(UK) Reprise	10 11 69	2	9
Green Manalishi			
(UK) Reprise	5 30 70	10	9
Albatross			
(UK) CBS (reissue)	6 2 73	2	8
FLEETWOODS			
Come Softly to Me			
(US) Dolphin	3 16 59	1	10
(UK) London	4 25 59	6	8
Mr. Blue			
(US) Dolton	9 21 59	1	14
Tragedy			
(US) Dolton	5 22 61	10	4
FLOWERPOT MEN			
Let's Go to San Francisco			
(UK) Deram	9 9 67	4	7
FLOYD, EDDIE			
Knock on Wood			
(UK) Atlantic	4 15 67	19	5
Bring It On Home to Me			
(US) Stax	12 7 68	17	5
FLYING MACHINE			
Smile a Little Smile for Me			
(US) Congress	10 25 69	5	8
FOCUS			
Sylvia			
(UK) Polydor	2 10 73	4	6
Hocus Pocus			
(UK) Polydor	2 24 73	20	1
(US) Sire	5 12 73	9	7
FONTANA, WAYNE (*and **THE MINDBENDERS**)			
Um Um Um Um Um Um*			
(UK) Fontana	10 31 64	5	7
Game of Love*			
(UK) Fontana	2 13 65	2	7
(US) Fontana	4 3 65	1	8
Just a Little Bit Too Late*			
(UK) Fontana	7 10 65	20	1
Come On Home			
(UK) Fontana	6 4 66	16	3

LABEL	DATE OF CHART ENTRY	HIGHEST POSITION REACHED	NUMBER OF WEEKS IN CHARTS
Pamela Pamela			
(UK) Fontana	1 7 67	11	6
FONTANE SISTERS			
Hearts of Stone			
(US) Dot	1 1 55	1	14
Rock Love			
(US) Dot	3 12 55	19	1
Seventeen			
(US) Dot	8 27 55	6	13
Daddy-O			
(US) Dot	12 3 55	11	5
Eddie My Love			
(US) Dot	3 24 56	12	7
FORD, CLINTON			
Too Many Beautiful Girls			
(UK) Oriole	8 19 61	20	1
FORD, EMILE, AND THE CHECKMATES			
What Do You Want to Make Those Eyes at Me For?			
(UK) Pye	10 31 59	1	17
Slow Boat to China			
(UK) Pye	1 30 60	4	10
You'll Never Know What You're Missing till You Try			
(UK) Pye	6 5 60	18	2
Them There Eyes			
(UK) Pye	10 24 60	20	1
Counting Teardrops			
(UK) Pye	12 25 60	6	6
FORD, FRANKIE			
Sea Cruise			
(US) Ace	3 30 59	14	5
FORD, TENNESSEE ERNIE			
Give Me Your Word			
(UK) Capitol	2 21 55	1	24
Ballad of Davy Crockett			
(US) Capitol	3 19 55	6	15
(UK) Capitol	1 13 56	3	7
Sixteen Tons			
(US) Capitol	11 19 55	1	17
(UK) Capitol	1 6 56	1	11
FORTUNE, LANCE			
Be Mine			
(UK) Pye	2 13 60	5	6
FORTUNES			
You've Got Your Troubles			
(UK) Decca	7 17 65	2	9
(US) Press	9 18 65	7	6
Here It Comes Again			
(UK) Decca	10 21 65	4	7

LABEL	DATE OF CHART ENTRY	HIGHEST POSITION REACHED	NUMBER OF WEEKS IN CHARTS
This Golden Ring			
(UK) Decca	3 12 66	15	2
Here Comes That Rainy Day Feeling Again			
(US) Capitol	7 3 71	15	5
Freedom Come, Freedom Go			
(UK) Capitol	10 2 71	6	7
Storm in a Teacup			
(UK) Capitol	2 12 72	7	6
FOUNDATIONS			
Baby, Now That I've Found You			
(UK) Pye	10 21 67	1	9
(US) UNI	1 20 68	11	8
Back on My Feet Again			
(UK) Pye	2 17 68	18	4
Build Me Up Buttercup			
(UK) Pye	12 7 68	2	9
(US) UNI	2 1 69	3	10
In the Bad Bad Old Days			
(UK) Pye	3 22 69	8	7
FOUR ACES			
Mr. Sandman			
(US) Decca	1 1 55	10	7
(UK) Brunswick	1 7 55	9	5
Melody of Love			
(US) Decca	1 29 55	11	13
Stranger in Paradise			
(UK) Brunswick	5 20 55	6	6
Love Is a Many Splendored Thing			
(US) Decca	9 3 55	1	20
(UK) Brunswick	11 18 55	2	13
Woman in Love			
(US) Decca	12 24 55	19	1
(UK) Brunswick	10 26 56	19	1
FOUR JACKS AND A JILL			
Master Jack			
(US) RCA	6 8 68	18	1
FOUR LADS			
Moments to Remember			
(US) Columbia	9 10 55	3	23
No, Not Much			
(US) Columbia	2 11 56	3	15
Standing on the Corner			
(US) Columbia	5 19 56	3	13
Who Needs You			
(US) Columbia	2 23 57	14	7
FOURMOST			
Hello Little Girl			
(UK) Parlophone	10 5 63	9	7

LABEL	DATE OF CHART ENTRY	HIGHEST POSITION REACHED	NUMBER OF WEEKS IN CHARTS
I'm in Love			
(UK) Parlophone	2 1 64	17	4
A Little Lovin'			
(UK) Parlophone	5 2 64	6	8
FOUR PENNIES			
Juliet			
(UK) Philips	4 25 64	1	10
I Found Out the Hard Way			
(UK) Philips	8 15 64	14	3
Black Girl			
(UK) Philips	11 28 64	20	2
Until It's Time for You to Go			
(UK) Philips	11 6 65	19	3
FOUR PREPS			
Twenty-Six Miles			
(US) Capitol	2 24 58	4	9
Big Man			
(US) Capitol	5 19 58	5	9
(UK) Capitol	6 20 58	2	12
Down by the Station			
(US) Capitol	1 18 60	13	8
More Money for You and Me (medley)			
(US) Capitol	9 25 61	17	1
FOUR SEASONS (*featuring **FRANKIE VALLI**)			
Sherry			
(US) Vee Jay	9 8 62	1	10
(UK) Stateside	10 20 62	8	10
Big Girls Don't Cry			
(US) Vee Jay	10 27 62	1	13
(UK) Stateside	1 27 63	13	5
Walk Like a Man			
(US) Vee Jay	2 2 63	1	9
(UK) Stateside	4 13 63	12	6
Candy Girl			
(US) Vee Jay	7 27 63	3	8
Dawn (Go Away)			
(US) Philips	2 15 64	3	8
Stay			
(US) Vee Jay	3 21 64	16	4
Ronnie*			
(US) Philips	4 25 64	6	6
Rag Doll*			
(US) Philips	6 27 64	1	10
(UK) Philips	9 4 64	2	9
Save It for Me*			
(US) Philips	9 19 64	10	4
Big Man in Town*			
(US) Philips	12 5 64	20	2

LABEL	DATE OF CHART ENTRY	HIGHEST POSITION REACHED	NUMBER OF WEEKS IN CHARTS
Bye Bye Baby*			
(US) Philips	2 6 65	12	3
Let's Hang On*			
(US) Philips	10 30 65	3	12
(UK) Philips	*12 4 65*	*4*	*11*
Working My Way Back to You*			
(US) Philips	2 19 66	9	4
Opus 17 (Don't Worry 'bout Me)*			
(US) Philips	6 4 66	13	5
(UK) Philips	*6 25 66*	*20*	*1*
I've Got You Under My Skin*			
(US) Philips	9 24 66	9	5
(UK) Philips	*10 15 66*	*12*	*5*
Tell It to the Rain*			
(US) Philips	1 7 67	10	4
Beggin'*			
(US) Philips	4 8 67	16	2
C'Mon Marianne*			
(US) Philips	7 1 67	9	5
[see also: **WONDER WHO?**]			
FOUR TOPS			
Baby I Need Your Loving			
(US) Motown	9 19 64	11	5
I Can't Help Myself			
(US) Motown	5 29 65	1	11
(UK) Tamla Motown (reissue)	*4 4 70*	*10*	*5*
It's the Same Old Song			
(US) Motown	8 7 65	5	7
Something About You			
(US) Motown	11 27 65	19	3
Shake Me, Wake Me (When It's Over)			
(US) Motown	3 19 66	18	2
Reach Out I'll Be There			
(US) Motown	9 24 66	1	9
(UK) Tamla Motown	*10 15 66*	*1*	*11*
Standing in the Shadows of Love			
(US) Motown	12 31 66	6	7
(UK) Tamla Motown	*1 14 67*	*6*	*4*
Bernadette			
(US) Motown	3 25 67	4	6
(UK) Tamla Motown	*4 15 67*	*8*	*5*
Seven Rooms of Gloom			
(US) Motown	6 10 67	14	4
(UK) Tamla Motown	*7 1 67*	*12*	*5*
You Keep Running Away			
(US) Motown	10 14 67	19	1
Walk Away Renee			
(UK) Tamla Motown	*12 23 67*	*3*	*8*
(US) Motown	2 24 68	14	4

LABEL	DATE OF CHART ENTRY	HIGHEST POSITION REACHED	NUMBER OF WEEKS IN CHARTS
If I Were a Carpenter			
(UK) *Tamla Motown*	3 23 68	7	6
(US) Motown	6 8 68	20	2
Yesterday's Dream			
(UK) *Tamla Motown*	9 7 68	20	1
What Is Man?			
(UK) *Tamla Motown*	6 28 69	16	2
Do What You Gotta Do			
(UK) *Tamla Motown*	10 11 69	20	1
It's All in the Game			
(UK) *Tamla Motown*	6 20 70	5	9
Still Water (Love)			
(US) Motown	10 3 70	11	7
(UK) *Tamla Motown*	10 17 70	10	6
Simple Game			
(UK) *Tamla Motown*	10 9 71	3	8
Keeper of the Castle			
(US) Dunhill	12 16 72	10	6
(UK) *Probe*	12 16 72	18	1
Ain't No Woman (Like the One I've Got)			
(UK) *Dunhill*	3 10 73	4	9
Are You Man Enough			
(US) Dunhill	8 25 73	15	3
[see also: SUPREMES]			

FOXX, INEZ AND CHARLIE

Mockingbird			
(US) Symbol	8 17 63	7	6

FRANCIS, CONNIE

Who's Sorry Now			
(US) MGM	3 3 58	4	11
(UK) *MGM*	4 11 58	1	20
I'm Sorry I Made You Cry			
(UK) *MGM*	7 4 58	12	8
Stupid Cupid			
(UK) *MGM* (b/w Carolina Moon)	8 22 58	1	17
(US) MGM	9 8 58	17	4
I'll Get By			
(UK) *MGM*	11 21 58	19	1
Fallin'			
(UK) *MGM*	11 28 58	20	1
You Always Hurt the One You Love			
(UK) *MGM*	1 10 59	12	5
My Happiness			
(US) MGM	12 22 58	2	11
(UK) *MGM*	2 21 59	3	11
Lipstick on Your Collar (b/w*)			
(US) MGM	6 8 59	5	10
(UK) *MGM*	7 11 59	4	13
Frankie*			
(US) MGM	6 8 59	9	7

LABEL	DATE OF CHART ENTRY	HIGHEST POSITION REACHED	NUMBER OF WEEKS IN CHARTS
Plenty Good Lovin'			
(UK) *MGM*	9 5 59	*14*	*3*
Among My Souvenirs			
(UK) *MGM*	*12 12 59*	*8*	*5*
(US) MGM	12 21 59	7	6
Mama			
(US) MGM (b/w**)	3 28 60	8	5
(UK) *MGM* (b/w *Robot Man*)	*5 15 60*	*2*	*13*
Teddy**			
(US) MGM	4 4 60	17	1
Everybody's Somebody's Fool			
(US) MGM (b/w***)	5 30 60	1	12
(UK) *MGM*	*8 14 60*	*6*	*10*
Jealous of You***			
(US) MGM	6 20 60	19	2
My Heart Has a Mind of Its Own			
(US) MGM	9 28 60	1	12
(UK) *MGM*	*10 30 60*	*2*	*7*
Many Tears Ago			
(US) MGM	11 22 60	7	9
(UK) *MGM*	*1 15 61*	*13*	*2*
Where the Boys Are			
(US) MGM	2 6 61	4	9
(UK) *MGM*	*3 19 61*	*7*	*6*
Breakin' In a Brand New Heart			
(US) MGM	5 1 61	7	6
(UK) *MGM*	*5 25 61*	*14*	*1*
Together			
(US) MGM	7 10 61	6	8
(UK) *MGM*	*9 9 61*	*10*	*6*
(He's My) Dreamboat			
(US) MGM	10 23 61	14	3
Baby's First Christmas†			
(UK) *MGM*	*12 9 61*	*17*	*1*
When the Boy in Your Arms			
(US) MGM (b/w†)	12 18 61	10	6
Don't Break the Heart That Loves You			
(US) MGM	3 3 62	1	8
Secondhand Love			
(US) MGM	6 2 62	7	5
Vacation			
(US) MGM	8 18 62	9	4
(UK) *MGM*	*8 18 62*	*10*	*4*
I'm Gonna Be Warm This Winter			
(US) MGM	1 26 63	18	1
Follow the Boys			
(US) MGM	4 6 63	17	3

FRANKLIN, ARETHA

I Never Loved A Man the Way I Love You

(US) Atlantic	3 25 67	9	7

LABEL	DATE OF CHART ENTRY	HIGHEST POSITION REACHED	NUMBER OF WEEKS IN CHARTS
Respect			
(US) Atlantic	5 13 67	1	9
(UK) Atlantic	7 8 67	10	5
Baby I Love You			
(US) Atlantic	8 12 67	4	7
Natural Woman			
(US) Atlantic	10 14 67	8	6
Chain of Fools			
(US) Atlantic	12 23 67	2	9
(Sweet Sweet Baby) Since You've Been Gone			
(US) Atlantic (b/w*)	3 9 68	5	8
Ain't No Way*			
(US) Atlantic	5 4 68	16	2
Think			
(US) Atlantic	5 25 68	7	8
House That Jack Built			
(US) Atlantic (b/w**)	8 31 68	6	6
I Say a Little Prayer**			
(UK) Atlantic	8 24 68	4	8
(US) Atlantic	9 14 68	10	5
See Saw			
(US) Atlantic	12 7 68	14	5
The Weight			
(US) Atlantic	3 22 69	19	2
Share Your Love with Me			
(US) Atlantic	9 6 69	13	3
Eleanor Rigby			
(US) Atlantic	12 6 69	17	2
Call Me/Son of a Preacher Man			
(US) Atlantic	3 21 70	13	4
Don't Play That Song			
(US) Atlantic	9 5 70	11	5
(UK) Atlantic	9 12 70	13	5
You're All I Need			
(US) Atlantic	4 3 71	19	1
Bridge over Troubled Water/Brand New Me			
(US) Atlantic	5 1 71	6	8
Spanish Harlem			
(US) Atlantic	8 14 71	2	9
(UK) Atlantic	10 23 71	14	3
Rock Steady			
(US) Atlantic	11 20 71	9	5
Day Dreaming			
(US) Atlantic	4 1 72	5	9
Angel			
(US) Atlantic	9 1 73	20	1
Until You Come Back (That's What I'm Gonna Do)			
(US) Atlantic	12 29 73	19	1

FRED, JOHN, AND HIS PLAYBOY BAND
Judy in Disguise (with Glasses)

LABEL	DATE OF CHART ENTRY	HIGHEST POSITION REACHED	NUMBER OF WEEKS IN CHARTS
(US) Paula	12 23 67	1	11
(UK) Pye	*1 20 68*	*3*	*7*

FREDDIE AND THE DREAMERS
If You Gotta Make a Fool of Somebody

(UK) Columbia	*6 1 63*	*3*	*9*
I'm Telling You Now			
(UK) Columbia	*8 17 63*	*2*	*8*
(US) Tower	3 27 65	1	7
You Were Made for Me			
(UK) Columbia	*11 23 63*	*3*	*10*
Over You			
(UK) Columbia	*2 29 64*	*13*	*6*
I Love You Baby			
(UK) Columbia	*6 6 64*	*16*	*3*
I Understand			
(UK) Columbia	*12 5 64*	*5*	*8*
Do the Freddie			
(US) Mercury	6 5 65	18	1

FREE
All Right Now

(UK) Island	*6 20 70*	*2*	*11*
(US) A&M	9 19 70	4	10
My Brother Jake			
(UK) Island	*5 15 71*	*4*	*7*
Little Bit of Love			
(UK) Island	*6 17 72*	*13*	*5*
Wishing Well			
(UK) Island	*1 20 73*	*7*	*5*
All Right Now			
(UK) Island (reissue)	*8 11 73*	*15*	*3*

FREEMAN, BOBBY
Do You Want to Dance?

(US) Josie	5 26 58	5	11
C'mon and Swim			
(US) Autumn	8 8 64	5	6

FREEMAN, ERNIE
Raunchy

(US) Imperial	11 25 57	12	9

FREE MOVEMENT
I've Found Someone of My Own

(US) Decca	10 9 71	5	7

FRIEND AND LOVER
Reach out of the Darkness

(US) Verve Forecast	6 22 68	10	6

FRIENDS OF DISTINCTION
Grazin' in the Grass

(US) RCA	5 17 69	6	8
Going in Circles			
(US) RCA	11 1 69	15	6

LABEL	DATE OF CHART ENTRY	HIGHEST POSITION REACHED	NUMBER OF WEEKS IN CHARTS
Love Me or Let Me Be Lonely			
(US) RCA	4 4 70	6	8
FRIJID PINK			
House of the Rising Sun			
(US) Parrot	3 14 70	7	7
(UK) Deram	4 25 70	4	8
FROMAN, JANE			
I Wonder			
(UK) Capitol	6 17 55	14	4
FULLER, BOBBY, FOUR			
I Fought the Law			
(US) Mustang	2 26 66	9	5
FURY, BILLY			
Maybe Tomorrow			
(UK) Decca	4 11 59	17	4
Colette			
(UK) Decca	3 6 60	18	2
That's Love			
(UK) Decca	6 5 60	20	1
Halfway to Paradise			
(UK) Decca	5 21 61	4	18
Jealousy			
(UK) Decca	9 9 61	4	7
I'd Never Find Another You			
(UK) Decca	12 9 61	4	12
Letter Full of Tears			
(UK) Decca	3 17 62	20	1
Last Night Was Made for Love			
(UK) Decca	5 19 62	4	11
Once upon a Dream			
(UK) Decca	8 11 62	7	8
Because of Love			
(UK) Decca	11 10 62	18	1
Like I've Never Been Gone			
(UK) Decca	3 2 63	3	10
When Will You Say I Love You?			
(UK) Decca	5 25 63	3	9
In Summer			
(UK) Decca	8 3 63	5	8
Somebody Else's Girl			
(UK) Decca	10 12 63	18	2
Do You Really Love Me Too (Fool's Errand)			
(UK) Decca	1 11 64	13	5
I Will			
(UK) Decca	5 9 64	14	6
It's Only Make Believe			
(UK) Decca	8 1 64	10	5
I'm Lost Without You			
(UK) Decca	2 6 65	16	3

LABEL	DATE OF CHART ENTRY	HIGHEST POSITION REACHED	NUMBER OF WEEKS IN CHARTS
In Thoughts of You			
(UK) Decca	8 7 65	9	5
GALLERY			
Nice to Be with You			
(US) Sussex	5 27 72	4	7
GARDNER, DON; and FORD, DEE DEE			
I Need Your Loving			
(US) Fire	7 28 62	20	2
GARFUNKEL, ART			
All I Know			
(US) Columbia	10 13 73	9	7
[see also: **SIMON AND GARFUNKEL**]			
GARLAND, JUDY			
The Man That Got Away			
(UK) Philips	6 10 55	18	2
GARNETT, GALE			
We'll Sing in the Sunshine			
(US) RCA	9 14 64	4	9
GAYE, MARVIN			
Pride and Joy			
(US) Tamla	7 6 63	10	4
You're a Wonderful One			
(US) Tamla	4 4 64	15	5
Once upon a Time (with **MARY WELLS**)			
(US) Motown (b/w*)	6 6 64	19	3
What's the Matter with You Baby (with **MARY WELLS**)*			
(US) Motown	7 4 64	17	1
Try It Baby			
(US) Tamla	7 4 64	15	5
How Sweet It Is (to Be Loved By You)			
(US) Tamla	1 2 65	6	7
I'll Be Doggone			
(US) Tamla	4 17 65	8	6
Ain't That Peculiar			
(US) Tamla	10 30 65	8	7
It Takes Two (with **KIM WESTON**)			
(US) Tamla	2 18 67	14	3
(UK) Motown	2 18 67	16	5
Ain't No Mountain High Enough (with **TAMMI TERRELL**)			
(US) Tamla	7 15 67	19	2
Your Precious Love (with **TAMMI TERRELL**)			
(US) Tamla	10 14 67	5	7
If I Could Build My Whole World Around You (with **TAMMI TERRELL**)			
(US) Tamla	12 30 67	10	4
Ain't Nothing Like the Real Thing (with **TAMMI TERRELL**)			
(US) Tamla	5 18 68	8	5
You're All I Need to Get By (with **TAMMI TERRELL**)			
(US) Tamla	8 24 68	7	5
(UK) Motown	11 16 68	19	1

LABEL	DATE OF CHART ENTRY	HIGHEST POSITION REACHED	NUMBER OF WEEKS IN CHARTS
I Heard It Through the Grapevine			
(US) Tamla	11 30 68	1	13
(UK) Motown	*3 1 69*	*1*	*10*
Too Busy Thinking About My Baby			
(US) Tamla	5 24 69	4	10
(UK) Motown	*8 16 69*	*5*	*8*
That's the Way Love Is			
(US) Tamla	9 27 69	7	6
Onion Song (with **TAMMI TERRELL**)			
(UK) Motown	*11 29 69*	*9*	*8*
Abraham, Martin and John			
(UK) Tamla Motown	*5 30 70*	*9*	*7*
What's Going On			
(US) Tamla	3 13 71	2	11
Mercy Mercy (The Ecology)			
(US) Tamla	7 24 71	4	8
Inner City Blues (Make Me Want to Holler)			
(US) Tamla	10 30 71	9	4
Trouble Man			
(US) Tamla	1 13 73	7	6
Let's Get It On			
(US) Tamla	8 4 73	1	15
[see also: **DIANA ROSS**]			

G-CLEFS
I Understand (Just How You Feel)			
(US) Terrace	10 23 61	9	7
(UK) London	*12 16 61*	*20*	*1*

GENE AND DEBBE
Playboy			
(US) TRX	4 13 68	17	3

GENTRY, BOBBIE
Ode to Billie Joe			
(US) Capitol	8 19 67	1	10
(UK) Capitol	*10 7 67*	*13*	*6*
I'll Never Fall in Love Again			
(UK) Capitol	*9 13 69*	*1*	*10*
[see also: **GLEN CAMPBELL**]			

GENTRYS
Keep On Dancing			
(US) MGM	10 2 65	4	7

GEORDIE
All Because of You			
(UK) EMI	*4 14 73*	*6*	*6*
Can You Do It			
(UK) EMI	*6 23 73*	*13*	*4*

GEORGE, BARBARA
I Know			
(US) AFO	1 6 62	3	8

LABEL	DATE OF CHART ENTRY	HIGHEST POSITION REACHED	NUMBER OF WEEKS IN CHARTS

GERRARD, DANYEL
Butterfly
| (UK) CBS | 10 2 71 | 11 | 5 |

GERRY AND THE PACEMAKERS
How Do You Do It?
| (UK) Columbia | 3 23 63 | 1 | 10 |
| (US) Laurie (reissue) | 8 15 64 | 10 | 5 |

I Like It
| (UK) Columbia | 6 8 63 | 1 | 12 |
| (US) Laurie (reissue) | 10 31 64 | 17 | 2 |

You'll Never Walk Alone
| (UK) Columbia | 10 19 63 | 1 | 14 |

I'm the One
| (UK) Columbia | 1 25 64 | 2 | 9 |

Don't Let the Sun Catch You Crying
| (UK) Columbia | 4 25 64 | 6 | 6 |
| (US) Laurie | 6 13 64 | 4 | 7 |

I'll Be There
| (US) Laurie | 1 19 65 | 14 | 3 |
| (UK) Columbia | 4 3 65 | 12 | 4 |

Ferry 'Cross the Mersey
| (UK) Columbia | 1 9 65 | 8 | 7 |
| (US) Laurie | 2 27 65 | 6 | 7 |

GETZ, STAN; and BYRD, CHARLIE
Desafinado
| (US) Verve | 11 10 62 | 15 | 5 |
| (UK) HMV | 12 15 62 | 13 | 5 |

GETZ, STAN; and GILBERTO, ASTRUD
Girl from Ipanema
| (US) Verve | 6 27 64 | 5 | 8 |

GIBB, ROBIN
Saved by the Bell
| (UK) Polydor | 7 19 69 | 2 | 10 |
[see also: BEE GEES]

GIBBS, GEORGIA
Tweedle Dee
| (US) Mercury | 2 5 55 | 3 | 17 |
| (UK) Mercury | 4 22 55 | 20 | 1 |

Dance with Me Henry
| (US) Mercury | 4 2 55 | 2 | 16 |

GIBSON, DON
Oh Lonesome Me
| (US) Victor | 4 14 58 | 8 | 11 |

Sea of Heartbreak
| (UK) RCA | 9 2 61 | 14 | 7 |

GILKYSON, TERRY, & THE EASY RIDERS
Marianne
| (US) Columbia | 2 23 57 | 5 | 10 |

LABEL	DATE OF CHART ENTRY	HIGHEST POSITION REACHED	NUMBER OF WEEKS IN CHARTS
GILLIES, STUART			
Amanda			
(*UK*) *Philips*	*4 7 73*	*13*	*5*
GILMER, JIMMY, AND THE FIREBALLS			
Sugar Shack			
(US) Dot	9 28 63	1	12
Daisy Petal Pickin'			
(US) Dot	1 25 64	15	4
GLAHE, WILL			
Liechtensteiner Polka			
(US) London	12 16 57	19	2
GLAZER, TOM, and the CHILDREN'S CHORUS			
On Top of Spaghetti			
(US) Kapp	6 29 63	14	3
GLITTER, GARY			
Rock and Roll			
(*UK*) *Bell (pts. 1 & 2)*	*6 24 72*	*2*	*10*
(US) Bell (pt. 2)	8 26 72	7	5
I Didn't Know I Loved You Till I Saw You Rock and Roll			
(*UK*) *Bell*	*9 30 72*	*4*	*7*
Do You Wanna Touch Me			
(*UK*) *Bell*	*1 27 73*	*2*	*7*
Hello Hello I'm Back Again			
(*UK*) *Bell*	*4 7 73*	*2*	*10*
I'm the Leader of the Gang			
(*UK*) *Bell*	*7 21 73*	*1*	*8*
I Love You Love Me Love			
(*UK*) *Bell*	*11 17 73*	*1*	*12*
GODSPELL			
Day by Day			
(US) Bell	7 22 72	13	4
GOLDSBORO, BOBBY			
See the Funny Little Clown			
(US) United Artists	2 22 64	9	5
Little Things			
(US) United Artists	3 13 65	13	4
Honey			
(US) United Artists	4 6 68	1	11
(*UK*) *United Artists*	*5 4 68*	*2*	*11*
Autumn of My Life			
(US) United Artists	8 3 68	19	2
Watching Scotty Grow			
(US) United Artists	2 6 71	11	5
Summer (The First Time)			
(*UK*) *United Artists*	*8 18 73*	*9*	*5*
GOODWIN, RON			
Blue Star			
(*UK*) *Parlophone*	*10 28 55*	*20*	*1*

GOONS
I'm Walking Backwards for Christmas

LABEL	DATE OF CHART ENTRY	HIGHEST POSITION REACHED	NUMBER OF WEEKS IN CHARTS
(*UK*) Decca	7 6 56	4	8

Bloodnocks' Rock and Roll/Ying Tong Song

(*UK*) Decca	9 14 56	3	8

Ying Tong Song

(*UK*) Decca (*reissue*)	8 4 73	9	4

GORE, LESLEY
It's My Party

(US) Mercury	5 25 63	1	9
(*UK*) *Mercury*	7 6 63	9	6

Judy's Turn to Cry

(US) Mercury	7 27 63	5	7

She's a Fool

(US) Mercury	10 26 63	5	9

You Don't Own Me

(US) Mercury	1 18 64	2	8

That's the Way Boys Are

(US) Mercury	4 18 64	12	4

Maybe I Know

(US) Mercury	8 29 64	14	3
(*UK*) *Mercury*	10 24 64	20	1

Sunshine, Lollipops and Rainbows

(US) Mercury	7 24 65	13	3

California Nights

(US) Mercury	3 18 67	16	2

GORME, EYDIE
Yes My Darling Daughter

(*UK*) CBS	6 30 62	10	5

Blame It on the Bossa Nova

(US) Columbia	2 16 63	7	8

[see also: **STEVE LAWRENCE**]

GOULET, ROBERT
My Love Forgive Me

(US) Columbia	1 2 65	16	2

GRACIE, CHARLIE
Butterfly

(US) Cameo	3 2 57	7	12
(*UK*) *Parlophone*	5 17 57	12	3

Fabulous

(*UK*) *Parlophone*	6 21 57	8	13

Wanderin' Eyes

(*UK*) *London*	8 30 57	6	11

I Love You So Much It Hurts

(*UK*) *London*	8 30 57	14	2

GRAMMER, BILLY
Gotta Travel On

(US) Monument	12 15 58	4	12

LABEL	DATE OF CHART ENTRY	HIGHEST POSITION REACHED	NUMBER OF WEEKS IN CHARTS
GRAND FUNK RAILROAD			
We're an American Band			
(US) Capitol	8 25 73	1	10
GRANT, EARL			
The End			
(US) Decca	9 29 58	7	11
GRANT, GOGI			
Suddenly There's a Valley			
(US) Era	10 15 55	14	9
Wayward Wind			
(US) Era	5 19 56	1	19
(UK) London	*6 29 56*	*9*	*9*
GRASS ROOTS			
Let's Live for Today			
(US) Dunhill	6 10 67	8	6
Midnight Confession			
(US) Dunhill	9 28 68	5	10
I'd Wait a Million Years			
(US) Dunhill	8 30 69	15	4
Temptation Eyes			
(US) Dunhill	3 13 71	15	5
Sooner or Later			
(US) Dunhill	7 10 71	9	5
Two Divided by Love			
(US) Dunhill	11 20 71	16	3
GRAY, DOBIE			
The "In" Crowd			
(US) Charger	2 6 65	13	3
Drift Away			
(US) Decca	4 21 73	5	9
GREAN, CHARLES RANDOLPH, SOUNDS			
Quentin's Theme			
(US) Ranwood	7 19 69	13	5
GREAVES, R. B.			
Take a Letter Maria			
(US) Atco	11 8 69	2	10
GREGORY, IAN			
Time Will Tell			
(UK) Pye	*12 4 60*	*17*	*3*
GREEN, AL			
Tired of Being Alone			
(US) Hi	9 18 71	11	10
(UK) London	*10 23 71*	*4*	*6*
Let's Stay Together			
(US) Hi	12 25 71	1	12
(UK) London	*1 22 72*	*7*	*7*
Look What You Done for Me			
(US) Hi	4 15 72	4	9

LABEL	DATE OF CHART ENTRY	HIGHEST POSITION REACHED	NUMBER OF WEEKS IN CHARTS
I'm Still in Love with You			
(US) Hi	7 29 72	3	8
You Ought to Be with Me			
(US) Hi	11 18 72	3	8
Call Me (Come Back Home)			
(US) Hi	3 17 73	10	6
Here I Am (Come Take Me)			
(US) Hi	8 4 73	10	8
GREENBAUM, NORMAN			
Spirit in the Sky			
(US) Reprise	3 21 70	3	10
(UK) Reprise	*4 4 70*	*1*	*11*
GREENE, GARLAND			
Jealous Kind of Fellow			
(US) UNI	11 1 69	20	1
GREENE, LORNE			
Ringo			
(US) RCA	11 14 64	1	9
GREYHOUND			
Black and White			
(UK) Trojan	*7 3 71*	*6*	*8*
Moon River			
(UK) Trojan	*1 29 72*	*12*	*3*
I Am What I Am			
(UK) Trojan	*4 29 72*	*20*	*1*
GUESS WHO			
Those Eyes			
(US) RCA	5 3 69	6	9
Laughing			
(US) RCA	8 9 69	10	5
No Time			
(US) RCA	′1 31 70	5	7
American Woman			
(US) RCA (b/w No Sugar Tonight)	4 4 70	1	12
(UK) RCA	*7 4 70*	*19*	*1*
Hand-Me-Down World			
(US) RCA	8 29 70	17	3
Share the Land			
(US) RCA	11 21 70	10	5
Rain Dance			
(US) RCA	10 2 71	19	2
GUITAR, BONNIE			
Dark Moon			
(US) Dot	5 6 57	8	7
GUN			
Race with the Devil			
(UK) CBS	*12 7 68*	*8*	*7*

LABEL	DATE OF CHART ENTRY			HIGHEST POSITION REACHED	NUMBER OF WEEKS IN CHARTS
GUTHRIE, ARLO					
City of New Orleans					
(US) Reprise	10	7	72	18	4
HALEY, BILL, AND HIS COMETS					
Shake, Rattle and Roll					
(US) Decca	1	1	55	12	4
(UK) Brunswick	*1*	*7*	*55*	*4*	*11*
Dim Dim the Lights					
(US) Decca	1	1	55	11	7
Rock Around the Clock					
(UK) Brunswick	*1*	*7*	*55*	*17*	*2*
(US) Decca	5	21	55	1	22
(UK) Brunswick (re-entry)	*10*	*14*	*55*	*1*	*17*
(UK) Brunswick (re-entry)	*9*	*21*	*56*	*5*	*11*
(UK) MCA (reissue)	*4*	*6*	*68*	*20*	*1*
Mambo Rock					
(US) Decca	3	19	55	18	1
(UK) Brunswick	*4*	*15*	*55*	*14*	*2*
Razzle Dazzle					
(US) Decca	7	23	55	15	2
(UK) Brunswick	*9*	*28*	*56*	*13*	*4*
Burn That Candle					
(US) Decca	12	31	55	20	2
Rock-a-Beatin' Boogie					
(UK) Brunswick	*1*	*6*	*56*	*4*	*8*
See You Later Alligator					
(US) Decca	1	28	56	6	12
(UK) Brunswick	*3*	*9*	*56*	*7*	*11*
(UK) Brunswick (re-entry)	*9*	*28*	*56*	*12*	*6*
Saints Rock and Roll					
(UK) Brunswick	*6*	*1*	*56*	*5*	*22*
Rockin' Through the Rye					
(UK) Brunswick	*8*	*17*	*56*	*3*	*19*
Rip It Up					
(UK) Brunswick	*11*	*16*	*56*	*4*	*14*
Don't Knock the Rock					
(UK) Brunswick	*3*	*8*	*57*	*7*	*7*
Rock the Joint					
(UK) Brunswick	*2*	*1*	*57*	*20*	*1*
HALL, LARRY					
Sandy					
(US) Strand	12	28	59	15	5
HAMILTON IV, GEORGE					
Rose and Baby Ruth					
(US) ABC-Paramount	11	24	56	6	11
Why Don't They Understand					
(US) ABC-Paramount	1	27	58	17	2
Abilene					
(US) RCA	8	10	63	15	2

HAMILTON, ROY
Unchained Melody
(US) Epic — 4 30 55 — 9 — 13
Don't Let Go
(US) Epic — 2 10 58 — 13 — 4
You Can Have Her
(US) Epic — 3 6 61 — 12 — 2

HAMILTON, RUSS
We Will Make Love
(UK) Oriole (b/w*) — *6 7 57* — *2* — *16*
Rainbow*
(US) Kapp — 8 19 57 — 7 — 11
Wedding Ring
(UK) Oriole — *10 18 57* — *20* — *1*

HAMILTON, JOE FRANK AND REYNOLDS
Don't Pull Your Love
(US) Dunhill — 6 19 71 — 4 — 8

HAMMOND, ALBERT
It Never Rains in Southern California
(US) Mums — 11 25 72 — 5 — 8
Free Electric Band
(UK) Mums — *8 11 73* — *19* — *1*

HAPPENINGS
See You in September
(US) B. T. Puppy — 8 6 66 — 3 — 8
Go Away Little Girl
(US) B. T. Puppy — 10 22 66 — 12 — 4
I Got Rhythm
(US) B. T. Puppy — 5 6 67 — 3 — 7
My Mommy
(US) B. T. Puppy — 8 5 67 — 13 — 4

HARDY, FRANÇOISE
All over the World
(UK) Pye — *4 17 65* — *16* — *7*

HARNELL, JOE, AND ORCHESTRA
Fly Me to the Moon Bossa Nova
(US) Kapp — 2 9 63 — 14 — 4

HARPER'S BIZARRE
59th Street Bridge Song
(US) Warner Brothers — 3 25 67 — 13 — 4

HARRIS, ANITA
Just Loving You
(UK) CBS — *7 29 67* — *6* — *15*

HARRIS, JET
Theme from "The Man with the Golden Arm"
(UK) Decca — *9 1 62* — *12* — *7*

LABEL	DATE OF CHART ENTRY	HIGHEST POSITION REACHED	NUMBER OF WEEKS IN CHARTS
HARRIS, JET; and MEEHAN, TONY			
Diamonds			
(*UK*) *Decca*	1 20 63	1	10
Scarlett O'Hara			
(*UK*) *Decca*	5 4 63	2	10
Applejack			
(*UK*) *Decca*	9 14 63	4	7
HARRIS, MAX			
Gurney Slade			
(*UK*) *Philips*	11 27 60	10	4
HARRIS, RICHARD			
MacArthur Park			
(US) Dunhill	6 1 68	2	8
(*UK*) *RCA*	7 6 68	4	7
HARRIS, ROLF			
Tie Me Kangaroo Down Sport			
(*UK*) *Columbia*	7 24 60	7	8
(US) Epic	6 29 63	3	5
Sun Arise			
(*UK*) *Columbia*	11 10 62	3	12
Two Little Boys			
(*UK*) *Columbia*	11 29 69	1	15
HARRIS, THURSTON			
Little Bittie Pretty One			
(US) Aladdin	11 4 57	6	8
HARRISON, GEORGE			
My Sweet Lord			
(US) Apple (b/w Isn't It a Pity?)	12 5 70	1	12
(*UK*) *Apple*	1 23 71	1	12
What Is Life			
(US) Apple	3 13 71	10	6
Give Me Love			
(US) Apple	6 2 73	1	9
(*UK*) *Apple*	6 9 73	8	6
[see also: **BEATLES**]			
HARRISON, NOEL			
Windmills of Your Mind			
(*UK*) *Reprise*	3 15 69	8	9
HARRISON, WILBERT			
Kansas City			
(US) Fury	5 4 59	1	10
HARRY J AND THE ALL STARS			
The Liquidator			
(*UK*) *Trojan*	11 15 69	9	13
HART, FREDDIE			
Easy Loving			
(US) Capitol	10 30 71	17	5
HATHAWAY, DONNY (see **FLACK, ROBERTA**)			

184

LABEL	DATE OF CHART ENTRY	HIGHEST POSITION REACHED	NUMBER OF WEEKS IN CHARTS
HAVENS, RICHIE			
Here Comes the Sun			
(US) Stormy Forest	5 15 71	16	4
HAWKINS, EDWIN, SINGERS			
Oh Happy Day			
(US) Pavilion	5 10 69	4	3
(UK) Buddah	*5 31 69*	*2*	*8*
[see also: **MELANIE**]			
HAWKWIND			
Silver Machine			
(UK) United Artists	*7 22 72*	*3*	*10*
HAYES, BILL			
Ballad of Davy Crockett			
(US) Cadence	2 26 55	1	20
(UK) London	*1 6 56*	*2*	*9*
HAYES, ISAAC			
Theme from "Shaft"			
(US) Enterprise/MGM	10 23 71	1	10
(UK) Stax	*12 4 71*	*4*	*8*
HAYMAN, RICHARD; and AUGUST, JAN			
Theme from "Three Penny Opera"			
(US) Mercury	2 25 56	12	6
HAZLEWOOD, LEE (see **NANCY SINATRA**)			
HEAD, MURRAY (with the TRINIDAD SINGERS)			
Superstar			
(US) Decca (reissue)	5 22 71	14	5
HEAD, ROY			
Treat Her Right			
(US) Back Beat	9 25 65	2	7
HEATH, TED			
Faithful Hussar			
(UK) Decca	*8 3 56*	*18*	*3*
Swingin' Shepherd Blues			
(UK) Decca	*3 28 58*	*3*	*10*
HEBB, BOBBY			
Sunny			
(US) Philips	7 30 66	2	8
(UK) Philips	*10 1 66*	*12*	*3*
HEDGEHOPPERS ANONYMOUS			
It's Good News Week			
(UK) Decca	*10 21 65*	*5*	*6*
HEINZ			
Just Like Eddie			
(UK) Decca	*8 24 63*	*5*	*10*
HELMS, BOBBY			
My Special Angel			
(US) Decca	11 4 57	7	12

LABEL	DATE OF CHART ENTRY	HIGHEST POSITION REACHED	NUMBER OF WEEKS IN CHARTS
Jingle Bell Rock			
(US) Decca	1 6 58	6	3
Jacqueline			
(UK) Brunswick	8 8 58	20	1
HELMS, JIMMY			
Gonna Make You an Offer You Can't Refuse			
(UK) Cube	3 3 73	8	5
HENDERSON, JOE "MR. PIANO"			
Sing It with Joe			
(UK) Polygon	6 3 55	14	7
Trudie			
(UK) Pye Nixa	8 8 58	14	6
HENDERSON, JOE			
Snap Your Fingers			
(US) Todd	6 16 62	8	6
HENDRIX, JIMI, EXPERIENCE			
Hey Joe			
(UK) Polydor	1 21 67	6	5
Purple Haze			
(UK) Track	4 15 67	3	8
And the Wind Cries Mary			
(UK) Track	5 20 67	6	5
Burning of the Midnight Lamp			
(UK) Track	9 9 67	18	4
All Along the Watchtower			
(US) Reprise	10 19 68	20	2
(UK) Track	11 2 68	5	6
Voodoo Chile			
(UK) Track	11 7 70	1	10
HENRY, CLARENCE "FROGMAN"			
But I Do			
(US) Argo	3 27 61	4	7
(UK) Pye International	5 7 61	5	11
You Always Hurt the One You Love			
(US) Argo	6 5 61	12	5
(UK) Pye International	7 15 61	9	8
HERD			
From the Underworld			
(UK) Fontana	10 7 67	6	8
Paradise Lost			
(UK) Fontana	1 20 68	15	3
I Don't Want Our Loving to Die			
(UK) Fontana	5 4 68	5	8
HERMAN'S HERMITS			
I'm into Something Good			
(UK) Columbia	9 4 64	1	10
(US) MGM	11 21 64	13	6

186

LABEL	DATE OF CHART ENTRY	HIGHEST POSITION REACHED	NUMBER OF WEEKS IN CHARTS
Show Me Girl			
(*UK*) *Columbia*	12 5 64	19	3
Silhouettes			
(*UK*) *Columbia*	2 27 65	3	9
(US) MGM	4 17 65	5	9
Can't You Hear My Heartbeat?			
(US) MGM	3 6 65	2	8
Mrs. Brown You've Got a Lovely Daughter			
(US) MGM	4 17 65	1	10
Wonderful World			
(*UK*) *Columbia*	5 1 65	7	7
(US) MGM	6 12 65	4	6
I'm Henry VIII I Am			
(US) MGM	7 10 65	1	8
Just a Little Bit Better			
(*UK*) *Columbia*	9 18 65	15	5
(US) MGM	10 9 65	7	4
A Must to Avoid			
(*UK*) *Columbia*	1 8 66	6	7
(US) MGM	1 8 66	8	6
Listen People			
(US) MGM	2 26 66	3	6
You Won't Be Leaving			
(*UK*) *Columbia*	4 16 66	20	2
Leaning on a Lamp Post			
(US) MGM	4 23 66	9	5
This Door Swings Both Ways			
(*UK*) *Columbia*	7 9 66	18	2
(US) MGM	7 30 66	12	4
Dandy			
(US) MGM	10 15 66	5	6
No Milk Today*			
(*UK*) *Columbia*	10 15 66	7	7
There's a Kind of a Hush			
(US) MGM (b/w*)	3 11 67	4	6
(*UK*) *Columbia*	2 25 67	7	7
Don't Go Out in the Rain (You're Going to Melt)			
(US) MGM	7 22 67	18	1
I Can Take or Leave Your Loving			
(*UK*) *Columbia*	1 27 68	11	6
Sleepy Joe			
(*UK*) *Columbia*	5 11 68	12	6
Sunshine Girl			
(*UK*) *Columbia*	8 3 68	8	8
Something's Happening			
(*UK*) *Columbia*	1 4 69	6	9
My Sentimental Friend			
(*UK*) *Columbia*	5 3 69	2	7

LABEL	DATE OF CHART ENTRY	HIGHEST POSITION REACHED	NUMBER OF WEEKS IN CHARTS
Years May Come, Years May Go			
(UK) Columbia	2 21 70	7	7
[see also: PETER NOONE]			
HEYWOOD, EDDIE			
Soft Summer Breeze			
(US) Mercury	8 4 56	12	12
Canadian Sunset (with **HUGO WINTERHALTER)**			
(US) Victor	8 11 56	2	18
HIBBLER, AL			
Unchained Melody			
(US) Decca	4 9 55	5	18
(UK) Brunswick	5 13 55	2	17
He			
(US) Decca	10 1 55	7	20
After the Lights Go Down Low			
(US) Decca	9 15 56	15	5
HIGHWAYMEN			
Michael			
(US) United Artists	8 7 61	1	10
(UK) HMV	9 9 61	1	9
Cotton Fields			
(US) United Artists	1 13 62	13	7
HILL, BENNY			
Pepys' Diary/Gather in the Mushrooms			
(UK) Pye	2 5 61	13	5
Harvest of Love			
(UK) Pye	6 1 63	20	2
Ernie (the Fastest Milkman in the West)			
(UK) Columbia	11 20 71	1	10
HILL, VINCE			
Take Me to Your Heart Again			
(UK) Columbia	1 22 66	13	1
Edelweiss			
(UK) Columbia	2 18 67	2	11
Roses of Picardy			
(UK) Columbia	6 3 67	13	4
Look Around			
(UK) Columbia	10 30 71	12	6
HILLSIDE SINGERS			
I'd Like to Teach the World to Sing			
(US) Metromedia	1 1 72	13	5
HILLTOPPERS			
Kentuckian Song			
(US) Dot	8 13 55	20	1
Only You			
(US) Dot	11 12 55	9	12
(UK) London	1 27 56	3	21
Marianne			

188

LABEL	DATE OF CHART ENTRY	HIGHEST POSITION REACHED	NUMBER OF WEEKS IN CHARTS
(US) Dot	2 16 57	8	11
(UK) London	*4 5 57*	*20*	*1*
HILTON, RONNIE			
I Still Believe			
(UK) HMV	*1 7 55*	*4*	*8*
Veni Vidi Vici			
(UK) HMV	*1 7 55*	*12*	*4*
A Blossom Fell			
(UK) HMV	*3 11 55*	*10*	*7*
Stars Shine in Your Eyes			
(UK) HMV	*8 26 55*	*13*	*7*
Yellow Rose of Texas			
(UK) HMV	*11 11 55*	*15*	*2*
Young and Foolish			
(UK) HMV	*2 10 56*	*17*	*3*
No Other Love			
(UK) HMV	*4 20 56*	*1*	*13*
Who Are We			
(UK) HMV	*7 13 56*	*6*	*8*
Two Different Worlds			
(UK) HMV	*11 23 56*	*13*	*7*
Around the World			
(UK) HMV	*5 24 57*	*4*	*15*
HINTON, JOE			
Funny, How Time Slips Away			
(US) Back Beat	9 26 64	13	4
HIRT, AL			
Java			
(US) RCA	2 8 64	4	9
Cotton Candy			
(US) RCA	5 30 64	15	2
HOCKRIDGE, EDMUND			
Young and Foolish			
(UK) Nixa	*2 17 56*	*10*	*7*
Fountains of Rome			
(UK) Pye Nixa	*9 7 56*	*17*	*4*
HODGES, EDDIE			
I'm Gonna Knock on Your Door			
(US) Cadence	8 21 61	12	3
(UK) London	*9 23 61*	*20*	*1*
(Girls Girls Girls) Made to Love			
(US) Cadence	7 21 62	14	5
HOLDEN, ROD			
Love You So			
(US) Donna	5 16 60	7	7
HOLLIDAY, MICHAEL			
Nothin' to Do			
(UK) Columbia	*3 30 56*	*20*	*1*

LABEL	DATE OF CHART ENTRY	HIGHEST POSITION REACHED	NUMBER OF WEEKS IN CHARTS
Gal with the Yaller Shoes			
(UK) Columbia	6 15 56	13	3
Hot Diggity			
(UK) Columbia	6 22 56	14	4
Story of My Life			
(UK) Columbia	1 17 58	1	14
Stairway of Love			
(UK) Columbia	5 23 58	3	11
Starry Eyed			
(UK) Columbia	1 2 60	2	9

HOLLIES

LABEL	DATE OF CHART ENTRY	HIGHEST POSITION REACHED	NUMBER OF WEEKS IN CHARTS
Searchin'			
(UK) Parlophone	9 28 63	12	6
Stay			
(UK) Parlophone	12 14 63	8	10
Just One Look			
(UK) Parlophone	3 7 64	2	9
Here I Go Again			
(UK) Parlophone	5 30 64	4	7
We're Through			
(UK) Parlophone	10 3 64	7	7
Yes I Will			
(UK) Parlophone	2 20 65	9	7
I'm Alive			
(UK) Parlophone	6 12 65	1	10
Look Through Any Window			
(UK) Parlophone	9 11 65	4	8
If I Needed Someone			
(UK) Parlophone	1 15 66	20	1
I Can't Let Go			
(UK) Parlophone	3 5 66	2	6
Bus Stop			
(UK) Parlophone	6 25 66	5	7
(US) Imperial	9 3 66	5	6
Stop Stop Stop			
(UK) Parlophone	10 22 66	2	8
(US) Imperial	11 19 66	7	6
On a Carousel			
(UK) Parlophone	2 25 67	4	7
(US) Imperial	4 29 67	11	7
Carrie Anne			
(UK) Parlophone	6 10 67	3	8
(US) Epic	7 29 67	9	6
King Midas in Reverse			
(UK) Parlophone	10 14 67	18	3
Jennifer Eccles			
(UK) Parlophone	4 13 68	7	6
Listen to Me			
(UK) Parlophone	10 19 68	11	6

LABEL	DATE OF CHART ENTRY	HIGHEST POSITION REACHED	NUMBER OF WEEKS IN CHARTS
Sorry Suzanne			
(UK) Parlophone	3 15 69	3	7
He Ain't Heavy He's My Brother			
(UK) Parlophone	10 11 69	3	8
(US) Epic	2 28 70	7	7
I Can't Tell the Bottom from the Top			
(UK) Parlophone	5 2 70	7	5
Gasoline Alley Bred			
(UK) Parlophone	10 17 70	14	4
Long Cool Woman			
(US) Epic	7 22 72	2	9
HOLLOWAY, BRENDA			
Every Little Bit Hurts			
(US) Tamla	5 30 64	13	4
HOLLY, BUDDY			
Peggy Sue			
(US) Coral	12 2 57	3	13
(UK) Coral	1 3 58	6	12
Listen to Me			
(UK) Coral	3 14 58	16	1
Rave On			
(UK) Coral	6 27 58	5	12
Early in the Morning			
(UK) Coral	8 29 58	17	2
It Doesn't Matter Any More			
(UK) Coral	3 7 59	1	19
(US) Coral	3 16 59	13	4
Peggy Sue Got Married			
(UK) Coral	9 12 59	14	8
Baby I Don't Care			
(UK) Coral	7 2 61	13	7
Reminiscing			
(UK) Coral	10 6 62	17	2
Brown Eyed Handsome Man			
(UK) Coral	3 16 63	3	10
Bo Diddley			
(UK) Coral	6 15 63	4	8
Wishing			
(UK) Coral	9 14 63	10	7
[see also: **CRICKETS**]			
HOLLYWOOD ARGYLES			
Alley-Oop			
(US) Lute	6 13 60	1	10
HOLLYWOOD FLAMES			
Buzz Buzz Buzz			
(US) Ebb	1 20 58	11	3
HOLMAN, EDDIE			
Hey There Lonely Girl			
(US) ABC	1 24 70	2	8

LABEL	DATE OF CHART ENTRY	HIGHEST POSITION REACHED	NUMBER OF WEEKS IN CHARTS
HOLMES, CLINT			
Playground in My Mind			
(US) Epic	5 26 73	2	10
HOMBRES			
Let It Out			
(US) Verve Forecast	10 28 67	12	5
HOMER AND JETHRO			
Battle of Kookamouga			
(US) RCA	9 21 59	14	5
HONDELLS			
Little Honda			
(US) Mercury	10 17 64	9	5
HONEYBUS			
I Can't Let Maggie Go			
(UK) Deram	*4 14 68*	*8*	*6*
HONEYCOMBS			
Have I the Right			
(UK) Pye	*8 8 64*	*1*	*11*
(US) Interphon	10 17 64	5	7
That's the Way			
(UK) Pye	*9 4 65*	*12*	*7*
HONEY CONE			
Want Ads			
(US) Hot Wax	5 8 71	1	11
Stick Up			
(US) Hot Wax	9 4 71	11	7
One Monkey Don't Stop No Show			
(US) Hot Wax	1 1 72	15	4
HOPKIN, MARY			
Those Were the Days			
(UK) Apple	*9 14 68*	*1*	*14*
(US) Apple	10 12 68	2	11
Goodbye			
(UK) Apple	*4 19 69*	*2*	*8*
(US) Apple	5 17 69	13	4
Temma Harbour			
(UK) Apple	*2 7 70*	*6*	*6*
Knock Knock Who's There?			
(UK) Apple	*3 28 70*	*2*	*7*
Think About Your Children			
(UK) Apple	*11 14 70*	*19*	*2*
HORTON, JOHNNY			
Battle of New Orleans			
(US) Columbia	5 18 59	1	14
(UK) Philips	*7 18 59*	*16*	*1*
Sink the Bismarck			
(US) Columbia	3 28 60	3	10

LABEL	DATE OF CHART ENTRY	HIGHEST POSITION REACHED	NUMBER OF WEEKS IN CHARTS
North to Alaska			
(US) Columbia	11 7 60	4	14
(UK) Philips	*1 8 61*	*15*	*4*
HOT BUTTER			
Popcorn			
(UK) Pye International	*7 29 72*	*5*	*8*
(US) Musicor	9 16 72	10	6
HOT CHOCOLATE			
Love Is Life			
(UK) RAK	*8 22 70*	*6*	*8*
I Believe in Love			
(UK) RAK	*9 11 71*	*8*	*6*
Brother Louie			
(UK) RAK	*4 28 73*	*7*	*6*
HOTLEGS			
Neanderthal Man			
(UK) Fontana	*7 25 70*	*2*	*9*
HOTSHOTS			
Snoppy Versus the Red Baron			
(UK) Mooncrest	*6 16 73*	*4*	*8*
HUDSON FORD			
Pick Up the Pieces			
(UK) A&M	*9 1 73*	*8*	*4*
(see also: **STRAWBS**)			
HUGHES, JIMMY			
Steal Away			
(US) Fame	8 1 64	17	3
HUMAN BEINZ			
Nobody But Me			
(US) Capitol	1 13 68	8	8
HUMBLE PIE			
Natural Born Bugie			
(UK) Immediate	*8 30 69*	*4*	*7*
HUMPERDINCK, ENGELBERT			
Release Me			
(UK) Decca	*2 11 67*	*1*	*15*
(US) Parrot	5 6 67	4	8
There Goes My Everything			
(UK) Decca	*6 3 67*	*2*	*13*
(US) Parrot	7 29 67	20	1
The Last Waltz			
(UK) Decca	*8 26 67*	*1*	*21*
Am I That Easy to Forget			
(UK) Decca	*1 20 68*	*3*	*9*
(US) Parrot	1 27 68	18	3
Man Without Love			
(UK) Decca	*5 4 68*	*2*	*9*
(US) Parrot	6 22 68	19	1

LABEL	DATE OF CHART ENTRY	HIGHEST POSITION REACHED	NUMBER OF WEEKS IN CHARTS
Les Bicyclettes de Belsize			
(*UK*) *Decca*	*10 12 68*	*5*	*7*
The Way It Used to Be			
(*UK*) *Decca*	*2 15 69*	*3*	*9*
I'm a Better Man			
(*UK*) *Decca*	*8 23 69*	*16*	*4*
Winterworld of Love			
(*UK*) *Decca*	*11 22 69*	*7*	*9*
(US) Parrot	*1 24 70*	*16*	*2*
Another Time Another Place			
(*UK*) *Decca*	*10 2 71*	*13*	*4*
Too Beautiful to Last			
(*UK*) *Decca*	*3 25 72*	*14*	*4*
100 PROOF AGED IN SOUL			
Somebody's Been Sleepin'			
(US) Hot Wax	10 24 70	8	6
HUNTER, IVORY JOE			
Since I Met You Baby			
(US) Atlantic	12 14 56	12	9
HUNTER, TAB			
Young Love			
(US) Dot	1 19 57	1	14
(*UK*) *London*	*2 8 57*	*1*	*17*
Ninety-Nine Ways			
(*UK*) *London*	*4 12 57*	*5*	*10*
(US) Dot	4 13 57	11	5
HUSKY, FERLIN			
Gone			
(US) Capitol	3 30 57	4	13
Wings of a Dove			
(US) Capitol	1 9 61	12	8
HYLAND, BRIAN			
Itsy Bitsy Teenie Weenie Yellow Polka Dot Bikini			
(*UK*) *London*	*7 10 60*	*9*	*8*
(US) Leader	7 11 60	1	10
Let Me Belong to You			
(US) ABC-Paramount	9 25 61	20	1
Ginny Come Lately			
(*UK*) *HMV*	*5 19 62*	*5*	*12*
Sealed with a Kiss			
(US) ABC-Paramount	7 7 62	3	8
(*UK*) *HMV*	*8 18 62*	*3*	*10*
Joker Went Wild			
(US) Philips	9 3 66	20	1
Gypsy Woman			
(US) UNI	11 7 70	3	9
HYMAN, DICK, TRIO			
Theme from "Three Penny Opera"			
(US) MGM	2 11 56	9	11
(*UK*) *MGM*	*3 16 56*	*9*	*9*

194   ROCK ALMANAC

LABEL	DATE OF CHART ENTRY	HIGHEST POSITION REACHED	NUMBER OF WEEKS IN CHARTS
IAN, JANIS			
Society's Child			
(US) Verve	7 8 67	14	3
IDES OF MARCH			
Vehicle			
(US) Warner Brothers	4 25 70	2	7
IFIELD, FRANK			
I Remember You			
(*UK*) *Columbia*	7 14 62	1	21
(US) Vee Jay	9 29 62	5	5
Lovesick Blues			
(*UK*) *Columbia*	10 27 62	1	15
Wayward Wind			
(*UK*) *Columbia*	2 3 63	1	10
Nobody's Darling but Mine			
(*UK*) *Columbia*	4 20 63	4	10
I'm Confessin'			
(*UK*) *Columbia*	7 6 63	1	12
Don't Blame Me			
(*UK*) *Columbia*	1 18 64	8	7
IKETTES			
I'm Blue (The Gong-Gong Song)			
(US) Atco	2 17 62	19	3
IMPALAS			
Sorry, I Ran All the Way Home			
(US) Cub	4 20 59	2	10
IMPRESSIONS			
Gypsy Woman			
(US) ABC-Paramount	12 4 61	20	2
It's All Right			
(US) ABC-Paramount	10 26 63	4	8
Talking About My Baby			
(US) ABC-Paramount	2 1 64	12	5
I'm So Proud			
(US) ABC-Paramount	5 9 64	14	4
Keep On Pushing			
(US) ABC-Paramount	7 11 64	10	5
You Must Believe Me			
(US) ABC-Paramount	10 3 64	15	4
Amen			
(US) ABC-Paramount	12 26 64	7	5
People Get Ready			
(US) ABC-Paramount	3 20 65	14	2
We're a Winner			
(US) ABC	2 17 68	14	4
[see also: **JERRY BUTLER**]			
INGMANN, JORGEN			
Apache			
(US) Atco	2 27 61	2	10

INGRAM, LUTHER
(If Loving You Is Wrong) I Don't Want to Be Right

(US) Koko	6 24 72	3	11

INK SPOTS
Melody of Love

(UK) Parlophone	*4 29 55*	*14*	*4*

INTRUDERS
Cowboys to Girls

(US) Gamble	4 13 68	6	9

IRISH ROVERS
Unicorn

(US) Decca	4 20 68	7	7

IRWIN, BIG DEE (with **LITTLE EVA**)
Swinging on a Star

(UK) Colpix	*12 21 63*	*7*	*9*

ISLANDERS
Enchanted Sea

(US) Mayflower	11 9 59	15	3

ISLEY BROTHERS
Twist and Shout

(US) Wand	7 28 62	17	4

This Old Heart of Mine

(US) Tamla	4 2 66	12	4
(UK) Tamla Motown	*11 2 68*	*3*	*9*

I Guess I'll Always Love You

(UK) Tamla Motown	*2 1 69*	*11*	*5*

It's Your Thing

(US) T-Neck	4 5 69	2	10

Behind a Painted Smile

(UK) Tamla Motown	*5 3 69*	*5*	*7*

Put Yourself in My Place

(UK) Tamla Motown	*9 27 69*	*13*	*2*

Love the One You're With

(US) T-Neck	8 7 71	18	2

That Lady

(US) T-Neck	9 8 73	6	10
(UK) Epic	*10 20 73*	*14*	*2*

IVES, BURL
A Little Bitty Tear

(US) Decca	1 13 62	9	8
(UK) Brunswick	*2 10 62*	*12*	*7*

Funny Way of Laughin'

(US) Decca	4 28 62	10	5

Call Me Mr. In-Between

(US) Decca	8 25 62	19	1

IVY LEAGUE
Funny How Love Can Be

(UK) Piccadilly	*2 13 65*	*8*	*6*

LABEL	DATE OF CHART ENTRY	HIGHEST POSITION REACHED	NUMBER OF WEEKS IN CHARTS
Tossing and Turning			
(UK) Piccadilly	7 10 65	3	8
IVY THREE			
Yogi			
(US) Shell	8 29 60	8	6
JACKSON, DEON			
Love Makes the World Go Round			
(US) Carla	3 12 66	11	5
JACKSON, JERMAINE			
Daddy's Home			
(US) Motown	2 10 73	9	7
[see also: **JACKSON FIVE**]			
JACKSON, MICHAEL			
Got to Be There			
(US) Motown	11 13 71	4	11
(UK) Tamla Motown	2 26 72	5	5
Rockin' Robin			
(US) Motown	3 25 72	2	9
(UK) Tamla Motown	6 10 72	3	7
I Wanna Be Where You Are			
(US) Motown	7 8 72	16	3
Ain't No Sunshine			
(UK) Tamla Motown	9 2 72	8	6
Ben			
(US) Motown	9 16 72	1	9
(UK) Tamla Motown	12 2 72	7	8
(see also: **JACKSON FIVE**)			
JACKSON, STONEWALL			
Waterloo			
(US) Columbia	6 22 59	4	9
JACKSON FIVE			
I Want You Back			
(US) Motown	12 13 69	1	13
(UK) Tamla Motown	2 14 70	2	9
ABC			
(US) Motown	3 21 70	1	11
(UK) Tamla Motown	5 23 70	8	5
The Love You Save			
(US) Motown (b/w I Found That Girl)			
	6 6 70	1	11
(UK) Tamla Motown	8 15 70	7	4
I'll Be There			
(US) Motown	9 26 70	1	14
(UK) Tamla Motown	12 5 70	4	11
Mama's Pearl			
(US) Motown	2 13 71	2	7
Never Can Say Goodbye			
(US) Motown	4 10 71	2	10

LABEL	DATE OF CHART ENTRY	HIGHEST POSITION REACHED	NUMBER OF WEEKS IN CHARTS
Maybe Tomorrow			
(US) Motown	8 21 71	20	1
Sugar Daddy			
(US) Motown	1 8 72	10	5
Little Bitty Pretty One			
(US) Motown	5 13 72	13	4
Lookin' Through the Windows			
(US) Motown	8 19 72	16	2
(UK) Tamla Motown	*11 25 72*	*9*	*3*
Corner of the Sky			
(US) Motown	12 9 72	18	2
Doctor My Eyes			
(UK) Tamla Motown	*2 24 73*	*9*	*5*
Hallelujah Day			
(UK) Tamla Motown	*6 30 73*	*20*	*2*
JACKY			
White Horses			
(UK) Philips	*4 27 68*	*10*	*9*
[see also: **JACKIE LEE**]			
JACOBS, DICK			
Petticoats of Portugal			
(US) Coral	12 8 56	20	1
JAGGERZ			
The Rapper			
(US) Kama Sutra	2 21 70	2	9
JAMES, DICK			
Robin Hood			
(UK) Parlophone	*1 20 56*	*14*	*8*
Garden of Eden			
(UK) Parlophone	*1 25 57*	*18*	*2*
JAMES, JONI			
How Important Can It Be			
(US) MGM	2 19 55	8	13
You Are My Love			
(US) MGM	11 5 55	15	6
There Goes My Heart			
(US) MGM	11 17 58	19	1
JAMES, SONNY			
Young Love			
(US) Capitol	1 12 57	2	14
(UK) Capitol	*2 8 57*	*11*	*7*
JAMES, TOMMY			
Draggin' the Line			
(US) Roulette	7 10 71	4	8
[see also: **TOMMY JAMES AND THE SHONDELLS**]			
JAMES, TOMMY, AND THE SHONDELLS			
Hanky Panky			
(US) Roulette	6 25 66	1	8

LABEL	DATE OF CHART ENTRY	HIGHEST POSITION REACHED	NUMBER OF WEEKS IN CHARTS
I Think We're Alone Now			
(US) Roulette	3 18 67	4	10
Mirage			
(US) Roulette	5 20 67	10	5
Gettin' Together			
(US) Roulette	9 23 67	18	2
Mony Mony			
(US) Roulette	5 18 68	3	9
(UK) Roulette	*7 6 68*	*1*	*11*
Crimson and Clover			
(US) Roulette	1 4 69	1	13
Sweet Cherry Wine			
(US) Roulette	4 12 69	7	6
Crystal Blue Persuasion			
(US) Roulette	6 28 69	2	11
Ball of Fire			
(US) Roulette	11 8 69	19	2
JAN AND ARNIE			
Jennie Lee			
(US) Arwin	6 2 58	8	7
JAN AND DEAN			
Baby Talk			
(US) Dore	8 24 59	10	6
Surf City			
(US) Liberty	6 22 63	1	10
Honolulu Lulu			
(US) Liberty	9 28 63	11	5
Drag City			
(US) Liberty	1 4 64	10	5
Dead Man's Curve			
(US) Liberty	4 11 64	8	7
Little Old Lady from Pasadena			
(US) Liberty	7 11 64	3	7
Ride the Wild Surf			
(US) Liberty	10 24 64	16	2
JANKOWSKI, HORST			
A Walk in the Black Forest			
(US) Mercury	6 19 65	12	5
(UK) Mercury	*8 7 65*	*3*	*12*
JARMELS			
Little Bit of Soap			
(US) Laurie	9 11 61	12	2
JAY AND THE AMERICANS			
She Cried			
(US) United Artists	4 21 62	5	8
Come a Little Bit Closer			
(US) United Artists	10 24 64	3	7
Let's Lock the Door (and Throw Away the Key)			
(US) United Artists	1 23 65	11	5

LABEL	DATE OF CHART ENTRY	HIGHEST POSITION REACHED	NUMBER OF WEEKS IN CHARTS
Cara Mia			
(US) United Artists	6 26 65	4	8
Some Enchanted Evening			
(US) United Artists	9 25 65	13	5
Sunday and Me			
(US) United Artists	12 18 65	18	2
This Magic Moment			
(US) United Artists	2 1 69	6	8
Walkin' in the Rain			
(US) United Artists	1 31 70	19	2
JAY AND THE TECHNIQUES			
Apples, Peaches, Pumpkin Pie			
(US) Smash	8 26 67	6	9
Keep the Ball Rollin'			
(US) Smash	12 2 67	14	4
JAYNETTS			
Sally Go Round the Roses			
(US) Tuff	9 14 63	2	7
JEFFERSON AIRPLANE			
Somebody to Love			
(US) RCA	5 27 67	5	6
White Rabbit			
(US) RCA	7 15 67	8	5
JOE JEFFREY GROUP			
My Pledge of Love			
(US) Wand	7 26 69	14	4
JELLY BEANS			
I Wanna Love Him So Bad			
(US) Red Bird	7 25 64	9	5
JENSEN, KRIS			
Torture			
(US) Hickory	11 3 62	20	1
JETHRO TULL			
Living in the Past			
(*UK*) *Island*	*6 14 69*	*3*	*6*
(US) Chrysalis (reissue)	12 16 72	11	6
Sweet Dream			
(*UK*) *Chrysalis*	*11 5 69*	*7*	*5*
Witches Promise/Teacher			
(*UK*) *Chrysalis*	*1 31 70*	*4*	*5*
Life Is a Long Song			
(*UK*) *Chrysalis*	*9 25 71*	*11*	*5*
JIMENEZ, JOSE			
Astronaut			
(US) Kapp	10 2 61	19	1
JIVE FIVE			
My True Story			
(US) Beltone	8 28 61	3	6

LABEL	DATE OF CHART ENTRY	HIGHEST POSITION REACHED	NUMBER OF WEEKS IN CHARTS
JOHN, ELTON			
Your Song			
(US) UNI	1 9 71	8	7
(UK) DJM	*2 6 71*	*7*	*6*
Rocket Man			
(UK) DJM	*5 6 72*	*2*	*8*
(US) UNI	6 17 72	6	8
Honky Cat			
(US) UNI	9 9 72	8	4
Crocodile Rock			
(UK) DJM	*11 11 72*	*5*	*10*
(US) MCA	12 30 72	1	12
Daniel			
(UK) DJM	*1 27 73*	*4*	*6*
(US) MCA	*5 5 73*	*2*	*9*
Saturday Night's All Right for Fighting			
(UK) DJM	*7 14 73*	*7*	*5*
(US) MCA	8 25 73	12	6
Goodbye Yellow Brick Road			
(UK) DJM	*10 6 73*	*6*	*7*
(US) MCA	11 17 73	2	7
JOHN, LITTLE WILLIE			
Talk to Me Talk to Me			
(US) King	5 26 58	20	1
Sleep			
(US) King	10 31 60	13	4
JOHN, ROBERT			
The Lion Sleeps Tonight			
(US) Atlantic	2 5 72	3	11
JOHNNIE AND JOE			
Over the Mountain			
(US) Chess	7 1 57	8	7
JOHNNY AND THE HURRICANES			
Red River Rock			
(US) Warwick	8 24 59	5	10
(UK) London	*10 10 59*	*2*	*14*
Reveille Rock			
(UK) London	*12 26 59*	*8*	*4*
Beatnik Fly			
(US) Warwick	3 7 60	15	5
(UK) London	*3 13 60*	*9*	*10*
Down Yonder			
(UK) London	*6 5 60*	*9*	*5*
Rocking Goose			
(UK) London	*10 14 60*	*3*	*10*
Ja Da			
(UK) London	*2 12 61*	*14*	*3*
Old Smokey			
(UK) London	*7 2 61*	*12*	*3*

LABEL	DATE OF CHART ENTRY	HIGHEST POSITION REACHED	NUMBER OF WEEKS IN CHARTS
JOHNSON, BETTY			
I Dreamed			
(US) Bally	2 9 57	12	5
Little Blue Man			
(US) Atlantic	3 31 58	19	2
JOHNSON, BRYAN			
Looking High High High			
(*UK*) *Decca*	4 3 60	17	1
JOHNSON, JOHNNY, AND THE BANDWAGON			
Sweet Inspiration			
(*UK*) *Bell*	8 22 70	10	5
Blame It on the Pony Express			
(*UK*) *Bell*	12 19 70	7	8
[see also: **BANDWAGON**]			
JOHNSON, LAURIE			
Sucu Sucu			
(*UK*) *Pye*	9 30 61	5	8
JOHNSON, MARV			
You've Got What It Takes			
(US) United Artists	1 11 60	10	8
(*UK*) *London*	2 6 60	4	10
I Love the Way You Love			
(US) United Artists	3 28 60	9	8
Move Two Mountains			
(US) United Artists	10 17 60	20	1
I'll Pick a Rose for My Rose			
(*UK*) *Tamla Motown*	2 8 69	10	6
JOHNSON, TEDDY (see **PEARL CARR**)			
JOHNSTON BROTHERS			
Hernando's Hideaway			
(*UK*) *Decca*	10 7 55	1	13
JO JO GUNNE			
Run Run Run			
(*UK*) *Asylum*	4 15 72	6	7
JON AND ROBIN AND THE IN CROWD			
Do It Again a Little Bit Slower			
(US) Abnak	6 17 67	18	2
JONES, JACK			
Wives and Lovers			
(US) Kapp	12 21 63	14	4
The Race Is On			
(US) Kapp	4 10 65	15	3
JONES, JIMMY			
Handy Man			
(US) Cub	1 25 60	2	12
(*UK*) *MGM*	3 13 60	4	18

ROCK ALMANAC

LABEL	DATE OF CHART ENTRY	HIGHEST POSITION REACHED	NUMBER OF WEEKS IN CHARTS
Good Timin'			
(US) Cub	5 9 60	3	9
(*UK*) *MGM*	6 12 60	1	10
JONES, JOE			
You Talk Too Much			
(US) Roulette	10 24 60	3	6
JONES, PAUL			
High Time			
(*UK*) *HMV*	10 29 66	4	8
I've Been a Bad Bad Boy			
(*UK*) *HMV*	1 28 67	5	6
JONES, TOM			
It's Not Unusual			
(*UK*) *Decca*	2 20 65	1	9
(US) Parrot	5 15 65	10	6
What's New Pussycat?			
(US) Parrot	7 10 65	3	8
(*UK*) *Decca*	8 28 65	11	5
With These Hands			
(*UK*) *Decca*	7 31 65	13	4
Not Responsible			
(*UK*) *Decca*	6 4 66	18	4
Green Green Grass of Home			
(*UK*) *Decca*	11 19 66	1	15
(US) Parrot	1 28 67	11	5
Detroit City			
(*UK*) *Decca*	3 4 67	8	6
Funny Familiar Forgotten Feelings			
(*UK*) *Decca*	4 29 67	7	7
I'll Never Fall in Love Again			
(*UK*) *Decca*	8 5 67	2	10
(US) Parrot (reissue)	8 23 69	6	11
I'm Coming Home			
(*UK*) *Decca*	12 2 67	2	12
Delilah			
(*UK*) *Decca*	3 9 68	2	12
(US) Parrot	6 8 68	15	2
Help Yourself			
(*UK*) *Decca*	7 27 68	3	10
A Minute of Your Time			
(*UK*) *Decca*	12 14 68	15	7
Love Me Tonight			
(*UK*) *Decca*	5 17 69	9	6
(US) Parrot	6 21 69	13	6
Without Love (There Is Nothing)			
(*UK*) *Decca*	12 20 69	10	6
(US) Parrot	1 10 70	5	7
Daughters of Darkness			

LABEL	DATE OF CHART ENTRY	HIGHEST POSITION REACHED	NUMBER OF WEEKS IN CHARTS
(*UK*) Decca	*4 25 70*	5	9
(US) Parrot	*5 23 70*	13	4
I (Who Have Nothing)			
(US) Parrot	*9 5 70*	14	5
(*UK*) Decca	*9 5 70*	*16*	*1*
She's a Lady			
(*UK*) Decca	*1 30 71*	13	5
(US) Parrot	*2 27 71*	2	10
Till			
(*UK*) Decca	*10 30 71*	2	10
Young New Mexican Puppeteer			
(*UK*) Decca	*4 8 72*	6	6

JOPLIN, JANIS
Me and Bobby McGee

(US) Columbia	*2 27 71*	1	10

[see also: **BIG BROTHER AND THE HOLDING COMPANY**]

JUDGE DREAD
Big Six

(*UK*) Big Shot	*9 23 72*	*11*	8
Big Seven			
(*UK*) Big Shot	*12 23 72*	8	7
Big Eight			
(*UK*) Big Shot	*4 28 73*	14	5

JUICY LUCY
Who Do You Love

(*UK*) Vertigo	*4 4 70*	14	4

JUNE, ROSEMARY
I'll Be with You in Apple Blossom Time

(*UK*) Pye	*2 7 59*	*12*	4

JUSTICE, JIMMY
When My Little Girl Is Smiling

(*UK*) Pye	*4 21 62*	9	7
Ain't That Funny			
(*UK*) Pye	*6 23 62*	8	7
Spanish Harlem			
(*UK*) Pye	*9 15 62*	20	*1*

JUSTIS, BILL
Raunchy

(US) Phillips International	*11 25 57*	3	11
(*UK*) London	*2 14 58*	*11*	4

KAEMPFERT, BERT
Wonderland by Night

(US) Decca	*11 28 60*	1	13
Red Roses for a Blue Lady			
(US) Decca	*2 27 65*	11	7

KALIN TWINS
When

LABEL	DATE OF CHART ENTRY	HIGHEST POSITION REACHED	NUMBER OF WEEKS IN CHARTS
(US) Decca	7 7 58	5	9
(UK) *Brunswick*	7 25 58	1	16
Forget Me Not			
(US) Decca	10 27 58	12	6

KALLEN, KITTY
My Coloring Book

(US) RCA	2 2 63	18	1

KANE, EDEN
Well I Ask You

(UK) *Decca*	5 28 61	1	16

Get Lost

(UK) *Decca*	9 16 61	7	5

Forget Me Not

(UK) *Decca*	1 27 62	4	10

I Don't Know Why

(UK) *Decca*	5 26 62	7	8

Boys Cry

(UK) *Fontana*	2 22 64	8	7

KASENATZ KATZ SINGING ORCHESTRAL CIRCUS
Quick Joey Small

(UK) *Buddah*	2 1 69	19	1

KAYE SISTERS
Paper Roses

(UK) *Philips*	7 31 60	10	8

[see also: **FRANKIE VAUGHAN; THREE KAYES**]

K-DOE, ERNIE
Mother-in-Law

(US) Minit	4 10 61	1	9

KEATING, JOHNNY
Theme from "Z Cars"

(UK) *Piccadilly*	3 10 62	8	10

KEITH
98.6

(US) Mercury	1 21 67	7	6

KELLER, JERRY
Here Comes Summer

(US) Kapp	8 3 59	14	3
(UK) *London*	8 29 59	2	12

KELLY, GRACE (see **BING CROSBY**)

KELLY, KEITH
Ooh! La La

(UK) *Parlophone*	4 17 60	13	6

Listen Little Girl/Uh Huh

(UK) *Parlophone*	7 31 60	15	4

KENDRICKS, EDDIE
Keep on Truckin'

(US) Tamla	9 22 73	1	13
(UK) *Tamla Motown*	12 15 73	18	1

LABEL	DATE OF CHART ENTRY	HIGHEST POSITION REACHED	NUMBER OF WEEKS IN CHARTS
KENNER, CHRIS			
I Like It Like That			
(US) Instant	7 10 61	2	8
KENNY			
Heart of Stone			
(UK) RAK　　　　．	3 17 73	11	6
KIDD, JOHNNY, AND THE PIRATES			
Shakin' All Over			
(UK) HMV	6 26 60	3	12
Restless			
(UK) HMV	10 7 60	18	2
I'll Never Get Over You			
(UK) HMV	8 10 63	4	10
Hungry for Love			
(UK) HMV	12 7 63	20	1
KIM, ANDY			
Baby, I Love You			
(US) Steed	7 12 69	9	8
Be My Baby			
(US) Steed	12 12 70	17	2
KING, B. B.			
The Thrill Is Gone			
(US) Blues Way	2 14 70	15	4
KING, BEN E.			
First Taste of Love*			
(UK) London	1 15 61	16	3
Spanish Harlem			
(US) Atco (b/w*)	2 27 61	10	5
Stand by Me			
(US) Atco	5 29 61	4	7
Amor			
(US) Atco	9 4 61	18	1
Don't Play That Song			
(US) Atco	6 2 62	11	4
[see also: **DRIFTERS**]			
KING, CAROLE			
It Might As Well Rain Until September			
(UK) London	10 6 62	3	9
It's Too Late			
(US) Ode (b/w I Feel the Earth Move)			
	6 5 71	1	12
(UK) A&M	8 28 71	6	6
So Far Away/Smackwater Jack			
(US) Ode	9 25 71	14	5
Sweet Seasons			
(US) Ode	2 12 72	9	6

LABEL	DATE OF CHART ENTRY	HIGHEST POSITION REACHED	NUMBER OF WEEKS IN CHARTS
KING, CLAUDE			
Wolverton Mountain			
(US) Columbia	6 23 62	6	10
KING, DAVE			
Memories Are Made of This			
(UK) Decca	*2 17 56*	*5*	*13*
You Can't Be True to Two			
(UK) Decca	*4 20 56*	*11*	*7*
Story of My Life			
(UK) Decca	*1 24 58*	*20*	*1*
KING, JONATHAN			
Everyone's Gone to the Moon			
(UK) Decca	*8 7 65*	*4*	*7*
(US) Parrot	10 30 65	17	3
[see also: **WEATHERMEN**]			
KING, SOLOMON			
She Wears My Ring			
(UK) Columbia	*1 20 68*	*3*	*11*
KING BROTHERS			
White Sports Coat			
(UK) Parlophone	*6 7 57*	*6*	*11*
In the Middle of an Island			
(UK) Parlophone	*9 20 57*	*19*	*3*
Standing on the Corner			
(UK) Parlophone	*4 17 60*	*9*	*5*
KING CURTIS			
Soul Twist			
(US) Enjoy	4 28 62	17	2
KING FLOYD			
Groove Me			
(US) Chimneyville	12 26 70	6	10
KING HARVEST			
Dancing in the Moonlight			
(US) Perception	1 27 73	13	7
KINGSMEN			
Louie Louie			
(US) Wand	12 7 63	2	10
Money			
(US) Wand	4 11 64	16	4
Jolly Green Giant			
(US) Wand	2 6 65	4	7
KINGSTON TRIO			
Tom Dooley			
(US) Capitol	10 13 58	1	5
(UK) Capitol	*11 21 58*	*4*	*12*
Tijuana Jail			
(US) Capitol	4 6 59	12	5

LABEL	DATE OF CHART ENTRY	HIGHEST POSITION REACHED	NUMBER OF WEEKS IN CHARTS
MTA			
(US) Capitol	7 6 59	15	4
Worried Man			
(US) Capitol	10 19 59	20	1
Reverend Mr. Black			
(US) Capitol	4 27 63	8	6
KINKS			
You Really Got Me			
(UK) Pye	*8 22 64*	*1*	*9*
(US) Reprise	11 7 64	7	8
All Day and All of the Night			
(UK) Pye	*11 7 64*	*2*	*9*
(US) Reprise	1 23 65	7	6
Tired of Waiting for You			
(UK) Pye	*1 30 65*	*1*	*7*
(US) Reprise	4 3 65	6	6
Everybody's Gonna Be Happy			
(UK) Pye	*4 10 65*	*11*	*3*
Set Me Free			
(UK) Pye	*6 12 65*	*9*	*6*
See My Friend			
(UK) Pye	*8 21 65*	*10*	*4*
Till the End of the Day			
(UK) Pye	*12 25 65*	*8*	*8*
Well Respected Man			
(US) Reprise	1 29 66	13	5
Dedicated Follower of Fashion			
(UK) Pye	*3 12 66*	*4*	*8*
Sunny Afternoon			
(UK) Pye	*6 18 66*	*1*	*9*
(US) Reprise	9 10 66	14	4
Dead End Street			
(UK) Pye	*12 3 66*	*5*	*9*
Waterloo Sunset			
(UK) Pye	*5 20 67*	*2*	*7*
Autumn Almanac			
(UK) Pye	*10 28 67*	*3*	*7*
Days			
(UK) Pye	*8 3 68*	*12*	*6*
Lola			
(UK) Pye	*7 11 70*	*2*	*10*
(US) Reprise	10 10 70	9	6
Apeman			
(UK) Pye	*1 2 71*	*5*	*9*
Supersonic Rocketship			
(UK) RCA	*6 17 72*	*16*	*3*
KIRBY, KATHY			
Dance On			
(UK) Decca	*8 31 63*	*11*	*5*

LABEL	DATE OF CHART ENTRY	HIGHEST POSITION REACHED	NUMBER OF WEEKS IN CHARTS
Secret Love			
(UK) Decca	11 16 63	4	11
Let Me Go Lover			
(UK) Decca	3 7 64	10	6
You're the One			
(UK) Decca	5 30 64	17	2
KISSON, MAC AND KATIE			
Chirpy Chirpy Cheep Cheep			
(US) ABC	10 2 71	20	2
KITT, EARTHA			
Under the Bridges of Paris			
(UK) HMV	4 4 55	7	9
KNICKERBOCKERS			
Lies			
(US) Challenge	1 22 66	20	1
KNIGHT, GLADYS, AND THE PIPS			
Letter Full of Tears			
(US) Fury	2 10 62	19	1
Take Me in Your Arms and Love Me			
(UK) Tamla Motown	7 22 67	13	3
I Heard It Through the Grapevine			
(US) Soul	11 25 67	2	11
End of Our Road			
(US) Soul	3 9 68	15	4
Nitty Gritty			
(US) Soul	9 13 69	19	1
Friendship Train			
(US) Soul	12 13 69	17	3
If I Were Your Woman			
(US) Soul	1 9 71	9	7
I Don't Want to Do Wrong			
(US) Soul	7 3 71	17	5
Help Me Make It Through the Night			
(UK) Tamla Motown	12 9 72	11	8
Neither of Us (Wants to Say Goodbye)			
(US) Soul	3 3 73	2	9
Daddy Could Swear I Declare			
(US) Soul	7 7 73	19	1
Midnight Train to Georgia			
(US) Buddah	9 29 73	1	12
I've Got to Use My Imagination			
(US) Buddah	12 22 73	14	2
KNIGHT, JEAN			
Mr. Big Stuff			
(US) Stax	6 26 71	2	11
KNIGHT, ROBERT			
Everlasting Love			
(US) Rising Sons	11 11 67	13	4

LABEL	DATE OF CHART ENTRY	HIGHEST POSITION REACHED	NUMBER OF WEEKS IN CHARTS
Love on a Mountain Top			
(*UK*) *Monument*	*12 15 73*	*10*	*9*
KNIGHT, SONNY			
Confidential			
(US) Dot	12 15 56	20	2
KNOX, BUDDY			
Party Doll			
(US) Roulette	3 9 57	2	13
Hula Love			
(US) Roulette	9 30 57	12	8
KOKOMO			
Asia Minor			
(US) Felsted	3 27 61	8	5
KONGOS, JOHN			
He's Gonna Step on You Again			
(*UK*) *Fly*	*6 12 71*	*4*	*8*
Tokoloshe Man			
(*UK*) *Fly*	*11 27 71*	*4*	*7*
KRAMER, BILLY J., AND THE DAKOTAS			
Do You Want to Know a Secret?			
(*UK*) *Parlophone*	*5 11 63*	*2*	*12*
Bad to Me			
(*UK*) *Parlophone*	*8 10 63*	*1*	*9*
(US) Imperial (b/w*)	6 20 64	9	5
I'll Keep You Satisfied			
(*UK*) *Parlophone*	*11 16 63*	*4*	*6*
Little Children*			
(*UK*) *Parlophone*	*3 7 64*	*1*	*9*
(US) Imperial	5 16 64	7	9
From a Window			
(*UK*) *Parlophone*	*8 8 64*	*10*	*4*
Trains Boats and Planes			
(*UK*) *Parlophone*	*5 29 65*	*12*	*4*
KRISTOFFERSON, KRIS			
Why Me			
(US) Monument	11 3 73	16	3
KUBAN, BOB, AND THE IN-MEN			
Cheater			
(US) Musicland USA	2 26 66	12	4
KUNZ, CHARLIE			
Piano Medley			
(*UK*) *Decca*	*1 14 55*	*16*	*1*
LAINE, CLEO			
You'll Answer to Me			
(*UK*) *Fontana*	*9 16 61*	*4*	*9*
LAINE, FRANKIE			
Rain Rain Rain			
(*UK*) *Philips*	*1 7 55*	*8*	*5*

LABEL	DATE OF CHART ENTRY	HIGHEST POSITION REACHED	NUMBER OF WEEKS IN CHARTS
In the Beginning			
(UK) Philips	3 11 55	20	1
Cool Water			
(UK) Philips	6 24 55	2	22
Strange Lady in Town			
(UK) Philips	7 15 55	6	13
Humming Bird			
(UK) Philips	11 11 55	16	1
Hawkeye			
(UK) Philips	11 25 55	7	8
Sixteen Tons			
(UK) Philips	1 20 56	10	3
Woman In Love			
(UK) Philips	9 14 56	1	19
Moonlight Gambler			
(UK) Philips	12 28 56	13	9
(US) Columbia	12 29 56	3	13
Love Is a Golden Ring			
(UK) Philips	5 10 57	19	2
Rawhide			
(UK) Philips	11 14 59	11	11
LANG, DON			
Cloudburst			
(UK) HMV	11 4 55	16	4
Witch Doctor			
(UK) HMV	5 23 58	5	10
LANSON, SNOOKY			
It's Almost Tomorrow			
(US) Dot	12 17 55	20	1
LANZA, MARIO			
Drinking Song			
(UK) HMV	2 4 55	13	1
I'll Walk with God			
(UK) HMV	2 18 55	18	1
Serenade			
(UK) HMV	4 22 55	15	3
I'll Walk with God (re-entry)			
(UK) HMV	5 6 55	20	1
LARKS			
The Jerk			
(US) Money	12 19 64	7	7
LA ROSA, JULIUS			
Domani			
(US) Cadence	7 30 55	13	4
Torero			
(UK) RCA	8 1 58	15	3
LA SALLE, DENISE			
Trapped by a Thing Called Love			
(US) Westbound	10 9 71	13	5

LABEL	DATE OF CHART ENTRY	HIGHEST POSITION REACHED	NUMBER OF WEEKS IN CHARTS
LAWRENCE, LEE			
Suddenly There's a Valley			
(*UK*) *Columbia*	*12 2 55*	*14*	*3*
LAWRENCE, STEVE			
Party Doll			
(US) Coral	3 16 57	10	11
Pretty Blue Eyes			
(US) ABC-Paramount	12 14 59	9	11
Footsteps			
(US) ABC-Paramount	4 4 60	7	6
(*UK*) *HMV*	*4 10 60*	*9*	*9*
Portrait of My Love			
(US) United Artists	4 24 61	9	6
Go Away Little Girl			
(US) Columbia	12 8 62	1	12
I Want to Stay Here (with **EYDIE GORME**)			
(*UK*) *CBS*	*8 31 63*	*3*	*8*
LAWRENCE, VICKI			
The Night the Lights Went Out in Georgia			
(US) Bell	3 24 73	1	10
LEANDROS, VICKY			
Come What May			
(*UK*) *Philips*	*4 22 72*	*2*	*8*
LED ZEPPELIN			
Whole Lotta Love			
(US) Atlantic	12 20 69	4	9
Immigrant Song			
(US) Atlantic	1 16 71	16	3
Black Dog			
(US) Atlantic	2 12 72	15	2
D'Yer Mak'Er			
(US) Atlantic	12 29 73	20	1
LEE, BRENDA			
Sweet Nothin's			
(US) Decca	2 29 60	4	11
(*UK*) *Brunswick*	*4 3 60*	*5*	*14*
I'm Sorry			
(US) Decca	6 20 60	1	13
(*UK*) *Brunswick (b/w*)*	*7 3 60*	*10*	*10*
That's All You Gotta Do*			
(US) Decca	6 27 60	6	6
I Want to Be Wanted			
(US) Decca	10 3 60	1	9
Rockin' Around the Christmas Tree			
(US) Decca	12 26 60	14	2
(*UK*) *Brunswick*	*12 8 62*	*5*	*5*
Emotions			
(US) Decca	1 23 61	7	6

LABEL	DATE OF CHART ENTRY	HIGHEST POSITION REACHED	NUMBER OF WEEKS IN CHARTS
Let's Jump the Broomstick			
(UK) Brunswick	2 12 61	15	3
You Can Depend on Me			
(US) Decca	4 10 61	6	7
Dum, Dum			
(US) Decca	7 3 61	4	9
Fool #1			
(US) Decca	10 30 61	3	8
(UK) Brunswick	11 18 61	18	2
Break It to Me Gently			
(US) Decca	1 27 62	4	9
Speak to Me Pretty			
(UK) Brunswick	4 21 62	3	8
Everybody Loves Me but You			
(US) Decca (b/w**)	5 5 62	6	6
Here Comes That Feeling**			
(UK) Brunswick	7 7 62	5	8
Heart in Hand			
(US) Decca (b/w***)	8 11 62	15	3
It Started All Over Again***			
(UK) Brunswick	10 6 62	15	5
All Alone Am I			
(US) Decca	10 20 62	3	9
(UK) Brunswick	1 27 63	7	8
Losing You			
(UK) Brunswick	4 20 63	10	8
(US) Decca	5 4 63	6	7
I Wonder			
(UK) Brunswick	7 27 63	14	5
Grass Is Greener			
(US) Decca	11 2 63	17	2
As Usual			
(US) Decca	12 28 63	12	6
(UK) Brunswick	1 18 64	5	10
Is It True?			
(UK) Brunswick	9 26 64	17	3
(US) Decca	11 14 64	17	3
Too Many Rivers			
(US) Decca	7 17 65	13	3
Coming On Strong			
(US) Decca	11 12 66	11	5
LEE, CURTIS			
Pretty Little Angel Eyes			
(US) Dunes	7 31 61	7	5
LEE, DICKEY			
Patches			
(US) Smash	9 8 62	6	9
I Saw Him Yesterday			
(US) Smash	1 12 63	14	5

LABEL	DATE OF CHART ENTRY	HIGHEST POSITION REACHED	NUMBER OF WEEKS IN CHARTS
Laurie			
(US) TCF-Hall	7 3 65	14	3
LEE, JACKIE			
The Duck			
(US) Mirwood	1 8 66	14	5
LEE, JACKIE			
Rupert			
(UK) Pye	*2 13 71*	*14*	*5*
[see also: **JACKY**]			
LEE, LEAPY			
Little Arrows			
(UK) MCA	*9 7 68*	*2*	*13*
(US) Decca	11 30 68	16	2
LEE, PEGGY			
Mr. Wonderful			
(UK) Brunswick	*5 24 57*	*5*	*13*
Fever			
(US) Capitol	7 28 58	8	7
(UK) Capitol	*8 22 58*	*5*	*8*
Is That All There Is?			
(US) Capitol	10 18 69	11	5
LEEDS UNITED FC			
Leeds United			
(UK) Chapter One	*5 13 72*	*10*	*5*
LEFT BANK			
Walk Away Renee			
(US) Smash	10 8 66	5	7
Pretty Ballerina			
(US) Smash	2 18 67	15	3
LEMON PIPERS			
Green Tambourine			
(US) Buddah	1 6 68	1	9
(UK) Pye International	*2 24 68*	*7*	*6*
LENNON, JOHN (*and the PLASTIC ONO BAND)			
Give Peace a Chance*			
(UK) Apple	*7 19 69*	*2*	*7*
(US) Apple	8 16 69	14	4
Cold Turkey*			
(UK) Apple	*11 5 69*	*14*	*5*
Instant Karma			
(UK) Apple	*2 21 70*	*5*	*6*
(US) Apple	3 14 70	3	10
Power to the People*			
(UK) Apple	*3 20 71*	*7*	*6*
(US) Apple	4 24 71	11	4
Imagine*			
(US) Apple	10 30 71	3	7

LABEL	DATE OF CHART ENTRY	HIGHEST POSITION REACHED	NUMBER OF WEEKS IN CHARTS
Happy Christmas (War Is Over)*			
(with the **HARLEM COMMUNITY CHOIR**)			
(UK) *Apple*	12 16 72	4	5
Mind Games			
(US) Apple	12 15 73	18	3
LENNON SISTERS			
Tonight You Belong to Me			
(US) Coral	10 20 56	15	4
LESTER, KETTY			
Love Letters			
(US) Era	3 24 62	5	7
(UK) *London*	5 5 62	4	7
LETTERMEN			
The Way You Look Tonight			
(US) Capitol	10 2 61	13	6
When I Fall in Love			
(US) Capitol	12 18 61	7	8
Come Back Silly Girl			
(US) Capitol	3 31 62	17	2
Theme from "Summer Place"			
(US) Capitol	7 31 65	16	2
Goin' out of My Head/Can't Take My Eyes Off You			
(US) Capitol	1 27 68	7	6
Hurt So Bad			
(US) Capitol	8 30 69	12	6
LEWIS, BARBARA			
Hello Stranger			
(US) Atlantic	6 8 63	3	7
Baby I'm Yours			
(US) Atlantic	8 7 65	11	5
Make Me Your Baby			
(US) Atlantic	10 23 65	11	4
LEWIS, BOBBY			
Tossin' and Turnin'			
(US) Beltone	6 12 61	1	15
One Track Mind			
(US) Beltone	9 18 61	9	3
LEWIS, GARY, AND THE PLAYBOYS			
This Diamond Ring			
(US) Liberty	1 30 65	1	9
Count Me In			
(US) Liberty	4 24 65	2	7
Save Your Heart for Me			
(US) Liberty	7 24 65	2	7
Everybody Loves a Clown			
(US) Liberty	10 16 65	4	6
She's Just My Style			
(US) Liberty	1 1 65	3	7

LABEL	DATE OF CHART ENTRY	HIGHEST POSITION REACHED	NUMBER OF WEEKS IN CHARTS
Sure Gonna Miss Her			
(US) Liberty	3 26 66	9	4
Green Grass			
(US) Liberty	5 28 66	8	5
My Heart's a Symphony			
(US) Liberty	8 13 66	13	4
(You Don't Have to) Paint Me a Picture			
(US) Liberty	10 29 66	15	2
Sealed with a Kiss			
(US) Liberty	8 17 68	19	3
LEWIS, JERRY			
Rock-a-Bye Your Baby to a Dixie Melody			
(US) Decca	12 22 56	12	9
(UK) Brunswick	2 8 57	12	5
LEWIS, JERRY LEE			
Whole Lotta Shakin' Goin' On			
(US) Sun	8 19 57	3	13
(UK) London	10 4 57	8	7
Great Balls of Fire			
(US) Sun	12 9 57	2	11
(UK) London	12 20 57	1	11
Breathless			
(US) Sun	3 17 58	7	6
(UK) London	4 18 58	8	5
High School Confidential			
(UK) London	1 24 59	10	5
Lovin' Up a Storm			
(UK) London	5 2 59	20	1
What'd I Say			
(UK) London	4 30 61	8	7
LEWIS, LINDA			
Rock a Doodle			
(UK) Raft	7 7 73	15	3
LEWIS, RAMSEY TRIO			
"In" Crowd			
(US) Argo	9 4 65	5	8
Hang On Sloopy			
(US) Cadet	12 11 65	11	4
Wade in the Water			
(US) Cadet	9 10 66	19	2
LEYTON, JOHN			
Johnny Remember Me			
(UK) Top Rank	7 29 61	1	12
Wild Wind			
(UK) Top Rank	9 30 61	2	7
Son This Is She			
(UK) HMV	12 9 61	12	4
Lonely City			
(UK) HMV	5 26 62	14	5

LABEL	DATE OF CHART ENTRY	HIGHEST POSITION REACHED	NUMBER OF WEEKS IN CHARTS
LIBERACE			
Unchained Melody			
(UK) Philips	6 17 55	20	1
LIEUTENANT PIGEON			
Mouldy Old Dough			
(UK) Decca	9 23 72	1	11
Desperate Dan			
(UK) Decca	1 13 73	17	3
LIGHTFOOT, GORDON			
If You Could Read My Mind			
(US) Reprise	2 6 71	5	8
LIMMIE AND THE FAMILY COOKING			
You Can Do Magic			
(UK) Avco	8 4 73	3	7
LIND, BOB			
Elusive Butterfly			
(US) World Pacific	2 19 66	5	7
(UK) Fontana	3 26 66	5	5
LINDEN, KATHY			
Billy			
(US) Felsted	4 21 58	12	4
Goodbye Jimmy Goodbye			
(US) Felsted	5 25 59	11	4
LINDISFARNE			
Meet Me on the Corner			
(UK) Charisma	3 11 72	5	6
Lady Eleanor			
(UK) Charisma	5 20 72	3	6
LINDSAY, MARK			
Arizona			
(US) Columbia	1 24 70	10	7
[see also: **PAUL REVERE AND THE RAIDERS**]			
LITTLE ANTHONY AND THE IMPERIALS			
Tears on My Pillow			
(US) End	9 8 58	4	10
I'm on the Outside (Looking In)			
(US) DCP	10 3 64	15	2
Goin' out of My Head			
(US) DCP	12 5 64	6	9
Hurt So Bad			
(US) DCP	2 27 65	10	5
Take Me Back			
(US) DCP	8 17 65	16	3
LITTLE CAESAR AND THE ROMANS			
Those Oldies but Goodies			
(US) Del Fi	6 12 61	9	6
LITTLE DIPPERS			
Forever			
(US) University	2 22 60	9	6

LABEL	DATE OF CHART ENTRY	HIGHEST POSITION REACHED	NUMBER OF WEEKS IN CHARTS
LITTLE EVA			
The Locomotion			
(US) Dimension	7 28 62	1	10
(*UK*) *London*	*9 22 62*	*2*	*12*
(*UK*) *London* (*reissue*)	*8 19 72*	*11*	*5*
Keep Your Hands Off			
(US) Dimension	12 1 62	12	6
Let's Turkey Trot			
(US) Dimension	3 23 63	20	1
(*UK*) *London*	*3 30 63*	*13*	*5*
[see also: **BIG DEE IRWIN**]			
LITTLE PEGGY MARCH			
I Will Follow Him			
(US) RCA	4 13 63	1	9
LITTLE RICHARD			
Long Tall Sally			
(US) Specialty	4 21 56	13	7
(*UK*) *London*	*2 15 57*	*3*	*14*
The Girl Can't Help It			
(*UK*) *London* (*b/w**)	*3 15 57*	*9*	*10*
She's Got It*			
(*UK*) *London*	*3 22 57*	*15*	*4*
Jenny Jenny			
(US) Specialty	7 1 57	14	8
(*UK*) *London*	*9 13 57*	*11*	*5*
Lucille			
(*UK*) *London*	*7 5 57*	*10*	*7*
Keep a'Knockin'			
(US) Specialty	10 14 57	8	7
Good Golly Miss Molly			
(*UK*) *London*	*3 7 58*	*8*	*7*
(US) Specialty	3 10 58	10	3
Baby Face			
(*UK*) *London*	*1 10 59*	*2*	*11*
By the Light of the Silvery Moon			
(*UK*) *London*	*4 4 59*	*15*	*3*
Bamalama Loo			
(*UK*) *London*	*6 27 64*	*20*	*1*
LITTLE TONY			
Too Good			
(*UK*) *Decca*	*1 2 60*	*13*	*4*
LIVINGSTONE, DANDY			
Suzanne Beware of the Devil			
(*UK*) *Horse*	*9 23 72*	*14*	*5*
LOBO			
Me and You and a Dog Named Boo			
(US) Big Tree	5 1 71	5	8
(*UK*) *Philips*	*7 3 71*	*4*	*9*

LABEL	DATE OF CHART ENTRY	HIGHEST POSITION REACHED	NUMBER OF WEEKS IN CHARTS
I'd Love You to Want Me			
(US) Big Tree	10 28 72	2	7
Don't Expect Me to Be Your Friend			
(US) Big Tree	1 27 73	8	7
LOCKLIN, HANK			
Please Help Me I'm Falling			
(US) RCA	7 4 60	8	10
(UK) RCA	*9 4 60*	*10*	*10*
LOGGINS AND MESSINA			
Your Mama Don't Dance			
(US) Columbia	12 23 72	4	8
Thinking of You			
(US) Columbia	5 19 73	18	3
My Music			
(US) Columbia	12 8 73	16	3
LOLITA			
Sailor (Your Home Is in the Sea)			
(US) Kapp	11 28 60	5	10
LONDON, JULIE			
Cry Me a River			
(US) Liberty	12 10 55	13	8
LONDON, LAURIE			
He's Got the Whole World in His Hands			
(UK) Parlophone	*11 29 57*	*12*	*8*
(US) Capitol	3 31 58	2	13
LONG, SHORTY			
Here Comes the Judge			
(US) Soul	6 15 68	8	7
LOOKING GLASS			
Brandy (You're a Fine Girl)			
(US) Epic	7 8 72	1	11
LOPEZ, TRINI			
If I Had a Hammer			
(US) Reprise	8 17 63	3	8
(UK) Reprise	*9 21 63*	*4*	*11*
Lemon Tree			
(US) Reprise	2 20 65	20	2
LORDAN, JERRY			
Who Could Be Bluer?			
(UK) Parlophone	*2 20 60*	*14*	*6*
LOREN, SOPHIA (see **PETER SELLERS**)			
LOS BRAVOS			
Black Is Black			
(UK) Decca	*7 16 66*	*2*	*9*
(US) Press	9 17 66	4	6
I Don't Care			
(UK) Decca	*10 8 66*	*16*	*3*

LABEL	DATE OF CHART ENTRY	HIGHEST POSITION REACHED	NUMBER OF WEEKS IN CHARTS
LOS INDIOS TABAJERAS			
Maria Elena			
(US) RCA	10 26 63	6	6
(UK) RCA	*11 16 63*	*5*	*11*
LOS MACHUCAMBOS			
Pepito			
(UK) Decca	*8 26 61*	*19*	*2*
LOSS, JOE			
Theme from "Maigret"			
(UK) HMV	*4 21 62*	*20*	*1*
Must Be Madison			
(UK) HMV	*11 17 62*	*20*	*2*
LOUDERMILK, JOHN D.			
The Language of Love			
(UK) RCA	*1 20 62*	*13*	*3*
LOVE AFFAIR			
Everlasting Love			
(UK) CBS	*1 13 68*	*1*	*10*
Rainbow Valley			
(UK) CBS	*5 11 68*	*5*	*8*
A Day Without Love			
(UK) CBS	*10 5 68*	*6*	*7*
One Road			
(UK) CBS	*3 15 69*	*16*	*3*
Bringing On Back the Good Times			
(UK) CBS	*8 2 69*	*9*	*5*
LOVE SCULPTURE			
Sabre Dance			
(UK) Parlophone	*12 14 68*	*6*	*8*
LOVE UNLIMITED			
Walking in the Rain with the One I Love			
(US) UNI	5 27 72	14	4
(UK) UNI	*7 8 72*	*14*	*4*
LOVIN' SPOONFUL			
Do You Believe in Magic			
(US) Kama Sutra	9 25 65	9	5
You Didn't Have to Be So Nice			
(US) Kama Sutra	1 8 66	10	4
Daydream			
(US) Kama Sutra	3 19 66	2	8
(UK) Pye	*4 23 66*	*2*	*8*
Did You Ever Have to Make Up Your Mind			
(US) Kama Sutra	5 21 66	2	7
Summer in the City			
(US) Kama Sutra	7 30 66	1	8
(UK) Kama Sutra	*7 30 66*	*8*	*7*
Rain on the Roof			
(US) Kama Sutra	11 5 66	10	5

LABEL	DATE OF CHART ENTRY	HIGHEST POSITION REACHED	NUMBER OF WEEKS IN CHARTS
Nashville Cats			
(US) Kama Sutra	1 14 67	8	4
Darlin' Be Home Soon			
(US) Kama Sutra	3 11 67	15	2
Six o'Clock			
(US) Kama Sutra	6 3 67	18	2
LOWE, JIM			
Green Door			
(US) Dot	10 6 56	1	20
Four Walls			
(US) Dot	2 9 57	20	1
LUKE, ROBIN			
Susie Darlin			
(US) Dot	9 15 58	5	9
LULU			
Shout (with the **LUVVERS)**			
(*UK*) *Decca*	6 6 64	7	7
Leave a Little Love			
(*UK*) *Decca*	7 3 65	8	5
The Boat That I Row			
(*UK*) *Columbia*	4 29 67	6	6
Let's Pretend			
(*UK*) *Columbia*	7 29 67	11	4
To Sir with Love			
(US) Epic	10 7 67	1	11
Me, the Peaceful Heart			
(*UK*) *Columbia*	3 9 68	9	5
Boys			
(*UK*) *Columbia*	6 29 68	15	2
I'm a Tiger			
(*UK*) *Columbia*	11 23 68	11	10
Boom Bang-a-Bang			
(*UK*) *Columbia*	3 29 69	4	7
LUMAN, BOB			
Let's Think About Livin'			
(*UK*) *Warner Brothers*	9 23 60	7	9
(US) Warner Brothers	10 3 60	7	7
LUNDBERG, VICTOR			
Open Letter to My Teenage Son			
(US) Liberty	11 25 67	10	3
LYMAN, ARTHUR			
Yellow Bird			
(US) Hi Fi	6 19 61	4	7
LYMON, FRANKIE, AND THE TEENAGERS			
Why Do Fools Fall in Love?			
(US) Gee	3 3 56	7	13
(*UK*) *Columbia*	7 6 56	*1*	*14*
I Want You to Be My Girl			
(US) Gee	6 9 56	17	1

LABEL	DATE OF CHART ENTRY	HIGHEST POSITION REACHED	NUMBER OF WEEKS IN CHARTS
Baby Baby			
(UK) Columbia	4 12 57	4	9
I'm Not a Juvenile Delinquent			
(UK) Columbia	4 12 57	12	4
LYNCH, KENNY			
Up on the Roof			
(UK) HMV	1 6 63	10	6
You Can Never Stop Me Loving You			
(UK) HMV	7 13 63	10	7
LYNN, BARBARA			
You'll Lose a Good Thing			
(US) Jamie	7 28 62	8	5
LYNN, TAMMI			
I'm Gonna Run Away from You			
(UK) Mojo (reissue)	6 5 71	4	8
LYNN, VERA			
My Son, My Son			
(UK) Decca	1 7 55	14	2
House with Love in It			
(UK) Decca	11 30 56	17	6
Travellin' Home			
(UK) Decca	7 5 57	20	1
LYON, BARBARA			
Stowaway			
(UK) Columbia	6 24 55	12	8
LYTTLETON, HUMPHREY			
Bad Penny Blues			
(UK) Parlophone	7 13 56	19	2
MACK, LONNIE			
Memphis			
(US) Fraternity	6 29 63	5	8
MACKENZIE, GIZELLE			
Hard to Get			
(US) X	6 25 55	5	15
MACKINTOSH, KEN			
Raunchy			
(UK) HMV	2 14 58	19	2
MACRAE, GORDON			
The Secret			
(US) Capitol	10 20 58	18	1
MACRAE, JOSH			
Talkin' Army Blues			
(UK) Rank	6 19 60	12	13
Wild Side of Life			
(UK) Rank	11 20 60	13	6
Messing About on the River			
(UK) Rank	1 22 61	15	3

LABEL	DATE OF CHART ENTRY	HIGHEST POSITION REACHED	NUMBER OF WEEKS IN CHARTS
MADDOX, JOHNNY			
Crazy Otto Medley			
(US) Dot	2 12 55	2	16
MAESTRO, JOHNNY			
Model Girl			
(US) Coed	3 27 61	20	2
[see also: **CRESTS; BROOKLYN BRIDGE**]			
MAIN INGREDIENT			
Everybody Plays the Fool			
(US) RCA	9 16 72	3	8
MAJOR LANCE			
Monkey Time			
(US) Okeh	8 24 63	8	6
Hey Little Girl			
(US) Okeh	11 16 63	13	4
Um Um Um Um Um Um			
(US) Okeh	1 18 64	5	8
Matador			
(US) Okeh	5 2 64	20	2
MAKEBA, MIRIAM			
Pata Pata			
(US) Reprise	11 18 67	12	4
MALO			
Suavecitio			
(US) Warner Brothers	4 29 72	18	2
MALTBY, RICHARD			
Man with the Golden Arm			
(US) Vik	4 28 56	14	3
MAMAS AND PAPAS			
California Dreamin'			
(US) Dunhill	2 19 66	4	10
Monday Monday			
(US) Dunhill	4 23 66	1	8
(UK) RCA	*5 21 66*	*3*	*10*
I Saw Her Again			
(US) Dunhill	7 9 66	5	6
(UK) RCA	*8 13 66*	*11*	*6*
Words of Love			
(US) Dunhill	12 31 66	5	7
Dedicated to the One I Love			
(US) Dunhill	3 11 67	2	8
(UK) RCA	*4 22 67*	*2*	*10*
Creeque Alley			
(US) Dunhill	5 20 67	5	4
(UK) RCA	*8 5 67*	*9*	*6*
Twelve Thirty			
(US) Dunhill	9 16 67	20	2

LABEL	DATE OF CHART ENTRY	HIGHEST POSITION REACHED	NUMBER OF WEEKS IN CHARTS
MANCINI, HENRY			
Moon River			
(US) RCA	12 11 61	11	4
How Soon			
(UK) RCA	10 17 64	10	4
Love Theme from "Romeo and Juliet"			
(US) RCA	5 24 69	1	11
Love Story			
(US) RCA	2 20 71	13	5
MANN, BARRY			
Who Put the Bomp in the Bomp Bomp Bomp			
(US) ABC-Paramount	9 4 61	7	5
MANN, JOHNNY, SINGERS			
Up, Up and Away			
(UK) Liberty	7 29 67	6	7
MANN, MANFRED			
5–4–3–2–1			
(UK) HMV	2 1 64	5	7
Hubble Toil and Trouble			
(UK) HMV	4 25 64	11	4
Do Wah Diddy Diddy			
(UK) HMV	7 25 64	1	10
(US) Ascot	9 19 64	1	10
Sha La La			
(UK) HMV	10 24 64	3	7
(US) Ascot	12 5 64	12	7
Come Tomorrow			
(UK) HMV	1 23 65	4	7
Oh No, Not My Baby			
(UK) HMV	5 1 65	11	5
If You Gotta Go, Go Now			
(UK) HMV	9 23 65	2	8
Pretty Flamingo			
(UK) HMV	4 30 66	1	7
Just Like a Woman			
(UK) Fontana	8 20 66	7	6
Semi-detached Suburban Mr. Jones			
(UK) Fontana	11 5 66	2	8
Ha! Ha! Said the Clown			
(UK) Fontana	4 8 67	4	7
The Mighty Quinn			
(UK) Fontana	2 3 68	1	8
(US) Mercury	3 23 68	10	5
My Name Is Jack			
(UK) Fontana	6 29 68	8	5
Fox on the Run			
(UK) Fontana	1 18 69	5	6
Ragamuffin Man			
(UK) Fontana	5 17 69	8	6

LABEL	DATE OF CHART ENTRY	HIGHEST POSITION REACHED	NUMBER OF WEEKS IN CHARTS
Joybringer			
(*UK*) *Vertigo*	8 22 73	9	5
MANTOVANI			
Lonely Ballerina			
(*UK*) *Decca*	2 11 55	16	4
Around the World			
(*UK*) *Decca*	6 7 57	20	1
Exodus			
(*UK*) *Decca*	3 26 61	20	1
MARATHONS			
Peanut Butter			
(US) Arvee	6 19 61	20	1
MARBLES			
Only One Woman			
(*UK*) *Polydor*	10 19 68	5	8
MARCELS			
Blue Moon			
(*UK*) *Pye International*	3 26 61	1	10
(US) Colpix	3 27 61	1	9
Heartaches			
(US) Colpix	11 13 61	7	4
MARDI GRAS			
Too Busy Thinkin' 'Bout My Baby			
(*UK*) *Bell*	9 16 72	19	1
MARESCA, ERNIE			
Shout Shout (Knock Yourself Out)			
(US) Seville	5 5 62	6	6
MARINI, MARINO			
Volare			
(*UK*) *Durium*	10 10 58	13	5
Come Prima			
(*UK*) *Durium*	10 10 58	2	17
MARKETTS			
Out of Limits			
(US) Warner Brothers	1 11 64	3	7
Batman Theme			
(US) Warner Brothers	3 5 66	17	3
[see also: **ROUTERS**]			
MAR-KEYS			
Last Night			
(US) Satellite	7 24 61	3	7
MARKHAM, PIGMEAT			
Here Comes the Judge			
(US) Chess	7 27 68	19	1
(*UK*) *Chess*	8 3 68	19	3
MARMALADE			
Lovin' Things			
(*UK*) *CBS*	6 15 68	6	6

LABEL	DATE OF CHART ENTRY	HIGHEST POSITION REACHED	NUMBER OF WEEKS IN CHARTS
Ob-la-di Ob-la-da			
(UK) CBS	12 21 68	1	10
Baby Make It Soon			
(UK) CBS	7 5 69	9	7
Reflections of My Life			
(UK) Deram	1 10 70	3	7
(US) London	4 18 70	10	8
Rainbow			
(UK) Decca	8 1 70	3	8
My Little One			
(UK) Decca	5 1 71	15	3
Cousin Norman			
(UK) Decca	9 11 71	6	7
Radancer			
(UK) Decca	4 22 72	6	6

MARTHA AND THE VANDELLAS [*MARTHA REEVES AND THE VANDELLAS]

Heat Wave			
(US) Gordy	8 24 63	4	9
Quicksand			
(US) Gordy	12 21 63	8	4
Dancing in the Street			
(US) Gordy	9 19 64	2	8
(UK) Tamla Motown (reissue)	2 1 69	4	7
Nowhere to Run			
(US) Gordy	3 27 65	8	5
I'm Ready for Love			
(US) Gordy	11 26 66	9	4
Jimmy Mack			
(US) Gordy	4 1 67	10	7
Honey Chile			
(US) Gordy	12 16 67	11	6
Forget Me Not*			
(UK) Tamla Motown	2 27 71	11	3

MARTIN, BOBBI

Don't Forget I Still Love You			
(US) Coral	1 16 65	19	1
For the Love of Him			
(US) United Artists	4 25 70	13	3

MARTIN, DEAN

Naughty Lady of Shady Lane			
(UK) Capitol	1 28 55	5	10
Mambo Italiano			
(UK) Capitol	2 4 55	14	2
Let Me Go Lover			
(UK) Capitol	2 25 55	3	9
Under the Bridges of Paris			
(UK) Capitol	4 4 55	6	8
Memories Are Made of This			

LABEL	DATE OF CHART ENTRY	HIGHEST POSITION REACHED	NUMBER OF WEEKS IN CHARTS
(US) Capitol	22 17 55	1	16
(UK) Capitol	2 10 56	1	14
Young and Foolish			
(UK) Capitol	3 2 56	20	1
Return to Me			
(US) Capitol	4 28 58	4	13
(UK) Capitol	6 27 58	2	16
Volare			
(US) Capitol	8 18 58	15	4
(UK) Capitol	8 29 58	2	12
Everybody Loves Somebody			
(US) Reprise	7 18 64	1	11
(UK) Reprise	9 18 64	12	7
The Door Is Still Open to My Heart			
(US) Reprise	10 24 64	6	5
I Will			
(US) Reprise	11 27 65	10	5
Gentle on My Mind			
(UK) Reprise	3 1 69	2	12
MARTIN, TONY			
Stranger in Paradise			
(UK) HMV	4 22 55	7	13
Walk Hand in Hand			
(US) RCA	6 23 56	10	2
(UK) HMV	7 13 56	2	14
MARTIN, VINCE (with **THE TARRIERS**)			
Cindy Oh Cindy			
(US) Glory	11 3 56	12	10
MARTINDALE, WINK			
Deck of Cards			
(US) Dot	10 12 59	7	9
(UK) London	12 19 59	19	1
(UK) London (reissue)	5 18 63	5	13
MARTINO, AL			
Man from Laramie			
(UK) Capitol	9 23 55	19	3
I Love You Because			
(US) Capitol	5 18 63	3	7
Painted, Tainted Rose			
(US) Capitol	9 7 63	15	3
I Love You More Every Day			
(US) Capitol	2 29 64	9	5
Tears and Roses			
(US) Capitol	6 20 64	20	1
Spanish Eyes			
(US) Capitol	1 8 66	15	4
(UK) Capitol (reissue)	7 28 73	5	13
MARVELETTES			
Please Mr. Postman			
(US) Tamla	11 6 61	1	11

LABEL	DATE OF CHART ENTRY	HIGHEST POSITION REACHED	NUMBER OF WEEKS IN CHARTS
Playboy			
(US) Tamla	6 2 62	7	7
Beechwood 4-5789			
(US) Tamla	9 15 62	17	3
Don't Mess with Bill			
(US) Tamla	2 5 66	7	6
Hunter Gets Captured by the Game			
(US) Tamla	3 4 67	13	3
When You're Young and in Love			
(UK) Motown	*7 15 67*	*13*	*1*
My Baby Must Be a Magician			
(US) Tamla	2 10 68	17	2
MARVIN, HANK (see CLIFF RICHARD)			
MARVIN, LEE			
Wanderin' Star			
(UK) Paramount	*2 14 70*	*1*	*11*
MASEKELA, HUGH			
Grazing in the Grass			
(US) UNI	6 29 68	1	9
MASON, BARBARA			
Yes, I'm Ready			
(US) Arctic	6 26 65	5	7
MATHIS, JOHNNY			
It's Not for Me to Say			
(US) Columbia	6 10 57	5	17
Wonderful Wonderful			
(US) Columbia	7 22 57	17	3
Chances Are			
(US) Columbia	9 30 57	5	17
A Certain Smile			
(US) Columbia	7 21 58	19	1
(UK) Fontana	*10 3 58*	*4*	*14*
Winter Wonderland			
(UK) Fontana	*12 26 58*	*17*	*1*
Someone			
(UK) Fontana	*8 1 59*	*8*	*12*
Small World			
(US) Columbia	8 10 59	20	1
Misty			
(US) Columbia	11 2 59	12	7
(UK) Fontana	*1 30 60*	*13*	*4*
Best of Everything			
(UK) Fontana	*11 28 59*	*18*	*1*
My Love for You			
(UK) Fontana	*9 30 60*	*14*	*7*
Gina			
(US) Columbia	10 20 62	6	7
What Will Mary Say			
(US) Columbia	2 23 63	9	7

LABEL	DATE OF CHART ENTRY	HIGHEST POSITION REACHED	NUMBER OF WEEKS IN CHARTS
MATTHEWS SOUTHERN COMFORT			
Woodstock			
(UK) UNI	10 17 70	1	8
MAUGHAN, SUSAN			
Bobby's Girl			
(UK) Philips	11 3 62	3	13
MAURIAT, PAUL			
Love Is Blue			
(US) Philips	1 27 68	1	13
(UK) Philips	3 23 68	12	5
MAXWELL, ROBERT, HIS HARP, HIS ORCHESTRA			
Shangri-La			
(US) Decca	4 25 64	15	4
MAY, BILLY			
Main Title: Man with the Golden Arm			
(UK) Capitol	5 4 56	9	6
MAYFIELD, CURTIS			
Move On Up			
(UK) Buddah	8 28 71	12	3
Freddie's Dead			
(US) Curtom	10 14 72	4	7
Superfly			
(US) Curtom	12 16 72	8	8
MCBETH, DAVID			
Mr. Blue			
(UK) Pye	10 31 59	14	2
MCBRIDE, FRANKIE			
Five Little Fingers			
(UK) Emerald	10 14 67	19	1
MCCARTNEY, PAUL			
Another Day			
(UK) Apple	3 6 71	2	9
(US) Apple (b/w Oh Woman Oh Why Oh Why)			
	3 20 71	5	9
Uncle Albert/Admiral Halsey (with **LINDA MCCARTNEY**)			
(US) Apple	8 28 71	1	10
[see also: **PAUL MCCARTNEY'S WINGS; WINGS; BEATLES**]			
MCCARTNEY'S, PAUL, WINGS			
My Love			
(UK) Apple	4 21 73	9	6
(US) Apple	5 12 73	1	10
Live and Let Die			
(UK) Apple	6 16 73	9	7
(US) Apple	8 4 73	2	8
Helen Wheels			
(UK) Apple	11 24 73	12	4
(US) Apple	12 22 73	16	2
[see also: **WINGS**]			

LABEL	DATE OF CHART ENTRY	HIGHEST POSITION REACHED	NUMBER OF WEEKS IN CHARTS
MCCOYS			
Hang On Sloopy			
(US) Bang	9 11 65	1	9
(*UK*) *Immediate*	9 18 65	5	9
Fever			
(US) Bang	12 4 65	7	7
MCCRACKLIN, JIMMY			
The Walk			
(US) Checker	3 10 58	7	5
MCDANIELS, GENE			
One Hundred Pounds of Clay			
(US) Liberty	4 10 61	3	10
Tower of Strength			
(US) Liberty	10 23 61	5	8
Chip Chip			
(US) Liberty	2 17 62	10	5
MCDEVITT, CHARLES (with **NANCY WHISKEY**)			
Freight Train			
(*UK*) *Oriole*	4 19 57	6	14
MCGOVERN, MAUREEN			
Morning After			
(US) 20th Century	7 21 73	1	9
MCGRIFF, JIMMY			
I've Gotta Woman			
(US) Sue	11 24 62	20	1
MCGUINNESS, FLINT			
When I'm Dead Gone			
(*UK*) *Capitol*	12 5 70	2	10
Malt and Barley Blues			
(*UK*) *Capitol*	5 15 71	5	7
MCGUIRE, BARRY			
Eve of Destruction			
(US) Dunhill	9 4 65	1	8
(*UK*) *RCA*	9 18 65	3	10
MCGUIRE SISTERS			
Sincerely			
(US) Coral	1 15 55	1	17
(*UK*) *Vogue-Coral*	7 15 55	14	4
No More			
(*UK*) *Vogue-Coral*	4 4 55	20	1
Something's Gotta Give			
(US) Coral	6 11 65	6	11
He			
(US) Coral	11 19 55	12	8
Picnic			
(US) Coral	5 26 56	13	8
Sugartime			
(US) Coral	1 20 58	5	15
(*UK*) *Vogue-Coral*	2 21 58	14	4

LABEL	DATE OF CHART ENTRY	HIGHEST POSITION REACHED	NUMBER OF WEEKS IN CHARTS
May You Always			
(US) Coral	1 26 59	11	4
Just for Old Times' Sake			
(US) Coral	5 15 61	20	1
MCKENZIE, SCOTT			
San Francisco			
(US) Ode	6 17 67	4	8
(UK) CBS	7 15 67	1	14
MCLAIN, TOMMY			
Sweet Dreams			
(US) MSL	8 6 66	15	4
MCLEAN, DON			
American Pie			
(US) United Artists	12 18 71	1	14
(UK) United Artists	2 5 72	2	11
Vincent			
(US) United Artists	4 15 72	12	6
(UK) United Artists	5 27 72	1	9
MCNAMARA, ROBIN			
Lay a Little Lovin' on Me			
(US) Steed	8 1 70	11	5
MCPHATTER, CLYDE			
A Lover's Question			
(US) Atlantic	11 10 58	6	14
Lover Please			
(US) Mercury	3 31 62	7	8
MEDICINE HEAD			
One and One Is One			
(UK) Polydor	5 19 73	3	7
Rising Sun			
(UK) Polydor	8 18 73	11	5
MELACHRINO, GEORGE			
Autumn Concerto			
(UK) HMV	10 19 56	19	4
MEL AND TIM			
Backfield in Motion			
(US) Bamboo	11 8 69	10	9
Start All Over Again			
(US) Stax	10 28 72	19	3
MELANIE			
Lay Down (Candles in the Rain) (with the **EDWIN HAWKINS SINGERS**)			
(US) Buddah	6 6 70	6	10
Ruby Tuesday			
(UK) Buddah	10 24 70	9	7
Brand New Key			
(US) Neighborhood	12 4 71	1	12
(UK) Buddah	1 15 72	4	7

LABEL	DATE OF CHART ENTRY	HIGHEST POSITION REACHED	NUMBER OF WEEKS IN CHARTS
MELVIN, HAROLD, AND THE BLUE NOTES			
If You Don't Know Me by Now			
(US) Phil. International	11 11 72	3	8
(*UK*) *CBS*	*1 27 73*	*9*	*4*
The Love I Lost (pt. 1)			
(US) Phil. International	11 10 73	7	9
MENDES, SERGIO, AND BRASIL '66			
Look of Love			
(US) A&M	6 8 68	4	8
Fool on the Hill			
(US) A&M	8 31 68	6	6
Scarborough Fair			
(US) A&M	12 14 68	16	2
MENZIES, IAN			
Fish Man			
(*UK*) *Pye Nixa*	*9 18 60*	*15*	*3*
MERCY			
Love (Can Make You Happy)			
(US) Sundi	5 3 69	2	9
MERSEYBEATS			
I Think of You			
(*UK*) *Fontana*	*2 1 64*	*5*	*11*
Don't Turn Around			
(*UK*) *Fontana*	*5 2 64*	*13*	*5*
Wishin' and Hopin'			
(*UK*) *Fontana*	*7 18 64*	*13*	*6*
[see also: **THE MERSEYS**]			
MERSEYS			
Sorrow			
(*UK*) *Pye*	*4 18 64*	*10*	*6*
MICHAELS, LEE			
Do You Know What I Mean			
(US) A&M	9 11 71	6	10
MICKEY AND SYLVIA			
Love Is Strange			
(US) Groove	2 9 57	13	8
MIDDLE OF THE ROAD			
Chirpy Chirpy Cheep Cheep			
(*UK*) *RCA*	*6 12 71*	*1*	*12*
Tweedle Tweedle Dee			
(*UK*) *RCA*	*9 18 71*	*2*	*9*
Soley Soley			
(*UK*) *RCA*	*12 18 71*	*5*	*8*
MIDLER, BETTE			
Do You Want to Dance			
(US) Atlantic	2 24 73	17	4
Boogie Woogie Bugle Boy			
(US) Atlantic	6 30 73	8	6

LABEL	DATE OF CHART ENTRY	HIGHEST POSITION REACHED	NUMBER OF WEEKS IN CHARTS
MIGIL FIVE			
Mockingbird Hill			
(UK) Pye	4 18 64	10	6
MIKI AND GRIFF			
Hold Back Tomorrow			
(UK) Pye	10 3 59	20	1
Little Bitty Tear			
(UK) Pye	3 24 62	19	1
MILES, GARY			
Look for a Star			
(US) Liberty	7 25 60	16	3
MILLER, CHUCK			
House of Blue Lights			
(US) Mercury	7 2 55	9	10
MILLER, GARY			
Yellow Rose of Texas			
(UK) Nixa	10 21 55	13	5
Robin Hood			
(UK) Nixa	1 13 56	10	6
Garden of Eden			
(UK) Pye-Nixa	1 11 57	14	2
Story of My Life			
(UK) Pye-Nixa	1 17 58	14	5
MILLER, JODY			
Queen of the House			
(US) Capitol	5 29 65	12	3
MILLER, MITCH			
Yellow Rose of Texas			
(US) Columbia	8 6 55	1	19
(UK) Philips	10 7 55	2	13
Song for a Summer Night			
(US) Columbia	8 25 56	10	9
Children's Marching Song			
(US) Columbia	2 9 59	16	5
MILLER, NED			
From a Jack to a King			
(US) Fabor (reissue)	2 2 63	6	6
(UK) London	3 16 63	2	13
MILLER, ROGER			
Dang Me			
(US) Smash	7 11 64	7	6
Chug-A-Lug			
(US) Smash	10 17 64	9	5
King of the Road			
(US) Smash	2 20 65	4	9
(UK) Philips	4 17 65	1	9
Engine, Engine #9			
(US) Smash	5 29 65	7	4

LABEL	DATE OF CHART ENTRY	HIGHEST POSITION REACHED	NUMBER OF WEEKS IN CHARTS
England Swings			
(US) Smash	12 4 65	8	6
(*UK*) *Philips*	*1 22 66*	*13*	*2*
Little Green Apples			
(*UK*) *Mercury*	*5 11 68*	*19*	*2*
MILLER, STEVE			
The Joker			
(US) Capitol	12 8 73	4	4
MILLER, SUZI			
Happy Days, Lonely Nights			
(*UK*) *Decca*	*1 21 55*	*14*	*2*
MILLIE (see **MILLIE SMALL**)			
MILLS, GARY			
Look for a Star			
(*UK*) *Top Rank*	*7 3 60*	*5*	*8*
Top Teen Baby			
(*UK*) *Top Rank*	*10 21 60*	*20*	*1*
MILLS, HAYLEY			
Let's Get Together			
(US) Vista	10 2 61	8	7
(*UK*) *Decca*	*10 14 61*	*11*	*5*
MIMMS, GARNET, AND THE ENCHANTERS			
Cry Baby			
(US) United Artists	9 14 63	4	8
MINDBENDERS			
A Groovy Kind of Love			
(*UK*) *Fontana*	*1 29 66*	*2*	*10*
(US) Fontana	5 7 66	2	8
Ashes to Ashes			
(*UK*) *Fontana*	*9 17 66*	*14*	*3*
[see also: **FONTANA, WAYNE, AND THE MINDBENDERS**]			
MINEO, SAL			
Start Movin'			
(US) Epic	6 3 57	10	6
(*UK*) *Philips*	*7 26 57*	*16*	*6*
MINGRABI, MARCELLO			
Zorba's Dance			
(*UK*) *Durium*	*8 14 65*	*6*	*10*
MIRACLES			
Shop Around			
(US) Tamla	1 9 61	2	9
You've Really Got a Hold on Me			
(US) Tamla	1 26 63	8	7
Mickey's Monkey			
(US) Tamla	9 14 63	8	5
Ooo Baby Baby			
(US) Tamla	5 1 65	16	3

LABEL	DATE OF CHART ENTRY	HIGHEST POSITION REACHED	NUMBER OF WEEKS IN CHARTS
Tracks of My Tears			
(US) Tamla	8 28 65	16	4
(UK) Tamla Motown (reissue)	5 31 69	9	6
My Girl Has Gone			
(US) Tamla	11 20 65	14	2
Going to A Go-Go			
(US) Tamla	2 12 66	11	2
(Come Round Here) I'm the One You Need			
(US) Tamla	12 3 66	17	3
(UK) Tamla Motown (reissue)	2 20 71	13	4
[see also: SMOKEY ROBINSON AND THE MIRACLES]			
MITCHELL, GUY			
Singing the Blues			
(US) Columbia	11 3 56	1	20
(UK) Philips	12 7 56	1	20
Knee Deep in the Blues			
(US) Columbia	2 16 57	16	3
(UK) Philips	2 22 57	3	11
Rock-a-Billy			
(UK) Philips	4 26 57	1	11
(US) Columbia	4 27 57	13	7
Call Rosie on the Phone			
(UK) Philips	10 18 57	17	3
Heartaches by the Number			
(US) Columbia	11 2 59	1	12
(UK) Philips	11 28 59	5	8
MITCHELL, JONI			
Big Yellow Taxi			
(UK) Reprise	7 25 70	11	5
MIXTURES			
The Pushbike Song			
(UK) Polydor	1 23 71	2	13
MODUGNO, DOMENICO			
Volare			
(US) Decca	8 11 58	1	13
(UK) Oriole	9 5 58	10	8
MOJOS			
Everything's All Right			
(UK) Decca	4 11 64	9	6
MOMENTS			
Love on a Two Way Street			
(US) Stang	5 2 70	3	10
MONKEES			
Last Train to Clarksville			
(US) Colgems	10 1 66	1	10
I'm a Believer			
(US) Colgems	12 17 66	1	12
(UK) RCA	1 14 67	1	11

LABEL	DATE OF CHART ENTRY	HIGHEST POSITION REACHED	NUMBER OF WEEKS IN CHARTS
(I'm Not Your) Steppin' Stone			
(US) Colgems	1 14 67	20	1
A Little Bit Me, A Little Bit You			
(US) Colgems	4 1 67	2	8
(UK) RCA	4 8 67	3	8
Alternate Title			
(UK) RCA	7 1 67	2	8
Pleasant Valley Sunday			
(US) Colgems (b/w*)	8 5 67	3	6
(UK) RCA	8 26 67	11	4
Words*			
(US) Colgems	8 19 67	11	4
Daydream Believer			
(US) Colgems	11 25 67	1	10
(UK) RCA	12 2 67	5	12
Valleri			
(US) Colgems	3 16 68	3	6
(UK) RCA	4 6 68	12	5
D. W. Washburn			
(US) Colgems	7 6 68	19	2
(UK) RCA	7 6 68	17	2
MONOTONES			
Book of Love			
(US) Argo	4 14 58	5	9
MONRO, MATT			
Portrait of My Love			
(UK) Parlophone	12 18 60	5	8
My Kind of Girl			
(UK) Parlophone	2 26 61	5	8
(US) Warwick	7 31 61	18	3
Softly as I Leave You			
(UK) Parlophone	3 3 62	10	8
From Russia with Love			
(UK) Parlophone	11 30 63	20	1
Walk Away			
(UK) Parlophone	10 10 64	5	10
Yesterday			
(UK) Parlophone	10 30 65	8	7
MONROE, GERRY			
Sally			
(UK) Chapter One	6 13 70	4	9
My Prayer			
(UK) Chapter One	12 5 70	9	7
It's a Sin to Tell a Lie			
(UK) Chapter One	5 8 71	13	4
MONTE, LOU			
Lazy Mary			
(US) Victor	3 24 58	12	7
Pepino the Italian Mouse			
(US) Reprise	12 29 62	5	5

LABEL	DATE OF CHART ENTRY	HIGHEST POSITION REACHED	NUMBER OF WEEKS IN CHARTS
MONTENEGRO, HUGO			
The Good, the Bad and the Ugly			
(US) RCA	4 20 68	2	10
(UK) RCA	*10 19 68*	*1*	*15*
MONTEZ, CHRIS			
Let's Dance			
(US) Monogram	9 15 62	4	7
(UK) London	*10 20 62*	*2*	*14*
(UK) London (reissue)	*11 4 72*	*9*	*5*
Some Kinda Fun			
(UK) London	*1 27 63*	*10*	*5*
The More I See You			
(US) A&M	6 11 66	16	3
(UK) Pye	*7 16 66*	*3*	*9*
MOODY BLUES			
Go Now			
(UK) Decca	*1 2 65*	*1*	*9*
(US) London	4 3 65	10	6
Nights in White Satin			
(UK) Deram	*2 17 68*	*19*	*1*
(US) Deram (reissue)	9 16 72	2	12
(UK) Deram (reissue)	*12 16 72*	*9*	*6*
Question			
(UK) Threshold	*5 9 70*	*2*	*9*
Isn't Life Strange?			
(UK) Threshold	*5 27 72*	*13*	*4*
I'm Just a Singer (in a Rock and Roll Band)			
(US) Threshold	3 3 73	12	4
MOONEY, ART			
Honey Babe			
(US) MGM	4 30 55	6	16
Nuttin for Christmas (with **BARRY GORDON**)			
(US) MGM	12 24 55	7	3
MOORE, BOB			
Mexico			
(US) Monument	9 25 61	7	7
MORGAN, JANE			
Fascination			
(US) Kapp	9 23 57	11	12
The Day the Rains Came Down			
(UK) London	*12 12 58*	*4*	*11*
MORGAN, JAYE P.			
That's All I Want from You			
(US) Victor	1 1 55	5	14
Danger, Heartbreak Ahead			
(US) Victor	4 9 55	18	1
Longest Walk			
(US) Victor	9 10 55	13	7

LABEL	DATE OF CHART ENTRY	HIGHEST POSITION REACHED	NUMBER OF WEEKS IN CHARTS
MORMON TABERNACLE CHOIR			
Battle Hymn of the Republic			
(US) Columbia	10 5 59	13	5
MORRISON, VAN			
Brown-Eyed Girl			
(US) Bang	9 9 67	10	6
Domino			
(US) Warner Brothers	12 19 70	9	4
[see also: **THEM**]			
MOTHERLODE			
When I Die			
(US) Buddah	10 4 69	18	2
MOTOWN SPINNERS (see **SPINNERS**)			
MOTT THE HOOPLE			
All the Young Dudes			
(*UK*) *CBS*	8 19 72	*3*	*6*
Honaloochie Boogie			
(*UK*) *CBS*	7 7 73	*12*	*3*
All the Way from Memphis			
(*UK*) *CBS*	9 22 73	*10*	*4*
Roll Away the Stone			
(*UK*) *CBS*	12 1 73	*8*	*9*
MOUTH AND MACNEAL			
How Do You Do			
(US) Philips	7 1 72	8	8
MOVE			
Night of Fear			
(*UK*) *Deram*	*1 14 67*	*2*	*7*
I Can Hear the Grass Grow			
(*UK*) *Deram*	*4 22 67*	*5*	*6*
Flowers in the Rain			
(*UK*) *Regal Zonophone*	*9 16 67*	*2*	*10*
Fire Brigade			
(*UK*) *Regal Zonophone*	*2 17 68*	*3*	*8*
Blackberry Way			
(*UK*) *Regal Zonophone*	*1 18 69*	*1*	*8*
Curly			
(*UK*) *Regal Zonophone*	*8 9 69*	*12*	*7*
Brontasaurus			
(*UK*) *Regal Zonophone*	*5 9 70*	*7*	*6*
Tonight			
(*UK*) *Harvest*	*7 17 71*	*11*	*5*
California Man			
(*UK*) *Harvest*	*5 27 72*	*7*	*8*
[see also: **ELECTRIC LIGHT ORCHESTRA; WIZARD; ROY WOOD**]			
MR. BLOE			
Groovin' with Mr. Bloe			
(*UK*) *DJM*	*5 30 70*	*2*	*10*

LABEL	DATE OF CHART ENTRY	HIGHEST POSITION REACHED	NUMBER OF WEEKS IN CHARTS
MUD			
Crazy			
(UK) RAK	4 7 73	12	5
Hypnosis			
(UK) RAK	8 4 73	16	2
Dyna-Mite			
(UK) RAK	11 3 73	4	7
MUDLARKS			
Lollipop			
(UK) Columbia	5 2 58	2	9
Book of Love			
(UK) Columbia	6 13 58	8	7
MUNGO JERRY			
In the Summertime			
(UK) Dawn	6 6 70	1	13
(US) Janus	8 8 70	3	8
Baby Jump			
(UK) Dawn	2 20 71	1	8
Lady Rose			
(UK) Dawn	6 5 71	5	7
You Don't Have to Be in the Army (to Fight in the War)			
(UK) Dawn	10 9 71	13	3
Alright, Alright, Alright			
(UK) Dawn	7 21 73	3	6
MURMAIDS			
Popsicles and Icicles			
(US) Chattahoochee	12 14 63	3	9
MURRAY, ANNE			
Snowbird			
(US) Capitol	9 5 70	8	8
Danny's Song			
(US) Capitol	3 3 73	7	9
MURRAY, RUBY			
Heartbeat			
(UK) Columbia	1 7 55	3	11
Softly Softly			
(UK) Columbia	1 28 55	1	23
Happy Days and Lonely Nights			
(UK) Columbia	2 4 55	6	8
If Anyone Finds This I Love You			
(UK) Columbia	3 11 55	4	11
Let Me Go Lover			
(UK) Columbia	3 4 55	5	7
Evermore			
(UK) Columbia	7 1 55	3	17
I'll Come When You Call			
(UK) Columbia	10 14 55	6	7
You Are My First Love			
(UK) Columbia	8 31 56	16	2

LABEL	DATE OF CHART ENTRY	HIGHEST POSITION REACHED	NUMBER OF WEEKS IN CHARTS
Real Love			
(UK) Columbia	12 12 58	18	3
Goodbye Jimmy Goodbye			
(UK) Columbia	6 20 59	10	7
MUSIC EXPLOSION			
Little Bit O' Soul			
(US) Laurie	6 3 67	2	11
MUSIC MACHINE			
Talk Talk			
(US) Original Sound	12 31 66	15	4
MYSTICS			
Hushabye			
(US) Laurie	6 29 59	20	1
NAPOLEON XIV			
They're Coming to Take Me Away, Ha Ha			
(US) Warner Brothers	7 30 66	3	4
(UK) Warner Brothers	8 20 66	4	6
NASH, JOHNNY			
Hold Me Tight			
(UK) Regal Zonophone	8 24 68	5	10
(US) JAD	10 19 68	5	9
You Got Soul			
(UK) Major Minor	1 25 69	6	6
Cupid			
(UK) Major Minor	4 19 69	6	6
Stir It Up			
(UK) CBS	4 22 72	13	5
(US) Epic	3 31 73	12	5
I Can See Clearly Now			
(UK) CBS	7 8 72	5	9
(US) Epic	10 21 72	1	10
There Are More Questions than Answers			
(UK) CBS	10 14 72	9	6
NASHVILLE TEENS			
Tobacco Road			
(UK) Decca	7 25 64	6	8
(US) London	10 24 64	14	4
Google Eyes			
(UK) Decca	11 7 64	10	3
NAZARETH			
Broken Down Angel			
(UK) Mooncrest	5 19 73	9	5
Bad Bad Boy			
(UK) Mooncrest	7 28 73	10	5
This Flight Tonight			
(UK) Mooncrest	10 27 73	11	5
NELSON, RICKY [RICK after 1961]			
Teenager's Romance			
(US) Verve (b/w*)	5 27 57	8	9

LABEL	DATE OF CHART ENTRY	HIGHEST POSITION REACHED	NUMBER OF WEEKS IN CHARTS
I'm Walkin'*			
(US) Verve	6 3 57	17	3
You're My One and Only Love			
(US) Verve	9 30 57	16	3
Be Bop Baby			
(US) Imperial	10 21 57	5	13
Stood Up			
(US) Imperial (b/w**)	1 6 58	5	8
Waiting in School**			
(US) Imperial	1 13 58	18	3
Believe What You Say			
(US) Imperial (b/w***)	4 14 58	8	3
My Bucket's Got a Hole in It*			
(US) Imperial	4 14 58	18	2
Poor Little Fool			
(US) Imperial	7 7 58	1	12
(UK) London	*8 22 58*	*4*	*13*
Lonesome Town			
(US) Imperial (b/w†)	10 27 58	7	14
I Got a Feeling†			
(US) Imperial	11 3 58	10	8
Someday			
(UK) London	*11 21 58*	*9*	*9*
Never Be Anyone Else but You			
(US) Imperial } (b/w††)	3 9 59	6	9
(UK) London }	*4 18 59*	*3*	*18*
It's Late††			
(US) Imperial	3 23 59	9	6
Sweeter than You			
(US) Imperial } (b/w†††)	7 20 59	9	5
(UK) London }	*9 5 59*	*9*	*8*
Just a Little Too Much†††			
(US) Imperial	7 27 59	9	5
I Wanna Be Loved			
(US) Imperial	12 21 59	20	1
Young Emotions			
(US) Imperial	5 23 60	12	6
Travelin' Man			
(US) Imperial } (b/w◇)	5 8 61	1	12
(UK) London }	*5 14 61*	*3*	*15*
Hello Mary Lou ◇			
(US) Imperial	5 15 61	9	8
A Wonder Like You			
(US) Imperial (b/w ◇ ◇)	11 6 61	11	4
Everlovin' ◇ ◇			
(US) Imperial	11 13 61	16	2
(UK) London	*12 2 61*	*20*	*1*
Young World			
(US) Imperial	3 24 62	5	7
(UK) London	*5 5 62*	*19*	*2*

LABEL	DATE OF CHART ENTRY	HIGHEST POSITION REACHED	NUMBER OF WEEKS IN CHARTS
Teen Age Idol			
(US) Imperial	9 1 62	5	6
It's Up to You			
(US) Imperial	1 5 63	6	6
Fools Rush In			
(US) Decca	10 19 63	12	6
(UK) Brunswick	*11 2 63*	*12*	*5*
For You			
(US) Decca	1 18 64	6	6
(UK) Brunswick	*2 15 64*	*14*	*4*
Garden Party			
(US) Decca	9 30 72	6	8
NELSON, SANDY			
Teen Beat			
(US) Original Sound	9 21 59	4	10
(UK) Top Rank	*10 31 59*	*7*	*11*
Let There Be Drums			
(US) Imperial	12 4 61	7	7
(UK) London	*12 9 61*	*2*	*11*
NEON PHILHARMONIC			
Morning Girl			
(US) Warner Brothers/Seven Arts	6 7 69	17	2
NERVOUS NORVUS			
Transfusion			
(US) Dot	6 16 56	13	5
NEVILLE, AARON			
Tell It Like It Is			
(US) Parlo	12 24 66	2	9
NEWBEATS			
Bread and Butter			
(US) Hickory	8 29 64	2	8
(UK) Hickory	*10 3 64*	*15*	*3*
Everything's All Right			
(US) Hickory	11 28 64	16	3
Run Baby Run			
(US) Hickory	11 13 65	12	5
(UK) London (reissue)	*11 13 71*	*10*	*6*
NEW CHRISTY MINSTRELS			
Green Green			
(US) Columbia	8 10 63	14	3
Today			
(US) Columbia	6 6 64	17	3
NEW COLONY SIX			
Things I'd Like to Say			
(US) Mercury	3 15 69	16	3
NEWLEY, ANTHONY			
Idle on Parade			
(UK) Decca EP	*5 2 59*	*13*	*2*

LABEL	DATE OF CHART ENTRY	HIGHEST POSITION REACHED	NUMBER OF WEEKS IN CHARTS
I've Waited So Long			
(UK) Decca	5 2 59	4	13
Personality			
(UK) Decca	6 20 59	6	10
Why			
(UK) Decca	1 9 60	1	12
Do You Mind?			
(UK) Decca	3 20 60	2	11
If She Should Come to You			
(UK) Decca	7 17 60	7	9
Strawberry Fair			
(UK) Decca	11 20 60	3	6
And the Heavens Cried			
(UK) Decca	3 5 61	8	7
Pop Goes the Weasel/Bee-Bum			
(UK) Decca	6 4 61	9	6
NEWMAN, THUNDERCLAP			
Something in the Air			
(UK) Track	6 21 69	1	8
NEW SEEKERS			
Look What They've Done to My Song Ma			
(US) Elektra	10 10 70	14	4
Never-Ending Song of Love			
(UK) Philips	7 24 71	2	12
I'd Like to Teach the World to Sing			
(UK) Polydor	12 25 71	1	14
(US) Elektra	12 25 71	7	7
Beg, Steal or Borrow			
(UK) Polydor	3 4 72	2	8
Circles			
(UK) Polydor	7 1 72	4	8
Come Softly to Me			
(UK) Polydor	1 20 73	20	1
Pinball Wizard/See Me Feel Me			
(UK) Polydor	3 10 73	16	4
You Won't Find Another Fool Like Me			
(UK) Polydor	12 1 73	1	12
NEWTON, WAYNE			
Danke Schoen			
(US) Capitol	8 17 63	13	4
Daddy Don't You Walk So Fast			
(US) Chelsea	6 24 72	4	10
NEWTON-JOHN, OLIVIA			
If Not for You			
(UK) Pye International	4 3 71	7	6
Banks of the Ohio			
(UK) Pye International	11 13 71	6	8
What Is Life?			
(UK) Pye International	4 1 72	16	4

LABEL	DATE OF CHART ENTRY	HIGHEST POSITION REACHED	NUMBER OF WEEKS IN CHARTS
Take Me Home Country Roads			
(UK) *Pye International*	2 10 73	15	4
Let Me Be There			
(US) MCA	12 29 73	17	1
NEW VAUDEVILLE BAND			
Winchester Cathedral			
(UK) *Fontana*	9 24 66	4	9
(US) Fontana	11 12 66	1	11
Peek a Boo			
(UK) *Fontana*	2 11 67	7	7
Finchley Central			
(UK) *Fontana*	5 27 67	11	6
NEW WORLD			
Rose Garden			
(UK) *RAK*	3 13 71	15	5
Tom Tom Turnaround			
(UK) *RAK*	7 10 71	6	10
Kara Kara			
(UK) *RAK*	1 8 72	17	1
Sister Jane			
(UK) *RAK*	5 27 72	9	6
NEW YORK CITY			
I'm Doing Fine Now			
(US) Chelsea	6 2 73	17	5
(UK) *RCA*	8 25 73	20	2
NICHOLLS, SUE			
Where Will You Be?			
(UK) *Pye*	7 20 68	17	2
NILSSON			
Everybody's Talkin'			
(US) RCA	9 20 69	6	6
Without You			
(US) RCA	1 29 72	1	11
(UK) *RCA*	2 19 72	1	13
Coconut			
(US) RCA	7 29 72	8	6
NINA AND FREDERICK			
Little Donkey			
(UK) *Columbia*	11 20 60	5	6
Sucu Sucu			
(UK) *Columbia*	10 7 61	17	2
1910 FRUITGUM COMPANY			
Simon Says			
(US) Buddah	2 17 68	4	9
(UK) *Pye International*	4 6 68	2	12
1, 2, 3			
(US) Buddah	8 31 68	5	6
Indian Giver			
(US) Buddah	3 1 69	5	7

LABEL	DATE OF CHART ENTRY	HIGHEST POSITION REACHED	NUMBER OF WEEKS IN CHARTS
NITTY GRITTY DIRT BAND			
Mr. Bojangles			
(US) Liberty	1 30 71	9	8
NOBLES, CLIFF, & CO.			
The Horse			
(US) Phil-LA of Soul	6 15 68	2	9
NOONE, PETER, AND HERMAN'S HERMITS			
Lady Barbara			
(UK) RAK	*12 12 70*	*13*	*6*
Oh You Pretty Thing			
(UK) RAK	*5 29 71*	*12*	*5*
[see also: **HERMAN'S HERMITS**]			
NUTTY SQUIRRELS			
Uh! Oh! (pt. 1)			
(US) Hanover	12 7 59	14	5
OCEAN			
Put Your Hand in the Hand			
(US) Kama Sutra	4 10 71	2	9
O'CONNOR, DES			
Careless Hands			
(UK) Columbia	*11 25 67*	*6*	*9*
I Pretend			
(UK) Columbia	*6 15 68*	*1*	*15*
1, 2, 3, O'Leary			
(UK) Columbia	*11 30 68*	*4*	*9*
Dick-a-Dum-Dum			
(UK) Columbia	*5 31 69*	*14*	*3*
Loneliness			
(UK) Columbia	*12 20 69*	*18*	*2*
Tips of My Fingers			
(UK) Columbia	*10 17 70*	*15*	*4*
OFARIM, ESTHER AND ABI			
Cinderella Rockafella			
(UK) Fontana	*2 24 68*	*1*	*9*
One More Dance			
(UK) Philips	*7 6 68*	*13*	*4*
OHIO EXPRESS			
Yummy Yummy Yummy			
(US) Buddah	6 1 68	4	8
(UK) Pye International	*6 29 68*	*5*	*9*
Chewy Chewy			
(US) Buddah	11 16 68	15	7
OHIO PLAYERS			
Funky Worm			
(US) Westbound	5 12 73	15	3
O'JAYS			
Backstabbers			
(US) Philadelphia International	8 26 72	3	8
(UK) CBS	*10 14 72*	*14*	*3*

LABEL	DATE OF CHART ENTRY	HIGHEST POSITION REACHED	NUMBER OF WEEKS IN CHARTS
Love Train			
(US) Philadelphia International	2 17 73	1	9
(UK) CBS	3 24 73	9	6
O'KAYSIONS			
Girl Watchers			
(US) ABC	9 14 68	5	9
O'KEEFE, DANNY			
Good Time Charlie's Got the Blues			
(US) Signpost	10 14 72	9	5
OLIVER			
Good Morning Starshine			
(US) Jubilee	6 14 69	3	9
(UK) CBS	8 30 69	3	9
Jean			
(US) Crewe	9 13 69	2	9
OLYMPICS			
Western Movies			
(US) Demon	8 18 58	8	6
(UK) HMV	10 10 58	12	7
ORBISON, ROY			
Only the Lonely			
(US) Monument	7 4 60	2	10
(UK) London	8 14 60	1	16
Blue Angel			
(UK) London (b/w Today's Teardrops)			
	10 30 60	13	8
(US) Monument	10 31 60	9	4
Runnin' Scared			
(US) Monument	5 8 61	1	9
(UK) London	5 21 61	9	10
Crying			
(US) Monument	9 4 61	2	8
Dream Baby			
(US) Monument	3 17 62	4	6
(UK) London	3 17 62	2	10
In Dreams			
(US) Monument	3 2 62	7	8
(UK) London	3 30 63	6	16
Falling			
(UK) London	6 8 63	9	9
Blue Bayou			
(UK) London (b/w*)	9 28 63	3	12
Mean Woman Blues*			
(US) Monument	10 5 63	5	8
Pretty Paper			
(US) Monument	12 28 63	15	3
(UK) London	11 28 64	6	6
Borne on the Wind			
(UK) London	3 7 64	15	3

LABEL	DATE OF CHART ENTRY	HIGHEST POSITION REACHED	NUMBER OF WEEKS IN CHARTS
It's Over			
(US) Monument	5 2 64	9	6
(UK) London	5 9 64	1	13
Oh, Pretty Woman			
(US) Monument	9 12 64	1	11
(UK) London	9 18 64	1	12
Good Night			
(UK) London	2 20 65	14	5
Crawlin' Back			
(UK) London	12 4 65	19	1
Lana			
(UK) London	7 2 66	15	5
Too Soon to Know			
(UK) London	8 27 66	3	10
There Won't Be Many Coming Home			
(UK) London	12 17 66	18	2
ORIGINALS			
Baby, I'm for Real			
(US) Soul	11 8 69	14	6
Bells			
(US) Soul	4 11 70	12	3
ORLANDO, TONY			
Bless You			
(UK) Fontana	9 30 61	7	8
(US) Epic	10 2 61	15	2
[see also: **DAWN**]			
ORLONS			
Wah-Watusi			
(US) Cameo	6 30 62	2	9
Don't Hang Up			
(US) Cameo	11 10 62	4	8
South Street			
(US) Cameo	3 16 63	3	7
Not Me			
(US) Cameo	7 6 63	12	14
Crossfire			
(US) Cameo	11 2 63	19	1
OSMOND, DONNY			
Sweet and Innocent			
(US) MGM	5 8 71	7	9
Go Away Little Girl			
(US) MGM	8 28 71	1	11
Hey Girl/I Knew You When			
(US) MGM	12 11 71	9	7
Puppy Love			
(US) MGM	3 11 72	3	8
(UK) MGM	6 24 72	1	12
Too Young			
(US) MGM	7 1 72	13	5
(UK) MGM	9 23 72	5	5

LABEL	DATE OF CHART ENTRY	HIGHEST POSITION REACHED	NUMBER OF WEEKS IN CHARTS
Why			
(US) MGM (b/w Lonely Boy)	10 7 72	13	4
(UK) MGM	11 18 72	3	9
Twelfth of Never			
(UK) MGM	3 10 73	1	9
(US) MGM	4 7 73	8	6
Young Love			
(UK) MGM	8 18 73	1	7
When I Fall in Love			
(UK) MGM	11 17 73	4	8
OSMOND, LITTLE JIMMY			
Long-Haired Lover from Liverpool			
(UK) MGM	12 9 72	1	14
Tweedle Dee			
(UK) MGM	4 7 73	4	7
OSMOND, MARIE			
Paper Roses			
(US) MGM	10 13 73	5	9
(UK) MGM	11 24 73	2	10
OSMONDS			
One Bad Apple			
(US) MGM	1 30 71	1	10
Double Lovin'			
(US) MGM	6 12 71	14	4
Yo Yo			
(US) MGM	9 25 71	3	10
Down by the Lazy River			
(US) MGM	2 5 72	4	10
Hold Her Tight			
(US) MGM	7 22 72	14	4
Crazy Horses			
(UK) MGM	11 18 72	2	12
(US) MGM	11 25 72	14	4
Going Home			
(UK) MGM	7 21 73	4	6
Let Me In			
(UK) MGM	11 3 73	2	9
O'SULLIVAN, GILBERT			
Nothing Rhymed			
(UK) MAM	12 12 70	8	7
We Will			
(UK) MAM	8 28 71	16	4
No Matter How I Try			
(UK) MAM	12 4 71	5	9
Alone Again (Naturally)			
(UK) MAM	3 11 72	3	7
(US) MAM	7 8 72	1	13
Ooh-Wakka-Doo-Wakka-Day			
(UK) MAM	6 24 72	8	6

LABEL	DATE OF CHART ENTRY	HIGHEST POSITION REACHED	NUMBER OF WEEKS IN CHARTS
Clair			
(*UK*) *MAM*	*10 21 72*	*1*	*8*
(US) MAM	11 25 72	2	10
Get Down			
(*UK*) *MAM*	*3 24 73*	*1*	*8*
(US) MAM	7 28 73	7	8
Out of the Question			
(US) MAM	5 5 73	17	3
Ooh Baby			
(*UK*) *MAM*	*9 29 73*	*18*	*3*
Why Oh Why Oh Why			
(*UK*) *MAM*	*11 17 73*	*6*	*10*
OTIS, JOHNNY, SHOW with **MARIE ADAMS**			
Ma (He's Making Eyes at Me)			
(*UK*) *Capitol*	*11 22 57*	*2*	*15*
Bye Bye Baby			
(*UK*) *Capitol*	*2 7 58*	*20*	*1*
Willie and the Hand Jive			
(US) Capitol	7 21 58	9	8
OUTSIDERS			
Time Won't Let Me			
(US) Capitol	4 2 66	5	7
Respectable			
(US) Capitol	9 3 66	15	2
OVERLANDERS			
Michelle			
(*UK*) *Pye*	*1 22 66*	*1*	*7*
OWEN, REG			
Manhattan Spiritual			
(US) Palette	1 12 59	10	7
(*UK*) *Pye International*	*3 7 59*	*18*	*3*
PACIFIC GAS AND ELECTRIC			
Are You Ready?			
(US) Columbia	7 11 70	14	5
PAGE, PATTI			
Cross of Gold			
(US) Mercury	12 3 55	16	3
Go On with the Wedding			
(US) Mercury	2 4 56	11	4
Allegheny Moon			
(US) Mercury	7 7 56	2	17
Mama from the Train			
(US) Mercury	11 24 56	11	8
Old Cape Cod			
(US) Mercury	6 10 57	7	12
Left Right Out of Your Heart			
(US) Mercury	8 4 58	13	2
Hush Hush Sweet Charlotte			
(US) Columbia	6 12 65	8	5

LABEL	DATE OF CHART ENTRY	HIGHEST POSITION REACHED	NUMBER OF WEEKS IN CHARTS
PAPER DOLLS			
Something Here in My Heart			
(*UK*) *Pye*	4 20 68	*11*	*5*
PARADE			
Sunshine Girl			
(US) A&M	5 27 67	20	1
PARAGONS			
Diamonds and Pearls			
(US) Milestone	10 10 60	18	3
PARIS SISTERS			
I Love How You Love Me			
(US) Gregmark	10 9 61	5	8
PARK, SIMON, ORCHESTRA			
Eye Level			
(*UK*) *Columbia*	9 22 73	*1*	*10*
PARKER, FESS			
Ballad of Davy Crockett			
(US) Columbia	3 12 55	*5*	17
PARKER, ROBERT			
Barefootin'			
(US) Nola	5 28 66	7	7
(*UK*) *Island*	9 3 66	*19*	*1*
PARKINSON, JIMMY			
The Great Pretender			
(*UK*) *Columbia*	3 2 56	*9*	*10*
Middle of the House			
(*UK*) *Columbia*	12 7 56	*20*	*1*
PARKS, MICHAEL			
Long Lonesome Highway			
(US) MGM	4 18 70	20	2
PARLIAMENTS			
(I Wanna) Testify			
(US) Revilot	9 2 67	20	2
PARSONS, BILL			
All American Boy			
(US) Fraternity	1 19 59	2	9
PARTRIDGE, DON			
Rosie			
(*UK*) *Columbia*	2 24 68	*4*	*9*
Blue Eyes			
(*UK*) *Columbia*	6 8 68	*3*	*8*
PARTRIDGE FAMILY (featuring **DAVID CASSIDY**)			
I Think I Love You			
(US) Bell	10 31 70	1	14
(*UK*) *Bell*	2 27 71	*18*	*1*
Doesn't Somebody Want to Be Wanted			
(US) Bell	2 27 71	6	10

250

LABEL	DATE OF CHART ENTRY	HIGHEST POSITION REACHED	NUMBER OF WEEKS IN CHARTS
I'll Meet You Halfway			
(US) Bell	5 29 71	9	5
I Woke Up This Morning			
(US) Bell	9 11 71	13	6
It's One of Those Nights (Yes Love)			
(US) Bell	1 22 72	20	2
(UK) Bell	*3 18 72*	*11*	*4*
Breaking Up Is Hard to Do			
(UK) Bell	*5 15 72*	*3*	*9*
Lookin' Through the Eyes of Love			
(UK) Bell	*2 17 73*	*9*	*5*
Walking in the Rain			
(UK) Bell	*6 2 73*	*10*	*5*
PATIENCE AND PRUDENCE			
Tonight You Belong to Me			
(US) Liberty	9 1 56	6	14
Gonna Get Along Without You Now			
(US) Liberty	12 15 56	12	8
PAUL, BILLY			
Me and Mrs. Jones			
(US) Philadelphia International	12 2 72	1	11
(UK) Epic	*1 27 73*	*12*	*4*
PAUL, LES; and FORD, MARY			
Hummingbird			
(US) Capitol	7 23 55	8	9
PAUL AND PAULA			
Hey Paula			
(US) Philips	1 19 63	1	10
(UK) Philips	*3 2 63*	*8*	*7*
Young Lovers			
(US) Philips	4 6 63	6	5
(UK) Philips	*5 11 63*	*9*	*8*
PAYNE, FREDA			
Band of Gold			
(US) Invictus	6 20 70	3	11
(UK) Invictus	*9 12 70*	*1*	*11*
Bring the Boys Home			
(US) Invictus	7 17 71	12	5
PEACHES AND HERB			
Close Your Eyes			
(US) Date	4 29 67	8	5
For Your Love			
(US) Date	8 5 67	20	1
Love Is Strange			
(US) Date	11 4 67	13	3
PEARSON, JOHNNY			
Sleepy Shores			
(UK) Penny Farthing	*12 25 71*	*8*	*7*

LABEL	DATE OF CHART ENTRY	HIGHEST POSITION REACHED	NUMBER OF WEEKS IN CHARTS
PEDDLERS			
Birth			
(*UK*) *CBS*	9 20 69	*17*	*1*
PEERS, DONALD			
Please Don't Go			
(*UK*) *Columbia*	2 1 69	4	9
PENGUINS			
Earth Angel			
(US) Dootone	1 15 55	8	11
PEOPLE			
I Love You			
(US) Capitol	6 15 68	14	6
PERICOLI, EMILIO			
Al Dila			
(US) Warner Brothers	6 16 62	6	7
PERKINS, CARL			
Blue Suede Shoes			
(US) Sun	3 17 56	4	14
(*UK*) *London*	5 18 56	10	7
PERSUADERS			
Thin Line Between Love and Hate			
(US) Atco	10 16 71	15	3
PETER AND GORDON			
World Without Love			
(*UK*) *Columbia*	3 28 64	*1*	9
(US) Capitol	5 23 64	1	8
Nobody I Know			
(*UK*) *Columbia*	6 20 64	*10*	5
(US) Capitol	7 18 64	12	4
I Don't Want to See You Again			
(US) Capitol	10 31 64	16	2
I Go to Pieces			
(US) Capitol	2 6 65	9	5
True Love Ways			
(*UK*) *Columbia*	4 24 65	*2*	*10*
(US) Capitol	5 22 65	14	5
To Know You Is to Love You			
(*UK*) *Columbia*	7 3 65	*5*	*6*
Baby I'm Yours			
(*UK*) *Columbia*	11 13 65	*19*	*1*
Woman			
(US) Capitol	3 19 66	14	5
Lady Godiva			
(*UK*) *Columbia*	10 15 66	*16*	*3*
(US) Capitol	11 19 66	6	6
Knight in Rusty Armor			
(US) Capitol	2 21 67	15	3

LABEL	DATE OF CHART ENTRY	HIGHEST POSITION REACHED	NUMBER OF WEEKS IN CHARTS
PETER, PAUL AND MARY			
If I Had a Hammer			
(US) Warner Brothers	9 22 62	10	5
Puff			
(US) Warner Brothers	3 30 63	2	10
Blowin' in the Wind			
(US) Warner Brothers	7 20 63	2	8
(UK) Warner Brothers	*11 9 63*	*13*	*5*
Don't Think Twice It's All Right			
(US) Warner Brothers	10 12 63	9	4
I Dig Rock & Roll Music			
(US) Warner Brothers	9 16 67	9	5
Leaving on a Jet Plane			
(US) Warner Brothers	11 22 69	1	12
(UK) Warner Brothers	*1 24 70*	*2*	*9*
PETERS AND LEE			
Welcome Home			
(UK) Philips	*6 9 73*	*1*	*15*
PETERSON, PAUL			
She Can't Find Her Keys			
(US) Colpix	4 28 62	19	1
My Dad			
(US) Colpix	12 29 62	6	7
PETERSON, RAY			
Tell Laura I Love Her			
(US) RCA	7 11 60	7	7
Corinna, Corinna			
(US) Dunes	12 26 60	9	7
PHILLIPS, LITTLE ESTHER			
Release Me			
(US) Lenox	11 24 62	8	7
PHILLIPS, PHIL			
Sea of Love			
(US) Mercury	8 10 59	2	9
PIAF, EDITH			
Milord			
(UK) Columbia	*11 13 60*	*17*	*2*
PICKETT, BOBBY "BORIS," AND THE CRYPT KICKERS			
Monster Mash			
(US) Garpax	9 22 62	1	9
(US) Parrot (reissue)	7 14 73	10	7
(UK) London (reissue)	*9 22 73*	*3*	*6*
PICKETT, WILSON			
In the Midnight Hour			
(UK) Atlantic	*10 14 65*	*12*	*4*
634-5789			
(US) Atlantic	3 19 66	13	4

LABEL	DATE OF CHART ENTRY	HIGHEST POSITION REACHED	NUMBER OF WEEKS IN CHARTS
Land of a Thousand Dances			
(US) Atlantic	8 20 66	6	5
Funky Broadway			
(US) Atlantic	9 2 67	8	6
She's Lookin' Good			
(US) Atlantic	5 25 68	15	2
Hey Jude			
(UK) Atlantic	2 15 69	16	1
Engine Number 9			
(US) Atlantic	11 14 70	14	4
Don't Let the Green Grass Fool You			
(US) Atlantic	2 27 71	17	3
Don't Knock My Love (pt. 1)			
(US) Atlantic	6 5 71	13	5
PICKETYWITCH			
That Same Old Feeling			
(UK) Pye	2 28 70	5	8
(It's Like a) Sad Old Kinda Movie			
(UK) Pye	7 18 70	16	2
PIGLETS			
Johnny Reggae			
(UK) Bell	11 6 71	3	7
PILTDOWN MAN			
McDonald's Cave			
(UK) Capitol	10 7 60	12	6
Piltdown Rides Again			
(UK) Capitol	1 1 61	16	2
Goodnight Mrs. Flintstone			
(UK) Capitol	3 5 61	18	3
PINK FLOYD			
Arnold Layne			
(UK) Columbia	4 22 67	20	1
See Emily Play			
(UK) Columbia	7 8 67	6	7
Money			
(US) Harvest	7 7 73	13	5
PINKERTON'S ASSORTED COLOURS			
Mirror Mirror			
(UK) Decca	2 12 66	9	4
PIONEERS			
Let Your Yeah Be Yeah			
(UK) Trojan	8 21 71	5	6
PIPKINS			
Gimme Dat Ding			
(UK) Columbia	4 11 70	6	6
(US) Capitol	6 27 70	9	5

LABEL	DATE OF CHART ENTRY	HIGHEST POSITION REACHED	NUMBER OF WEEKS IN CHARTS
PIPS			
Every Beat of My Heart			
(US) Vee Jay	6 12 61	6	7
[see also: **GLADYS KNIGHT AND THE PIPS**]			
PITNEY, GENE			
Town Without Pity			
(US) Musicor	1 20 62	13	4
The Man Who Shot Liberty Valance			
(US) Musicor	6 2 62	4	6
Only Love Can Break a Heart			
(US) Musicor	10 13 62	2	8
Half Heaven Half Heartache			
(US) Musicor	1 12 63	12	6
Mecca			
(US) Musicor	4 20 63	12	5
24 Hours from Tulsa			
(US) Musicor	11 30 63	17	2
(UK) United Artists	12 14 63	5	12
That Girl Belongs to Yesterday			
(UK) United Artists	3 14 64	8	7
It Hurts to Be in Love			
(US) Musicor	9 19 64	7	6
I'm Gonna Be Strong			
(US) Musicor	11 14 64	9	7
(UK) Stateside	11 21 64	2	10
I Must Be Seeing Things			
(UK) Stateside	2 27 65	6	6
Last Chance to Turn Around			
(US) Musicor	6 12 65	13	4
Lookin' Through the Eyes of Love			
(UK) Stateside	6 19 65	3	8
Princess in Rags			
(UK) Stateside	11 20 65	9	8
Backstage			
(UK) Stateside	2 26 66	4	6
Nobody Needs Your Love			
(UK) Stateside	6 18 66	2	9
Just One Smile			
(UK) Stateside	11 26 66	8	6
Somethin's Gotten Hold of My Heart			
(UK) Stateside	11 25 67	5	9
Somewhere in the Country			
(UK) Stateside	5 4 68	19	2
She's a Heartbreaker			
(US) Musicor	7 13 68	16	3

PLASTIC ONO BAND (see **JOHN LENNON**)

PLASTIC PENNY

LABEL	DATE OF CHART ENTRY	HIGHEST POSITION REACHED	NUMBER OF WEEKS IN CHARTS
Everything I Am			
(UK) *Page One*	*1 27 68*	*6*	*5*
PLATTERS			
Only You			
(US) Mercury	10 8 55	5	18
(UK) *Mercury (b/w*)*	*9 7 56*	*5*	*11*
The Great Pretender*			
(US) Mercury	12 30 55	1	17
Magic Touch			
(US) Mercury	4 7 56	4	12
My Prayer			
(US) Mercury	7 21 56	1	16
(UK) *Mercury*	*11 2 56*	*4*	*10*
You'll Never Know			
(US) Mercury	10 20 56	14	6
I'm Sorry			
(US) Mercury	4 27 57	19	2
(UK) *Mercury*	*5 31 57*	*18*	*2*
Twilight Time			
(US) Mercury	4 14 58	1	13
(UK) *Mercury*	*6 6 58*	*3*	*12*
Smoke Gets in Your Eyes			
(US) Mercury	12 8 58	1	13
(UK) *Mercury*	*1 17 59*	*1*	*19*
Enchanted			
(US) Mercury	4 20 59	12	7
Harbor Lights			
(UK) *Mercury*	*1 30 60*	*12*	*5*
(US) Mercury	2 29 60	8	8
With This Ring			
(US) Musicor	4 15 67	14	3
PLAYMATES			
Jo Ann			
(US) Roulette	2 17 58	20	1
Beep Beep			
(US) Roulette	11 10 58	4	11
What Is Love			
(US) Roulette	8 17 59	15	4
POINTER SISTERS			
Yes We Can			
(US) Blue Thumb	9 22 73	11	7
PONITAILS			
Born Too Late			
(US) ABC-Paramount	8 11 58	7	9
(UK) *HMV*	*9 19 58*	*5*	*10*
POOLE, BRIAN, AND THE TREMELOES			
Twist and Shout			
(UK) *Decca*	*7 13 63*	*4*	*10*

256   ROCK ALMANAC

LABEL	DATE OF CHART ENTRY	HIGHEST POSITION REACHED	NUMBER OF WEEKS IN CHARTS
Do You Love Me?			
(*UK*) *Decca*	*9 21 63*	*1*	*11*
Candy Man			
(*UK*) *Decca*	*2 15 64*	*6*	*7*
Someone, Someone			
(*UK*) *Decca*	*5 30 64*	*2*	*10*
Three Bells			
(*UK*) *Decca*	*1 30 65*	*17*	*2*
[see also: **TREMELOES**]			
POPPY FAMILY			
Which Way You Goin' Billy?			
(US) London	5 16 70	2	8
(*UK*) *Decca*	*9 12 70*	*7*	*7*
POSEY, SANDY			
Born a Woman			
(US) MGM	8 27 66	12	7
Single Girl			
(US) MGM	12 24 66	12	4
(*UK*) *MGM*	*1 28 67*	*15*	*7*
I Take It Back			
(US) MGM	7 15 67	12	5
POURCEL, FRANK			
Only You			
(US) Capitol	5 11 59	9	7
POWELL, COZY			
Dance with the Devil			
(*UK*) *RAK*	*12 22 73*	*3*	*10*
POWERS, JOEY			
Midnight Mary			
(US) Amy	12 28 63	10	4
PRADO, PEREZ			
Cherry Pink and Apple Blossom White			
(*UK*) *HMV*	*3 25 55*	*1*	*17*
(US) Victor	3 26 55	1	22
Patricia			
(US) Victor	6 30 58	1	15
(*UK*) *RCA*	*8 8 58*	*8*	*11*
PREMIERS			
Farmer John			
(US) Warner Brothers	8 1 64	19	1
PRESIDENTS			
5-10-15-20- (25-30 Years of Love)			
(US) Sussex	11 21 70	11	7
PRESLEY, ELVIS			
Heartbreak Hotel			
(US) Victor	3 24 56	1	18
(*UK*) *HMV*	*5 11 56*	*2*	*19*

LABEL	DATE OF CHART ENTRY	HIGHEST POSITION REACHED	NUMBER OF WEEKS IN CHARTS
Blue Suede Shoes			
(UK) HMV	5 25 56	9	8
I Want You, I Need You, I Love You			
(US) Victor	6 9 56	3	16
(UK) HMV	8 17 56	14	6
Hound Dog			
(US) Victor ⎫ (b/w*)	8 11 56	2	16
(UK) HMV ⎬	9 21 56	2	22
Don't Be Cruel*			
(US) Victor	8 18 56	1	19
Love Me Tender			
(US) Victor	10 20 56	1	17
(UK) HMV	12 7 56	11	9
Blue Moon			
(UK) HMV	11 16 56	9	8
Love Me			
(US) Victor EP	12 8 56	6	12
Too Much			
(US) Victor	2 2 57	2	11
(UK) HMV	5 10 57	6	8
All Shook Up			
(US) Victor	4 13 57	1	17
(UK) HMV	6 28 57	1	18
Teddy Bear			
(US) Victor	7 1 57	1	16
(UK) RCA	7 12 57	3	18
Paralysed			
(UK) HMV	8 30 57	8	8
Let's Have a Party			
(UK) RCA (b/w**)	10 4 57	2	14
Jailhouse Rock			
(US) Victor	10 14 57	1	16
(UK) RCA	1 24 58	1	13
Got a Lot of Living to Do*			
(UK) RCA	10 18 57	17	3
Tryin' to Get to You			
(UK) HMV (b/w***)	11 1 57	16	3
Lawdy Miss Clawdy*			
(UK) HMV	11 8 57	15	3
Santa Bring My Baby			
(UK) RCA	11 15 57	7	7
Jailhouse Rock			
(UK) RCA EP	1 31 58	18	3
Don't			
(US) Victor ⎫ (b/w†)	2 3 58	1	11
(UK) RCA ⎬	2 28 58	2	10
I Beg of You†			
(US) Victor	2 3 58	8	3
Wear My Ring Around Your Neck			

LABEL	DATE OF CHART ENTRY	HIGHEST POSITION REACHED	NUMBER OF WEEKS IN CHARTS
(US) Victor	4 21 58	3	10
(UK) RCA	*5 2 58*	*3*	*7*
Hard Headed Woman			
(US) Victor	6 30 58	2	8
(UK) RCA	*7 25 58*	*2*	*8*
King Creole			
(UK) RCA	*10 3 58*	*2*	*10*
I Got Stung			
(US) RCA ⎱ (b/w††)	11 10 58	8	10
(UK) RCA ⎰	*1 24 59*	*1*	*12*
One Night††			
(US) RCA	11 17 58	4	11
A Fool such as I			
(US) RCA ⎱ (b/w†††)	4 6 59	2	9
(UK) RCA ⎰	*4 25 59*	*1*	*14*
I Need Your Love Tonight†††			
(US) RCA	4 6 59	4	8
Big Hunk of Love			
(US) RCA ⎱ (b/w ◊)	7 20 59	1	9
(UK) RCA ⎰	*7 25 59*	*4*	*8*
My Wish Came True ◊			
(US) RCA	8 3 59	12	4
Stuck on You			
(UK) RCA ⎱ (b/w ◊ ◊)	*4 3 60*	*2*	*8*
(US) RCA ⎰	4 11 60	1	11
Fame and Fortune ◊ ◊			
(US) RCA	4 25 60	17	5
The Girl of My Best Friend/Mess of Blues			
(UK) RCA	*7 24 60*	*2*	*15*
It's Now or Never			
(US) RCA	7 25 60	1	14
(UK) RCA	*10 30 60*	*1*	*13*
Are You Lonesome Tonight?			
(US) RCA ⎱ (b/w ◊ ◊ ◊)	12 21 60	1	12
(UK) RCA ⎰	*1 8 61*	*1*	*8*
I Gotta Know ◊ ◊ ◊			
(US) RCA	12 12 60	20	1
Wooden Heart			
(UK) RCA	*2 26 61*	*1*	*15*
Surrender			
(US) RCA	2 27 61	1	9
(UK) RCA	*5 14 61*	*1*	*11*
Flaming Star			
(US) RCA EP	5 1 61	14	3
I Feel So Bad			
(US) RCA	5 22 61	5	6
(UK) RCA (b/w Wild in the Country)			
	9 2 61	*2*	*8*
Little Sister			
(US) RCA (b/wº)	9 4 61	5	7

LABEL	DATE OF CHART ENTRY	HIGHEST POSITION REACHED	NUMBER OF WEEKS IN CHARTS
(Marie's the Name) His Latest Flame⁰			
(US) RCA	9 18 61	4	2
(UK) RCA	10 28 61	1	8
Can't Help Falling in Love			
(US) RCA	12 18 61	2	10
(UK) RCA (b/w Rock A-Hula Baby)			
	2 3 62	1	17
Good Luck Charm			
(US) RCA	3 24 62	1	10
(UK) RCA	5 12 62	1	13
She's Not You			
(US) RCA	8 18 62	5	7
(UK) RCA	9 8 62	1	10
Return to Sender			
(US) RCA	10 27 62	2	12
(UK) RCA	12 8 62	1	10
One Broken Heart for Sale			
(US) RCA	3 2 63	11	5
(UK) RCA	3 16 63	12	4
(You're the) Devil in Disguise			
(US) RCA	7 13 63	3	8
(UK) RCA	7 13 63	1	9
Bossa Nova Baby			
(UK) RCA	11 2 63	13	4
(US) RCA	11 9 63	8	4
Kiss Me Quick			
(UK) RCA	12 28 63	14	6
Kissin' Cousins			
(US) RCA	3 14 64	12	4
(UK) RCA	7 4 64	10	5
Viva Las Vegas			
(UK) RCA	3 28 64	17	4
Such a Night			
(US) RCA	8 22 64	16	2
(UK) RCA	8 29 64	13	5
Ain't That Loving You Baby			
(US) RCA (b/w⁰⁰)	11 7 64	16	3
(UK) RCA	11 7 64	15	3
Ask Me⁰⁰			
(US) RCA	11 21 64	12	4
Do the Clam			
(UK) RCA	3 20 65	19	2
Crying in the Chapel			
(US) RCA	5 15 65	3	10
(UK) RCA	6 5 65	1	11
(Such An) Easy Question			
(US) RCA	7 10 65	11	4
I'm Yours			
(US) RCA	10 2 65	11	4

LABEL	DATE OF CHART ENTRY	HIGHEST POSITION REACHED	NUMBER OF WEEKS IN CHARTS
Tell Me Why			
(UK) RCA	*11 27 65*	*15*	*4*
Puppet on a String			
(US) RCA	12 18 65	14	3
Love Letters			
(UK) RCA	*7 16 66*	*6*	*7*
(US) RCA	7 23 66	19	2
All That I Am			
(UK) RCA	*11 5 66*	*18*	*1*
If Every Day Was like Christmas			
(UK) RCA	*12 10 66*	*13*	*3*
Guitar Man			
(UK) RCA	*3 23 68*	*19*	*2*
U. S. Male			
(UK) RCA	*5 25 68*	*15*	*3*
If I Can Dream			
(US) RCA	1 11 69	12	6
(UK) RCA	*3 8 69*	*11*	*6*
In the Ghetto			
(US) RCA	5 24 69	3	9
(UK) RCA	*5 24 69*	*2*	*11*
Suspicious Minds			
(US) RCA	9 27 69	1	11
(UK) RCA	*12 6 69*	*2*	*11*
Don't Cry Daddy			
(US) RCA (b/w Rubberneckin')	1 3 70	6	7
(UK) RCA	*3 7 70*	*8*	*7*
Kentucky Rain			
(US) RCA	3 14 70	16	3
The Wonder of You			
(US) RCA (b/w Mama Liked the Roses)			
	6 13 70	9	7
(UK) RCA	*7 11 70*	*1*	*16*
You Don't Have to Say You Love Me			
(US) RCA (b/w Patch It Up)	11 21 70	11	4
(UK) RCA	*1 16 71*	*9*	*6*
I've Lost You			
(UK) RCA	*11 28 70*	*9*	*8*
There Goes My Everything			
(UK) RCA	*3 27 71*	*6*	*6*
Rags to Riches			
(UK) RCA	*5 29 71*	*9*	*6*
Heartbreak Hotel			
(UK) RCA (reissue)	*8 7 71*	*10*	*5*
I Just Can't Help Believing			
(UK) RCA	*12 25 71*	*6*	*8*
Until It's Time for You to Go			
(UK) RCA	*4 15 72*	*5*	*5*
American Trilogy			
(UK) RCA	*7 1 72*	*8*	*5*

LABEL	DATE OF CHART ENTRY	HIGHEST POSITION REACHED	NUMBER OF WEEKS IN CHARTS
Burning Love			
(US) RCA	9 23 72	2	9
(UK) RCA	*10 7 72*	*7*	*6*
Always on My Mind			
(UK) RCA	*1 6 73*	*9*	*5*
Separate Ways			
(UK) RCA	*2 3 73*	*20*	*1*
Steamroller Blues			
(US) RCA (b/w°°°)	5 26 73	17	2
Fool°°°			
(US) RCA	5 26 73	17	2
(UK) RCA	*9 1 73*	*15*	*5*
PRESTON, BILLY			
That's the Way God Planned It			
(UK) Apple	*7 12 69*	*11*	*6*
Outa-Space			
(US) A&M	6 3 72	2	8
Will It Go Round in Circles			
(US) A&M	6 2 73	1	11
Space Race			
(US) A&M	10 20 73	4	9
PRESTON, JOHNNY			
Running Bear			
(US) Mercury	12 28 59	1	12
(UK) Mercury	*2 6 60*	*1*	*11*
Cradle of Love			
(US) Mercury	4 11 60	7	9
(UK) Mercury	*5 1 60*	*2*	*9*
Feel So Fine			
(US) Mercury	8 1 60	14	5
PRESTON, MIKE			
Mr. Blue			
(UK) Decca	*10 24 59*	*9*	*7*
Marry Me			
(UK) Decca	*3 12 61*	*13*	*3*
PRETTY THINGS			
Don't Bring Me Down			
(UK) Fontana	*11 14 64*	*10*	*5*
Honey I Need			
(UK) Fontana	*3 13 65*	*13*	*3*
PRICE, ALAN			
I Put a Spell on You			
(UK) Decca	*4 16 66*	*9*	*5*
Hi-Lili-Hi-Lo			
(UK) Decca	*8 6 66*	*11*	*7*
Simon Smith and His Dancing Bear			
(UK) Decca	*3 18 67*	*4*	*7*
The House That Jack Built			
(UK) Decca	*8 12 67*	*4*	*7*

LABEL	DATE OF CHART ENTRY	HIGHEST POSITION REACHED	NUMBER OF WEEKS IN CHARTS
Don't Stop the Carnival			
(*UK*) Decca	2 10 68	13	4
[see also: **ANIMALS; FAME AND PRICE**]			
PRICE, LLOYD			
Stagger Lee			
(US) ABC-Paramount	1 19 59	1	12
(*UK*) HMV	2 14 59	6	13
Where Were You on Our Wedding Day?			
(*UK*) HMV	5 9 59	15	5
Personality			
(US) ABC-Paramount	5 25 59	2	11
(*UK*) HMV	6 6 59	9	9
I'm Gonna Get Married			
(US) ABC-Paramount	8 24 59	3	10
(*UK*) HMV	9 19 59	20	2
Come into My Heart			
(US) ABC-Paramount	12 7 59	20	1
Lady Luck			
(US) ABC-Paramount	2 22 60	14	7
Question			
(US) ABC-Paramount	8 8 60	19	1
PRICE, RAY			
For the Good Times			
(US) Columbia	12 19 70	11	6
PRIMA, LOUIS			
Wonderland by Night			
(US) Dot	12 19 60	15	6
[see also: **KEELEY SMITH**]			
PRINCE BUSTER			
Al Capone			
(*UK*) Blue Beat	4 1 67	18	2
PROBY, P. J.			
Hold Me			
(*UK*) Decca	6 27 64	3	8
Together			
(*UK*) Decca	9 18 64	8	6
Somewhere			
(*UK*) Liberty	12 19 64	6	8
I Apologise			
(*UK*) Liberty	3 6 65	11	5
Let the Water Run Down			
(*UK*) Liberty	7 31 65	19	1
Maria			
(*UK*) Liberty	12 4 65	8	6
PROCOL HARUM			
A Whiter Shade of Pale			
(*UK*) Deram	6 3 67	1	11
(US) Deram	7 8 67	5	9
(*UK*) MagniFly (*reissue*)	5 27 72	13	4

LABEL	DATE OF CHART ENTRY	HIGHEST POSITION REACHED	NUMBER OF WEEKS IN CHARTS
Homburg			
(*UK*) *Regal Zonophone*	*10 14 67*	*7*	*7*
Conquistador			
(US) A&M	7 15 72	16	4
PROVINE, DOROTHY			
Don't Bring Lulu			
(*UK*) *Warner Brothers*	*1 6 62*	*14*	*2*
PUCKETT, GARY (see **UNION GAP**)			
PURIFY, JAMES AND BOBBY			
I'm Your Puppet			
(US) Bell	10 29 66	6	7
PURSELL, BILL			
Our Winter Love			
(US) Columbia	3 9 63	9	6
PYRAMIDS			
Penetration			
(US) Best	3 7 64	18	2
PYTHON LEE JACKSON			
In a Broken Dream			
(*UK*) *Young Blood*	*10 7 72*	*3*	*6*
QUATRO, SUZIE			
Can the Can			
(*UK*) *RAK*	*5 26 73*	*1*	*7*
48 Crash			
(*UK*) *RAK*	*8 4 73*	*3*	*5*
Daytona Demon			
(*UK*) *RAK*	*11 17 73*	*14*	*4*
? AND THE MYSTERIANS			
96 Tears			
(US) Cameo	9 24 66	1	11
QUIN-TONES			
Down the Aisle of Love			
(US) Hunt	9 15 58	20	1
RADHA KRISHNA TEMPLE			
Hare Krishna Mantra			
(*UK*) *Apple*	*9 20 69*	*12*	*5*
RAIDERS (see **PAUL REVERE**)			
RAINDROPS			
The Kind of Boy You Can't Forget			
(US) Jubilee	9 28 63	17	1
RAINWATER, MARVIN			
Whole Lotta Woman			
(*UK*) *MGM*	*3 14 58*	*1*	*14*
I Dig You Baby			
(*UK*) *MGM*	*6 20 58*	*19*	*1*
RAMRODS			
Riders in the Sky			
(*UK*) *London*	*2 5 61*	*7*	*9*

LABEL	DATE OF CHART ENTRY	HIGHEST POSITION REACHED	NUMBER OF WEEKS IN CHARTS
RAN-DELLS			
Martian Hop			
(US) Chairman	9 21 63	16	3
RANDY AND THE RAINBOWS			
Denise			
(US) Rust	8 17 63	10	5
RARE EARTH			
Get Ready			
(US) Rare Earth	5 9 70	4	11
(I Know) I'm Losing You			
(US) Rare Earth	9 12 70	7	6
Born to Wander			
(US) Rare Earth	1 30 71	17	2
I Just Want to Celebrate			
(US) Rare Earth	8 28 71	7	6
Hey Big Brother			
(US) Rare Earth	1 15 72	19	2
RASCALS (see **YOUNG RASCALS**)			
RASPBERRIES			
Go All the Way			
(US) Capitol	9 2 72	5	8
I Wanna Be with You			
(US) Capitol	1 13 73	16	3
RATTLES			
The Witch			
(*UK*) *Decca*	*10 31 70*	*8*	*5*
RAWLS, LOU			
Love Is a Hurtin' Thing			
(US) Capitol	10 29 66	13	5
Your Good Thing (Is About to End)			
(US) Capitol	9 13 69	18	3
Natural Man			
(US) MGM	11 27 71	17	3
RAY, JOHNNIE			
If You Believe			
(*UK*) *Philips*	*4 8 55*	*7*	*11*
Paths of Paradise			
(*UK*) *Philips*	*5 20 55*	*20*	*1*
Hernando's Hideaway			
(*UK*) *Philips*	*10 7 55*	*11*	*5*
Hey There			
(*UK*) *Philips*	*10 14 55*	*5*	*9*
Song of the Dreamer			
(*UK*) *Philips*	*10 28 55*	*10*	*5*
Who's Sorry Now			
(*UK*) *Philips*	*2 17 56*	*17*	*2*
Ain't Misbehavin'			
(*UK*) *Philips*	*4 20 56*	*17*	*4*

LABEL	DATE OF CHART ENTRY	HIGHEST POSITION REACHED	NUMBER OF WEEKS IN CHARTS
Just Walkin' in the Rain			
(US) Columbia	9 22 56	2	20
(*UK*) *Philips*	*10 12 56*	*1*	*18*
You Don't Owe Me a Thing			
(*UK*) *Philips* ⎫ (b/w*)	*1 25 57*	*12*	*10*
(US) Columbia ⎭	2 9 57	10	6
Look Homeward Angel*			
(*UK*) *Philips*	*3 22 57*	*7*	*10*
Yes Tonight Josephine			
(*UK*) *Philips*	*5 10 57*	*1*	*15*
(US) Columbia	5 27 57	18	1
Build Your Love			
(*UK*) *Philips*	*9 13 57*	*17*	*3*
RAYBURN, MARGIE			
I'm Available			
(US) Liberty	11 25 57	16	5
RAYS			
Silhouettes			
(US) Cameo	10 28 57	3	15
REBELS			
Wild Weekend			
(US) Swan	2 16 63	8	6
REDBONE			
Witch Queen of New Orleans			
(*UK*) *Epic*	*10 9 71*	*2*	*8*
REDDING, OTIS			
My Girl			
(*UK*) *Atlantic*	*1 8 66*	*11*	*7*
Tramp (with **CARLA THOMAS**)			
(*UK*) *Stax*	*8 19 67*	*18*	*1*
(Sittin' on the) Dock of the Bay			
(US) Volt	2 17 68	1	12
(*UK*) *Stax*	*3 9 68*	*3*	*8*
Hard to Handle			
(*UK*) *Atlantic*	*8 31 68*	*15*	*6*
REDDY, HELEN			
I Don't Know How to Love Him			
(US) Capitol	5 22 71	13	5
I Am Woman			
(US) Capitol	10 28 72	1	11
Peaceful			
(US) Capitol	4 14 73	12	4
Delta Dawn			
(US) Capitol	8 11 73	1	10
Leave Me Alone (Ruby Red)			
(US) Capitol	11 24 73	3	6
REED, JERRY			
Amos Moses			
(US) RCA	2 20 71	8	7

LABEL	DATE OF CHART ENTRY	HIGHEST POSITION REACHED	NUMBER OF WEEKS IN CHARTS
When You're Hot You're Hot			
(US) RCA	6 12 71	9	6
REED, LOU			
Walk on the Wild Side			
(US) RCA	4 21 73	16	4
(UK) RCA	*5 26 73*	*10*	*4*
REESE, DELLA			
Don't You Know			
(US) RCA	10 19 59	2	10
Not One Minute More			
(US) RCA	1 4 60	16	4
REEVES, JIM			
Four Walls			
(US) Victor	5 20 57	12	7
He'll Have to Go			
(US) RCA	1 21 60	2	16
(UK) RCA	*4 10 60*	*11*	*15*
You're the Only Good Thing That's Happened to Me			
(UK) RCA	*12 2 61*	*12*	*1*
Welcome to My World			
(UK) RCA	*6 29 63*	*6*	*10*
I Love You Because			
(UK) RCA	*3 14 64*	*5*	*26*
I Won't Forget You			
(UK) RCA	*7 4 64*	*3*	*19*
There's a Heartache Following Me			
(UK) RCA	*11 14 64*	*6*	*9*
It Hurts So Much			
(UK) RCA	*2 13 65*	*8*	*6*
Not Until the Next Time			
(UK) RCA	*5 15 65*	*13*	*5*
Is It Really Over?			
(UK) RCA	*12 4 65*	*17*	*2*
Distant Drums			
(UK) RCA	*9 3 66*	*1*	*19*
I Won't Come In While He's There			
(UK) RCA	*2 11 67*	*12*	*5*
When Two Worlds Collide			
(UK) RCA	*8 2 69*	*17*	*2*
But You Love Me, Daddy			
(UK) RCA	*12 27 69*	*15*	*6*
REEVES, MARTHA (see **MARTHA AND THE VANDELLAS**)			
REFLECTIONS			
(Just like) Romeo and Juliet			
(US) Golden World	5 16 64	6	5
REGAN, JOAN			
Prize of Gold			
(UK) Decca	*3 25 55*	*6*	*9*
May You Always			
(UK) HMV	*6 6 59*	*12*	*8*

LABEL	DATE OF CHART ENTRY	HIGHEST POSITION REACHED	NUMBER OF WEEKS IN CHARTS
Happy Anniversary			
(*UK*) *HMV*	*2 13 60*	*20*	*1*
REGENTS			
Barbara Ann			
(US) Gee	5 29 61	13	6
REID, NEIL			
Mother of Mine			
(*UK*) *Decca*	*12 25 71*	*2*	*15*
RENAY, DIANE			
Navy Blue			
(US) 20th Century Fox	2 22 64	6	6
RENE AND RENE			
The More I Love You			
(US) White Whale	1 4 69	14	3
REPARATA AND THE DELRONS			
Captain of Your Ship			
(*UK*) *Bell*	*4 6 68*	*13*	*5*
REVERE, PAUL, AND THE RAIDERS FEATURING MARK LINDSAY			
Just Like Me			
(US) Columbia	1 15 66	11	5
Kicks			
(US) Columbia	4 9 66	4	9
Hungry			
(US) Columbia	7 9 66	6	6
Great Airplane Strike			
(US) Columbia	10 29 66	20	1
Good Thing			
(US) Columbia	12 31 66	4	7
Him or Me—What's It Gonna Be?			
(US) Columbia*	5 20 67	5	5
I Had a Dream			
(US) Columbia	9 16 67	17	3
Too Much Talk			
(US) Columbia	3 9 69	19	3
Mr. Sun, Mr. Moon			
(US) Columbia	4 5 69	18	3
Let Me			
(US) Columbia	7 5 69	20	2
Indian Reservations			
(US) Columbia**	6 12 71	1	12
[*no label credit to **MARK LINDSAY**; **label credit: **RAIDERS**]			
REYNOLDS, DEBBIE			
Tammy			
(US) Coral	8 5 57	1	18
(*UK*) *Vogue-Coral*	*9 6 57*	*2*	*15*
REYNOLDS, JODY			
Endless Sleep			
(US) Demon	6 16 58	5	9

LABEL	DATE OF CHART ENTRY	HIGHEST POSITION REACHED	NUMBER OF WEEKS IN CHARTS
RICH, CHARLIE			
Behind Closed Doors			
(US) Epic	6 30 73	15	4
Most Beautiful Girl			
(US) Epic	11 17 73	1	7
RICHARD, CLIFF (and **THE SHADOWS** through 1967)			
Move It			
(UK) Columbia	9 26 58	2	11
High Class Baby			
(UK) Columbia	11 28 58	7	9
Never Mind/Mean Streak			
(UK) Columbia	4 25 59	8	10
Livin' Doll			
(UK) Columbia	7 11 59	1	18
Travellin' Light			
(UK) Columbia	10 10 59	1	14
A Voice in the Wilderness			
(UK) Columbia	1 16 60	2	10
Expresso Bongo			
(UK) Columbia EP	1 16 60	8	4
Fall in Love with You/Willie and the Hand Jive			
(UK) Columbia	3 20 60	2	11
Please Don't Tease			
(UK) Columbia	6 26 60	1	14
Nine Times out of Ten			
(UK) Columbia	9 18 60	2	9
I Love You			
(UK) Columbia	11 27 60	2	11
Theme for a Dream			
(UK) Columbia	2 19 61	4	9
Gee Whiz, It's You			
(UK) Columbia	3 26 61	8	7
A Girl Like You			
(UK) Columbia	6 11 61	3	11
When the Girl in Your Arms Is the Girl in Your Heart			
(UK) Columbia	10 14 61	2	9
The Young Ones			
(UK) Columbia	1 13 62	1	15
Do You Want to Dance/I'm Looking out the Window			
(UK) Columbia	5 12 62	2	12
It'll Be Me			
(UK) Columbia	9 8 62	2	9
The Next Time/Bachelor Boy			
(UK) Columbia	12 8 62	1	14
Summer Holiday			
(UK) Columbia	3 2 63	1	11
Lucky Lips			
(UK) Columbia	5 18 63	4	8
It's All in the Game			
(UK) Columbia	8 31 63	2	9

LABEL	DATE OF CHART ENTRY	HIGHEST POSITION REACHED	NUMBER OF WEEKS IN CHARTS
Don't Talk to Him			
(UK) Columbia	11 16 63	2	9
I'm the Lonely One			
(UK) Columbia	2 15 64	8	4
Constantly			
(UK) Columbia	5 9 64	4	8
On the Beach			
(UK) Columbia	7 11 64	7	8
Twelfth of Never			
(UK) Columbia	10 17 64	8	6
I Could Easily Fall			
(UK) Columbia	12 12 64	6	8
The Minute You're Gone			
(UK) Columbia	3 27 65	1	9
On My Word			
(UK) Columbia	6 26 65	12	5
Wind Me Up			
(UK) Columbia	11 20 65	2	12
Blue Turns to Grey			
(UK) Columbia	4 2 66	15	6
Visions			
(UK) Columbia	7 30 66	7	8
Time Drags By			
(UK) Columbia	10 29 66	10	4
In the Country			
(UK) Columbia	12 31 66	6	6
It's All Over			
(UK) Columbia	4 1 67	9	6
The Day I Met Marie			
(UK) Columbia	9 9 67	10	8
All My Love			
(UK) Columbia	11 25 67	8	8
Congratulations			
(UK) Columbia	3 30 68	1	9
Good Times			
(UK) Columbia	3 8 69	12	7
Big Ship			
(UK) Columbia	6 14 69	8	5
Throw Down a Line (with **HANK MARVIN**)			
(UK) Columbia	9 20 69	7	6
With the Eyes of a Child			
(UK) Columbia	12 20 69	20	2
Goodbye Sam Hello Samantha			
(UK) Columbia	6 13 70	6	10
Sunny Honey Girl			
(UK) Columbia	2 20 71	19	1
Sing a Song of Freedom			
(UK) Columbia	11 27 71	13	4
Living in Harmony			
(UK) Columbia	9 16 72	12	4

LABEL	DATE OF CHART ENTRY	HIGHEST POSITION REACHED	NUMBER OF WEEKS IN CHARTS
Power to All Our Friends			
(UK) EMI	3 17 73	4	7
RIDDLE, NELSON			
Lisbon Antigua			
(US) Capitol	1 21 56	2	19
RIGHTEOUS BROTHERS			
You've Lost That Lovin' Feeling			
(US) Philles	1 2 65	1	12
(UK) London	1 23 65	1	7
Just Once in My Life			
(US) Philles	4 24 65	9	6
Unchained Melody			
(US) Philles	8 7 65	4	8
(UK) London	9 11 65	14	3
Ebb Tide			
(US) Philles	12 18 65	5	6
(You're My) Soul and Inspiration			
(US) Verve	3 19 66	1	10
(UK) Verve	5 7 66	15	4
He			
(US) Verve	7 2 66	18	2
You've Lost That Lovin' Feeling			
(UK) London (re-entry)	3 1 69	10	7
RILEY, JEANNIE C.			
Harper Valley PTA			
(US) Plantation	8 31 68	1	11
(UK) Polydor	11 30 68	12	4
RIOS, MIGUEL			
Song of Joy			
(US) A&M	7 4 70	14	5
(UK) A&M	8 8 70	16	2
RIP CHORDS			
Hey Little Cobra			
(US) Columbia	1 11 64	4	8
RITTER, TEX			
Wayward Wind			
(UK) Capitol	6 29 56	8	11
Hillbilly Heaven			
(US) Capitol	8 28 61	20	1
RIVERS, JOHNNY			
Memphis			
(US) Imperial	6 20 64	2	8
Maybellene			
(US) Imperial	9 5 64	12	4
Mountain of Love			
(US) Imperial	11 21 64	9	6
Midnight Special			
(US) Imperial	3 13 65	20	2

LABEL	DATE OF CHART ENTRY	HIGHEST POSITION REACHED	NUMBER OF WEEKS IN CHARTS
Seventh Son			
(US) Imperial	6 19 65	7	7
Secret Agent Man			
(US) Imperial	4 2 66	3	7
I Washed My Hands in Muddy Water			
(US) Imperial	7 16 66	19	1
Poor Side of Town			
(US) Imperial	10 8 66	1	10
Baby I Need Your Lovin'			
(US) Imperial	2 18 67	3	8
Tracks of My Tears			
(US) Imperial	6 24 67	10	4
Summer Rain			
(US) Imperial	12 16 67	14	5
Rockin' Pneumonia and the Boogie Woogie Flu			
(US) United Artists	12 2 72	6	10
RIVIERAS			
California Sun			
(US) Riviera	2 15 64	5	6
ROBBINS, MARTY			
White Sports Coat			
(US) Columbia	4 29 57	3	15
El Paso			
(US) Columbia	12 7 59	1	12
(UK) Fontana	1 23 60	17	2
Don't Worry (Like All the Other Times)			
(US) Columbia	2 20 61	3	10
Devil Woman			
(US) Columbia	9 1 62	16	3
(UK) CBS	10 27 62	5	11
Ruby Ann			
(US) Columbia	12 22 62	18	1
ROBERTS, AUSTIN			
Something's Wrong with Me			
(US) Chelsea	11 25 72	12	7
ROBERTS, MALCOLM			
May I Have the Next Dream with You			
(UK) Major Minor	11 23 68	8	8
Love Is All			
(UK) Major Minor	11 29 69	12	5
ROBERTSON, DON			
Happy Whistler			
(US) Capitol	5 12 56	9	11
(UK) Capitol	5 18 56	8	7
ROBIC, IVO			
Morgen			
(US) Laurie	9 21 59	13	6
ROBINSON, FLOYD			
Makin' Love			

LABEL	DATE OF CHART ENTRY	HIGHEST POSITION REACHED	NUMBER OF WEEKS IN CHARTS
(US) RCA	9 28 59	20	1
(UK) RCA	10 17 59	8	7

SMOKEY ROBINSON AND THE MIRACLES
The Love I Saw in You Was Just a Mirage

(US) Tamla	4 8 67	20	1

I Second That Emotion

(US) Tamla	12 2 67	4	10

If You Can Wait

(US) Tamla	3 30 68	11	6

Don't Cry

(US) Tamla	2 15 69	8	6

Tears of a Clown

(UK) Tamla Motown	8 15 70	1	10
(US) Tamla	11 7 70	1	12

I Don't Blame You at All

(US) Tamla	5 15 71	18	1
(UK) Tamla Motown	6 26 71	11	5

[see also: **MIRACLES**]

ROCK-A-TEENS
Woo-Hoo

(US) Roulette	11 23 59	16	1

ROCKIN' BERRIES
He's in Town

(UK) Pye	10 31 64	3	7

Poor Man's Son

(UK) Piccadilly	5 22 65	5	7

LORD ROCKINGHAM'S XI
Hoots Mon

(UK) Decca	10 24 58	1	16

Wee Tom

(UK) Decca	2 7 59	11	3

ROCKY FELLERS
Killer Joe

(US) Scepter	5 11 63	16	3

RODGERS, CLODAGH
Come Back and Shake Me

(UK) RCA	4 19 69	3	8

Goodnight Midnight

(UK) RCA	7 26 69	4	8

Jack in the Box

(UK) RCA	3 27 71	4	6

RODGERS, JIMMIE
Honeycomb

(US) Roulette	9 2 57	1	15

Kisses Sweeter than Wine

(US) Roulette	12 9 57	7	10
(UK) Columbia	12 20 57	7	10

Oh Oh I'm Falling in Love Again

(UK) Columbia	4 4 58	18	5

LABEL	DATE OF CHART ENTRY	HIGHEST POSITION REACHED	NUMBER OF WEEKS IN CHARTS
Secretly			
(US) Roulette	5 26 58	4	10
Are You Really Mine			
(US) Roulette	8 25 58	10	4
Bimbambay			
(US) Roulette	12 8 58	11	7
English Country Garden			
(UK) Columbia	6 30 62	5	9
RODGERS, JULIE			
The Wedding			
(UK) Mercury	9 4 64	3	13
(US) Mercury	12 19 64	10	5
Like a Child			
(UK) Mercury	1 2 65	20	1
ROE, TOMMY			
Shelia			
(US) ABC-Paramount	8 18 62	1	10
(UK) HMV	9 22 62	3	10
The Folk Singer			
(UK) HMV	3 30 63	4	9
Everybody			
(UK) HMV	10 12 63	9	5
(US) ABC-Paramount	11 9 63	3	8
Sweet Pea			
(US) ABC	7 16 66	8	7
Hooray for Hazel			
(US) ABC	10 15 66	6	7
Dizzy			
(US) ABC	3 1 69	1	10
(UK) Stateside	5 10 69	1	10
Jam Up Jelly Tight			
(US) ABC	12 27 69	8	7
RODGERS, EILEEN			
Miracle of Love			
(US) Columbia	10 6 56	19	2
ROGERS, KENNY, AND THE FIRST EDITION			
Ruby, Don't Take Your Love to Town			
(US) Reprise	7 19 69	6	6
(UK) Reprise	11 15 69	2	14
Something's Burning			
(UK) Reprise	3 7 70	8	8
(US) Reprise	4 18 70	11	5
Tell It All Brother			
(US) Reprise	8 15 70	17	3
[see also: **FIRST EDITION**]			
ROLLING STONES			
I Wanna Be Your Man			
(UK) Decca	12 7 63	12	9

LABEL	DATE OF CHART ENTRY	HIGHEST POSITION REACHED	NUMBER OF WEEKS IN CHARTS
Not Fade Away			
(*UK*) *Decca*	*3 7 64*	*3*	9
It's All Over Now			
(*UK*) *Decca*	*7 11 64*	*1*	*11*
Time Is on My Side			
(US) London	11 14 64	6	8
Little Red Rooster			
(*UK*) *Decca*	*11 28 64*	*1*	*8*
Heart of Stone			
(US) London	1 20 65	19	1
The Last Time			
(*UK*) *Decca*	*3 13 65*	*1*	*9*
(US) London	4 17 65	9	5
(I Can't Get No) Satisfaction			
(US) London	6 26 65	1	10
(*UK*) *Decca*	*8 28 65*	*1*	*10*
Get off of My Cloud			
(US) London	10 16 65	1	9
(*UK*) *Decca*	*10 30 65*	*1*	*8*
As Tears Go By			
(US) London	1 8 66	6	5
19th Nervous Breakdown			
(*UK*) *Decca*	*2 12 66*	*2*	*7*
(US) London	3 5 66	2	8
Paint It Black			
(*UK*) *Decca*	*5 21 66*	*1*	*7*
(US) London	5 21 66	1	9
Mother's Little Helper			
(US) London	7 23 66	8	6
Have You Seen Your Mother Baby			
(*UK*) *Decca*	*10 1 66*	*5*	*6*
(US) London	10 15 66	9	5
Let's Spend the Night Together/Ruby Tuesday			
(*UK*) *Decca*	*1 28 67*	*3*	*7*
(US) London	2 4 67	1	8
Dandelion/We Love You			
(*UK*) *Decca*	*8 26 67*	*8*	*6*
(US) London	9 30 67	14	3
Jumping Jack Flash			
(*UK*) *Decca*	*6 1 68*	*1*	*9*
(US) London	6 22 68	3	9
Honky Tonk Women			
(*UK*) *Decca*	*7 12 69*	*1*	*12*
(US) London	8 2 69	1	12
Brown Sugar			
(*UK*) *Rolling Stones* (b/w Bitch/Let It Rock)			
	5 1 71	*2*	*9*
(US) Rolling Stones	5 8 71	1	10
Tumbling Dice			

LABEL	DATE OF CHART ENTRY	HIGHEST POSITION REACHED	NUMBER OF WEEKS IN CHARTS
(UK) *Rolling Stones*	4 29 72	*5*	6
(US) Rolling Stones	5 13 72	7	6
Angie			
(UK) *Rolling Stones*	9 8 73	*5*	*5*
(US) Rolling Stones	9 29 73	1	10

ROMEO, MAX
Wet Dream

(UK) *Unity*	8 2 69	*10*	6

RONDO, DON
Two Different Worlds

(US) Jubilee	11 17 56	19	2

White Silver Sands

(US) Jubilee	7 5 57	10	8

RONETTES
Be My Baby

(US) Philles	9 14 63	2	9
(UK) *London*	10 26 63	*4*	*7*

Baby I Love You

(UK) *London*	2 1 64	*11*	*7*

RONNIE AND THE HI-LITES
I Wish That We Were Married

(US) Joy	5 12 62	16	3

RONNY AND THE DAYTONAS
G.T.O.

(US) Mala	8 29 64	4	8

ROOFTOP SINGERS
Walk Right In

(US) Vanguard	1 19 63	1	9
(UK) *Fontana*	2 17 63	*10*	*6*

Tom Cat

(US) Vanguard	5 4 63	20	1

ROSE, DAVID, AND ORCHESTRA
Stripper

(US) MGM	9 2 62	1	11

ROSE GARDEN
Next Plane to London

(US) Atco	12 30 67	17	1

ROSIE AND THE ORIGINALS
Angel Baby

(US) Highland	12 26 60	5	9

ROSS, DIANA
Reach Out and Touch (Somebody's Hand)

(US) Motown	6 6 70	20	1

Ain't No Mountain High Enough

(US) Motown	8 22 70	1	11
(UK) *Tamla Motown*	9 26 70	*6*	*7*

Remember Me

(US) Motown	1 30 71	16	3
(UK) *Tamla Motown*	4 17 71	*7*	*7*

LABEL	DATE OF CHART ENTRY	HIGHEST POSITION REACHED	NUMBER OF WEEKS IN CHARTS
I'm Still Waiting			
(*UK*) *Tamla Motown*	*7 31 71*	*1*	*11*
Surrender			
(*UK*) *Tamla Motown*	*11 20 71*	*10*	*5*
Doobedood'n doobe			
(*UK*) *Tamla Motown*	*6 3 72*	*12*	*3*
Touch Me in the Morning			
(US) Motown	7 21 73	1	12
(*UK*) *Tamla Motown*	*7 28 73*	*9*	*6*
You're a Special Part of Me (with **MARVIN GAYE**)			
(US) Motown	10 27 73	12	4
[see also: **DIANA ROSS AND THE SUPREMES; SUPREMES**]			

ROSS, DIANA, AND THE SUPREMES

Reflections			
(US) Motown	8 19 67	2	8
(*UK*) *Tamla Motown*	*9 16 67*	*5*	*8*
In and out of Love			
(US) Motown	12 2 67	9	4
(*UK*) *Tamla Motown*	*12 9 67*	*13*	*7*
Love Child			
(US) Motown	10 26 68	1	14
(*UK*) *Tamla Motown*	*12 7 68*	*15*	*9*
I'm Gonna Make You Love Me (with the **TEMPTATIONS**)			
(US) Motown	12 14 68	2	11
(*UK*) *Tamla Motown*	*2 8 69*	*3*	*7*
I'm Livin' in Shame			
(US) Motown	2 8 69	10	4
(*UK*) *Tamla Motown*	*5 10 69*	*14*	*3*
I Second that Emotion (with the **TEMPTATIONS**)			
(*UK*) *Tamla Motown*	*10 4 69*	*18*	*2*
Someday We'll Be Together			
(US) Motown	11 29 69	1	12
(*UK*) *Tamla Motown*	*1 17 70*	*13*	*5*

ROSS, JACK

Cinderella			
(US) Dot	4 21 62	16	2

ROSS, JACKIE

Selfish One			
(US) Chess	8 29 64	11	5

ROSS, SPENCER

Tracy's Theme			
(US) Columbia	2 1 60	13	7

ROSSO, NINI

Il Silenzio			
(*UK*) *Durium*	*9 18 65*	*8*	*7*

ROUTERS

Let's Go			
(US) Warner Brothers	12 15 62	19	2
[see also: **MARKETTS**]			

LABEL	DATE OF CHART ENTRY	HIGHEST POSITION REACHED	NUMBER OF WEEKS IN CHARTS
ROVER BOYS			
Graduation Days			
(US) ABC-Paramount	6 23 56	20	1
ROWLES, JOHN			
If I Only Had Time			
(*UK*) *MCA*	*3 30 68*	*3*	*11*
Not a Word to Mary			
(*UK*) *MCA*	*9 29 68*	*12*	*5*
ROXY MUSIC			
Virginia Plain			
(*UK*) *Island*	*9 2 72*	*4*	*6*
Pyjamarama			
(*UK*) *Island*	*3 31 73*	*10*	*6*
Street Life			
(*UK*) *Island*	*12 1 73*	*9*	*7*
ROYAL, BILLY JOE			
Down in the Boondocks			
(US) Columbia	8 7 65	9	6
I Knew You When			
(US) Columbia	10 30 65	14	4
Cherry Hill Park			
(US) Columbia	11 22 69	15	5
ROYAL AIR FORCE BAND			
Dambusters March			
(*UK*) *HMV*	*10 21 55*	*18*	*1*
ROYAL GUARDSMEN			
Snoopy vs. the Red Baron			
(US) Laurie	12 24 66	2	9
(*UK*) *Stateside*	*2 4 67*	*8*	*8*
Return of the Red Baron			
(US) Laurie	3 25 67	15	1
ROYAL SCOTS DRAGOON GUARDS BAND			
Amazing Grace			
(*UK*) *RCA*	*4 15 72*	*1*	*10*
(US) RCA	6 10 72	11	4
Little Drummer Boy			
(*UK*) *RCA*	*12 16 72*	*13*	*4*
ROYAL TEENS			
Short Shorts			
(US) ABC-Paramount	2 3 58	3	8
ROYALTONES			
Poor Boy			
(US) Jubilee	12 1 58	17	1
ROZA, LITA			
Hey There			
(*UK*) *Decca*	*10 7 55*	*17*	*2*
Jimmy Unknown			
(*UK*) *Decca*	*3 23 56*	*15*	*4*

LABEL	DATE OF CHART ENTRY	HIGHEST POSITION REACHED	NUMBER OF WEEKS IN CHARTS
RUBY AND THE ROMANTICS			
Our Day Will Come			
(US) Kapp	3 2 63	1	8
My Summer Love			
(US) Kapp	6 29 63	16	2
RUFFIN, BRUCE			
Rain			
(UK) Trojan	*5 22 71*	*19*	*2*
Mad About You			
(UK) Rhino	*7 22 72*	*9*	*5*
RUFFIN, DAVID			
My Whole World Ended (The Moment You Left Me)			
(US) Motown	3 8 69	9	5
RUFFIN, JIMMY			
What Becomes of the Broken Hearted			
(US) Soul	10 1 66	7	9
(UK) Tamla Motown	*12 3 66*	*8*	*7*
I've Passed This Way Before			
(US) Soul	1 14 67	17	3
Farewell Is a Lonely Sound			
(UK) Tamla Motown	*3 28 70*	*8*	*8*
It's Wonderful to Be Loved by You			
(UK) Tamla Motown	*10 31 70*	*6*	*9*
I'll Say Forever My Love			
(UK) Tamla Motown (reissue)	*7 18 70*	*7*	*8*
RUNDGREN, TODD (*as **RUNT**)			
We Gotta Get You a Woman			
(US) Ampex*	1 30 71	20	3
I Saw the Light			
(US) Bearsville	6 3 72	16	4
Hello It's Me			
(US) Bearsville	11 24 73	5	6
RUSH, MERRILEE			
Angel of the Morning			
(US) Bell	6 8 68	7	8
RUSSELL, LEON			
Tight Rope			
(US) Shelter	10 7 72	11	5
RYAN, BARRY			
Eloise			
(UK) MGM	*11 2 68*	*2*	*8*
RYAN, MARION			
Love Me Forever			
(UK) Pye Nixa	*1 24 58*	*5*	*10*
It's You That I Love			
(UK) Pye	*12 18 60*	*20*	*1*
RYAN, PAUL AND BARRY			
Don't Bring Me Your Heartaches			
(UK) Decca	*11 27 65*	*13*	*4*

LABEL	DATE OF CHART ENTRY	HIGHEST POSITION REACHED	NUMBER OF WEEKS IN CHARTS
Have Pity on the Boy			
(UK) *Decca*	2 12 66	18	2
I Love Her			
(UK) *Decca*	5 28 66	17	3
RYDELL, BOBBY			
Kissin' Time			
(US) Cameo	8 24 59	11	5
We Got Love			
(US) Cameo	11 16 59	6	9
Wild One			
(US) Cameo (b/w*)	2 22 60	2	10
(UK) *Columbia*	3 13 60	12	7
Little Bitty Girl*			
(US) Cameo	3 21 60	19	2
Swinging School			
(US) Cameo (b/w**)	5 23 60	5	6
Ding-a-Ling**			
(US) Cameo	5 30 60	18	2
Volare			
(US) Cameo	8 15 60	4	8
Sway			
(US) Cameo	11 21 60	14	6
(UK) *Columbia*	1 1 61	14	2
Good Time Baby			
(US) Cameo	2 20 61	11	5
I've Got Bonnie			
(US) Cameo	4 7 62	18	1
I'll Never Dance Again			
(US) Cameo	6 30 62	14	4
Cha Cha Cha			
(US) Cameo	11 3 62	10	6
Wildwood Days			
(US) Cameo	6 22 63	17	1
Forget Him			
(UK) *Cameo Parkway*	6 15 63	14	7
(US) Cameo	12 21 63	4	18
RYDER, MITCH, AND THE DETROIT WHEELS			
Jenny Take a Ride			
(US) New Voices	1 22 66	10	4
Little Lain Lupe Lu			
(US) New Voices	4 9 66	17	3
Devil with a Blue Dress On/Good Golly Miss Molly			
(US) New Voices	11 5 66	4	11
Sock It to Me Baby			
(US) New Voices	2 25 66	6	7
SADLER, BARRY			
Ballad of the Green Berets			
(US) RCA	2 19 66	1	11

LABEL	DATE OF CHART ENTRY	HIGHEST POSITION REACHED	NUMBER OF WEEKS IN CHARTS
SAFARIS			
Image of a Girl			
(US) Eldo	7 11 60	6	8
SAILCAT			
Motorcycle Mama			
(US) Elektra	8 12 72	12	5
ST. CECILIA			
Leap Up and Down (Wave Your Knickers in the Air)			
(UK) Polydor	*7 17 71*	*12*	*7*
ST. LOUIS UNION			
Girl			
(UK) Decca	*2 5 66*	*11*	*5*
ST. PETERS, CRISPIAN			
You Were on My Mind			
(UK) Decca	*1 29 66*	*2*	*8*
Pied Piper			
(UK) Decca	*4 16 66*	*5*	*8*
(US) Jamie	7 16 66	4	6
SAINTE MARIE, BUFFY			
Soldier Blue			
(UK) RCA	*8 14 71*	*7*	*8*
SAKAMOTO, KYU			
Sukiyaki			
(US) Capitol	5 25 63	1	10
(UK) HMV	*7 20 63*	*6*	*8*
SAKHARIN			
Sugar Sugar			
(UK) RCA	*5 8 71*	*12*	*5*
SAM AND DAVE			
Soul Man			
(US) Stax	10 7 67	2	10
Thank You			
(US) Stax	3 9 68	9	5
Soul Sister, Brown Sugar			
(UK) Stax	*2 8 69*	*15*	*4*
SAM THE SHAM AND THE PHARAOHS			
Wooly Bully			
(US) MGM	5 8 65	2	12
(UK) MGM	*7 17 65*	*11*	*6*
Lil' Red Riding Hood			
(US) MGM	7 9 66	2	9
SAMMES, MICHAEL, SINGERS			
Somewhere My Love			
(UK) HMV	*7 22 67*	*14*	*1*
SANDFORD, CHRIS			
Not Too Little, Not Too Much			
(UK) Decca	*12 21 63*	*17*	*5*

LABEL	DATE OF CHART ENTRY	HIGHEST POSITION REACHED	NUMBER OF WEEKS IN CHARTS
SANDPIPERS			
Guantanamera			
(US) A&M	9 3 66	9	5
(*UK*) *Pye*	*10 1 66*	*7*	*9*
Come Saturday Morning			
(US) A&M	5 30 70	17	3
SANDS, JODIE			
With All My Heart			
(US) Chancellor	6 24 57	20	1
Someday			
(*UK*) *HMV*	*10 17 58*	*14*	*8*
SANDS, TOMMY			
Teen-Age Crush			
(US) Capitol	3 2 57	3	11
Goin' Steady			
(US) Capitol	6 24 57	19	1
SANTAMARIA, MONGO			
Watermelon Man			
(US) Battle	4 20 63	10	4
SANTANA			
Evil Ways			
(US) Columbia	3 7 70	9	6
Black Magic Woman			
(US) Columbia	12 5 70	4	9
Oye Como Va			
(US) Columbia	3 27 71	13	3
Everybody's Everything			
(US) Columbia	11 13 71	12	4
SANTO AND JOHNNY			
Sleep Walk			
(US) Canadian-American	8 24 59	1	11
(*UK*) *Pye*	*10 10 59*	*14*	*2*
SARNE, MIKE			
Come Outside			
(*UK*) *Parlophone*	*5 26 62*	*1*	*14*
Will I What?			
(*UK*) *Parlophone*	*9 15 62*	*18*	*3*
SARSTEDT, PETER			
Where Do You Go To (My Lovely)?			
(*UK*) *United Artists*	*2 8 69*	*1*	*10*
Frozen Orange Juice			
(*UK*) *United Artists*	*6 28 69*	*10*	*4*
SAVAGE, EDNA			
Arrivederci Darling			
(*UK*) *Parlophone*	*1 13 56*	*19*	*1*
SAXON, AL			
Only Sixteen			
(*UK*) *Fontana*	*8 29 59*	*17*	*1*

LABEL	DATE OF CHART ENTRY	HIGHEST POSITION REACHED	NUMBER OF WEEKS IN CHARTS
SAYER, LEO			
The Show Must Go On			
(UK) Chrysalis	*12 22 73*	2	9
SCAFFOLD			
Thank U Very Much			
(UK) Columbia	*12 9 67*	4	8
Lily the Pink			
(UK) Columbia	*11 23 68*	1	12
SCOTT, BOBBY			
Chain Gang			
(US) Paramount	2 11 56	15	4
SCOTT, FREDDIE			
Hey Girl			
(US) Colpix	8 24 63	10	5
SCOTT, JACK			
My True Love			
(US) Carlton	7 28 58	3	10
(UK) London	*10 17 58*	9	7
Goodbye Baby			
(US) Carlton	1 12 59	8	7
What in the World's Come Over You			
(US) Top Rank	1 25 60	5	10
(UK) Rank	*2 27 60*	6	8
Burning Bridges			
(US) Top Rank	5 16 60	3	10
SCOTT, LINDA			
I've Told Every Little Star			
(US) Canadian-American	4 17 61	3	7
(UK) Columbia	*5 28 61*	9	5
Don't Bet Money Honey			
(US) Canadian-American	8 14 61	9	5
I Don't Know Why			
(US) Canadian-American	12 11 61	12	4
SEALS AND CROFT			
Summer Breeze			
(US) Warner Brothers	11 11 72	6	6
Hummingbird			
(US) Warner Brothers	3 31 73	20	1
Diamond Girl			
(US) Warner Brothers	7 7 73	6	7
SEARCHERS			
Sweets for My Sweet			
(UK) Pye	*7 13 63*	1	11
Sugar and Spice			
(UK) Pye	*11 2 63*	2	6
Needles and Pins			
(UK) Pye	*1 25 64*	1	9
(US) Kapp	3 28 64	13	5

LABEL	DATE OF CHART ENTRY	HIGHEST POSITION REACHED	NUMBER OF WEEKS IN CHARTS
Don't Throw Your Love Away			
(*UK*) *Pye*	4 18 64	1	8
(US) Kapp	7 4 64	16	3
Someday We're Gonna Love Again			
(*UK*) *Pye*	7 25 64	11	5
When You Walk in the Room			
(*UK*) *Pye*	10 3 64	3	8
What Have They Done to the Rain			
(*UK*) *Pye*	12 19 64	13	6
Love Potion #9			
(US) Kapp	12 26 64	3	8
Goodbye My Love			
(US) Pye	3 13 65	4	5
He's Got No Love			
(*UK*) *Pye*	7 24 65	12	5
Take Me for What I'm Worth			
(*UK*) *Pye*	1 22 66	20	1
SECOMBE, HARRY			
On with the Motley			
(*UK*) *Philips*	12 9 55	16	3
If I Ruled the World			
(*UK*) *Philips*	12 21 63	20	1
This Is My Song			
(*UK*) *Philips*	3 11 67	2	9
[see also: **GOONS**]			
SECRETS			
The Boy Next Door			
(US) Philips	12 28 63	18	2
SEDAKA, NEIL			
Diary			
(US) RCA	1 26 59	14	3
I Go Ape			
(*UK*) *RCA*	5 2 59	9	10
Oh, Carol			
(US) RCA	11 2 59	9	8
(*UK*) *RCA*	11 14 59	3	13
(*UK*) *RCA* (*reissue*)	12 2 72	19	1
Stairway to Heaven			
(US) RCA	4 25 60	9	7
(*UK*) *RCA*	5 8 60	13	6
You Mean Everything to Me			
(US) RCA	9 26 60	17	3
Calendar Girl			
(US) RCA	1 16 61	4	8
(*UK*) *RCA*	1 22 61	10	9
Little Devil			
(*UK*) *RCA*	5 14 61	12	6
(US) RCA	5 22 61	11	3

LABEL	DATE OF CHART ENTRY	HIGHEST POSITION REACHED	NUMBER OF WEEKS IN CHARTS
Happy Birthday Sweet 16			
(US) RCA	12 11 61	6	8
(UK) RCA	*12 16 61*	*4*	*12*
Breaking Up Is Hard to Do			
(US) RCA	7 14 62	1	10
(UK) RCA	*8 11 62*	*7*	*10*
Next Door to an Angel			
(US) RCA	10 27 62	5	6
Alice in Wonderland			
(US) RCA	3 9 63	17	3
That's When the Music Takes Me			
(UK) RCA	*3 24 73*	*18*	*1*
SEEKERS			
I'll Never Find Another You			
(UK) Columbia	*1 30 65*	*1*	*11*
(US) Capitol	4 17 65	4	9
World of Our Own			
(UK) Columbia	*5 1 65*	*3*	*11*
(US) Capitol	7 10 65	19	2
The Carnival Is Over			
(UK) Columbia	*11 6 65*	*1*	*14*
Someday One Day			
(UK) Columbia	*4 9 66*	*11*	*6*
Walk with Me			
(UK) Columbia	*9 24 66*	*10*	*6*
Morningtown Ride			
(UK) Columbia	*12 3 66*	*2*	*10*
Georgy Girl			
(US) Capitol	1 7 67	2	10
(UK) Columbia	*3 4 67*	*3*	*7*
When Will the Good Apple Fall			
(UK) Columbia	*10 7 67*	*11*	*6*
SEGER, BOB			
Ramblin' Gamblin' Man			
(US) Capitol	2 1 69	17	5
SELLERS, PETER			
Any Old Iron			
(UK) Parlophone	*9 20 57*	*17*	*2*
Goodness Gracious Me (with **SOPHIA LOREN**)			
(UK) Parlophone	*11 13 60*	*5*	*9*
Hard Day's Night			
(UK) Parlophone	*1 8 66*	*14*	*4*
[see also: **GOONS**]			
SENATOR BOBBY			
Wild Thing			
(US) Parkway	2 4 67	20	2
SENSATIONS			
Let Me In			
(US) Argo	2 24 62	4	8

LABEL	DATE OF CHART ENTRY	HIGHEST POSITION REACHED	NUMBER OF WEEKS IN CHARTS
SERENDIPITY SINGERS			
Don't Let the Rain Come Down			
(US) Philips	3 28 64	6	9
SEVERINE			
Un Banc, Une Arbre, Une Rue			
(*UK*) *Philips*	*5 15 71*	*9*	*4*
SEVILLE, DAVID (*and **THE CHIPMUNKS**)			
Witch Doctor			
(US) Liberty	4 21 58	1	14
(*UK*) *London*	*5 23 58*	*11*	*5*
Chipmunk Song*			
(US) Liberty	12 15 58	1	7
Alvin's Harmonica*			
(US) Liberty	3 2 59	3	7
Ragtime Cowboy Joe*			
(US) Liberty	7 27 59	16	3
(*UK*) *London*	*8 1 59*	*11*	*5*
SHADES OF BLUE			
Oh How Happy			
(US) Impact	6 4 66	12	6
SHADOWS			
Apache			
(*UK*) *Columbia*	*7 17 60*	*1*	*15*
Man of Mystery			
(*UK*) *Columbia*	*11 6 60*	*2*	*9*
F.B.I.			
(*UK*) *Columbia*	*1 29 61*	*4*	*11*
Frightened City			
(*UK*) *Columbia*	*4 30 61*	*3*	*11*
Kon-Tiki			
(*UK*) *Columbia*	*9 2 61*	*1*	*9*
The Savage			
(*UK*) *Columbia*	*11 11 61*	*9*	*5*
Wonderful Land			
(*UK*) *Columbia*	*3 3 62*	*1*	*16*
Guitar Tango			
(*UK*) *Columbia*	*8 11 62*	*4*	*9*
Dance On			
(*UK*) *Columbia*	*12 22 62*	*1*	*9*
Footapper			
(*UK*) *Columbia*	*3 16 63*	*1*	*10*
Atlantis			
(*UK*) *Columbia*	*6 15 63*	*2*	*11*
Shindig			
(*UK*) *Columbia*	*9 28 63*	*6*	*7*
Geronimo			
(*UK*) *Columbia*	*12 14 63*	*11*	*5*
Theme for Young Lovers			
(*UK*) *Columbia*	*3 21 64*	*12*	*6*

LABEL	DATE OF CHART ENTRY	HIGHEST POSITION REACHED	NUMBER OF WEEKS IN CHARTS
Rise and Fall of Flingel Bunt			
(UK) Columbia	5 23 64	5	8
Genie with the Light Brown Lamp			
(UK) Columbia	1 9 65	17	2
Mary Anne			
(UK) Columbia	2 27 65	17	4
Stingray			
(UK) Columbia	6 26 65	19	1
Don't Make My Baby Blue			
(UK) Columbia	8 14 64	10	5
War Lord			
(UK) Columbia	12 25 65	18	2
[see also: **CLIFF RICHARD**]			
SHADOWS OF KNIGHT			
Gloria			
(US) Dunwich	4 23 66	10	6
SHAG			
Loop di Love			
(UK) UK	10 28 72	4	7
SHAND, JIMMY			
Bluebell Polka			
(UK) Parlophone	12 23 55	18	2
SHANGRI-LAS			
Remember (Walking in the Sand)			
(US) Red Bird	9 5 64	5	8
(UK) Red Bird	11 14 64	14	3
Leader of the Pack			
(US) Red Bird	10 24 64	1	9
(UK) Red Bird	1 30 65	11	4
(UK) Kama Sutra (reissue)	11 4 72	3	6
Give Him a Great Big Kiss			
(US) Red Bird	1 30 65	18	2
I Can Never Go Home Any More			
(US) Red Bird	11 27 65	6	6
SHANNON, DEL			
Runaway			
(US) Big Top	4 3 61	1	10
(UK) London	4 23 61	1	17
Hats Off to Larry			
(US) Big Top	6 26 61	5	9
(UK) London	9 2 61	9	8
So Long Baby			
(UK) London	12 9 61	10	8
Hey Little Girl			
(UK) London	3 31 62	2	11
Swiss Maid			
(UK) London	10 20 62	2	14
Little Town Flirt			

LABEL	DATE OF CHART ENTRY	HIGHEST POSITION REACHED	NUMBER OF WEEKS IN CHARTS
(UK) London	1 27 63	4	8
(US) Big Top	2 16 63	12	3
Two Kinds of Teardrops			
(UK) London	5 4 63	5	10
Keep Searchin'			
(US) Amy	1 2 65	9	7
(UK) Stateside	1 23 65	3	8
SHAPIRO, HELEN			
Don't Treat Me Like a Child			
(UK) Columbia	4 14 61	4	8
You Don't Know			
(UK) Columbia	7 2 61	1	14
Walkin' Back to Happiness			
(UK) Columbia	9 23 61	1	16
Tell Me What He Said			
(UK) Columbia	2 24 62	2	12
Little Miss Lonely			
(UK) Columbia	7 28 62	8	7
SHARP, DEE DEE			
Mashed Potato Time			
(US) Cameo	3 31 62	2	12
Gravy			
(US) Cameo	7 7 62	9	5
Ride			
(US) Cameo	11 17 62	5	6
Do the Bird			
(US) Cameo	3 30 63	10	5
SHAW, SANDIE			
(There's) Always Something There to Remind Me			
(UK) Pye	10 17 64	1	7
Girl Don't Come			
(UK) Pye	12 19 64	3	9
I'll Stop at Nothing			
(UK) Pye	2 27 65	4	7
Long Live Love			
(UK) Pye	5 22 65	1	9
Message Understood			
(UK) Pye	10 7 65	6	5
Tomorrow			
(UK) Pye	2 12 66	9	5
Nothing Comes Easy			
(UK) Pye	6 4 66	14	4
Puppet on a String			
(UK) Pye	3 25 67	1	13
You've Not Changed			
(UK) Pye	10 21 67	18	4
Monsieur Dupont			
(UK) Pye	3 1 69	6	8

LABEL	DATE OF CHART ENTRY	HIGHEST POSITION REACHED	NUMBER OF WEEKS IN CHARTS
SHEARING, GEORGE (See **NAT "KING" COLE**)			
SHELTON, ANNE			
Arrivederci Darling			
(*UK*) *HMV*	*12 16 55*	*17*	*4*
Seven Days			
(*UK*) *Philips*	*4 20 56*	*20*	*2*
Lay Down Your Arms			
(*UK*) *Philips*	*8 31 56*	*1*	*13*
Sailor			
(*UK*) *Philips*	*1 15 61*	*7*	*5*
SHEP AND THE LIMELITES			
Daddy's Home			
(US) Hull	4 24 61	2	8
SHEPHERD SISTERS			
Alone			
(US) Lance	11 18 57	20	1
(*UK*) *HMV*	*11 22 57*	*14*	*3*
SHERMAN, ALLAN			
Hello Muddah, Hello Faddah			
(US) Warner Brothers	8 10 63	2	8
(*UK*) *Warner Brothers*	*10 5 63*	*14*	*5*
SHERMAN, BOBBY			
Little Woman			
(US) Metromedia	9 13 69	3	9
La La La (If I Had You)			
(US) Metromedia	12 20 69	9	6
Easy Come Easy Go			
(US) Metromedia	3 14 70	9	8
Julie, Do Ya Love Me			
(US) Metromedia	8 29 70	5	9
Cried Like a Baby			
(US) Metromedia	3 13 71	16	3
SHIELDS			
You Cheated			
(US) Dot	10 6 58	15	4
SHIRELLES			
Will You Love Me Tomorrow			
(US) Scepter	12 26 60	1	12
(*UK*) *Top Rank*	*1 29 61*	*3*	*11*
Dedicated to the One I Love			
(US) Scepter	2 13 61	3	11
Mama Said			
(US) Scepter	5 1 61	4	7
Baby, It's You			
(US) Scepter	1 13 62	8	9
Soldier Boy			
(US) Scepter	4 14 62	1	10

LABEL	DATE OF CHART ENTRY	HIGHEST POSITION REACHED	NUMBER OF WEEKS IN CHARTS
Everybody Loves a Lover			
(US) Scepter	1 19 63	19	2
Foolish Little Girl			
(US) Scepter	4 27 63	4	7
SHOCKING BLUE			
Venus			
(US) Colossus	12 27 69	1	11
(UK) Penny Farthing	*2 14 70*	*8*	*5*
SHONDELL, TROY			
This Time			
(US) Liberty	10 2 61	6	10
(UK) London	*11 25 61*	*14*	*1*
SHOWSTOPPERS			
Ain't Nothing but a Houseparty			
(UK) Beacon	*3 30 68*	*11*	*9*
SIFFRE, LABI			
It Must Be Love			
(UK) Pye International	*12 11 71*	*14*	*6*
Crying, Laughing, Loving, Lying			
(UK) Pye International	*4 15 72*	*11*	*4*
SILHOUETTES			
Get a Job			
(US) Ember	1 27 58	1	9
SILKIE			
You've Got to Hide Your Love Away			
(US) Fontana	11 13 65	10	4
HARRY SIMEONE CHORALE			
Little Drummer Boy			
(US) 20th Century Fox	1 5 59	13	2
(US) 20th Century Fox (re-entry)	12 28 59	15	1
SIMMONS, GENE			
Haunted House			
(US) Hi	9 5 64	11	6
SIMON, CARLY			
That's the Way I've Always Heard It Should Be			
(US) Elektra	6 26 71	10	6
Anticipation			
(US) Elektra	1 22 72	13	6
You're So Vain			
(US) Elektra	12 23 72	1	12
(UK) Elektra	*1 2 73*	*3*	*8*
The Right Thing to Do			
(UK) Elektra	*5 12 73*	*17*	*1*
(US) Elektra	5 19 73	17	2
SIMON, JOE			
Chokin' Kind			
(US) SS7	4 26 69	13	5

LABEL	DATE OF CHART ENTRY	HIGHEST POSITION REACHED	NUMBER OF WEEKS IN CHARTS
Drowning in the Sea of Love			
(US) Spring	1 1 72	11	7
Power of Love			
(US) Spring	9 9 72	11	4
Step by Step			
(UK) Mojo	*7 14 73*	*14*	*3*
Theme from "Cleopatra Jones"			
(US) Spring	8 22 73	18	3
SIMON, PAUL			
Mother and Child Reunion			
(UK) CBS	*2 26 72*	*5*	*7*
(US) Columbia	3 4 72	4	8
Me and Julio Down by the Schoolyard			
(UK) CBS	*5 27 72*	*15*	*3*
Kodachrome			
(US) Columbia	9 6 73	2	18
Take Me to the Mardi Gras			
(UK) CBS	*6 30 73*	*7*	*5*
Loves Me Like a Rock			
(US) Columbia	8 25 73	2	10
SIMON AND GARFUNKEL			
Sounds of Silence			
(US) Columbia	12 18 65	1	8
Homeward Bound			
(US) Columbia	3 5 66	5	7
(UK) CBS	*4 16 66*	*9*	*7*
I Am a Rock			
(US) Columbia	5 21 66	3	8
(UK) CBS	*7 2 66*	*17*	*2*
Hazy Shade of Winter			
(US) Columbia	11 26 66	13	4
At the Zoo			
(US) Columbia	4 15 67	16	3
Scarborough Fair			
(US) Columbia	3 23 68	11	5
Mrs. Robinson			
(US) Columbia	5 11 68	1	10
(UK) CBS	*7 20 68*	*4*	*7*
Mrs. Robinson			
(UK) CBS EP	*2 8 69*	*9*	*1*
The Boxer			
(US) Columbia	4 19 69	7	8
(UK) CBS	*5 10 69*	*6*	*7*
Bridge over Troubled Water			
(US) Columbia	2 14 70	1	12
(UK) CBS	*2 28 70*	*1*	*13*
Cecilia			
(US) Columbia	5 2 70	4	9

LABEL	DATE OF CHART ENTRY	HIGHEST POSITION REACHED	NUMBER OF WEEKS IN CHARTS
El Condor Pasa			
(US) Columbia	10 24 70	18	3
[see also: **PAUL SIMON; ART GARFUNKEL**]			
SIMONE, NINA			
I Loves You Porgy			
(US) Bethlehem	10 5 59	18	2
Ain't Got No—I Got Life			
(UK) RCA	*11 16 68*	*2*	*12*
To Love Somebody			
(UK) RCA	*2 1 69*	*5*	*5*
SINATRA, FRANK			
Learnin' the Blues			
(US) Capitol	5 28 55	2	18
(UK) Capitol	*8 5 55*	*2*	*15*
You My Love			
(UK) Capitol	*6 10 55*	*13*	*6*
Not As a Stranger			
(UK) Capitol	*9 2 55*	*18*	*1*
Love and Marriage			
(US) Capitol	11 12 55	5	14
(UK) Capitol	*1 13 56*	*3*	*8*
Love Is the Tender Trap			
(UK) Capitol	*1 20 56*	*2*	*9*
Songs for Swingin' Lovers			
(UK) Capitol (LP)	*6 22 56*	*12*	*5*
Hey Jealous Lover			
(US) Capitol	11 3 56	6	14
Can I Steal a Little Love			
(US) Capitol	3 2 57	20	1
All the Way			
(US) Capitol	12 2 57	15	7
(UK) Capitol	*12 13 57*	*3*	*16*
Witchcraft			
(UK) Capitol	*2 14 58*	*12*	*6*
(US) Capitol	2 24 58	20	1
High Hopes			
(UK) Capitol	*9 19 59*	*9*	*10*
River, Stay 'Way from My Door			
(UK) Capitol	*6 12 60*	*16*	*2*
Nice 'n' Easy			
(UK) Capitol	*9 11 60*	*20*	*1*
Ole McDonald			
(UK) Capitol	*11 20 60*	*14*	*4*
Granada			
(UK) Reprise	*9 23 61*	*13*	*3*
Strangers in the Night			
(UK) Reprise	*5 21 66*	*1*	*13*
(US) Reprise	6 4 66	1	8
That's Life			
(US) Reprise	12 3 66	4	8

LABEL	DATE OF CHART ENTRY	HIGHEST POSITION REACHED	NUMBER OF WEEKS IN CHARTS
My Way			
(*UK*) *Reprise*	5 10 69	5	9
Love's Been Good to Me			
(*UK*) *Reprise*	10 25 69	8	7
Somethin' Stupid (with **NANCY SINATRA**)			
(US) Reprise	4 1 67	1	10
(*UK*) *Reprise*	4 1 67	1	11
My Way			
(*UK*) *Reprise (re-entry)*	1 2 71	18	1
I Will Drink the Wine			
(*UK*) *Reprise*	3 20 71	16	2
SINATRA, NANCY			
These Boots Are Made for Walkin'			
(*UK*) *Reprise*	2 5 66	1	10
(US) Reprise	2 12 66	1	10
How Does That Grab You Darlin'			
(US) Reprise	5 7 66	7	4
(*UK*) *Reprise*	5 14 66	19	1
Sugar Town			
(US) Reprise	12 10 66	5	8
(*UK*) *Reprise*	2 4 67	8	5
Love Eyes			
(US) Reprise	4 22 67	15	2
You Only Live Twice			
(*UK*) *Reprise*	7 15 67	11	4
Jackson (with **LEE HAZLEWOOD**)			
(US) Reprise	7 22 67	14	4
Lady Bird (with **LEE HAZLEWOOD**)			
(US) Reprise	11 18 67	20	1
Did You Ever? (with **LEE HAZLEWOOD**)			
(*UK*) *Reprise*	9 4 71	2	9
[see also: **FRANK SINATRA**]			
SINGING DOGS			
Oh Susanna			
(*UK*) *Nixa*	11 25 55	13	4
SINGING NUN			
Dominique			
(US) Philips	11 16 63	1	11
(*UK*) *Philips*	12 14 63	7	7
SIR DOUGLAS QUINTET			
She's About a Mover			
(US) Tribe	5 22 65	13	4
(*UK*) *London*	7 10 65	15	3
SKELLERN, PETER			
You're a Lady			
(*UK*) *Decca*	9 30 72	3	7
SKIP AND FLIP			
It Was I			
(US) Brent	8 10 59	11	6

LABEL	DATE OF CHART ENTRY	HIGHEST POSITION REACHED	NUMBER OF WEEKS IN CHARTS
Cherry Pie			
(US) Brent	5 2 60	11	6
SKYLARK			
Wildflower			
(US) Capitol	4 21 73	9	9
SKYLINERS			
Since I Don't Have You			
(US) Calico	3 30 59	12	6
SLADE			
Get Down and Get with It			
(*UK*) *Polydor*	8 7 71	*16*	*4*
Coz I Luv You			
(*UK*) *Polydor*	*11 6 71*	*1*	*9*
Look Wot You Dun			
(*UK*) *Polydor*	*2 12 72*	*4*	*8*
Take Me Back Home			
(*UK*) *Polydor*	*6 10 72*	*1*	*9*
Mama Weer All Crazee Now			
(*UK*) *Polydor*	*9 2 72*	*1*	*7*
Gudbuy t' Jane			
(*UK*) *Polydor*	*11 25 72*	*2*	*9*
Cum On Feel the Noize			
(*UK*) *Polydor*	*3 3 73*	*1*	*8*
Skweeze Me Pleeze Me			
(*UK*) *Polydor*	*6 30 73*	*1*	*6*
My Friend Stan			
(*UK*) *Polydor*	*10 6 73*	*2*	*6*
Merry Christmas Everybody			
(*UK*) *Polydor*	*12 8 73*	*1*	*6*
SLEDGE, PERCY			
When a Man Loves a Woman			
(US) Atlantic	5 7 66	1	8
(*UK*) *Atlantic*	*5 28 66*	*4*	*9*
Warm and Tender Love			
(US) Atlantic	8 27 66	17	2
It Tears Me Up			
(US) Atlantic	12 17 66	20	1
Take Time to Know Her			
(US) Atlantic	4 27 68	11	5
SLIM HARPO			
Baby Scratch My Back			
(US) Excello	3 19 66	16	3
SLY AND THE FAMILY STONE			
Dance to the Music			
(US) Epic	3 9 68	8	9
(*UK*) *CBS*	*8 3 68*	*7*	*7*
Everyday People			
(US) Epic	1 18 69	1	11
Hot Fun in the Summertime			
(US) Epic	9 27 69	2	8

LABEL	DATE OF CHART ENTRY	HIGHEST POSITION REACHED	NUMBER OF WEEKS IN CHARTS
Thank You (Falettin Me Be Mice Elf Agin)/Everybody Is a Star			
(US) Epic	1 24 70	1	8
Family Affair			
(US) Epic	11 20 71	1	11
(UK) Epic	*2 5 72*	*15*	*3*
Runnin' Away			
(UK) Epic	*5 6 72*	*17*	*2*
If You Want Me to Stay			
(US) Epic	8 4 73	12	8
SMALL, MILLIE			
My Boy Lollipop			
(UK) Fontana	*4 11 64*	*2*	*10*
(US) Smash	6 13 64	2	7
SMALL FACES			
Whatcha Gonna Do About It			
(UK) Decca	*9 30 65*	*14*	*5*
Sha La La La Lee			
(UK) Decca	*2 19 66*	*3*	*8*
Hey Girl			
(UK) Decca	*5 21 66*	*10*	*5*
All or Nothing			
(UK) Decca	*8 20 66*	*1*	*8*
My Mind's Eye			
(UK) Decca	*11 26 66*	*4*	*8*
Here Comes the Nice			
(UK) Immediate	*6 24 67*	*12*	*6*
Itchycoo Park			
(UK) Immediate	*8 19 67*	*3*	*11*
(US) Immediate	1 27 68	16	3
Tin Soldier			
(UK) Immediate	*12 23 67*	*9*	*8*
Lazy Sunday			
(UK) Immediate	*4 27 68*	*2*	*7*
Universal			
(UK) Immediate	*7 27 68*	*16*	*5*
SMITH			
Baby It's You			
(US) Dunhill	10 11 69	5	9
SMITH, HUEY, AND THE CLOWNS			
Don't You Just Know It			
(US) Ace	4 7 58	9	7
SMITH, HURRICANE			
Don't Let It Die			
(UK) Columbia	*6 19 71*	*2*	*8*
Oh Babe, What Would You Say			
(UK) Columbia	*5 13 72*	*4*	*8*
(US) Capitol	1 13 73	3	8
SMITH, KEELEY			
That Old Black Magic (with **LOUIS PRIMA**)			
(US) Capitol	12 15 58	18	1

LABEL	DATE OF CHART ENTRY	HIGHEST POSITION REACHED	NUMBER OF WEEKS IN CHARTS
You're Breaking My Heart			
(*UK*) *Reprise*	4 3 65	*14*	*5*
SMITH, O. C.			
Son of Hickory Hollers Tramp			
(*UK*) *CBS*	6 15 68	2	9
Little Green Apples			
(US) Columbia	9 28 68	2	10
SMITH, SAMMI			
Help Me Make It Through the Night			
(US) Mega	2 13 71	8	7
SMITH, SOMETHIN', AND THE REDHEADS			
It's a Sin to Tell a Lie			
(US) Epic	5 14 55	7	16
SMITH, WHISTLING JACK			
I Was Kaiser Bill's Batman			
(*UK*) *Deram*	3 18 67	5	7
(US) Deram	6 3 67	20	1
SMITH BROTHERS			
I'm in Favour of Friendship			
(*UK*) *Decca*	7 22 55	20	1
SOMMERS, JOANIE			
Johnny Get Angry			
(US) Warner Brothers	6 30 62	7	7
SONNY			
Laugh at Me			
(*UK*) *Atlantic*	9 4 65	9	6
(US) Atco	9 11 65	10	5
[see also: **SONNY AND CHER**]			
SONNY AND CHER			
I Got You Babe			
(US) Atco	8 7 65	1	8
(*UK*) *Atlantic*	8 21 65	*1*	*10*
Baby Don't Go			
(US) Reprise	9 25 65	8	5
(*UK*) *Reprise*	9 30 65	11	5
Just You			
(US) Atco	10 9 65	20	1
But You're Mine			
(US) Atco	10 30 65	15	4
(*UK*) *Atlantic*	11 6 65	*17*	*2*
What Now My Love			
(US) Atco	2 19 66	14	3
(*UK*) *Atlantic*	3 12 66	*13*	*5*
Little Man			
(*UK*) *Atlantic*	9 17 66	*4*	*6*
The Beat Goes On			
(US) Atco	2 4 67	6	6

LABEL	DATE OF CHART ENTRY	HIGHEST POSITION REACHED	NUMBER OF WEEKS IN CHARTS
All I Ever Need Is You			
(US) Kapp	11 27 71	7	7
(UK) MCA	1 29 72	8	7
A Cowboy's Work Is Never Done			
(US) Kapp	3 25 72	8	8
[see also: CHER; SONNY]			
SOUL, JIMMY			
If You Wanna Be Happy			
(US) S.P.Q.R.	4 27 63	1	9
SOUL SURVIVORS			
Expressway to Your Heart			
(US) Crimson	10 7 67	4	9
SOUNDS NICE			
Love at First Sight			
(UK) Parlophone	10 4 69	18	3
SOUNDS ORCHESTRAL			
Cast Your Fate to the Wind			
(UK) Piccadilly	1 2 65	5	10
(US) Parkway	4 24 65	10	6
SOUTH, JOE			
Games People Play			
(US) Capitol	2 15 69	12	6
(UK) Capitol	3 15 69	6	8
Walk a Mile in My Shoes			
(US) Capitol	1 31 70	12	6
SOUTHLANDERS			
Alone			
(UK) Decca	11 29 57	17	6
SPANKY AND OUR GANG			
Sunday Will Never Be the Same			
(US) Mercury	6 10 67	9	5
Lazy Day			
(US) Mercury	11 18 67	14	5
Like to Get to Know You			
(US) Mercury	5 18 68	17	4
SPENCE, JOHNNY			
Theme from "Dr. Kildare"			
(UK) Parlophone	3 31 62	15	6
SPINNERS (*MOTOWN SPINNERS; †DETROIT SPINNERS)			
It's a Shame			
(US) V.I.P.	10 3 70	14	3
(UK) Tamla Motown*	12 19 70	20	2
I'll Be Around/How Could I Let You Get Away			
(US) Atlantic	10 28 72	3	7
Could It Be I'm Falling in Love			
(US) Atlantic	2 3 73	4	8
(UK) Atlantic†	5 12 73	11	5

LABEL	DATE OF CHART ENTRY	HIGHEST POSITION REACHED	NUMBER OF WEEKS IN CHARTS
One of a Kind (Love Affair)			
(US) Atlantic	6 9 73	11	5
Ghetto Child			
(UK) Atlantic†	*10 13 73*	*7*	*6*
SPIRAL STAIRCASE			
More Today than Yesterday			
(US) Columbia	5 31 69	12	4
SPOTNIKS			
Hava Nagila			
(UK) Oriole	*2 17 63*	*13*	*4*
SPRINGFIELD, DUSTY			
I Only Want to Be with You			
(UK) Philips	*12 7 63*	*4*	*12*
(US) Philips	2 22 64	12	4
Stay Awhile			
(UK) Philips	*2 29 64*	*13*	*6*
I Just Don't Know What to Do with Myself			
(UK) Philips	*7 21 64*	*3*	*9*
Wishin' and Hopin'			
(US) Philips	7 18 64	6	7
Losing You			
(UK) Philips	*11 21 64*	*9*	*5*
In the Middle of Nowhere			
(UK) Philips	*7 10 65*	*8*	*6*
Some of Your Lovin'			
(UK) Philips	*10 7 65*	*8*	*6*
Little by Little			
(UK) Philips	*2 19 66*	*17*	*3*
You Don't Have to Say You Love Me			
(UK) Philips	*4 9 66*	*1*	*10*
(US) Philips	6 11 66	4	8
Goin' Back			
(UK) Philips	*7 16 66*	*10*	*7*
All I See Is You			
(UK) Philips	*9 24 66*	*9*	*7*
(US) Philips	10 22 66	20	1
I'll Try Anything			
(UK) Philips	*3 14 67*	*13*	*4*
Give Me Time			
(UK) Philips	*7 8 67*	*19*	*1*
I Close My Eyes			
(UK) Philips	*7 27 68*	*4*	*6*
Son of a Preacher Man			
(UK) Philips	*12 21 68*	*9*	*6*
(US) Atlantic	1 4 69	10	6
[see also: **SPRINGFIELDS**]			
SPRINGFIELD, RICK			
Speak to the Sky			
(US) Capitol	9 23 72	14	5

LABEL	DATE OF CHART ENTRY	HIGHEST POSITION REACHED	NUMBER OF WEEKS IN CHARTS
SPRINGFIELDS			
Bambino			
(*UK*) *Philips*	*1 6 62*	*15*	*1*
Silver Threads and Golden Needles			
(US) Philips	9 22 62	20	2
Island of Dreams			
(*UK*) *Philips*	*1 20 63*	*5*	*15*
Say I Won't Be There			
(*UK*) *Philips*	*4 13 63*	*5*	*8*
SPRINGWATER			
I Will Return			
(*UK*) *Polydor*	*11 6 71*	*5*	*6*
STAFFORD, JO			
Suddenly There's a Valley			
(US) Columbia	11 12 55	16	3
(*UK*) *Philips*	*12 9 55*	*12*	*6*
It's Almost Tomorrow			
(US) Columbia	1 21 56	19	2
STAFFORD, TERRY			
Suspicion			
(US) Crusader	3 21 64	3	9
STAMPEDERS			
Sweet City Woman			
(US) Bell	9 25 71	8	7
STANDELLS			
Dirty Water			
(US) Tower	7 2 66	11	4
STANG, ARNOLD			
Ivy Will Cling			
(*UK*) *Fontana*	*12 5 59*	*18*	*1*
STAPLE SINGERS			
Respect Yourself			
(US) Stax	11 27 71	12	6
I'll Take You There			
(US) Stax	4 29 72	1	10
If You're Ready Go with Me			
(US) Stax	11 24 73	9	6
STAPLETON, CYRIL			
Elephant Tango			
(*UK*) *Decca*	*5 27 55*	*19*	*4*
Blue Star			
(*UK*) *Decca*	*9 23 55*	*2*	*12*
The Italian Theme			
(*UK*) *Decca*	*4 6 56*	*18*	*1*
Children's Marching Song			
(US) London	2 2 59	13	4
STARDUST, ALVIN			
My Coo Coo Ca Choo			
(*UK*) *Magnet*	*11 24 73*	*2*	*11*

LABEL	DATE OF CHART ENTRY	HIGHEST POSITION REACHED	NUMBER OF WEEKS IN CHARTS
STARGAZERS			
Somebody			
(*UK*) *Decca*	3 11 55	20	1
Crazy Otto Rag			
(*UK*) *Decca*	6 3 55	18	3
Close the Door			
(*UK*) *Decca*	9 9 55	6	9
Twenty Tiny Fingers			
(*UK*) *Decca*	11 11 55	4	11
STARR, EDWIN			
SOS/Headline News			
(*UK*) *Polydor* (*reissue*)	1 18 69	11	5
25 Miles			
(US) Gordy	3 29 69	6	6
War			
(US) Gordy	8 1 70	1	11
(*UK*) *Tamla Motown*	10 24 70	3	8
STARR, KAY			
Rock and Roll Waltz			
(US) Victor	1 7 56	1	18
(*UK*) *HMV*	2 17 56	1	18
STARR, RINGO			
It Don't Come Easy			
(*UK*) *Apple*	4 24 71	4	8
(US) Apple	5 15 71	4	9
Back Off Boogaloo			
(*UK*) *Apple*	4 8 72	2	7
(US) Apple	4 22 72	9	5
Photograph			
(US) Apple	10 27 73	1	9
(*UK*) *Apple*	11 10 73	8	5
STATLER BROTHERS			
Flowers on the Wall			
(US) Columbia	12 25 65	4	5
STATUS QUO			
Pictures of Matchstick Men			
(*UK*) *Pye International*	2 10 68	7	7
(US) Cadet Concept	7 27 68	12	4
Ice in the Sun			
(*UK*) *Pye International*	9 21 68	8	6
Down the Dustpipe			
(*UK*) *Pye*	6 20 70	12	6
Paper Plane			
(*UK*) *Vertigo*	1 27 73	8	5
Mean Girl			
(*UK*) *Pye*	5 26 73	20	1
Caroline			
(*UK*) *Vertigo*	9 29 73	5	8

LABEL	DATE OF CHART ENTRY	HIGHEST POSITION REACHED	NUMBER OF WEEKS IN CHARTS
STEALERS WHEEL			
Stuck in the Middle with You			
(US) A&M	4 14 73	6	9
(UK) A&M	*6 2 73*	*8*	*6*
STEAM			
Na Na Hey Hey Kiss Him Goodbye			
(US) Fontana	11 15 69	1	11
(UK) Fontana	*3 7 70*	*9*	*5*
STEELE, TOMMY			
Rock with the Cave Man			
(UK) Decca	*11 2 56*	*13*	*3*
Singing the Blues			
(UK) Decca	*12 21 56*	*1*	*10*
Knee Deep in the Blues			
(UK) Decca	*2 22 57*	*15*	*4*
Butterfingers			
(UK) Decca	*5 17 57*	*8*	*15*
Shiralee			
(UK) Decca	*8 23 57*	*11*	*3*
Water Water/Handful of Songs			
(UK) Decca	*8 30 57*	*5*	*13*
Nairobi			
(UK) Decca	*3 7 58*	*3*	*10*
Happy Guitar			
(UK) Decca	*4 25 58*	*20*	*1*
Only Man on the Island			
(UK) Decca	*7 18 58*	*16*	*3*
Come On, Let's Go			
(UK) Decca	*11 21 58*	*9*	*11*
Give Give Give/Tallahassie Lassie			
(UK) Decca	*8 15 59*	*17*	*3*
Little White Bull			
(UK) Decca	*11 28 59*	*6*	*10*
What a Mouth			
(UK) Decca	*6 26 60*	*5*	*7*
The Writing on the Wall			
(UK) Decca	*8 12 61*	*18*	*1*
STEELEYE SPAN			
Gaudete			
(UK) Chrysalis	*12 22 73*	*14*	*3*
STEELY DAN			
Do It Again			
(US) ABC	1 20 73	6	7
Reeling in the Years			
(US) ABC	4 28 73	11	6
STEPPENWOLF			
Born to Be Wild			
(US) Dunhill	8 3 68	2	9

LABEL	DATE OF CHART ENTRY	HIGHEST POSITION REACHED	NUMBER OF WEEKS IN CHARTS
Magic Carpet Ride			
(US) Dunhill	11 2 68	3	9
Rock Me			
(US) Dunhill	3 22 69	10	6
STEVENS, CAT			
Matthew and Son			
(UK) Deram	*1 14 67*	*2*	*7*
I'm Gonna Get Me a Gun			
(UK) Deram	*4 22 67*	*6*	*5*
A Bad Night			
(UK) Deram	*8 26 67*	*20*	*1*
Lady D'Arbanville			
(UK) Island	*7 11 70*	*8*	*8*
Wild World			
(US) A&M	3 27 71	11	5
Peace Train			
(US) A&M	10 16 71	7	8
Morning Has Broken			
(UK) Island	*1 15 72*	*9*	*4*
(US) A&M	5 6 72	6	8
Sitting			
(US) A&M	12 30 72	16	3
Can't Keep It In			
(UK) Island	*1 20 73*	*13*	*4*
STEVENS, CONNIE			
Sixteen Reasons			
(US) Warner Brothers	4 4 60	3	11
(UK) Warner Brothers	*5 15 60*	*12*	*4*
[see also: **ED BYRNES**]			
STEVENS, DODIE			
Pink Shoelaces			
(US) Crystalette	3 16 59	3	12
STEVENS, RAY			
Ahab the Arab			
(US) Mercury	7 14 62	5	8
Harry the Hairy Ape			
(US) Mercury	7 13 63	17	3
Gitarzan			
(US) Monument	5 3 69	8	8
Everything Is Beautiful			
(US) Barnaby	5 2 70	1	9
(UK) CBS	*5 23 70*	*6*	*8*
Bridget the Midget			
(UK) CBS	*3 20 71*	*2*	*9*
STEVENSON, B. W.			
My Maria			
(US) RCA	9 8 73	9	7
STEWART, BILLY			
Summertime			
(US) Chess	8 20 66	10	4

LABEL	DATE OF CHART ENTRY	HIGHEST POSITION REACHED	NUMBER OF WEEKS IN CHARTS
STEWART, ROD			
Maggie May /Reason to Believe			
(US) Mercury	9 4 71	1	13
(UK) Mercury	*8 19 72*	*1*	*7*
You Wear It Well			
(UK) Mercury	*8 19 72*	*1*	*7*
(US) Mercury	10 7 72	13	3
Angel/What Made Milwaukee Famous			
(UK) Mercury	*11 25 72*	*4*	*5*
Oh No, Not My Baby			
(UK) Mercury	*9 15 73*	*6*	*5*
[see also: **FACES; PYTHON LEE JACKSON**]			
STEWART, SANDY			
My Coloring Book			
(US) Colpix	2 2 63	20	1
STILLS, STEPHEN			
Love the One You're With			
(US) Atlantic	1 16 71	14	4
[see also: **CROSBY, STILLS & NASH; CROSBY, STILLS, NASH & YOUNG; BUFFALO SPRINGFIELD**]			
STOLLER, RHET			
Chariot			
(UK) Decca	*1 8 61*	*19*	*1*
STOLOFF, MORRIS			
Moonglow/Theme from "Picnic"			
(US) Decca	5 5 56	2	17
(UK) Brunswick	*6 1 56*	*7*	*8*
STONE PONEYS			
Different Drum			
(US) Capitol	12 30 67	13	6
STORIES			
Brother Louie			
(US) Kama Sutra	7 28 73	1	11
STORM, GALE			
I Hear You Knocking			
(US) Dot	10 29 55	2	17
Teen-Age Prayer			
(US) Dot (b/w*)	12 31 55	9	11
Memories Are Made of This*			
(US) Dot	1 7 56	16	2
Why Do Fools Fall in Love			
(US) Dot	3 10 56	15	9
Ivory Tower			
(US) Dot	5 12 56	10	11
Dark Moon			
(US) Dot	5 13 57	5	14
STRANGELOVES			
I Want Candy			
(US) Bang	7 24 65	11	4

LABEL	DATE OF CHART ENTRY	HIGHEST POSITION REACHED	NUMBER OF WEEKS IN CHARTS
STRAWBERRY ALARM CLOCK			
Incense and Peppermint			
(US) UNI	10 21 67	1	12
STRAWBS			
Lay Down			
(UK) A&M	*11 25 72*	*12*	*3*
Part of the Union			
(UK) A&M	*1 27 73*	*2*	*9*
STREISAND, BARBRA			
People			
(US) Columbia	5 30 64	5	9
Second Hand Rose			
(UK) CBS	*2 19 66*	*14*	*2*
Stoney End			
(US) Columbia	12 26 70	6	8
STRING-A-LONGS			
Wheels			
(UK) London	*2 12 61*	*12*	*5*
(US) Warwick	2 13 61	3	8
STRUNK, JUD			
Daisy a Day			
(US) MGM	5 5 73	14	4
STYLISTICS			
You Are Everything			
(US) Avco	12 11 71	9	10
Betcha by Golly Wow			
(US) Avco	3 25 72	3	10
(UK) Avco	*7 22 72*	*13*	*4*
I'm Stone in Love with You			
(UK) Avco	*11 11 72*	*9*	*5*
(US) Avco	11 18 72	10	6
Break Up to Make Up			
(US) Avco	3 10 73	5	7
Rock'n Roll Baby			
(US) Avco	12 8 73	14	4
SUGARLOAF			
Green-Eyed Lady			
(US) Liberty	9 26 70	3	10
SUNNY AND THE SUNGLOWS			
Talk to Me			
(US) Tear Drop	10 19 63	11	5
SUNNY SIDERS			
Hey Mr. Banjo			
(US) Kapp	6 4 55	20	4
SUPREMES			
Where Did Our Love Go?			
(US) Motown	7 25 64	1	11
(UK) Stateside	*9 11 64*	*3*	*10*

LABEL	DATE OF CHART ENTRY	HIGHEST POSITION REACHED	NUMBER OF WEEKS IN CHARTS
Baby Love			
(US) Motown	10 17 64	1	10
(UK) Stateside	*10 31 64*	*1*	*10*
Come See About Me			
(US) Motown	11 28 64	1	11
Stop! In the Name of Love			
(US) Motown	3 6 65	1	9
(UK) Tamla Motown	*4 10 65*	*6*	*6*
Back in My Arms Again			
(US) Motown	5 15 65	1	8
Nothing but Heartaches			
(US) Motown	8 21 65	11	4
I Hear a Symphony			
(US) Motown	11 6 65	1	8
My World Is Empty Without You			
(US) Motown	2 5 66	5	6
Love Is Like an Itching in My Heart			
(US) Motown	5 14 66	9	5
You Can't Hurry Love			
(US) Motown	8 27 66	1	9
(UK) Tamla Motown	*9 17 66*	*3*	*8*
You Keep Me Hangin' On			
(US) Motown	11 12 66	1	8
(UK) Tamla Motown	*12 10 66*	*8*	*7*
Love Is Here and Now You're Gone			
(US) Motown	2 11 67	1	8
(UK) Tamla Motown	*3 25 67*	*17*	*3*
The Happening			
(US) Motown	4 15 67	1	8
(UK) Tamla Motown	*5 27 67*	*6*	*8*
Up the Ladder to the Roof			
(US) Motown	4 4 70	10	6
(UK) Tamla Motown	*5 30 70*	*6*	*6*
Stoned Love			
(US) Motown	12 5 70	7	8
(UK) Tamla Motown	*1 30 71*	*3*	*9*
River Deep Mountain High (with the FOUR TOPS)			
(US) Motown	12 26 70	14	5
(UK) Tamla Motown	*7 10 71*	*11*	*6*
Nathan Jones			
(US) Motown	6 12 71	16	4
(UK) Tamla Motown	*9 4 71*	*5*	*7*
Floy Joy			
(US) Motown	2 26 72	16	3
(UK) Tamla Motown	*3 18 72*	*9*	*6*
Automatically Sunshine			
(UK) Tamla Motown	*7 29 72*	*10*	*4*

[see also: **DIANA ROSS AND THE SUPREMES**]

SURFARIS
Wipe Out

LABEL	DATE OF CHART ENTRY	HIGHEST POSITION REACHED	NUMBER OF WEEKS IN CHARTS
(US) Dot	7 6 63	2	9
(UK) London	8 3 63	5	9
(US) Dot (reissue)	9 17 66	16	4
SWEET			
Funny Funny			
(UK) RCA	4 10 71	13	6
Co-Co			
(UK) RCA	6 19 71	2	10
Poppa Joe			
(UK) RCA	2 26 72	11	5
Little Willy			
(UK) RCA	6 24 72	4	8
(US) Bell (reissue)	4 7 73	3	9
Wig Wam Bam			
(UK) RCA	9 23 72	4	7
Blockbuster			
(UK) RCA	1 13 73	1	10
Hell Raiser			
(UK) RCA	5 5 73	2	6
Ballroom Blitz			
(UK) RCA	9 22 73	2	6
SWEET INSPIRATIONS			
Sweet Inspiration			
(US) Atlantic	4 27 68	18	3
SWINGING BLUE JEANS			
Hippy Hippy Shake			
(UK) HMV	1 4 64	2	9
Good Golly Miss Molly			
(UK) HMV	4 4 64	11	5
You're No Good			
(UK) HMV	6 20 64	3	7
SWINGING MEDALLIONS			
Double Shot (of My Baby's Love)			
(US) Smash	6 18 66	17	3
SYLVIA			
Pillow Talk			
(US) Vibration	5 5 73	3	11
(UK) London	7 21 73	14	4
SYNDICATE OF SOUND			
Little Girl			
(US) Bell	7 2 66	8	4
TAMS			
What Kind of Fool (Do You Think I Am)			
(US) ABC-Paramount	2 1 64	9	5
Hey Girl Don't Bother Me			
(UK) Probe (reissue)	8 21 71	1	11
TARRIERS			
Banana Boat Song			

306   ROCK ALMANAC

LABEL	DATE OF CHART ENTRY	HIGHEST POSITION REACHED	NUMBER OF WEEKS IN CHARTS
(US) Glory	12 29 56	6	20
(UK) Philips	*3 8 57*	*8*	*6*

[see also: **VINCE MARTIN**]

TAYLOR, FELICE
I Feel Love Coming On

(UK) President	*11 18 67*	*11*	*6*

TAYLOR, JAMES
Fire and Rain

(US) Warner Brothers	10 10 70	3	10

You've Got a Friend

(US) Warner Brothers	6 26 71	1	10
(UK) Warner Brothers	*9 11 71*	*4*	*9*

Don't Let Me Be Lonely Tonight

(US) Warner Brothers	1 6 73	14	4

TAYLOR, JOHNNIE
Who's Making Love

(US) Stax	11 16 68	5	9

Take Care of Your Homework

(US) Stax	2 22 69	20	1

I Believe in You (You Believe in Me)

(US) Stax	7 28 73	11	8

Cheaper to Keep Her

(US) Stax	11 10 73	15	4

TAYLOR, LITTLE JOHNNY
Part-Time Love

(US) Galaxy	10 5 63	19	2

TAYLOR, R. DEAN
Gotta See Jane

(UK) Tamla Motown	*7 20 68*	*17*	*3*

Indiana Wants Me

(US) Rare Earth	10 17 70	5	8
(UK) Tamla Motown	*5 1 71*	*2*	*9*

TAYLOR, VINCE
I'll Be Your Hero/Jet Black Machine

(UK) Palette	*9 18 60*	*15*	*4*

T-BONES
No Matter What Shape (Your Stomach's In)

(US) Liberty	1 8 66	3	8

TEDDY BEARS
To Know Him Is to Love Him

(US) Dore	20 20 58	1	15
(UK) London	*1 10 59*	*2*	*10*

TEE SET
Ma Belle Amie

(US) Colossus	2 14 70	5	8

TEMPERANCE SEVEN
You're Driving Me Crazy

(UK) Parlophone	*3 26 61*	*1*	*10*

LABEL	DATE OF CHART ENTRY	HIGHEST POSITION REACHED	NUMBER OF WEEKS IN CHARTS
Pasadena			
(UK) *Parlophone*	6 4 61	4	12
Hardhearted Hannah			
(UK) *Parlophone*	9 30 61	19	2
The Charleston			
(UK) *Parlophone*	12 2 61	14	2
TEMPO, NINO; and STEVENS, APRIL			
Deep Purple			
(US) Atco	10 12 63	1	9
(UK) *London*	12 7 63	17	2
Whispering			
(US) Atco	1 4 64	11	6
(UK) *London*	2 8 64	20	1
TEMPTATIONS			
The Way You Do the Things You Do			
(US) Gordy	3 28 64	11	6
My Girl			
(US) Gordy	1 30 65	1	10
It's Growing			
(US) Gordy	5 1 65	18	3
Since I Lost My Baby			
(US) Gordy	8 28 65	17	2
My Baby			
(US) Gordy	11 20 65	13	2
Ain't Too Proud to Beg			
(US) Gordy	6 25 66	13	5
Beauty Is Only Skin Deep			
(US) Gordy	9 10 66	3	6
(UK) *Tamla Motown*	11 12 66	18	1
(I Know) I'm Losing You			
(US) Gordy	12 10 66	8	6
(UK) *Tamla Motown*	1 14 67	19	2
All I Need Is You			
(US) Gordy	5 27 67	8	5
You're My Everything			
(US) Gordy	8 26 67	6	6
(Loneliness Made Me Realize) It's You That I Need			
(US) Gordy	10 28 67	14	5
I Wish It Would Rain			
(US) Gordy	1 27 68	4	5
I Could Never Love Another			
(US) Gordy	6 1 68	13	5
Cloud Nine			
(US) Gordy	12 7 68	6	8
(UK) *Tamla Motown*	9 13 69	15	3
Runaway Child, Running Wild			
(US) Gordy	3 8 69	6	8
Get Ready			
(UK) *Tamla Motown* (reissue)	3 22 69	10	5

LABEL	DATE OF CHART ENTRY	HIGHEST POSITION REACHED	NUMBER OF WEEKS IN CHARTS
Don't Let the Joneses Get You Down			
(US) Gordy	6 28 69	20	1
I Can't Get Next to You			
(US) Gordy	9 6 69	1	13
(UK) Tamla Motown	*1 31 70*	*13*	*5*
Psychedelic Shack			
(US) Gordy	2 7 70	7	7
Ball of Confusion			
(US) Gordy	6 13 70	3	11
(UK) Tamla Motown	*10 10 70*	*7*	*7*
Just My Imagination			
(US) Gordy	2 27 71	1	11
(UK) Tamla Motown	*6 19 71*	*8*	*8*
Superstar (Remember How You Got Where You Are)			
(US) Gordy	12 18 71	18	2
Take a Look Around			
(UK) Tamla Motown	*5 6 72*	*13*	*5*
Papa Was a Rolling Stone			
(US) Gordy	11 4 72	1	9
(UK) Tamla Motown	*1 20 73*	*14*	*4*
Masterpiece			
(US) Gordy	3 31 73	7	6
[see also: **SUPREMES**]			
10 CC			
Donna			
(UK) UK	*10 7 72*	*2*	*9*
Rubber Bullets			
(UK) UK	*6 2 73*	*1*	*9*
The Dean and I			
(UK) UK	*9 8 73*	*10*	*4*
TEN YEARS AFTER			
Love Like a Man			
(UK) Deram	*7 18 70*	*10*	*6*
TERRELL, TAMMI (see **MARVIN GAYE**)			
TERRY DACTYL AND THE DINOSAURS			
Seaside Shuffle			
(UK) UK (reissue)	*7 22 72*	*2*	*8*
TEX, JOE			
Hold What You've Got			
(US) Dial	1 16 65	5	6
Skinny Legs and All			
(US) Dial	12 9 67	10	7
I Gotcha			
(US) Dial	3 11 72	2	13
THEM			
Baby Please Don't Go			
(UK) Decca	*1 16 65*	*10*	*6*
Here Comes the Night			
(UK) Decca	*4 3 65*	*2*	*8*

	DATE OF CHART ENTRY	HIGHEST POSITION REACHED	NUMBER OF WEEKS IN CHARTS
THIN LIZZY			
Whisky in the Jar			
(*UK*) *Decca*	2 10 73	6	6
THOMAS, B. J.			
I'm So Lonesome I Could Cry (with the **TRIUMPHS**)			
(US) Scepter	3 19 66	8	8
Hooked on a Feeling			
(US) Scepter	12 28 68	5	7
Raindrops Keep Falling on My Head			
(US) Scepter	12 6 69	1	15
I Just Can't Help Believing			
(US) Scepter	7 25 70	9	7
No Love at All			
(US) Scepter	4 10 71	16	2
Rock and Roll Lullaby			
(US) Scepter	3 18 72	15	4
THOMAS, CARLA			
Gee Whiz			
(US) Atlantic	3 13 61	10	5
B-A-B-Y			
(US) Stax	10 15 66	14	4
[see also: **OTIS REDDING**]			
THOMAS, IRMA			
Wish Someone Would Care			
(US) Imperial	5 9 64	17	3
THOMAS, NICKY			
Love of the Common People			
(*UK*) *Trojan*	7 4 70	9	7
THOMAS, RUFUS			
Walking the Dog			
(US) Stax	11 16 63	10	6
Do the Funky Chicken			
(*UK*) *Stax*	5 23 70	18	2
THOMAS, TIMMY			
Why Can't We Live Together			
(US) Glades	1 6 73	3	8
(*UK*) *Mojo*	3 24 73	12	4
THOMPSON, SUE			
Sad Movies (Make Me Cry)			
(US) Hickory	10 9 61	5	7
Norman			
(US) Hickory	1 13 62	3	9
James (Hold the Ladder Steady)			
(US) Hickory	11 3 62	17	3
THORNE, KEN			
Theme from "Legion's Last Patrol"			
(*UK*) *HMV*	8 3 63	4	9

LABEL	DATE OF CHART ENTRY	HIGHEST POSITION REACHED	NUMBER OF WEEKS IN CHARTS
THREE DOG NIGHT			
One			
(US) Dunhill	6 7 69	5	10
Easy to Be Hard			
(US) Dunhill	8 23 69	4	10
Eli's Coming			
(US) Dunhill	11 15 69	10	10
Celebrate			
(US) Dunhill	3 14 70	15	5
Mama Told Me Not to Come			
(US) Dunhill	6 13 70	1	11
(UK) Stateside	*8 22 70*	*3*	*8*
Out in the Country			
(US) Dunhill	10 10 70	15	3
One Man Band			
(US) Dunhill	1 2 71	19	2
Joy to the World			
(US) Dunhill	4 3 71	1	13
Liar			
(US) Dunhill	8 7 71	7	7
Old Fashioned Love Song			
(US) Dunhill	11 27 71	4	8
Never Been to Spain			
(US) Dunhill	1 15 72	5	8
Family of Man			
(US) Dunhill	4 15 72	12	5
Black and White			
(US) Dunhill	9 2 72	1	6
Pieces of April			
(US) Dunhill	1 13 73	19	1
Shambala			
(US) Dunhill	6 9 73	3	11
Let Me Serenade You			
(US) Dunhill	12 1 73	17	2
THREE KAYES			
Ivory Tower			
(UK) HMV	*6 8 56*	*20*	*1*
[see also: **KAYE SISTERS**]			
TILLOTSON, JOHNNY			
Poetry in Motion			
(US) Cadence	10 31 60	2	9
(UK) London	*11 20 60*	*1*	*12*
Without You			
(US) Cadence	9 4 61	7	6
It Keeps Right On A-Hurtin'			
(US) Cadence	5 26 62	3	9
Send Me the Pillow You Dream On			
(US) Cadence	9 15 62	17	2
You Can Never Stop Me Loving You			
(US) Cadence	9 7 63	18	3

LABEL	DATE OF CHART ENTRY	HIGHEST POSITION REACHED	NUMBER OF WEEKS IN CHARTS
Talk Back Trembling Lips			
(US) MGM	12 14 63	7	6
TIN TIN			
Toast and Marmalade for Tea			
(US) Atco	5 29 71	20	1
TINY TIM			
Tip-Toe Through the Tulips			
(US) Reprise	6 29 68	17	1
TITANIC			
Sultana			
(UK) CBS	10 9 71	5	7
TODD, ART AND DOTTY			
Chanson d'Amour			
(US) Era	5 5 58	13	8
TOKENS			
Tonight I Fell in Love			
(US) Warwick	5 1 61	15	4
The Lion Sleeps Tonight			
(US) RCA	12 4 61	1	11
(UK) London	1 13 62	16	4
TOPOL			
If I Were a Rich Man			
(UK) CBS	6 17 67	9	3
TORME, MEL			
Mountain Greenery			
(UK) Vogue-Coral	5 18 56	4	17
Comin' Home Baby			
(UK) London	1 20 63	13	3
TORNADOES			
Telstar			
(UK) Decca	9 15 62	1	20
(US) London	11 24 62	1	11
Globetrotter			
(UK) Decca	1 20 63	5	7
Robot			
(UK) Decca	4 13 63	17	2
Ice Cream Man			
(UK) Decca	6 29 63	18	2
TOROK, MITCHELL			
When Mexico Gave Up the Rhumba			
(UK) Brunswick	10 5 56	6	15
TOWER OF POWER			
So Very Hard to Go			
(US) Warner Brothers	7 14 73	17	3
TOWNSEND, ED			
For Your Love			
(US) Capitol	5 12 58	15	6

LABEL	DATE OF CHART ENTRY	HIGHEST POSITION REACHED	NUMBER OF WEEKS IN CHARTS
TOYS			
A Lover's Concerto			
(US) DynoVoice	10 9 65	2	8
(*UK*) *Stateside*	11 20 65	5	9
Attack			
(US) DynoVoice	1 22 66	18	2
TRAFFIC			
Paper Sun			
(*UK*) *Island*	6 17 67	5	5
Hole in My Shoe			
(*UK*) *Island*	9 23 67	2	10
Here We Go Round the Mulberry Bush			
(*UK*) *Island*	12 9 67	8	7
TRASHMEN			
Surfin' Bird			
(US) Garrett	1 4 64	4	7
TRAVIS AND BOB			
Tell Him No			
(US) Sandy	4 13 59	8	6
TREMELOES			
Here Comes My Baby			
(*UK*) *CBS*	2 18 67	4	6
(US) Epic	5 13 67	13	5
Silence Is Golden			
(*UK*) *CBS*	5 6 67	1	10
(US) Epic	7 29 67	11	5
Even the Good Times Are Bad			
(*UK*) *CBS*	8 12 67	5	9
Suddenly You Love Me			
(*UK*) *CBS*	1 27 68	6	8
Helule Helule			
(*UK*) *CBS*	5 25 68	14	5
My Little Lady			
(*UK*) *CBS*	10 5 68	6	7
Hello World			
(*UK*) *CBS*	4 19 69	14	2
(Call Me) Number One			
(*UK*) *CBS*	11 1 69	2	11
Me and My Life			
(*UK*) *CBS*	9 26 70	4	9
TRENT, JACKIE			
Where Are You Now My Love			
(*UK*) *Pye*	5 8 65	1	7
T. REX			
Ride a White Swan			
(*UK*) *Fly*	11 21 70	2	14
Hot Love			
(*UK*) *Fly*	3 6 71	1	12

LABEL	DATE OF CHART ENTRY	HIGHEST POSITION REACHED	NUMBER OF WEEKS IN CHARTS
Get It On			
(UK) Fly	7 17 71	1	9
(US) Reprise (retitle: Bang A Gong)	2 19 72	10	6
Jeepster			
(UK) Fly	11 20 71	2	10
Telegram Sam			
(UK) T. Rex	1 29 72	1	7
Debora/One Inch Rock			
(UK) MagniFly (reissue)	4 15 72	7	6
Metal Guru			
(UK) T. Rex	5 13 73	1	8
Children of the Revolution			
(UK) T. Rex	9 16 72	2	7
Solid Gold Easy Action			
(UK) EMI	12 9 72	2	8
20th Century Boy			
(UK) EMI	3 10 73	3	6
Groover			
(UK) EMI	6 16 73	4	5
Truck On (Tyke)			
(UK) EMI	12 1 73	12	6
TROGGS			
Wild Thing			
(UK) Fontana	5 14 66	2	7
(US) Atco Fontana	7 9 66	1	8
With a Girl Like You			
(UK) Fontana	7 23 66	1	8
I Can't Control Myself			
(UK) Page One	10 8 66	2	9
Any Way That You Want Me			
(UK) Page One	12 31 66	8	6
Give It to Me			
(UK) Page One	3 11 67	12	4
Night of the Long Grass			
(UK) Page One	6 17 67	17	2
Love Is All Around			
(UK) Page One	11 4 67	5	7
(US) Fontana	5 4 68	7	5
TROY, DORIS			
Just One Look			
(US) Atlantic	7 13 63	10	6
TUCKER, TOMMY			
Hi-Heel Sneakers			
(US) Checker	3 14 64	11	4
TUNE WEAVERS			
Happy Happy Birthday Baby			
(US) Checker	9 30 57	5	9
TURNER, IKE AND TINA			
It's Gonna Work Out Fine			
(US) Sue	9 18 61	14	2

LABEL	DATE OF CHART ENTRY	HIGHEST POSITION REACHED	NUMBER OF WEEKS IN CHARTS
River Deep Mountain High			
(*UK*) *London*	*6 18 66*	*3*	*9*
A Love Like Yours			
(*UK*) *London*	*11 26 66*	*16*	*3*
Proud Mary			
(US) Liberty	3 6 71	4	7
Nutbush City Limits			
(*UK*) *United Artists*	*9 22 73*	*4*	*7*
TURNER, JESSE LEE			
Little Space Girl			
(US) Carlton	2 9 59	20	1
TURNER, SAMMY			
Lavender Blue			
(US) Big Top	7 27 59	3	8
Always			
(*UK*) *London*	*11 14 59*	*20*	*1*
(US) Big Top	11 30 59	19	1
TURNER, SPYDER			
Stand by Me			
(US) MGM	1 28 67	12	5
TURTLES			
It Ain't Me Babe			
(US) White Whale	9 4 65	8	5
You Baby			
(US) White Whale	3 26 66	20	1
Happy Together			
(US) White Whale	3 11 67	1	10
(*UK*) *London*	*4 15 67*	*12*	*6*
She'd Rather Be with Me			
(US) White Whale	6 3 67	3	6
(*UK*) *London*	*6 24 67*	*4*	*10*
You Know What I Mean			
(US) White Whale	9 9 67	12	4
She's My Girl			
(US) White Whale	12 16 67	14	3
Eleanore			
(US) White Whale	10 19 68	6	7
(*UK*) *London*	*11 16 68*	*7*	*5*
You Showed Me			
(US) White Whale	2 1 69	6	7
TWINKLE			
Terry			
(*UK*) *Decca*	*12 19 64*	*4*	*9*
TWITTY, CONWAY			
It's Only Make Believe			
(US) MGM	10 6 58	1	14
(*UK*) *MGM*	*11 14 58*	*1*	*14*
Hey Little Lucy			
(*UK*) *MGM*	*5 16 59*	*20*	*1*

LABEL	DATE OF CHART ENTRY	HIGHEST POSITION REACHED	NUMBER OF WEEKS IN CHARTS
Mona Lisa			
(UK) MGM	8 15 59	6	13
Danny Boy			
(US) MGM	11 2 59	10	7
Lonely Blue Boy			
(US) MGM	2 1 60	· 6	6
TYMES			
So Much in Love			
(US) Parkway	6 29 63	1	9
Wonderful Wonderful			
(US) Parkway	9 14 63	7	5
Somewhere			
(US) Parkway	2 1 64	19	1
People			
(UK) Direction	2 8 69	16	2
UNDISPUTED TRUTH			
Smiling Faces Sometimes			
(US) Gordy	8 21 71	3	9
UNION GAP (*GARY PUCKETT AND)			
Woman Woman			
(US) Columbia	12 16 67	4	11
Young Girl*			
(US) Columbia	3 23 68	2	11
(UK) CBS	5 4 68	1	'12
Lady Willpower*			
(US) Columbia	6 22 68	2	10
(UK) CBS	9 7 68	5	10
Over You*			
(US) Columbia	10 12 68	7	7
Don't Give In to Him*			
(US) Columbia	4 12 69	15	4
This Girl Is a Woman Now*			
(US) Columbia	9 13 69	9	7
UNIT 4+2			
Concrete and Clay			
(UK) Decca	3 20 65	1	9
(You've) Never Been In Love Like This Before			
(UK) Decca	6 5 65	14	4
UPSETTERS			
Return of Django			
(UK) Upsetter	10 18 69	5	8
VALANCE, RICKY			
Tell Laura I Love Her			
(UK) Columbia	8 21 60	1	11
VALE, JERRY			
You Don't Know Me			
(US) Columbia	8 18 56	14	10

LABEL	DATE OF CHART ENTRY	HIGHEST POSITION REACHED	NUMBER OF WEEKS IN CHARTS
VALENS, RICHIE			
Donna			
(US) Del-Fi	12 29 58	2	14
(*UK*) *London*	*3 28 59*	*20*	*2*
VALENTE, CATERINA			
The Breeze and I			
(US) Decca	4 16 55	3	11
(*UK*) *Polydor*	*8 19 55*	*5*	*14*
VALENTINE, DICKIE			
Finger of Suspicion			
(*UK*) *Decca*	*1 7 55*	*1*	*12*
Mr. Sandman			
(*UK*) *Decca*	*1 7 55*	*5*	*9*
A Blossom Fell			
(*UK*) *Decca*	*2 18 55*	*9*	*10*
I Wonder			
(*UK*) *Decca*	*6 3 55*	*4*	*15*
Christmas Alphabet			
(*UK*) *Decca*	*11 25 55*	*1*	*7*
Old Pianna Rag			
(*UK*) *Decca*	*12 16 55*	*20*	*3*
Christmas Island			
(*UK*) *Decca*	*12 14 56*	*8*	*3*
One More Sunrise			
(*UK*) *Pye*	*10 24 59*	*14*	*4*
VALINO, JOE			
Garden of Eden			
(US) Vik	11 24 56	12	9
VALLI, FRANKIE			
Can't Take My Eyes off You			
(US) Philips	6 10 67	2	11
I Make a Fool of Myself			
(US) Philips	9 30 67	18	2
You're Ready Now			
(*UK*) *Philips* (*reissue*)	*1 16 71*	*11*	*6*
[see also: **FOUR SEASONS**]			
VAN DYKE, LEROY			
Walk On By			
(US) Mercury	11 27 61	5	10
(*UK*) *Mercury*	*1 13 62*	*5*	*12*
VANILLA FUDGE			
(You Keep Me) Hangin' On			
(*UK*) *Atlantic*	*9 16 67*	*18*	*2*
(US) Atco (reissue)	8 3 68	6	7
VANITY FARE			
I Live for the Sun			
(*UK*) *Page One*	*9 28 68*	*20*	*1*
Early in the Morning			

LABEL	DATE OF CHART ENTRY	HIGHEST POSITION REACHED	NUMBER OF WEEKS IN CHARTS
(UK) *Page One*	8 9 69	10	6
(US) Page One	1 3 70	12	6
Hitchin' a Ride			
(UK) *Page One*	2 7 70	16	3
(US) Page One	6 13 70	5	9

VAUGHAN, FRANKIE

Happy Days and Lonely Nights			
(UK) *HMV*	1 28 55	12	3
Tweedle Dee			
(UK) *Philips*	4 22 55	17	1
Seventeen			
(UK) *Philips*	12 2 55	18	3
My Boy Flat Top			
(UK) *Philips*	2 3 56	20	2
Green Door			
(UK) *Philips*	11 9 56	2	15
Garden of Eden			
(UK) *Philips*	1 11 57	1	12
Man on Fire/Wanderin' Eyes			
(UK) *Philips*	10 4 57	6	11
Gotta Have Somethin' in the Bank Frank (with the **KAYE SISTERS**)			
(UK) *Philips*	11 1 57	8	8
Kisses Sweeter than Wine			
(UK) *Philips*	12 27 57	8	8
Can't Get Along Without You/We Are Not Alone			
(UK) *Philips*	3 7 58	11	3
Kewpie Doll			
(UK) *Philips*	5 16 58	10	9
Come Softly to Me			
(UK) *Philips*	4 25 59	9	8
Heart of a Man			
(UK) *Philips*	7 25 59	6	12
Tower of Strength			
(UK) *Philips*	11 11 61	1	12
Don't Stop, Twist			
(UK) *Philips*	2 10 62	14	5
Loop de Loop			
(UK) *Philips*	2 10 63	5	7
Hello Dolly			
(UK) *Philips*	6 27 64	18	3
There Must Be a Way			
(UK) *Philips*	9 16 67	7	14

VAUGHAN, MALCOLM

Every Day of My Life			
(UK) *HMV*	7 1 55	5	16
With Your Love			
(UK) *HMV*	1 27 56	18	3
St. Theresa of the Roses			
(UK) *HMV*	11 16 56	3	18

LABEL	DATE OF CHART ENTRY	HIGHEST POSITION REACHED	NUMBER OF WEEKS IN CHARTS
Chapel of the Roses			
(UK) HMV	5 10 57	13	7
My Special Angel			
(UK) HMV	11 29 57	3	14
To Be Loved			
(UK) HMV	4 4 58	14	8
More than Ever			
(UK) HMV	10 17 58	5	13
Wait for Me			
(UK) HMV	2 28 59	15	6
VAUGHAN, SARAH			
Make Yourself Comfortable			
(US) Mercury	1 1 55	8	9
How Important Can It Be			
(US) Mercury	3 5 55	18	1
Whatever Lola Wants			
(US) Mercury	4 23 55	12	11
Broken-Hearted Melody			
(US) Mercury	8 31 59	7	8
(UK) Mercury	9 26 59	9	10
Passing Strangers (with **BILLY ECKSTINE**)			
(UK) Mercury (reissue)	4 26 69	17	3
VAUGHN, BILLY			
Melody of Love			
(US) Dot	1 1 55	2	21
Shifting Whispering Sands			
(US) Dot	9 24 55	5	14
(UK) London	1 27 56	20	1
Theme from "Threepenny Opera"			
(UK) London	3 23 56	12	5
Sail Along Silv'ry Moon			
(US) Dot	1 27 58	5	13
Look for a Star			
(US) Dot	8 1 60	19	1
Swingin' Star			
(US) Dot	9 1 62	13	2
VEE, BOBBY			
Devil or Angel			
(US) Liberty	9 19 60	6	9
Rubber Ball			
(US) Liberty	12 19 60	6	9
(UK) London	1 8 61	3	7
More Than I Care to Say			
(UK) London	4 23 61	3	9
How Many Tears			
(UK) London	8 12 61	13	5
Take Good Care of My Baby			
(US) Liberty	9 4 61	1	8
(UK) London	10 28 61	1	11

LABEL	DATE OF CHART ENTRY	HIGHEST POSITION REACHED	NUMBER OF WEEKS IN CHARTS
Run to Him			
(US) Liberty	11 27 61	2	11
(UK) London	1 6 62	10	9
Please Don't Ask About Barbara			
(US) Liberty	3 31 62	15	2
Sharing You			
(US) Liberty	6 16 62	15	4
(UK) Liberty	6 16 62	10	8
Punish Me			
(US) Liberty	10 13 62	20	1
Forever Kind of Love			
(UK) Liberty	12 15 62	13	5
The Night Has a Thousand Eyes			
(US) Liberty	1 5 63	3	8
(UK) Liberty	2 17 63	3	8
Charms			
(US) Liberty	4 27 63	13	4
Come Back When You Grow Up (with the **STRANGERS**)			
(US) Liberty	8 26 67	3	9
VENTURES			
Walk Don't Run			
(US) Dolton	8 1 60	2	12
(UK) London	9 11 60	8	7
Perfidia			
(US) Dolton	11 28 60	15	6
(UK) London	12 4 60	5	7
Walk Don't Run			
(US) Dolton	8 8 64	8	5
Hawaii Five-0			
(US) Liberty	4 19 69	4	7
VERNE, LARRY			
Mr. Custer			
(US) Era	9 5 60	1	8
VERNON GIRLS			
Lover Please			
(UK) Decca	6 16 62	16	2
VIENNA PHILHARMONIC ORCHESTRA			
Theme from "Onedin Line"			
(UK) Decca	1 15 72	15	2
VILLAGE STOMPERS			
Washington Square			
(US) Epic	10 19 63	2	9
VINCENT, GENE			
Be-Bop-a-Lula			
(US) Capitol	7 14 56	9	10
(UK) Capitol	8 24 56	16	2
Blue Jean Bop			
(UK) Capitol	11 9 56	16	1

LABEL	DATE OF CHART ENTRY	HIGHEST POSITION REACHED	NUMBER OF WEEKS IN CHARTS
Lotta Lovin'			
(US) Capitol	10 7 57	14	7
Pistol Packing Mama			
(UK) Capitol	*6 12 60*	*11*	*4*
VINTON, BOBBY			
Roses Are Red			
(US) Epic	6 23 62	1	12
(UK) Columbia	*8 18 62*	*15*	*2*
Rain Rain Go Away			
(US) Epic	9 22 62	12	4
Blue on Blue			
(US) Epic	6 8 63	3	8
Blue Velvet			
(US) Epic	8 31 63	1	10
There! I've Said It Again			
(US) Epic	12 14 63	1	10
My Heart Belongs to Only You			
(US) Epic	3 21 64	9	4
Tell Me Why			
(US) Epic	6 6 64	13	4
Clinging Vine			
(US) Epic	9 5 64	17	3
Mr. Lonely			
(US) Epic	11 21 64	1	11
Long Lonely Nights			
(US) Epic	4 3 65	17	2
Coming Home Soldier			
(US) Epic	12 24 66	11	6
Please Love Me Forever			
(US) Epic	10 21 67	6	9
I Love How You Love Me			
(US) Epic	11 23 68	9	10
Sealed with a Kiss			
(US) Epic	8 19 72	19	2
VIPERS			
Don't You Rock Me Daddy-O			
(UK) Parlophone	*2 1 57*	*10*	*6*
Cumberland Gap			
(UK) Parlophone	*3 29 57*	*10*	*4*
VIRTUES			
Guitar Boogie Shuffle			
(US) Hunt	3 30 59	5	9
(UK) HMV	*5 16 59*	*19*	*3*
VISCOUNTS			
Shortnin' Bread			
(UK) Pye	*10 14 60*	*13*	*4*
Who Put the Bomp			
(UK) Nixa	*10 7 61*	*15*	*1*

LABEL	DATE OF CHART ENTRY	HIGHEST POSITION REACHED	NUMBER OF WEEKS IN CHARTS
VOGUES			
You're the One			
(US) Co and Co	10 16 65	4	6
Five O'Clock			
(US) Co and Co	12 25 65	4	9
Turn Around, Look at Me			
(US) Reprise	7 20 68	7	8
My Special Angel			
(US) Reprise	9 21 68	7	7
WADE, ADAM			
Take Good Care of Her			
(US) Coed	4 3 61	7	8
Writing on the Wall			
(US) Coed	6 5 61	5	7
As If I Didn't Know			
(US) Coed	8 21 61	10	4
WADSWORTH MANSION			
Sweet Mary			
(US) Sussex	2 13 71	7	5
WAINWRIGHT III, LOUDON			
Dead Skunk			
(US) Columbia	3 17 73	16	4
WALKER, JUNIOR, AND THE ALL STARS			
Shotgun			
(US) Soul	3 13 65	4	8
(I'm a) Road Runner			
(US) Soul	6 11 66	20	2
(UK) Tamla Motown	*4 26 69*	*12*	*6*
How Sweet It Is			
(US) Soul	9 24 66	18	1
What Does It Take to Win Your Love			
(US) Soul	6 28 69	4	9
(UK) Tamla Motown	*11 5 69*	*13*	*5*
These Eyes			
(US) Soul	12 13 69	16	3
Walk in the Night			
(UK) Tamla Motown	*9 23 72*	*16*	*4*
Take Me Girl I'm Ready			
(UK) Tamla Motown	*2 17 73*	*16*	*2*
WALKER, SCOTT			
Jackie			
(UK) Philips	*1 6 68*	*20*	*1*
Joanna			
(UK) Philips	*5 18 68*	*7*	*7*
Lights of Cincinnati			
(UK) Philips	*6 28 69*	*13*	*5*
[see also: **WALKER BROTHERS**]			

LABEL	DATE OF CHART ENTRY	HIGHEST POSITION REACHED	NUMBER OF WEEKS IN CHARTS
WALKER BROTHERS			
Love Her			
(*UK*) *Philips*	6 19 65	*20*	*1*
Make It Easy on Yourself			
(*UK*) *Philips*	8 28 65	*1*	*10*
(US) Smash	12 4 65	16	1
My Ship Is Coming In			
(*UK*) *Philips*	12 11 65	*3*	*10*
The Sun Ain't Gonna Shine Any More			
(*UK*) *Philips*	3 12 66	*1*	*8*
(US) Smash	5 14 66	13	4
(Baby) You Don't Have to Tell Me			
(*UK*) *Philips*	7 30 66	*13*	*2*
Another Tear Falls			
(*UK*) *Philips*	10 8 66	*12*	*3*
WALLACE, JERRY			
How Time Flies			
(US) Challenge	9 22 58	11	4
Primrose Lane			
(US) Challenge	9 21 59	8	11
In the Misty Moonlight			
(US) Challenge	9 12 64	19	2
WAR			
Slippin' into Darkness			
(US) United Artists	5 6 72	16	4
World Is a Ghetto			
(US) United Artists	1 20 73	7	6
Cisco Kid			
(US) United Artists	4 7 73	2	7
Gypsy Man			
(US) United Artists	8 18 73	8	6
[see also: **ERIC BURDON AND WAR**]			
WARD, BILLY			
Stardust			
(US) Liberty	7 29 57	13	11
(*UK*) *Brunswick*	9 13 57	*13*	*6*
WARD, CLIFFORD T.			
Gaye			
(*UK*) *Charisma*	7 21 73	*8*	*5*
WARD, MICHAEL			
Let There Be Peace on Earth			
(*UK*) *Philips*	10 27 73	*15*	*3*
WARD, ROBIN			
Wonderful Summer			
(US) Dot	11 23 63	14	5
WARWICK, DIONNE			
Anyone Who Had a Heart			
(US) Scepter	1 18 64	8	6

LABEL	DATE OF CHART ENTRY	HIGHEST POSITION REACHED	NUMBER OF WEEKS IN CHARTS
Walk On By			
(*UK*) *Pye International*	*5 2 64*	*9*	*9*
(US) Scepter	5 23 64	6	8
You'll Never Get to Heaven			
(*UK*) *Pye International*	*8 15 64*	*20*	*1*
Reach Out for Me			
(US) Scepter	11 28 64	20	1
Message to Michael			
(US) Scepter	4 30 66	8	6
Alfie			
(US) Scepter	6 24 67	15	4
I Say a Little Prayer			
(US) Scepter	11 18 67	4	8
Valley of the Dolls			
(US) Scepter	2 10 68	2	9
Do You Know the Way to San Jose?			
(US) Scepter	5 11 68	10	4
(*UK*) *Pye International*	*5 25 68*	*8*	*8*
Promises Promises			
(US) Scepter	11 30 68	19	2
This Girl's in Love with You			
(US) Scepter	3 1 69	7	7
You've Lost That Lovin' Feeling			
(US) Scepter	10 25 69	16	3
I'll Never Fall in Love Again			
(US) Scepter	1 17 70	6	7

WASHINGTON, DINAH
What a Difference a Day Makes			
(US) Mercury	7 27 59	8	8
Unforgettable			
(US) Mercury	11 9 59	17	3
September in the Rain			
(*UK*) *Mercury*	*11 25 61*	*16*	*2*
[see also: **BROOK BENTON**]			

WATTS 103rd STREET RHYTHM BAND (*featuring **CHARLES WRIGHT**)
Do Your Thing			
(US) Warner Brothers	4 19 69	11	4
Love Land			
(US) Warner Brothers*	7 4 70	16	3
Express Yourself			
(US) Warner Brothers*	10 3 70	12	5

WAYNE, THOMAS
Tragedy			
(US) Fernwood	3 9 59	5	8

WEATHERMEN
It's the Same Old Song			
(*UK*) *B&C*	*2 13 71*	*19*	*2*

LABEL	DATE OF CHART ENTRY	HIGHEST POSITION REACHED	NUMBER OF WEEKS IN CHARTS
WEBER, JOAN			
Let Me Go Lover			
(US) Columbia	1 1 55	1	10
(UK) Philips	2 18 55	16	1
WEEDON, BERT			
Guitar Boogie Shuffle			
(UK) Top Rank	5 9 59	6	8
Sorry Robbie			
(UK) Rank	11 13 60	18	1
WE FIVE			
You Were on My Mind			
(US) A&M	8 21 65	3	9
WEIR, FRANK			
Caribbean Holiday			
(UK) Oriole	8 28 60	18	4
WEISSBERG, ERIC, AND DELIVERANCE			
Dueling Banjos			
(US) Warner Brothers	2 3 73	2	10
(UK) Warner Brothers	4 21 73	17	2
WELCH, LENNY			
Since I Fell for You			
(US) Cadence	11 23 63	4	10
WELK, LAWRENCE			
Calcutta			
(US) Dot	1 9 61	1	11
(UK) RCA	2 5 61	19	1
WELLS, MARY			
The One Who Really Loves You			
(US) Motown	5 12 62	8	7
You Beat Me to the Punch			
(US) Motown	9 15 62	9	5
Two Lovers			
(US) Motown	12 29 62	7	7
Laughing Boy			
(US) Motown	3 30 63	15	2
My Guy			
(US) Motown	4 18 64	1	11
(UK) Stateside	6 6 64	5	8
(UK) Tamla Motown (reissue)	7 29 72	14	3
[see also: **MARVIN GAYE**]			
WEST, KEITH			
Excerpt from a Teenage Opera			
(UK) Parlophone	8 26 66	2	11
WESTON, KIM (see **MARVIN GAYE**)			
WHITCOMB, IAN			
You Turn Me On			
(US) Tower	6 26 65	8	6

LABEL	DATE OF CHART ENTRY	HIGHEST POSITION REACHED	NUMBER OF WEEKS IN CHARTS
WHITE, BARRY			
I'm Gonna Love You Just a Little Bit More Baby			
(US) 20th Century	5 19 73	3	9
Never Never Gonna Give Ya Up			
(US) 20th Century	12 1 73	10	5
WHITE, TONY JOE			
Polk Salad Annie			
(US) Monument (reissue)	8 2 69	8	6
WHITE PLAINS			
My Baby Loves Lovin'			
(UK) Deram	2 21 70	9	6
(US) Deram	6 13 70	13	6
I've Got You on My Mind			
(UK) Deram	5 16 70	17	4
Julie Do Ya Love Me?			
(UK) Deram	11 14 70	8	9
When You Are a King			
(UK) Deram	7 3 71	13	5
WHITFIELD, DAVID			
Santo Natale			
(UK) Decca	1 7 55	5	2
Beyond the Stars			
(UK) Decca	2 11 55	8	9
Mama			
(UK) Decca	5 27 55	12	11
Everywhere			
(UK) Decca	7 8 55	3	20
When You Lose the One You Love			
(UK) Decca	11 25 55	7	11
My September Love			
(UK) Decca	3 2 56	5	21
Adoration Waltz			
(UK) Decca	1 25 57	9	8
On the Street Where You Live			
(UK) Decca	6 20 58	16	8
WHITMAN, SLIM			
Rosemarie			
(UK) London	7 15 55	1	19
Indian Love Call			
(UK) London	7 29 55	8	12
China Doll			
(UK) London	9 23 55	15	2
Tumbling Tumbleweeds			
(UK) London	3 9 56	19	2
I'm a Fool			
(UK) London	4 13 56	16	3
Serenade			
(UK) London	8 3 56	8	8
I'll Take You Home Again, Kathleen			
(UK) London	4 19 57	5	11

LABEL	DATE OF CHART ENTRY	HIGHEST POSITION REACHED	NUMBER OF WEEKS IN CHARTS
WHITTAKER, ROGER			
Leavin' (Durham Town)			
(*UK*) *Columbia*	12 6 69	12	9
I Don't Believe in If Any More			
(*UK*) *Columbia* (*reissue*)	5 9 70	8	8
WHO			
I Can't Explain			
(*UK*) *Brunswick*	3 27 65	8	6
Anyway, Anyhow, Anywhere			
(*UK*) *Brunswick*	6 19 65	10	6
My Generation			
(*UK*) *Brunswick*	11 13 65	2	10
Substitute			
(*UK*) *Reaction*	3 19 66	5	9
I'm a Boy			
(*UK*) *Reaction*	9 10 66	2	10
Happy Jack			
(*UK*) *Reaction*	12 24 66	3	7
Pictures of Lily			
(*UK*) *Track*	5 6 67	4	6
I Can See for Miles			
(*UK*) *Track*	11 11 67	10	4
(US) Decca	11 11 67	9	5
Pinball Wizard			
(*UK*) *Track*	4 5 69	4	8
(US) Decca	5 17 69	19	3
The Seeker			
(*UK*) *Track*	5 16 70	19	1
See Me, Feel Me			
(US) Decca	11 28 70	12	2
Won't Get Fooled Again			
(*UK*) *Track*	7 31 71	9	5
(US) Decca	9 4 71	15	4
Let's See Action			
(*UK*) *Track*	11 27 71	16	3
Join Together			
(*UK*) *Track*	7 8 72	9	7
(US) Decca	9 2 72	17	2
5.15			
(*UK*) *Track*	10 20 73	20	1
WILDE, MARTY			
Endless Sleep			
(*UK*) *Philips*	7 18 58	4	12
Donna			
(*UK*) *Philips*	3 21 59	4	13
Teenager in Love			
(*UK*) *Philips*	6 6 59	2	13
Sea of Love			
(*UK*) *Philips*	9 26 59	4	12

LABEL	DATE OF CHART ENTRY	HIGHEST POSITION REACHED	NUMBER OF WEEKS IN CHARTS
Bad Boy			
(UK) *Philips*	12 5 59	6	8
Little Girl			
(UK) *Philips*	12 25 60	17	4
Rubber Ball			
(UK) *Philips*	1 15 61	10	4
Jezebel			
(UK) *Philips*	6 16 62	19	2
WILLIAMS, ANDY			
Canadian Sunset			
(US) Cadence	9 1 56	8	12
Butterfly			
(US) Cadence	3 2 57	1	13
(UK) *London*	4 26 57	1	12
I Like Your Kind of Love			
(US) Cadence	6 17 57	9	7
(UK) *London*	7 12 57	16	2
Are You Sincere?			
(US) Cadence	3 3 58	10	6
Promise Me Love			
(US) Cadence	10 6 58	17	2
Hawaiian Wedding Song			
(US) Cadence	2 2 59	11	10
Lonely Street			
(US) Cadence	9 28 59	5	10
Village of St. Bernadette			
(US) Cadence	1 4 60	7	7
Can't Get Used to Losing You			
(US) Columbia	3 30 63	2	9
(UK) *CBS*	4 20 63	2	11
Hopeless			
(US) Columbia	7 20 63	13	4
A Fool Never Learns			
(US) Columbia	2 8 64	13	5
Almost There			
(UK) *CBS*	9 23 65	2	10
Can't Keep My Eyes off You			
(UK) *CBS*	4 6 68	5	9
Happy Heart			
(UK) *CBS*	6 28 69	19	1
Can't Help Falling in Love			
(UK) *CBS*	3 14 70	3	11
It's So Easy			
(UK) *CBS*	9 5 70	13	4
Home Lovin' Man			
(UK) *CBS*	11 28 70	7	9
Love Story (Where Do I Begin)			
(US) Columbia	3 20 71	9	6
(UK) *CBS*	4 3 71	4	8

LABEL	DATE OF CHART ENTRY	HIGHEST POSITION REACHED	NUMBER OF WEEKS IN CHARTS
WILLIAMS, BILLY			
I'm Gonna Sit Right Down and Write Myself a Letter			
(US) Coral	7 8 57	6	12
WILLIAMS, DANNY			
Moon River			
(UK) HMV	*11 4 61*	*2*	*14*
Jeannie			
(UK) HMV	*2 10 62*	*14*	*4*
Wonderful World of the Young			
(UK) HMV	*4 28 62*	*8*	*7*
White on White			
(US) United Artists	4 25 64	9	5
WILLIAMS, LARRY			
Short Fat Fanny			
(US) Specialty	7 15 57	6	12
Bony Moronie			
(US) Specialty	12 30 57	18	4
(UK) London	*1 24 58*	*11*	*7*
WILLIAMS, MASON			
Classical Gas			
(US) Warner Brothers	7 20 68	2	8
(UK) Warner Brothers	*9 21 68*	*9*	*8*
WILLIAMS, MAURICE, AND THE ZODIACS			
Stay			
(US) Herald	10 31 60	1	8
(UK) Top Rank	*12 25 60*	*11*	*5*
WILLIAMS, OTIS, & THE CHARMS			
Ivory Tower			
(US) Deluxe	4 28 56	12	8
[see also: **CHARMS**]			
WILLIAMS, ROGER			
Autumn Leaves			
(US) Kapp	8 27 55	1	24
Near You			
(US) Kapp	9 22 58	10	9
Born Free			
(US) Kapp	11 5 66	7	9
WILLIS, CHUCK			
C C Rider			
(US) Atlantic	7 1 57	12	6
What Am I Living For			
(US) Atlantic	7 14 58	15	2
WILSON, AL			
Show and Tell			
(US) Rocky Road	12 15 73	8	3
WILSON, JACKIE			
Reet Petite			
(UK) Coral	*11 29 57*	*6*	*11*

LABEL	DATE OF CHART ENTRY	HIGHEST POSITION REACHED	NUMBER OF WEEKS IN CHARTS
Lonely Teardrops			
(US) Brunswick	12 26 58	7	12
That's Why			
(US) Brunswick	4 27 59	13	4
I'll Be Satisfied			
(US) Brunswick	8 3 59	20	1
Night			
(US) Brunswick (b/w*)	4 18 60	4	10
Doggin' Around*			
(US) Brunswick	5 9 60	15	1
(You Were Made) For All My Love			
(US) Brunswick (b/w**)	8 15 60	12	4
A Woman, A Love, A Friend**			
(US) Brunswick	8 15 60	15	2
My Empty Arms			
(US) Brunswick	1 23 61	9	4
Please Tell Me Why			
(US) Brunswick	4 17 61	20	1
I'm Comin' On Back to You			
(US) Brunswick	7 10 61	19	1
Baby Work Out			
(US) Brunswick	3 30 63	5	7
Whispers			
(US) Brunswick	11 5 66	11	5
(Your Love Keeps Lifting Me) Higher and Higher			
(US) Brunswick	9 9 67	6	7
(UK) MCA (reissue)	*5 31 69*	*11*	*6*
I Get the Sweetest Feeling			
(UK) MCA (reissue)	*8 26 72*	*9*	*6*
WILSON, J. FRANK			
Last Kiss			
(US) Josie	10 3 64	2	10
WILSON, NANCY			
(You Don't Know) How Glad I Am			
(US) Capitol	8 1 64	11	4
WINDING, KAI			
More			
(US) Verve	8 3 63	8	6
WINGS			
Give Ireland Back to the Irish			
(UK) Apple	*3 11 72*	*16*	*3*
Mary Had a Little Lamb			
(UK) Apple	*6 3 72*	*9*	*7*
Hi Hi Hi			
(UK) Apple (b/w C. Moon)	*1 6 73*	*5*	*6*
(US) Apple	1 13 73	10	5
[see also: **PAUL MCCARTNEY'S WINGS**]			
WINSTONS			
Color Him Father			
(US) Metromedia	6 28 69	7	7

LABEL	DATE OF CHART ENTRY	HIGHEST POSITION REACHED	NUMBER OF WEEKS IN CHARTS
WINTER, EDGAR, GROUP			
Frankenstein			
(US) Epic	4 28 73	1	10
(UK) Epic	*6 23 73*	*19*	*1*
Free Ride			
(US) Epic	9 29 73	14	4
WISDOM, NORMAN			
Wisdom of a Fool			
(UK) Columbia	*3 15 57*	*13*	*4*
WITHERS, BILL			
Ain't No Sunshine			
(US) Sussex	8 28 71	3	9
Lean on Me			
(US) Sussex	6 10 72	1	10
(UK) A&M	*9 9 72*	*18*	*2*
Use Me			
(US) Sussex	9 23 72	2	7
WIZZARD			
Ball Park Incident			
(UK) Harvest	*1 6 73*	*6*	*6*
See My Baby Jive			
(UK) Harvest	*4 28 73*	*1*	*10*
Angel Fingers			
(UK) Harvest	*9 1 73*	*1*	*8*
I Wish It Could Be Christmas Every Day			
(UK) Harvest	*12 8 73*	*4*	*6*
WONDER, STEVIE (*LITTLE)			
Fingertips (pt. 2)			
(US) Tamla*	7 6 63	1	10
Uptight (Everything's Alright)			
(US) Tamla	2 5 66	3	6
(UK) Tamla Motown	*2 26 66*	*14*	*3*
Nothing's Too Good for My Baby			
(US) Tamla	5 14 66	20	1
Blowin' in the Wind			
(US) Tamla	8 13 66	9	5
A Place in the Sun			
(US) Tamla	12 10 66	9	5
(UK) Tamla Motown	*1 21 67*	*20*	*1*
I Was Made to Love Her			
(US) Tamla	7 8 67	2	9
(UK) Tamla Motown	*8 5 67*	*5*	*9*
I'm Wondering			
(US) Tamla	10 28 67	12	3
Shoo-Be-Doo-Be-Doo-Da-Day			
(US) Tamla	5 4 68	9	6
For Once in My Life			
(US) Tamla	11 16 68	2	11
(UK) Tamla Motown	*1 4 69*	*3*	*11*

LABEL	DATE OF CHART ENTRY	HIGHEST POSITION REACHED	NUMBER OF WEEKS IN CHARTS
I Don't Know Why**			
(UK) Motown	4 19 69	14	4
My Cherie Amour			
(US) Tamla (b/w**)	7 5 69	4	8
(UK) Tamla Motown	8 2 69	4	9
Yester-Me, Yester-You, Yesterday			
(US) Tamla	11 22 69	7	6
(UK) Tamla Motown	11 22 69	2	9
Never Had a Dream Come True			
(UK) Tamla Motown	4 11 70	6	7
Signed Sealed Delivered (I'm Yours)			
(US) Tamla	7 18 70	3	10
(UK) Tamla Motown	8 1 70	15	5
Heaven Help Us All			
(US) Tamla	11 14 70	9	6
We Can Work It Out			
(US) Tamla	4 24 71	13	3
If You Really Love Me			
(US) Tamla	9 18 71	8	8
(UK) Tamla Motown	2 19 72	20	2
Superstition			
(US) Tamla	12 23 72	1	10
(UK) Tamla Motown	2 10 73	11	5
You Are the Sunshine of My Life			
(US) Tamla	4 14 73	1	10
(UK) Tamla Motown	5 26 73	7	5
Higher Ground			
(US) Tamla	9 8 73	4	9
Living in the City			
(US) Tamla	12 15 73	15	3
WONDER WHO?			
Don't Think Twice			
(US) Philips	12 11 65	12	4
WOOD, BRENTON			
Gimme Little Sign			
(US) Double Shot	9 23 67	9	7
(UK) Liberty	2 3 68	8	7
WOOD, ROY			
Dear Elaine			
(UK) Harvest	9 8 73	18	1
Forever			
(UK) Harvest	12 22 73	8	8
[see also: **WIZZARD, ELECTRIC LIGHT ORCHESTRA, MOVE**]			
WOOLEY, SHEB			
Purple People Eater			
(US) MGM	6 2 58	1	9
(UK) MGM	6 27 58	12	6
WRAY, LINK			
Rumble			
(US) Cadence	5 19 58	16	5

LABEL	DATE OF CHART ENTRY	HIGHEST POSITION REACHED	NUMBER OF WEEKS IN CHARTS
WRIGHT, BETTY			
Clean Up Woman			
(US) Alston	1 1 72	6	8
WRIGHT, CHARLES (see **WATTS 103rd STREET RHYTHM BAND**)			
WRIGHT, PERCY			
Man in the Raincoat			
(US) Unique	7 9 55	18	4
WRIGHT, RUBY			
Three Stars			
(*UK*) *Parlophone*	5 23 59	8	6
WYNETTE, TAMMY			
Stand by Your Man			
(US) Epic	2 1 69	19	1
WYNTER, MARK			
Image of a Girl			
(*UK*) *Decca*	8 21 60	11	7
Kicking Up the Leaves			
(*UK*) *Decca*	11 27 60	19	1
Dream Girl			
(*UK*) *Decca*	2 19 61	18	2
Venus in Blue Jeans			
(*UK*) *Pye*	10 20 62	4	9
Go Away Little Girl			
(*UK*) *Pye*	1 6 63	6	6
It's Almost Tomorrow			
(*UK*) *Pye*	11 30 63	4	12
YARBROUGH, GLENN			
Baby the Rain Must Fall			
(US) RCA	5 8 65	12	5
YARDBIRDS			
For Your Love			
(*UK*) *Columbia*	3 27 65	2	7
(US) Epic	6 12 65	6	7
Heart Full of Soul			
(*UK*) *Columbia*	6 26 65	2	9
(US) Epic	9 4 65	9	5
Evil Hearted You/Still I'm Sad			
(*UK*) *Columbia*	10 21 65	3	6
I'm a Man			
(US) Epic	12 11 65	17	1
Shapes of Things			
(*UK*) *Columbia*	3 12 66	3	7
(US) Epic	4 23 66	11	4
Over Under Sideways Down			
(*UK*) *Columbia*	6 11 66	10	5
(US) Epic	7 30 66	13	4
YES			
Roundabout			
(US) Atlantic	3 25 72	13	5

LABEL	DATE OF CHART ENTRY	HIGHEST POSITION REACHED	NUMBER OF WEEKS IN CHARTS
YOUNG, BARRY			
One Has My Name			
(US) Dot	12 18 65	13	3
YOUNG, FARON			
Hello Walls			
(US) Capitol	5 22 61	12	5
Four in the Morning			
(UK) Mercury	8 12 72	3	10
YOUNG, JIMMY			
Unchained Melody			
(UK) Decca	5 6 55	1	18
Man from Laramie			
(UK) Decca	9 16 55	1	12
Someone on Your Mind			
(UK) Decca	12 23 55	13	5
Chain Gang			
(UK) Decca	3 16 56	9	5
More			
(UK) Decca	10 12 56	4	14
Miss You			
(UK) Columbia	11 2 63	15	4
YOUNG, KAREN			
Nobody's Child			
(UK) Major Minor	9 27 69	6	13
YOUNG, KATHY, AND THE INNOCENTS			
1000 Stars			
(US) Indigo	11 14 60	3	12
YOUNG, NEIL			
Heart of Gold			
(US) Reprise	2 26 72	1	10
(UK) Reprise	4 1 72	10	5
[see also: **BUFFALO SPRINGFIELD** and **CROSBY, STILLS, NASH AND YOUNG**]			
YOUNGBLOODS			
Get Together			
(US) RCA (reissue)	8 16 69	5	9
YOUNG-HOLT LIMITED			
Soulful Street			
(US) Brunswick	12 21 68	3	9
YOUNG IDEA			
With a Little Help from My Friends			
(UK) Columbia	7 15 67	10	1
YOUNG RASCALS (*RASCALS)			
Good Lovin'			
(US) Atlantic	4 9 66	1	9
You Better Run			
(US) Atlantic	7 16 66	20	2

LABEL	DATE OF CHART ENTRY	HIGHEST POSITION REACHED	NUMBER OF WEEKS IN CHARTS
I've Been Lonely Too Long			
(US) Atlantic	3 18 67	16	3
Groovin'			
(US) Atlantic	5 6 67	1	10
(UK) Atlantic	*6 17 67*	*8*	*9*
Girl Like You			
(US) Atlantic	7 29 67	10	6
How Can I Be Sure			
(US) Atlantic	9 30 67	4	7
It's Wonderful			
(US) Atlantic	1 13 68	20	1
Beautiful Morning			
(US) Atlantic*	4 27 68	3	9
People Got to Be Free			
(US) Atlantic*	8 3 68	1	11
YURO, TIMI			
Hurt			
(US) Liberty	8 7 61	4	7
What's a Matter Baby			
(US) Liberty	8 25 62	12	3
ZACHARIAS, HELMUT			
When the White Lilacs Bloom Again			
(US) Decca	9 22 56	16	4
Tokyo Melody			
(UK) Polydor	*11 14 64*	*9*	*5*
ZACHARLE, JOHN			
Dinner with Drac			
(US) Cameo	3 24 58	6	3
ZAGER AND EVANS			
In the Year 2525			
(US) RCA	7 5 69	1	10
(UK) RCA	*8 16 69*	*1*	*9*
ZOMBIES			
She's Not There			
(UK) Decca	*9 4 64*	*12*	*6*
(US) Parrot	11 14 64	2	9
Tell Her No			
(US) Parrot	2 6 65	6	6
Time of the Season			
(US) Date	3 8 69	3	8

CHART TOPPERS
SINGLES, 1955–73

CHART TOPPERS
U. S. SINGLES, 1955–73

1955

Jan.	1	Chordettes	Mr. Sandman	Cadence	3
Jan.	22	Joan Weber	Let Me Go Lover	Columbia	2
Feb.	5	Fontane Sisters	Hearts of Stone	Dot	1
Feb.	12	McGuire Sisters	Sincerely	Coral	6
Mar.	26	Bill Hayes	Ballad of Davy Crockett	Cadence	5
May	30	Perez Prado	Cherry Pink and Apple Blossom White	Victor	10
July	9	Bill Haley and His Comets	Rock Around the Clock	Decca	8
Sept.	3	Mitch Miller	Yellow Rose of Texas	Columbia	5
Oct.	8	Four Aces	Love Is a Many Splendored Thing	Decca	1
Oct.	15	Mitch Miller	Yellow Rose of Texas	Columbia	1
Oct.	22	Four Aces	Love Is a Many Splendored Thing	Decca	1
Oct.	29	Roger Williams	Autumn Leaves	Kapp	2
Nov.	12	Four Aces	Love Is a Many Splendored Thing	Decca	3
Dec.	3	Tennessee Ernie Ford	Sixteen Tons	Capitol	6

1956

Jan.	14	Dean Martin	Memories Are Made of This	Capitol	5

Feb.	18	Platters	Great Pretender	Mercury	2
Mar.	3	Kay Starr	Rock and Roll Waltz	Victor	3
Mar.	24	Les Baxter	Poor People of Paris	Capitol	6
May	3	Elvis Presley	Heartbreak Hotel	Victor	7
June	16	Gogi Grant	Wayward Wind	Era	7
Aug.	4	Pat Boone	I Almost Lost My Mind	Dot	2
Aug.	18	Platters	My Prayer	Mercury	5
Sept.	15	Elvis Presley	Don't Be Cruel	Victor	7
Nov.	3	Jim Lowe	Green Door	Dot	3
Nov.	17	Elvis Presley	Love Me Tender	Victor	3
Dec.	8	Guy Mitchell	Singing the Blues	Columbia	2
Dec.	22	Elvis Presley	Love Me Tender	Victor	1
Dec.	29	Guy Mitchell	Singing the Blues	Columbia	7

1957

Feb.	9	Pat Boone	Don't Forbid Me	Dot	1
Feb.	16	Tab Hunter	Young Love	Dot	6
Mar.	30	Andy Williams	Butterfly	Cadence	3
Apr.	20	Elvis Presley	All Shook Up	Victor	8
June	10	Pat Boone	Love Letters in the Sand	Dot	5
July	15	Elvis Presley	Teddy Bear	Victor	7
Sept.	2	Debbie Reynolds	Tammy	Coral	5
Oct.	7	Jimmie Rodgers	Honeycomb	Roulette	2
Oct.	21	Everly Brothers	Wake Up Little Susie	Cadence	2
Nov.	4	Elvis Presley	Jailhouse Rock	Victor	6
Dec.	9	Sam Cooke	You Send Me	Keen	3
Dec.	30	Pat Boone	April Love	Dot	1

1958

Jan.	6	Danny and the Juniors	At the Hop	ABC-Paramount	7
Feb.	24	Silhouettes	Get a Job	Ember	2
Mar.	10	Elvis Presley	Don't	Victor	1
Mar.	17	Champs	Tequila	Challenge	5
Apr.	21	Platters	Twilight Time	Mercury	1

Apr.	28	David Seville	Witch Doctor	Liberty	3
May	19	Everly Brothers	All I Have to Do Is Dream	Cadence	3
June	9	Sheb Wooley	Purple People Eater	MGM	6
July	21	Coasters	Yakety Yak	Atco	1
July	28	Perez Prado	Patricia	Victor	1
Aug.	4	Ricky Nelson	Poor Little Fool	Imperial	2
Aug.	18	Domenico Modugno	Volaré	Decca	1
Aug.	25	Elegants	Little Star	Apt	1
Sept.	1	Domenico Modugno	Volaré	Decca	4
Sept.	29	Tommy Edwards	It's All in the Game	MGM	6
Nov.	10	Conway Twitty	It's Only Make Believe	MGM	1
Nov.	17	Kingston Trio	Tom Dooley	Capitol	1
Nov.	24	Conway Twitty	It's Only Make Believe	MGM	1
Dec.	1	Teddy Bears	To Know Him Is to Love Him	Dore	3
Dec.	22	David Seville and the Chipmunks	Chipmunk Song	Liberty	4

1959

Jan.	19	Platters	Smoke Gets in Your Eyes	Mercury	3
Feb.	9	Lloyd Price	Stagger Lee	ABC-Paramount	4
Mar.	9	Frankie Avalon	Venus	Chancellor	5
Apr.	13	Fleetwoods	Come Softly to Me	Dolphin	4
May	11	Dave "Baby" Cortez	Happy Organ	Clock	1
May	18	Wilbert Harrison	Kansas City	Fury	2
June	1	Johnny Horton	Battle of New Orleans	Columbia	6
July	13	Paul Anka	Lonely Boy	ABC-Paramount	4
Aug.	10	Elvis Presley	Big Hunk o'Love	RCA	2
Aug.	24	Browns	Three Bells	RCA	4
Sept.	21	Santo and Johnny	Sleep Walk	Canadian-American	2

Oct.	5	Bobby Darin	Mack the Knife	Atco	6
Nov.	16	Fleetwoods	Mr. Blue	Dolton	1
Nov.	23	Bobby Darin	Mack the Knife	Atco	3
Dec.	14	Guy Mitchell	Heartaches by the Number	Columbia	2
Dec.	28	Frankie Avalon	Why	Chancellor	1

1960

Jan.	4	Marty Robbins	El Paso	Columbia	2
Jan.	18	Johnny Preston	Running Bear	Mercury	3
Feb.	8	Mark Dinning	Teen Angel	MGM	2
Feb.	22	Percy Faith	Theme from Summer Place	Columbia	9
Apr.	25	Elvis Presley	Stuck on You	RCA	4
May	23	Everly Brothers	Cathy's Clown	Warner Brothers	5
June	27	Connie Francis	Everybody's Somebody's Fool	MGM	2
July	11	Hollywood Argyles	Alley-Oop	Lute	1
July	18	Brenda Lee	I'm Sorry	Decca	3
Aug.	8	Brian Hyland	Itsy Bitsy Teenie Weenie Yellow Polka Dot Bikini	Leader	1
Aug.	15	Elvis Presley	It's Now or Never	RCA	5
Sept.	19	Chubby Checker	The Twist	Parkway	1
Sept.	26	Connie Francis	My Heart Has a Mind of Its Own	MGM	2
Oct.	10	Larry Verne	Mr. Custer	Era	1
Oct.	17	Drifters	Save the Last Dance for Me	Atlantic	1
Oct.	24	Brenda Lee	I Want to Be Wanted	Decca	1
Oct.	31	Drifters	Save the Last Dance for Me	Atlantic	2
Nov.	14	Ray Charles	Georgia on My Mind	ABC-Paramount	1
Nov.	21	Maurice Williams and the Zodiacs	Stay	Herald	1
Nov.	28	Elvis Presley	Are You Lonesome Tonight	RCA	6

1961

Jan.	9	Bert Kaempfert	Wonderland by Night	Decca	3
Jan.	30	Shirelles	Will You Love Me Tomorrow	Scepter	2
Feb.	13	Lawrence Welk	Calcutta	Dot	2
Feb.	27	Chubby Checker	Pony Time	Parkway	3
Mar.	20	Elvis Presley	Surrender	RCA	2
Apr.	3	Marcels	Blue Moon	Colpix	3
Apr.	24	Del Shannon	Runaway	Big Top	4
May	22	Ernie K. Doe	Mother-in-Law	Minit	1
May	29	Ricky Nelson	Travelin' Man	Imperial	1
June	5	Roy Orbison	Runnin' Scared	Monument	1
June	12	Ricky Nelson	Travelin' Man	Imperial	1
June	19	Pat Boone	Moody River	Dot	1
June	26	Gary "U.S." Bonds	Quarter to Three	Le Grand	2
July	10	Bobby Lewis	Tossin' and Turnin'	Beltone	7
Aug.	28	Joe Dowell	Wooden Heart	Smash	1
Sept.	4	Highwaymen	Michael	United Artists	2
Sept.	18	Bobby Vee	Take Good Care of My Baby	Liberty	3
Oct.	9	Ray Charles	Hit the Road Jack	ABC-Paramount	2
Oct.	23	Dion	Runaround Sue	Laurie	2
Nov.	6	Jimmy Dean	Big Bad John	Columbia	5
Dec.	11	Marvelettes	Please Mr. Postman	Tamla	1
Dec.	18	Tokens	The Lion Sleeps Tonight	RCA	3

1962

Jan.	13	Chubby Checker	The Twist	Parkway	2
Jan.	27	Joey Dee and the Starliters	Peppermint Twist	Roulette	3
Feb.	17	Gene Chandler	Duke of Earl	Vee Jay	3
Mar.	10	Bruce Channel	Hey! Baby	Smash	3
Mar.	31	Connie Francis	Don't Break the Heart That Loves You	MGM	1

Apr.	7	Shelley Fabares	Johnny Angel	Colpix	2
Apr.	21	Elvis Presley	Good Luck Charm	RCA	2
May	5	Shirelles	Soldier Boy	Scepter	3
May	26	Acker Bilk	Stranger on the Shore	Atco	1
June	2	Ray Charles	I Can't Stop Loving You	ABC-Paramount	5
July	7	David Rose and Orchestra	The Stripper	MGM	1
July	14	Bobby Vinton	Roses Are Red	Epic	4
Aug.	11	Neil Sedaka	Breaking Up Is Hard to Do	RCA	2
Aug.	25	Little Eva	The Locomotion	Dimension	1
Sept.	1	Tommy Roe	Sheila	ABC-Paramount	2
Sept.	15	Four Seasons	Sherry	Vee Jay	5
Oct.	20	Bobby "Boris" Pickett and the Crypt Kickers	The Monster Mash	Garpax	2
Nov.	3	Crystals	He's a Rebel	Philles	2
Nov.	17	Four Seasons	Big Girls Don't Cry	Vee Jay	5
Dec.	22	Tornadoes	Telstar	London	3
1963					
Jan.	12	Steve Lawrence	Go Away Little Girl	Columbia	2
Jan.	26	Rooftop Singers	Walk Right In	Vanguard	2
Feb.	9	Paul and Paula	Hey Paula	Philips	3
Mar.	2	Four Seasons	Walk Like a Man	Vee Jay	3
Mar.	23	Ruby and the Romantics	Our Day Will Come	Kapp	1
Mar.	30	Chiffons	He's So Fine	Laurie	4
Apr.	27	Little Peggy March	I Will Follow Him	RCA	3
May	18	Jimmy Soul	If You Wanna Be Happy	S.P.Q.R.	2
June	1	Lesley Gore	It's My Party	Mercury	2
June	15	Kyu Sakamoto	Sukiyaki	Capitol	3

July	6	Essex	Easier Said Than Done	Roulette	2
July	20	Jan and Dean	Surf City	Liberty	2
Aug.	3	Tymes	So Much in Love	Parkway	1
Aug.	10	Stevie Wonder	Fingertips (pt. 2)	Tamla	3
Aug.	31	Angels	My Boyfriend's Back	Smash	3
Sept.	21	Bobby Vinton	Blue Velvet	Epic	3
Oct.	12	Jimmy Gilmer and the Fireballs	Sugar Shack	Dot	5
Nov.	16	Nino Tempo and April Stevens	Deep Purple	Atco	1
Nov.	23	Dale and Grace	I'm Leavin' It Up to You	Montel-Michele	2
Dec.	7	Singing Nun	Dominique	Philips	4

1964

Jan.	4	Bobby Vinton	There I've Said It Again	Epic	4
Feb.	1	Beatles	I Want to Hold Your Hand	Capitol	7
Mar.	21	Beatles	She Loves You	Swan	2
Apr.	4	Beatles	Can't Buy Me Love	Capitol	5
May	9	Louis Armstrong	Hello Dolly	Kapp	1
May	16	Mary Wells	My Guy	Motown	2
May	30	Beatles	Love Me Do	Tollie	1
June	6	Dixie Cups	Chapel of Love	Red Bird	3
June	27	Peter and Gordon	World Without Love	Capitol	1
July	4	Beach Boys	I Get Around	Capitol	2
July	18	Four Seasons	Rag Doll	Philips	2
Aug.	1	Beatles	Hard Day's Night	Capitol	2
Aug.	15	Dean Martin	Everybody Loves Somebody	Reprise	1
Aug.	22	Supremes	Where Did Our Love Go?	Motown	2
Sept.	5	Animals	House of the Rising Sun	MGM	3
Sept.	26	Roy Orbison	Oh Pretty Woman	Monument	3

Oct.	17	Manfred Mann	Do Wah Diddy Diddy	Ascot	2
Oct.	31	Supremes	Baby Love	Motown	4
Nov.	28	Shangri-Las	Leader of the Pack	Red Bird	1
Dec.	5	Lorne Greene	Ringo	RCA	1
Dec.	12	Bobby Vinton	Mr. Lonely	Epic	1
Dec.	19	Supremes	Come See About Me	Motown	1
Dec.	26	Beatles	I Feel Fine	Capitol	3

1965

Jan.	16	Supremes	Come See About Me	Motown	1
Jan.	23	Petula Clark	Downtown	Warner Brothers	2
Feb.	6	Righteous Brothers	You've Lost That Lovin' Feeling	Philles	2
Feb.	20	Gary Lewis and the Playboys	This Diamond Ring	Liberty	2
Mar.	6	Temptations	My Girl	Gordy	1
Mar.	13	Beatles	8 Days a Week	Capitol	2
Mar.	27	Supremes	Stop! In the Name of Love	Motown	2
Apr.	10	Freddie and the Dreamers	I'm Telling You Now	Tower	2
Apr.	24	Wayne Fontana and the Mindbenders	Game of Love	Fontana	1
May	1	Herman's Hermits	Mrs. Brown You've Got a Lovely Daughter	MGM	3
May	22	Beatles	Ticket to Ride	Capitol	1
May	29	Beach Boys	Help Me Rhonda	Capitol	2
June	12	Supremes	Back in My Arms Again	Motown	1
June	19	Four Tops	I Can't Help Myself	Motown	1
June	26	Byrds	Mr. Tambourine Man	Columbia	1
July	3	Four Tops	I Can't Help Myself	Motown	1

July	10	Rolling Stones	Satisfaction	London	4
Aug.	7	Herman's Hermits	I'm Henry VIII I Am	MGM	1
Aug.	14	Sonny and Cher	I Got You Babe	Atco	3
Sept.	4	Beatles	Help	Capitol	3
Sept.	25	Barry McGuire	Eve of Destruction	Dunhill	1
Oct.	2	McCoys	Hang On Sloopy	Bang	1
Oct.	9	Beatles	Yesterday	Capitol	4
Nov.	6	Rolling Stones	Get off of My Cloud	London	2
Nov.	20	Supremes	I Hear a Symphony	Motown	2
Dec.	4	Byrds	Turn Turn Turn	Columbia	3
Dec.	25	Dave Clark Five	Over and Over	Epic	1

1966

Jan.	1	Simon and Garfunkel	Sounds of Silence	Columbia	1
Jan.	8	Beatles	We Can Work It Out	Capitol	2
Jan.	22	Simon and Garfunkel	Sounds of Silence	Columbia	1
Jan.	29	Beatles	We Can Work It Out	Capitol	1
Feb.	5	Petula Clark	My Love	Warner Brothers	2
Feb.	19	Lou Christie	Lightning Strikes	MGM	1
Feb.	26	Nancy Sinatra	These Boots Are Made for Walking	Reprise	1
Mar.	5	Barry Sadler	Ballad of the Green Berets	RCA	5
Apr.	9	Righteous Brothers	You're My Soul and Inspiration	Verve	3
Apr.	30	Young Rascals	Good Lovin'	Atlantic	1
May	7	Mamas and Papas	Monday Monday	Dunhill	3
May	28	Percy Sledge	When a Man Loves a Woman	Atlantic	2
June	11	Rolling Stones	Paint It Black	London	2
June	25	Beatles	Paperback Writer	Capitol	1

			WEEKS AT NO. 1

				WEEKS AT NO. 1
July	2	Frank Sinatra	Strangers in the Night	Reprise	1
July	9	Beatles	Paperback Writer	Capitol	1
July	16	Tommy James and the Shondells	Hanky Panky	Roulette	2
July	30	Troggs	Wild Thing	Atco and Fontana	2
Aug.	13	Lovin' Spoonful	Summer in the City	Kama Sutra	3
Sept.	3	Donovan	Sunshine Superman	Epic	1
Sept.	10	Supremes	You Can't Hurry Love	Motown	2
Sept.	24	Association	Cherish	Valiant	3
Oct.	15	Four Tops	Reach Out I'll Be There	Motown	2
Oct.	29	? and the Mysterians	96 Tears	Cameo	1
Nov.	5	Monkees	Last Train to Clarksville	Colgems	1
Nov.	12	Johnny Rivers	Poor Side of Town	Imperial	1
Nov.	19	Supremes	You Keep Me Hanging On	Motown	2
Dec.	3	New Vaudeville Band	Winchester Cathedral	Fontana	1
Dec.	10	Beach Boys	Good Vibrations	Capitol	1
Dec.	17	New Vaudeville Band	Winchester Cathedral	Fontana	2
Dec.	31	Monkees	I'm a Believer	Colgems	7

1967

Feb.	18	Buckinghams	Kind of a Drag	USA	2
Mar.	4	Rolling Stones	Ruby Tuesday	London	1
Mar.	11	Supremes	Love Is Here and Now You're Gone	Motown	1
Mar.	18	Beatles	Penny Lane	Capitol	1
Mar.	25	Turtles	Happy Together	White Whale	3

Apr.	15	Frank and Nancy Sinatra	Something Stupid	Reprise	4
May	13	Supremes	The Happening	Motown	1
May	20	Young Rascals	Groovin'	Atlantic	2
June	3	Aretha Franklin	Respect	Atlantic	2
June	17	Young Rascals	Groovin'	Atlantic	2
July	1	Association	Windy	Warner Brothers	4
July	29	Doors	Light My Fire	Elektra	3
Aug.	19	Beatles	All You Need Is Love	Capitol	1
Aug.	26	Bobbie Gentry	Ode to Billie Joe	Capitol	4
Sept.	23	Box Tops	The Letter	Mala	4
Oct.	21	Lulu	To Sir, with Love	Epic	5
Nov.	25	Strawberry Alarm Clock	Incense and Peppermint	UNI	1
Dec.	2	Monkees	Daydream Believer	Colgems	4
Dec.	30	Beatles	Hello Goodbye	Capitol	3

1968

Jan.	20	John Fred and his Playboy Band	Judy in Disguise	Paula	2
Feb.	3	Lemon Pipers	Green Tambourine	Buddah	1
Feb.	10	Paul Mauriat	Love Is Blue	Philips	5
Mar.	16	Otis Redding	Dock of the Bay	Volt	4
Apr.	13	Bobby Goldsboro	Honey	United Artists	5
May	18	Archie Bell and the Drells	Tighten Up	Atlantic	2
June	1	Simon and Garfunkel	Mrs. Robinson	Columbia	3
June	22	Herb Alpert and the Tijuana Brass	This Guy's in Love with You	A & M	4
July	20	Hugh Masekela	Grazing in the Grass	UNI	2
Aug.	3	Doors	Hello I Love You	Elektra	2
Aug.	17	Rascals	People Got to Be Free	Atlantic	5

				WEEKS AT NO. 1
Sept.	21	Jeannie C. Riley	Harper Valley PTA	Plantation	1

Sept.	21	Jeannie C. Riley	Harper Valley PTA	Plantation	1
Sept.	28	Beatles	Hey Jude	Apple	9
Nov.	30	Diana Ross and the Supremes	Love Child	Motown	2
Dec.	14	Marvin Gaye	I Heard it Through the Grapevine	Tamla	7
1969					
Feb.	1	Tommy James and the Shondells	Crimson and Clover	Roulette	2
Feb.	15	Sly and the Family Stone	Everyday People	Epic	4
Mar.	15	Tommy Roe	Dizzy	ABC	4
Apr.	12	5th Dimension	Aquarius/Let the Sun Shine In	Soul City	6
May	24	Beatles	Get Back	Apple	5
June	28	Henry Mancini	Love Theme from *Romeo and Juliet*	RCA	2
July	12	Zager and Evans	In the Year 2525	RCA	6
Aug.	23	Rolling Stones	Honky Tonk Women	London	4
Sept.	20	Archies	Sugar Sugar	Calendar	4
Oct.	18	Temptations	I Can't Get Next to You	Gordy	2
Nov.	1	Elvis Presley	Suspicious Minds	RCA	1
Nov.	8	5th Dimension	Wedding Bell Blues	Soul City	3
Nov.	29	Beatles	Come Together/ Something	Apple	1
Dec.	6	Steam	Na Na Hey Hey Kiss Him Goodbye	Fontana	2
Dec.	20	Peter, Paul and Mary	Leaving on a Jet Plane	Warner Brothers	1
Dec.	27	Diana Ross and the Supremes	Someday We'll Be Together	Motown	1
1970					
Jan.	3	B. J. Thomas	Raindrops Keep Falling on My Head	Scepter	4

Jan.	31	Jackson 5	I Want You Back	Motown	1
Feb.	7	Shocking Blue	Venus	Colossus	1
Feb.	14	Sly and the Family Stone	Thank You Falettin Me Be Mice Elf Agin	Epic	2
Feb.	28	Simon and Garfunkel	Bridge over Troubled Water	Columbia	6
Apr.	11	Beatles	Let It Be	Apple	2
Apr.	25	Jackson 5	ABC	Motown	2
May	9	Guess Who	American Woman/ No Sugar Tonight	RCA	3
May	30	Ray Stevens	Everything Is Beautiful	Barnaby	2
June	13	Beatles	Long and Winding Road/For You Blue	Apple	2
June	27	Jackson 5	The Love You Save/I Found That Girl	Motown	2
July	11	Three Dog Night	Mama Told Me Not to Come	Dunhill	2
July	25	Carpenters	Close to You	A & M	4
Aug.	22	Bread	Make It with You	Elektra	1
Aug.	29	Edwin Starr	War	Gordy	3
Sept.	19	Diana Ross	Ain't No Mountain High Enough	Motown	3
Oct.	10	Neil Diamond	Cracklin' Rosie	UNI	1
Oct.	17	Jackson 5	I'll Be There	Motown	5
Nov.	21	Partridge Family	I Think I Love You	Bell	3
Dec.	12	Smokey Robinson and the Miracles	Tears of a Clown	Tamla	2
Dec.	26	George Harrison	My Sweet Lord/ Isn't It a Pity	Apple	4

1971

Jan.	23	Dawn	Knock Three Times	Bell	3
Feb.	13	Osmonds	One Bad Apple	MGM	5

				WEEKS AT NO. 1
Mar.	20	Janis Joplin	Me and Bobby McGee	Columbia	2
Apr.	3	Temptations	Just My Imagination	Gordy	2
Apr.	17	Three Dog Night	Joy to the World	Dunhill	6
May	29	Rolling Stones	Brown Sugar	Rolling Stones	2
June	12	Honey Cone	Want Ads	Hot Wax	1
June	19	Carole King	It's Too Late/I Feel the Earth Move	Ode	5
July	24	Raiders	Indian Reservation	Columbia	1
July	31	James Taylor	You've Got a Friend	Warner Brothers	1
Aug.	7	Bee Gees	How Can You Mend a Broken Heart	Atco	4
Sept.	4	Paul McCartney	Uncle Albert/ Admiral Halsey	Apple	1
Sept.	11	Donny Osmond	Go Away Little Girl	MGM	3
Oct.	2	Rod Stewart	Maggie May/ Reason to Believe	Mercury	5
Nov.	6	Cher	Gypsies, Tramps and Thieves	Kapp	2
Nov.	20	Isaac Hayes	Shaft	Enterprise/ MGM	2
Dec.	4	Sly and the Family Stone	Family Affair	Epic	3
Dec.	25	Melanie	Brand New Key	Neighbor- hood	3

1972

Jan.	15	Don McLean	American Pie	United Artists	4
Feb.	12	Al Green	Let's Stay Together	Hi	1
Feb.	19	Nilsson	Without You	RCA	4
Mar.	18	Neil Young	Heart of Gold	Reprise	1
Mar.	25	America	Horse with No Name	Warner Brothers	3

Apr.	15	Roberta Flack	First Time Ever I Saw Your Face	Atlantic	6
May	27	Chi-Lites	Oh Girl	Brunswick	1
June	3	Staple Singers	I'll Take You There	Stax	1
June	10	Sammy Davis, Jr.	Candy Man	MGM	3
July	1	Neil Diamond	Song Sung Blue	UNI	1
July	8	Bill Withers	Lean on Me	Sussex	3
July	29	Gilbert O'Sullivan	Alone Again (Naturally)	MAM	4
Aug.	26	Looking Glass	Brandy (You're a Fine Girl)	Epic	1
Sept.	2	Gilbert O'Sullivan	Alone Again (Naturally)	MAM	2
Sept.	16	Three Dog Night	Black and White	Dunhill	1
Sept.	23	Mac Davis	Baby Don't Get Hooked on Me	Columbia	3
Oct.	14	Michael Jackson	Ben	Motown	1
Oct.	21	Chuck Berry	My Ding-a-Ling	Chess	2
Nov.	4	Johnny Nash	I Can See Clearly Now	Epic	4
Dec.	2	Temptations	Papa Was a Rolling Stone	Gordy	1
Dec.	9	Helen Reddy	I Am Woman	Capitol	1
Dec.	16	Billy Paul	Me and Mrs. Jones	Philadelphia International	3

1973

Jan.	6	Carly Simon	You're So Vain	Elektra	3
Jan.	27	Stevie Wonder	Superstition	Tamla	1
Feb.	3	Elton John	Crocodile Rock	MCA	3
Feb.	24	Roberta Flack	Killing Me Softly	Atlantic	4
Mar.	24	O'Jays	Love Train	Philadelphia International	1
Mar.	31	Roberta Flack	Killing Me Softly	Atlantic	1
Apr.	7	Vicki Lawrence	The Night the Lights Went Out in Georgia	Bell	2

Apr.	21	Dawn	Tie a Yellow Ribbon Round the Old Oak Tree	Bell	4
May	19	Stevie Wonder	You Are the Sunshine of My Life	Tamla	1
May	26	Edgar Winter Group	Frankenstein	Epic	1
June	2	Paul McCartney and Wings	My Love	Apple	4
June	30	George Harrison	Give Me Love	Apple	1
July	7	Billy Preston	Will It Go Round in Circles	A & M	2
July	21	Jim Croce	Bad, Bad Leroy Brown	ABC	2
Aug.	4	Maureen McGovern	Morning After	20th Century	2
Aug.	18	Diana Ross	Touch Me in the Morning	Motown	1
Aug.	25	Stories	Brother Louie	Kama Sutra	2
Sept.	8	Marvin Gaye	Let's Get It On	Motown	1
Sept.	15	Helen Reddy	Delta Dawn	Capitol	1
Sept.	22	Marvin Gaye	Let's Get It On	Motown	1
Sept.	29	Grand Funk Railroad	We're an American Band	Capitol	1
Oct.	6	Cher	Half-Breed	MCA	2
Oct.	20	Rolling Stones	Angie	Rolling Stones	1
Oct.	27	Gladys Knight and the Pips	Midnight Train to Georgia	Buddah	2
Nov.	10	Eddie Kendricks	Keep On Truckin'	Tamla	2
Nov.	24	Ringo Starr	Photograph	Apple	1
Dec.	1	Carpenters	Top of the World	A & M	2
Dec.	15	Charlie Rich	Most Beautiful Girl in the World	Epic	2
Dec.	29	Jim Croce	Time in a Bottle	ABC	1

CHART TOPPERS, U.K. SINGLES
—1955–73

1955					WEEKS AT NO. 1
Jan.	7	Dickie Valentine	Finger of Suspicion	Decca	1
Jan.	14	Rosemary Clooney	Mambo Italiano	Philips	3
Feb.	4	Eddie Fisher	I Need You Now	HMV	2
Feb.	18	Ruby Murray	Softly Softly	Columbia	3
Mar.	11	Tennessee Ernie Ford	Give Me Your Word	Capitol	7
Apr.	29	Perez Prado	Cherry Pink and Apple Blossom White	HMV	2
May	13	Tony Bennett	Stranger in Paradise	Philips	2
May	27	Eddie Calvert	Cherry Pink and Apple Blossom White	Columbia	4
June	24	Jimmy Young	Unchained Melody	Decca	3
July	15	Alma Cogan	Dreamboat	HMV	2
July	29	Slim Whitman	Rosemarie	London	11
Oct.	14	Jimmy Young	Man from Laramie	Decca	4
Nov.	11	Johnston Brothers	Hernando's Hideaway	Decca	2
Nov.	25	Billy Haley and the Comets	Rock Around the Clock	Brunswick	3
Dec.	16	Dickie Valentine	Christmas Alphabet	Decca	3
1956					
Jan.	6	Billy Haley and the Comets	Rock Around the Clock	Brunswick	2
Jan.	20	Tennessee Ernie Ford	Sixteen Tons	Capitol	4
Feb.	17	Dean Martin	Memories Are Made of This	Capitol	4

Mar.	16	Dream Weavers	It's Almost Tomorrow	Brunswick	2
Mar.	30	Kay Starr	Rock and Roll Waltz	HMV	1
Apr.	6	Dream Weavers	It's Almost Tomorrow	Brunswick	1
Apr.	13	Winifred Attwell	Poor People of Paris	Decca	3
May	4	Ronnie Hilton	No Other Love	HMV	6
June	15	Pat Boone	I'll Be Home	London	5
July	20	Frankie Lymon and the Teenagers	Why Do Fools Fall in Love	Columbia	3
Aug.	10	Doris Day	Whatever Will Be Will Be	Philips	6
Sept.	21	Anne Shelton	Lay Down Your Arms	Philips	4
Oct.	19	Frankie Laine	Woman in Love	Philips	4
Nov.	16	Johnnie Ray	Just Walkin' in the Rain	Philips	7

1957

Jan.	4	Guy Mitchell	Singing the Blues	Philips	1
Jan.	11	Tommy Steele	Singing the Blues	Decca	1
Jan.	18	Guy Mitchell	Singing the Blues	Philips	1
Jan.	25	Frankie Vaughan	Garden of Eden	Philips	4
Feb.	22	Tab Hunter	Young Love	London	7
Apr.	12	Lonnie Donegan	Cumberland Gap	Pye Nixa	5
May	17	Guy Mitchell	Rock-a-Billy	Philips	1
May	24	Andy Williams	Butterfly	London	2
June	7	Johnnie Ray	Yes Tonight Josephine	Philips	3
June	28	Lonnie Donegan	Gamblin' Man/ Putting on the Style	Pye Nixa	2
July	12	Elvis Presley	All Shook Up	HMV	7
Aug.	30	Paul Anka	Diana	Columbia	9
Nov.	1	Crickets	That'll Be the Day	Vogue-Coral	3
Nov.	22	Harry Belafonte	Mary's Boy Child	RCA	7

1958

Jan.	10	Jerry Lee Lewis	Great Balls of Fire	London	2
Jan.	24	Elvis Presley	Jailhouse Rock	RCA	3
Feb.	14	Michael Holliday	The Story of My Life	Columbia	2
Feb.	28	Perry Como	Magic Moments	RCA	8
Apr.	25	Marvin Rainwater	Whole Lotta Woman	MGM	3
May	16	Connie Francis	Who's Sorry Now?	MGM	6
June	27	Vic Damone	On the Street Where You Live	Philips	2
July	4	Everly Brothers	All I Have to Do Is Dream/ Claudette	London	7
Aug.	22	Kalin Twins	When	Brunswick	5
Sept.	26	Connie Francis	Carolina Moon/ Stupid Cupid	MGM	6
Nov.	7	Tommy Edwards	It's All in the Game	MGM	3
Nov.	28	Lord Rockingham's XI	Hoots Mon	Decca	3
Dec.	19	Conway Twitty	It's Only Make Believe	MGM	5

1959

Jan.	24	Elvis Presley	I Got Stung One Night	RCA	5
Feb.	22	Platters	Smoke Gets in Your Eyes	Mercury	5
Apr.	4	Russ Conway	Side Saddle	Columbia	2
Apr.	18	Buddy Holly	It Doesn't Matter Any More	Coral	2
May	2	Elvis Presley	A Fool Such as I	RCA	7
June	20	Russ Conway	Roulette	Columbia	1
June	27	Bobby Darin	Dream Lover	London	5
Aug.	1	Cliff Richard	Livin' Doll	Columbia	4
Aug.	29	Craig Douglas	Only Sixteen	Top Rank	7
Oct.	17	Cliff Richard	Travellin' Light	Columbia	7
Dec.	5	Adam Faith	What Do You Want	Parlophone	5

1960

Jan.	9	Emile Ford	What Do You Want to Make Those Eyes at Me For?	Pye	1
Jan.	16	Anthony Newley	Why	Decca	6
Feb.	27	Adam Faith	Poor Me	Parlophone	1
Mar.	6	Johnny Preston	Running Bear	Mercury	2
Mar.	20	Lonnie Donegan	My Old Man's a Dustman	Pye	5
Apr.	24	Everly Brothers	Cathy's Clown	Warner Brothers	9
June	26	Jimmy Jones	Good Timin'	MGM	4
July	24	Cliff Richard	Please Don't Tease	Columbia	3
Aug.	14	Shadows	Apache	Columbia	6
Sept.	23	Ricky Valance	Tell Laura I Love Her	Columbia	2
Oct.	7	Roy Orbison	Only the Lonely	London	3
Oct.	30	Elvis Presley	It's Now or Never	RCA	8
Dec.	25	Johnny Tillotson	Poetry in Motion	London	3

1961

Jan.	15	Elvis Presley	Are You Lonesome Tonight?	RCA	4
Feb.	12	Everly Brothers	Walk Right Back	Warner Brothers	4
Mar.	12	Elvis Presley	Wooden Heart	RCA	3
Apr.	2	Allisons	Are You Sure?	Fontana	2
Apr.	16	Temperance Seven	You're Driving Me Crazy	Parlophone	2
Apr.	30	Marcels	Blue Moon	Pye Int.	2
May	14	Del Shannon	Runaway	London	1
May	14	Elvis Presley	Surrender	RCA	5
June	18	Del Shannon	Runaway	London	1
June	25	Everly Brothers	Temptation	Warner Brothers	4
July	29	Eden Kane	Well I Ask You	Decca	1
Aug.	5	Helen Shapiro	You Don't Know	Columbia	2
Aug.	19	John Leyton	Johnny Remember Me	Top Rank	5

Sept.	23	Shadows	Kon-Tiki	Columbia	1
Sept.	30	Highwaymen	Michael Row the Boat	HMV	1
Oct.	7	Helen Shapiro	Walkin' Back to Happiness	Columbia	4
Nov.	4	Elvis Presley	His Latest Flame	RCA	3
Nov.	25	Bobby Vee	Take Good Care of My Baby	London	1
Dec.	2	Frankie Vaughan	Tower of Strength	Philips	3
Dec.	23	Acker Bilk	Stranger on the Shore	Columbia	4

1962

Jan.	20	Cliff Richard	The Young Ones	Columbia	5
Feb.	24	Elvis Presley	Rock a Hula Baby/ Can't Help Falling in Love with You	RCA	4
Mar.	24	Shadows	Wonderful Land	Columbia	8
May	19	B. Bumble and the Stingers	Nut Rocker	Top Rank	1
May	26	Elvis Presley	Good Luck Charm	RCA	5
June	30	Mike Sarne	Come Outside	Parlophone	2
July	14	Ray Charles	I Can't Stop Loving You	HMV	2
July	28	Frank Ifield	I Remember You	Columbia	7
Sept.	15	Elvis Presley	She's Not You	RCA	3
Oct.	6	Tornadoes	Telstar	Decca	5
Nov.	10	Frank Ifield	Lovesick Blues	Columbia	5
Dec.	15	Elvis Presley	Return to Sender	RCA	3

1963

Jan.	6	Cliff Richard	The Next Time/ Bachelor Boy	Columbia	3
Jan.	27	Shadows	Dance On	Columbia	1
Feb.	3	Jet Harris/Tony Meehan	Diamonds	Decca	3
Feb.	24	Frank Ifield	Wayward Wind	Columbia	3
Mar.	16	Cliff Richard	Summer Holiday	Columbia	2
Mar.	30	Shadows	Foot Tapper	Columbia	1

Apr.	6	Gerry and the Pacemakers	How Do You Do It?	Columbia	4
May	4	Beatles	From Me to You	Parlophone	7
June	22	Gerry and the Pacemakers	I Like It	Columbia	4
July	20	Frank Ifield	Confessin'	Columbia	2
Aug.	3	Elvis Presley	Devil in Disguise	RCA	1
Aug.	10	Searchers	Sweets for My Sweet	Pye	2
Aug.	24	Billy J. Kramer and the Dakotas	Bad to Me	Parlophone	3
Sept.	14	Beatles	She Loves You	Parlophone	4
Oct.	12	Brian Poole and the Tremeloes	Do You Love Me	Decca	3
Nov.	2	Gerry and the Pacemakers	You'll Never Walk Alone	Columbia	4
Nov.	30	Beatles	She Loves You	Parlophone	2
Dec.	14	Beatles	I Want to Hold Your Hand	Parlophone	5

1964

Jan.	18	Dave Clark Five	Glad All Over	Columbia	2
Feb.	1	Searchers	Needles and Pins	Pye	3
Feb.	22	Bachelors	Diane	Decca	1
Feb.	29	Cilla Black	Anyone Who Had a Heart	Parlophone	3
Mar.	21	Billy J. Kramer and the Dakotas	Little Children	Parlophone	2
Apr.	4	Beatles	Can't Buy Me Love	Parlophone	3
Apr.	25	Peter and Gordon	World Without Love	Columbia	2
May	9	Searchers	Don't Throw Your Love Away	Pye	2
May	23	Four Pennies	Juliet	Philips	1
May	30	Cilla Black	You're My World	Parlophone	4
June	27	Roy Orbison	It's Over	London	2
July	11	Animals	The House of the Rising Sun	Columbia	1
July	18	Rolling Stones	It's All Over Now	Decca	1

July	25	Beatles	Hard Day's Night	Parlophone	3
Aug.	15	Manfred Mann	Doo Wab Diddy Diddy	HMV	2
Aug.	29	Honeycombs	Have I the Right?	Pye	2
Sept.	11	Kinks	You Really Got Me	Pye	2
Sept.	26	Herman's Hermits	I'm into Something Good	Columbia	2
Oct.	10	Roy Orbison	Oh, Pretty Woman	London	2
Oct.	24	Sandie Shaw	(There's) Always Something There to Remind Me	Pye	3
Nov.	14	Roy Orbison	Oh, Pretty Woman	London	1
Nov.	21	Supremes	Baby Love	Stateside	2
Dec.	5	Rolling Stones	Little Red Rooster	Decca	1
Dec.	12	Beatles	I Feel Fine	Parlophone	5

1965

Jan.	16	Georgie Fame	Yeh Yeh	Columbia	2
Jan.	30	Moody Blues	Go Now	Decca	1
Feb.	6	Righteous Brothers	You've Lost That Lovin' Feeling	London	2
Feb.	20	Kinks	Tired of Waiting for You	Pye	1
Feb.	27	Seekers	I'll Never Find Another You	Columbia	2
Mar.	13	Tom Jones	It's Not Unusual	Decca	1
Mar.	30	Rolling Stones	The Last Time	Decca	3
Apr.	10	Unit 4+2	Concrete and Clay	Decca	1
Apr.	17	Cliff Richard	The Minute You're Gone	Columbia	1
Apr.	24	Beatles	Ticket to Ride	Parlophone	3
May	15	Roger Miller	King of the Road	Philips	1
May	22	Jackie Trent	Where Are You Now My Love	Pye	1
May	29	Sandie Shaw	Long Live Love	Pye	3
June	19	Elvis Presley	Crying in the Chapel	RCA	2
June	26	Hollies	I'm Alive	Parlophone	3

July	24	Byrds	Mr. Tambourine Man	CBS	2
Aug.	7	Beatles	Help	Parlophone	3
Aug.	23	Sonny and Cher	I Got You Babe	Atlantic	2
Sept.	11	Rolling Stones	Satisfaction	Decca	2
Sept.	23	Walker Brothers	Make It Easy on Yourself	Philips	1
Sept.	30	Ken Dodd	Tears	Columbia	5
Nov.	6	Rolling Stones	Get off of My Cloud	Decca	3
Nov.	27	Seekers	The Carnival Is Over	Columbia	3
Dec.	18	Beatles	Day Tripper/We Can Work It Out	Parlophone	5

1966

Jan.	22	Spencer Davis Group	Keep On Runnin'	Fontana	1
Jan.	29	Overlanders	Michelle	Pye	3
Feb.	19	Nancy Sinatra	These Boots Are Made for Walking	Reprise	4
Mar.	17	Walker Brothers	Sun Ain't Gonna Shine Any More	Philips	4
Apr.	16	Spencer Davis	Somebody Help Me	Fontana	2
Apr.	30	Dusty Springfield	You Don't Have to Say You Love Me	Philips	1
May	7	Manfred Mann	Pretty Flamingo	HMV	3
May	28	Rolling Stones	Paint It Black	Decca	1
June	4	Frank Sinatra	Strangers in the Night	Reprise	3
June	25	Beatles	Paperback Writer	Parlophone	2
July	9	Kinks	Sunday Afternoon	Pye	2
July	23	Georgie Fame	Get Away	Columbia	1
July	30	Chris Farlowe	Out of Time	Immediate	1
Aug.	6	Troggs	With a Girl Like You	Fontana	2
Aug.	20	Beatles	Eleanor Rigby/ Yellow Submarine	Parlophone	4

Sept.	17	Small Faces	All or Nothing	Decca	1
Sept.	24	Jim Reeves	Distant Drums	RCA	5
Oct.	29	Four Tops	Reach Out I'll Be There	Tamla Motown	3
Nov.	19	Beach Boys	Good Vibrations	Capitol	2
Dec.	3	Tom Jones	Green Green Grass of Home	Decca	6

1967

Jan.	14	Monkees	I'm a Believer	RCA	4
Feb.	18	Pet Clark	This Is My Song	Pye	2
Mar.	4	Engelbert Humperdinck	Release Me	Decca	6
Apr.	15	Frank and Nancy Sinatra	Somethin' Stupid	Reprise	2
Apr.	29	Sandie Shaw	Puppet on a String	Pye	3
May	20	Tremeloes	Silence Is Golden	CBS	3
June	10	Procol Harum	A Whiter Shade of Pale	Deram	6
July	22	Beatles	All You Need Is Love	Parlophone	3
Aug.	12	Scott MacKenzie	San Francisco	CBS	4
Sept.	9	Engelbert Humperdinck	The Last Waltz	Decca	5
Oct.	14	Bee Gees	Massachusetts	Polydor	4
Nov.	11	Foundations	Baby Now That I've Found You	Pye	2
Nov.	25	Long John Baldry	Let the Heartaches Begin	Pye	2
Dec.	9	Beatles	Hello Goodbye	Parlophone	7

1968

Jan.	27	Georgie Fame	The Ballad of Bonnie and Clyde	CBS	1
Feb.	3	Love Affair	Everlasting Love	CBS	2
Feb.	17	Manfred Mann	The Mighty Quinn	Fontana	2
Mar.	2	Esther and Abi Ofarim	Cinderella Rockafella	Fontana	3
Mar.	23	Dave Dee & Co.	Legend of Xanadu	Fontana	1
Mar.	30	Beatles	Lady Madonna	Parlophone	2

Apr.	13	Cliff Richard	Congratulations	Columbia	2
Apr.	27	Louis Armstrong	Wonderful World	Stateside	4
May	25	Union Gap	Young Girl	CBS	4
June	22	Rolling Stones	Jumping Jack Flash	Decca	2
July	6	Equals	Baby Come Back	President	3
July	27	Des O'Connor	I Pretend	Columbia	1
Aug.	3	Tommy James and the Shondells	Mony Mony	Roulette	2
Aug.	17	The Crazy World of Arthur Brown	Fire	Track	1
Aug.	24	Tommy James and the Shondells	Mony Mony	Roulette	1
Aug.	31	Beach Boys	Do It Again	Capitol	1
Sept.	7	Bee Gees	I Gotta Get a Message to You	Polydor	1
Sept.	14	Beatles	Hey Jude	Apple	2
Sept.	28	Mary Hopkin	Those Were the Days	Apple	6
Nov.	9	Joe Cocker	With a Little Help from My Friends	Regal Zonophone	1
Nov.	16	Hugh Montenegro	The Good, the Bad and the Ugly	RCA	4
Dec.	14	Scaffold	Lily the Pink	Columbia	3

1969

Jan.	4	Marmalade	Ob-la-di Ob-la-da	CBS	3
Jan.	11	Scaffold	Lily the Pink	Columbia	1
Jan.	18	Marmalade	Ob-la-di Ob-la-da	CBS	2
Feb.	1	Fleetwood Mac	Albatross	Blue Horizon	1
Feb.	8	Move	Blackberry Way	Regal Zonophone	1
Feb.	15	Amen Corner	Half as Nice	Immediate	2
Mar.	1	Peter Sarstedt	Where Do You Go to My Lovely	United Artists	4
Mar.	29	Marvin Gaye	I Heard It thru the Grapevine	Tamla Motown	3
Apr.	19	Desmond Dekker & the Aces	The Israelites	Pyramid	1

Apr.	26	Beatles	Get Back	Apple	6
June	7	Tommy Roe	Dizzy	Stateside	1
June	24	Beatles	Ballad of John and Yoko	Apple	3
July	5	Thunderclap Newman	Something in the Air	Track	3
July	26	Rolling Stones	Honky Tonk Woman	Decca	5
Aug.	30	Zager and Evans	In the Year 2525	RCA	3
Sept.	20	Creedence Clearwater Revival	Bad Moon Rising	Liberty	3
Oct.	11	Jane Birkin and Serge Gainsbourg	Je T'aime Moi Non Plus	Major Minor	1
Oct.	18	Bobbie Gentry	I'll Never Fall in Love Again	Capitol	1
Oct.	25	Archies	Sugar Sugar	RCA	8
Dec.	20	Rolf Harris	Two Little Boys	Columbia	6

1970

Jan.	31	Edison Lighthouse	Love Grows	Bell	5
Mar.	7	Lee Marvin	Wanderin' Star	Paramount	3
Apr.	4	Simon and Garfunkel	Bridge over Troubled Water	CBS	3
Apr.	18	Dana	All Kinds of Everything	Rex	2
May	2	Norman Greenbaum	Spirit in the Sky	Reprise	2
May	16	England World Cup Squad	Back Home	Pye	3
June	6	Christie	Yellow River	CBS	1
June	13	Mungo Jerry	In the Summertime	Dawn	7
Aug.	1	Elvis Presley	The Wonder of You	RCA	6
Sept.	12	Smokey Robinson and the Miracles	The Tears of a Clown	Tamla Motown	1
Sept.	19	Freda Payne	Band of Gold	Invictus	6
Oct.	31	Matthews Southern Comfort	Woodstock	UNI	3
Nov.	21	Jimi Hendrix	Voodoo Chile	Track	1
Nov.	28	Dave Edmunds	I Hear You Knocking	MAM	6

1971

Jan.	9	Clive Dunn	Grandad	Columbia	3
Jan.	31	George Harrison	My Sweet Lord	Apple	5
Mar.	6	Mungo Jerry	Baby Jump	Dawn	2
Mar.	20	T Rex	Hot Love	Fly	6
May	1	Dave and Ansell Collins	Double Barrel	Technique	2
May	15	Dawn	Knock Three Times	Bell	5
June	19	Middle of the Road	Chirpy Chirpy Cheep Cheep	RCA	5
July	24	T Rex	Get It On	Fly	4
Aug.	21	Diana Ross	I'm Still Waiting	Tamla Motown	4
Sept.	18	Tams	Hey Girl Don't Bother Me	Probe	3
Oct.	9	Rod Stewart	Maggie May	Mercury	5
Nov.	13	Slade	Cos I Luv You	Polydor	4
Dec.	11	Benny Hill	Ernie	Columbia	4

1972

Jan.	8	New Seekers	I'd Like to Teach the World to Sing	Polydor	4
Feb.	5	T Rex	Telegram Sam	T Rex	2
Feb.	19	Chicory Tip	Son of My Father	CBS	3
Mar.	11	Nilsson	Without You	RCA	5
Apr.	15	Royal Scots Dragoon Guards Band	Amazing Grace	RCA	5
May	20	T Rex	Metal Guru	T Rex	4
June	17	Don McLean	Vincent	UA	2
July	1	Slade	Take Me Back 'Ome	Polydor	1
July	8	Donny Osmond	Puppy Love	MGM	5
Aug.	12	Alice Cooper	School's Out	Warner Brothers	3
Sept.	2	Rod Stewart	You Wear It Well	Mercury	1
Sept.	9	Slade	Mama Weer All Crazee Now	Polydor	3
Sept.	30	David Cassidy	How Can I Be Sure	Bell	2
Oct.	14	Lieutenant Pigeon	Mouldy Old Dough	Decca	4

Nov.	11	Gilbert O'Sullivan	Clair	MAM	2
Nov.	25	Chuck Berry	My Ding-a-Ling	Chess	4
Dec.	23	Little Jimmy Osmond	Long Haired Lover from Liverpool	MGM	5

1973

Jan.	27	Sweet	Blockbuster	RCA	5
Mar.	3	Slade	Cum On Feel the Noize	Polydor	4
Mar.	31	Donny Osmond	12th of Never	MGM	1
Apr.	7	Gilbert O'Sullivan	Get Down	MAM	2
Apr.	21	Dawn	Tie a Yellow Ribbon Round the Old Oak Tree	Bell	4
May	19	Wizzard	See My Baby Jive	Harvest	4
June	16	Suzie Quatro	Can the Can	RAK	1
June	23	10 cc	Rubber Bullets	UK	1
June	30	Slade	Skweeze Me, Pleeze Me	Polydor	3
July	21	Peters and Lee	Welcome Home	Philips	1
July	28	Gary Glitter	I'm the Leader of the Gang	Bell	4
Aug.	25	Donny Osmond	Young Love	MGM	4
Sept.	22	Wizzard	Angel Fingers	Harvest	1
Sept.	29	Simon Park Orchestra	Eye Level	Columbia	4
Oct.	27	David Cassidy	Daydreamer	Bell	3
Nov.	17	Gary Glitter	I Love You Love Me Love	Bell	4
Dec.	15	Slade	Merry Christmas Everybody	Polydor	5

ROLL CALL
OF HIT MAKERS
SINGLES

I. SINGLES, 1955–73

TOTAL NUMBER OF HITS	ARTIST	NUMBER OF HITS	
		IN USA	IN UK
85	Elvis Prelsey	56	69
48	Cliff Richard	–	48
39	Beatles	37	23
28	Pat Boone	23	22
	Connie Francis	22	19
	Ricky Nelson	27	9
	Diana Ross & the Supremes	24	28
27	Temptations	24	9
26	Lonnie Donegan	2	26
25	Beach Boys	20	12
	Perry Como	14	17
	Marvin Gaye	23	6
	Herman's Hermits/Peter Noone	14	18
24	Everly Brothers	17	19
	Brenda Lee	19	13
23	Aretha Franklin	23	4
22	Four Seasons/Frankie Valli	21	8
	Four Tops	17	15
	Hollies	6	21
	Frank Sinatra	9	19
21	Rolling Stones	17	17
	Stevie Wonder	19	12
19	Nat "King" Cole	11	10
	Billy Fury	–	19
	Tom Jones	10	19
	Gene Pitney	10	11
	Supremes	18	13

TOTAL NUMBER OF HITS		NUMBER OF HITS	
		IN USA	IN UK
18	Fats Domino	15	8
	Roy Orbison	10	16
	Frankie Vaughan	–	18
	Andy Williams	12	10
17	Paul Anka	16	7
	Ray Charles	16	5
	Dave Clark Five	14	9
	Duane Eddy	6	17
	Kinks	6	16
16	Eric Burdon & the Animals & War	11	11
	Brook Benton	16	–
	Sam Cooke	15	4
	Bobby Darin	14	10
	Adam Faith	–	16
	Manfred Mann	3	16
	Move/Wizzard/Roy Wood	–	16
	Three Dog Night	16	1
15	James Brown	15	1
	Buddy Holly/Crickets	5	15
	Dusty Springfield	5	14
	Who	5	14
	Jackie Wilson	13	3
14	Bee Gees	11	9
	Cilla Black	–	14
	David Cassidy/Partridge Family	6	10
	Chubby Checker	14	4
	Neil Diamond	14	4
	Gladys Knight & Pips	12	2
	Jim Reeves	2	13
	Smokey Robinson & Miracles	14	4
	Bobby Rydell	14	2
	Tommy Steele	–	14
	Bobby Vinton	14	1
13	Drifters	11	5
	Bill Haley & His Comets	7	11
	Impressions/Curtis Mayfield	12	1
	Jackson Five	11	7
	Bobby Vee	10	8
	Dionne Warwick	12	3

TOTAL NUMBER OF HITS		NUMBER OF HITS IN USA	IN UK
12	Russ Conway	–	12
	Dion & Belmonts/Di Mucci	12	2
	Fifth Dimension	12	2
	Dean Martin	6	10
	Johnny Mathis	8	6
	Johnnie Ray	3	12
	Johnny Rivers	12	–
	Neil Sedaka	10	9
	Simon & Garfunkel	11	6
	T. Rex	1	12
11	Chuck Berry	9	5
	Engelbert Humperdinck	5	11
	Frankie Laine	1	11
	Platters	11	6
	Paul Revere & Raiders	11	–
	Searchers	3	10
10	Bachelors	2	10
	Max Bygraves	–	10
	Alma Cogan	–	10
	Creedence Clearwater Revival	10	6
	Dave Dee, Dozy, Beaky, Mick & Titch	–	10
	Ronnie Hilton	–	10
	Tommy James & Shondells	10	1
	Gary Lewis & the Playboys	10	–
	Little Richard	4	9
	Monkees	9	7
	Ruby Murray	–	10
	Gilbert O'Sullivan	4	9
	Peter & Gordon	8	6
	Slade	–	10
	Small Faces	1	10
9	18 artists		
8	26 artists		
7	27 artists		
6	42 artists		
5	51 artists		
4	62 artists		

3	131 artists
2	210 artists
1	894 artists

CUMULATIVE STATISTICS

NUMBER OF HITS	NUMBER OF ARTISTS		
	ALL TOGETHER	IN USA	IN UK
one or more	1558	1138	902
only one	894	726	490
more than one	664	412	412
only two	210	158	160
from three to nine	357	197	192
from ten to nineteen	75	46	54
twenty or more	22	11	6

PREFACE TO THE LOG
OF AMERICAN AND BRITISH
TOP TWENTY ALBUMS

The following compilation is based on the weekly listings of
Billboard for the USA and *Music Week* (formerly *Record
Retailer*) for Britain, from January 1964 through December
1973.

Although the album was introduced as a commercial form
of reproducing music during the nineteen fifties, for more
than ten years the album charts were dominated by easy-listening music and movie sound tracks. This listing starts
when the Beatles established the album as a medium of teen
music in America.

For most of the period covered by these logs, the album
market in Britain was not as extensive as the American market, and the reliability of the list drops off outside the top
ten. For a period in 1969, *Record Retailer* acknowledged
this by reducing their list to fifteen albums a week, and in
March integrated budget and mid-price albums into the regular album list. So although we have listed every British top
twenty entry where possible, we have restricted the weeks-

in-chart figures to the top ten. To keep the over-all compilation consistent, we have had to adopt the same system for the American entries.

The *Billboard* lists never include budget-price albums, or TV-merchandised various-artists albums, which *Music Week* listed when they were first introduced to Britain, in 1972. We have indicated budget-price and TV albums with a dagger (†) after the label, and with a double dagger (‡) where their weeks-in-top-ten runs were prematurely ended by their being consigned to their own lists in *Music Week*.

Because of a print strike from February 6 to March 27, 1971, there were no British charts printed during this period. Records whose top ten careers were ended during this period are designated by a single asterisk beside their weeks-in-chart figure; albums that appeared in the top ten in the week after the strike have two asterisks. Records that appeared in the top ten both before and after the strike, and would presumably have been present throughout the eight-week period, have three asterisks.

Double and triple albums are noted accordingly: (DLP), (TLP).

THE LOG
OF AMERICAN AND BRITISH
TOP TWENTY ALBUMS, 1964–73

LABEL	DATE OF ENTRY TO TOP 20	HIGHEST POSITION REACHED	NUMBER OF WEEKS IN TOP 10
ADDERLY, JULIAN "CANNONBALL"			
Mercy Mercy Mercy			
(US) Capitol	3 25 67	13	–
ALICE COOPER			
School's Out			
(US) Warner Brothers	7 15 72	2	6
(UK) Warner Brothers	*7 22 72*	*4*	*10*
Billion Dollar Babies			
(US) Warner Brothers	3 24 73	1	10
(UK) Warner Brothers	*3 24 73*	*1*	*9*
Muscle of Love			
(US) Warner Brothers	12 22 73	15	–
ALLMAN, GREG			
Laid Back			
(US) Capricorn	12 29 73	19	–
ALLMAN BROTHERS BAND			
At the Fillmore East			
(US) Capricorn	8 7 71	13	–
Eat a Peach			
(US) Capricorn	3 25 72	4	10
Brothers and Sisters			
(US) Capricorn	8 25 73	1	15
ALPERT, HERB, AND THE TIJUANA BRASS			
Whipped Cream and Other Delights			
(US) A&M	6 26 65	1	61
Going Places			
(US) A&M	11 13 65	1	48
(UK) Pye	*1 27 66*	*5*	*41*
South of the Border			
(US) A&M	1 22 66	6	3
Lonely Bull			
(US) A&M	2 12 66	10	2
Tijuana Brass			
(US) A&M	4 2 66	17	–
What Now My Love			
(US) A&M	5 21 66	1	32
(UK) Pye	*6 2 66*	*18*	*–*
S.R.O.			
(US) A&M	12 17 66	2	19
(UK) Pye	*2 16 67*	*5*	*6*
Sounds Like			
(US) A&M	6 10 67	1	12
Ninth			
(US) A&M	12 30 67	4	10
Beat of the Brass			
(US) A&M	5 18 68	1	16
(UK) A&M	*8 14 68*	*4*	*2*
Early Alpert			
(UK) Marble Arch†	*3 5 69*	*4*	*1*

LABEL	CHART DATE OF TO TOP 20	POSITION HIGHEST REACHED	OF WEEKS NUMBER IN TOP 10
American			
(*UK*) *A&M*	*1 3 70*	*4*	*3*
Herb Alpert's Greatest Hits			
(*UK*) *A&M*	*6 6 70*	*8*	*1*
AMEN CORNER			
Explosion Company			
(*UK*) *Immediate*	*11 1 69*	*19*	–
AMERICA			
America			
(*UK*) *Warner Brothers*	*1 29 72*	*13*	–
(US) Warner Brothers	3 11 72	1	13
Homecoming			
(US) Warner Brothers	12 23 72	9	4
AMES, ED			
My Cup Runneth Over			
(US) RCA	3 18 67	4	10
Who Will Answer and Other Songs of Our Times			
(US) RCA	4 13 68	13	–
ANDERSON, LYNN			
Rose Garden			
(US) Columbia	2 27 71	19	–
ANIMALS			
Animals			
(US) MGM	10 3 64	7	4
(*UK*) *Columbia*	*11 12 64*	*6*	*13*
Animal Tracks			
(*UK*) *Columbia*	*5 20 65*	*6*	*14*
Best of the Animals			
(US) MGM	3 19 66	6	7
Most of the Animals			
(*UK*) *Columbia*	*4 21 66*	*4*	*10*
Animalisms			
(*UK*) *Decca*	*5 26 66*	*4*	*8*
Animalization			
(US) MGM	10 8 66	20	–
ARGENT			
All Together Now			
(*UK*) *Epic*	*5 6 72*	*13*	–
ARMSTRONG, LOUIS			
Hello Dolly			
(US) Kapp	5 23 64	1	19
(*UK*) *London*	*6 25 64*	*11*	–
ARNOLD, EDDY			
My World			
(US) RCA	12 11 65	7	6
ASSOCIATION			
And Then . . . Along Comes Mary			
(US) Valiant	10 8 66	4	7

LABEL	DATE OF ENTRY TO TOP 20	HIGHEST POSITION REACHED	NUMBER OF WEEKS IN TOP 10
Insight Out			
(US) Warner Brothers	8 12 67	8	4
Greatest Hits, Vol. 1			
(US) Warner Brothers	2 1 69	4	9
ATOMIC ROOSTER			
Death Walks Behind You			
(UK) Charisma	4 3 71	12	–
In Hearing of Atomic Rooster			
(UK) Pegasus	8 28 71	11	–
AUGER, BRIAN (See **JULIE DRISCOLL**)			
BACHARACH, BURT			
Burt Bacharach, Hitmaker			
(UK) London	5 20 65	3	9
Portrait in Music			
(UK) A&M	4 3 71	5	3**
Close to You/One Less Bell to Answer			
(US) A&M	7 3 71	18	–
BACHELORS			
The Bachelors and Sixteen Great Songs			
(UK) Decca	6 25 64	2	40
More Great Song Hits			
(UK) Decca	10 7 65	15	–
Hits of the Sixties			
(UK) Decca	7 21 66	12	–
Golden All Time Hits			
(UK) Decca	8 9 67	19	–
World of the Bachelors			
(UK) Decca†	3 5 69	8	5
World of the Bachelors, Vol. 2			
(UK) Decca†	8 30 69	11	–
BAEZ, JOAN			
Joan Baez in Concert			
(US) Vanguard	1 4 64	12	–
(UK) Fontana	4 15 65	8	4
Joan Baez in Concert, Part 2			
(US) Vanguard	1 4 64	7	8
(UK) Fontana	5 13 65	17	–
Joan Baez			
(UK) Fontana	7 16 64	9	1
Joan Baez No. 5			
(US) Vanguard	12 12 64	12	–
(UK) Fontana	5 13 65	20	–
Joan Baez in Concert, Vol. 5			
(UK) Fontana	7 8 65	3	15
Farewell Angelina			
(UK) Fontana	11 25 65	5	7
(US) Vanguard	11 27 65	10	1
Joan Baez			
(UK) Vanguard	7 30 69	15	–

LABEL	DATE OF ENTRY TO TOP 20	HIGHEST POSITION REACHED	NUMBER OF WEEKS IN TOP 10
Blessed Are			
(US) Vanguard	10 2 71	11	–
BALL, KENNY			
Golden Hits			
(*UK*) *Pye*	*1 2 64*	*8*	*2*
THE BAND			
The Band			
(US) Capitol	11 8 69	9	1
Stage Fright			
(US) Capitol	9 12 70	5	4
(*UK*) *Capitol*	*10 10 70*	*15*	*–*
Rock of Ages (DLP)			
(US) Capitol	10 7 72	6	7
BARRY, JOHN			
The Persuaders			
(*UK*) *CBS*	*2 19 72*	*18*	*–*
[see also: **ADAM FAITH**]			
BASSEY, SHIRLEY			
At the Pigalle			
(*UK*) *Columbia*	*12 2 65*	*15*	*–*
Something			
(*UK*) *United Artists*	*9 5 70*	*5*	*4*
Something Else			
(*UK*) *United Artists*	*5 15 71*	*7*	*2*
I, Capricorn			
(*UK*) *United Artists*	*2 26 72*	*13*	*–*
Never, Never, Never			
(*UK*) *United Artists*	*6 2 73*	*10*	*1*
BEACH BOYS			
Little Deuce Coupe			
(US) Capitol	1 4 64	4	8
Surfer Girl			
(US) Capitol	1 11 64	11	–
(*UK*) *Capitol*	*3 23 67*	*13*	*–*
Shut Down, Vol. 2			
(US) Capitol	5 9 64	13	–
All Summer Long			
(US) Capitol	8 8 64	4	16
Beach Boys' Concert			
(US) Capitol	11 21 64	1	21
Beach Boys Today			
(US) Capitol	4 24 64	4	14
(*UK*) *Capitol*	*4 21 66*	*6*	*5*
Summer Days (and Summer Nights)			
(US) Capitol	8 7 65	2	10
(*UK*) *Capitol*	*14 7 66*	*4*	*10*
Surfin' USA			
(*UK*) *Capitol*	*9 23 65*	*17*	*–*

LABEL	DATE OF ENTRY TO TOP 20	HIGHEST POSITION REACHED	NUMBER OF WEEKS IN TOP 10
Beach Boys' Party			
(US) Capitol	12 4 65	6	4
(UK) Capitol	*2 17 66*	*3*	*9*
Pet Sounds			
(US) Capitol	6 18 66	10	1
(UK) Capitol	*7 7 66*	*2*	*26*
Best of the Beach Boys			
(US) Capitol	8 13 66	8	6
(UK) Capitol	*11 10 66*	*2*	*56*
Best of the Beach Boys, Vol. 2			
(UK) Capitol	*10 25 67*	*3*	*10*
Smiley Smile			
(UK) Capitol	*11 15 67*	*9*	*4*
Wild Honey			
(UK) Capitol	*3 20 68*	*7*	*5*
Friends			
(UK) Capitol	*9 25 68*	*13*	–
Best of the Beach Boys, Vol. 3			
(UK) Capitol	*11 27 68*	*8*	*2*
20/20			
(UK) Capitol	*3 20 69*	*3*	*5*
Beach Boys' Greatest Hits			
(UK) Capitol	*9 19 70*	*5*	*5*
Surf's Up			
(UK) Stateside	*11 27 71*	*12*	–
Holland			
(UK) Reprise	*2 24 73*	*20*	–
BEATLES			
Please Please Me			
(UK) Parlophone	*1 2 64*	*2*	*23*
With the Beatles			
(UK) Parlophone	*1 2 64*	*1*	*39*
Meet the Beatles			
(US) Capitol	2 8 64	1	23
Introducing the Beatles			
(US) Vee Jay	2 22 64	2	15
Beatles' Second Album			
(US) Capitol	4 25 64	1	15
A Hard Day's Night			
(UK) Parlophone	*7 16 64*	*1*	*31*
(US) United Artists	7 18 64	1	28
Something New			
(US) Capitol	8 15 64	2	18
Beatles for Sale			
(UK) Parlophone	*12 10 64*	*1*	*37*
Beatle Story			
(US) Capitol	12 19 64	7	5
Beatles '65			
(US) Capitol	1 9 65	1	16

LABEL	DATE OF ENTRY TO TOP 20	HIGHEST POSITION REACHED	NUMBER OF WEEKS IN TOP 10
Beatles VI			
(US) Capitol	7 10 65	1	13
Help			
(UK) Parlophone	*8 12 65*	*1*	*30*
(US) Capitol	9 11 65	1	15
Rubber Soul			
(UK) Parlophone	*12 9 65*	*1*	*30*
(US) Capitol	1 8 66	1	14
Yesterday and Today			
(US) Capitol	7 16 66	1	9
Revolver			
(UK) Parlophone	*8 11 66*	*1*	*21*
(US) Capitol	9 10 66	1	14
Collection of Beatles Oldies			
(UK) Parlophone	*12 15 66*	*7*	*2*
Sgt. Pepper's Lonely Hearts Club Band			
(UK) Parlophone	*6 1 67*	*1*	*43*
(US) Capitol	6 24 67	1	33
Magical Mystery Tour			
(US) Capitol	12 30 67	1	14
Beatles (DLP)			
(UK) Apple	*12 4 68*	*1*	*18*
(US) Apple	12 14 68	1	15
Yellow Submarine (with **GEORGE MARTIN**)			
(UK) Apple	*2 5 69*	*3*	*6*
(US) Apple	2 15 69	2	6
Abbey Road			
(UK) Apple	*10 4 69*	*1*	*31*
(US) Apple	10 25 69	1	27
Hey Jude			
(US) Apple	3 21 70	2	11
Let It Be			
(UK) Apple	*5 23 70*	*1*	*18**
(US) Apple	6 6 70	1	10
Beatles 62/66 (DLP)			
(US) Apple	4 28 73	3	8
(UK) Apple	*5 5 73*	*3*	*14*
Beatles 67/70 (DLP)			
(US) Apple	4 28 73	1	11
(UK) Apple	*5 5 73*	*3*	*14*
[see also: **ART RUDY**]			
BECK, JEFF			
Truth			
(US) Epic	10 26 68	15	–
Beck-Ola			
(US) Epic	8 2 69	15	–
Jeff Beck Group			
(US) Epic	7 1 72	14	–

LABEL	DATE OF ENTRY TO TOP 20	HIGHEST POSITION REACHED	NUMBER OF WEEKS IN TOP 10
Beck, Bogart and Appice			
(US) Epic	5 19 73	12	–
BEE GEES			
. . . First			
(*UK*) *Polydor*	9 27 67	*11*	–
(US) Atco	8 30 67	7	5
Horizontal			
(US) Atco	3 2 68	12	–
(*UK*) *Polydor*	3 6 68	16	–
Idea			
(*UK*) *Polydor*	10 2 68	4	6
(US) Atco	10 12 68	17	–
Odessa			
(US) Atco	3 29 69	20	–
(*UK*) *Polydor*	4 2 69	10	1
Best of the Bee Gees			
(US) Atco	8 2 69	9	3
(*UK*) *Polydor*	11 8 69	7	5
BELAFONTE, HARRY			
Harry Belafonte at the Greek Theatre			
(US) RCA	5 23 64	17	–
BENNETT, TONY			
I Left My Heart in San Francisco			
(US) Columbia	1 11 64	17	–
(*UK*) *CBS*	5 27 65	*13*	–
Many Moods of Tony			
(US) Columbia	3 28 64	20	–
Tony Bennett's Greatest Hits, Vol. 3			
(US) Columbia	10 30 65	20	–
A String of Tony's Hits			
(*UK*) *CBS*	7 5 67	*9*	*1*
Movie Song Album			
(US) Columbia	6 11 66	18	–
Tony's Greatest Hits			
(*UK*) *CBS*	7 5 67	*19*	–
BERRY, CHUCK			
More			
(*UK*) *Pye*	1 2 64	*9*	*1*
The Latest and Greatest			
(*UK*) *Pye*	5 28 64	*8*	*5*
You Never Can Tell			
(*UK*) *Pye*	10 1 64	*18*	–
London Sessions			
(US) Chess	9 9 72	8	7
BIG BROTHER AND THE HOLDING COMPANY			
Cheap Thrills			
(US) Columbia	9 21 68	1	23

LABEL	DATE OF ENTRY TO TOP 20	HIGHEST POSITION REACHED	NUMBER OF WEEKS IN TOP 10
BLACK, CILLA			
Cilla			
(UK) *Parlophone*	2 11 65	5	6
Cilla Sings a Rainbow			
(UK) *Parlophone*	5 12 66	4	11
Sher-Oo			
(UK) *Parlophone*	4 24 68	7	1
BLACK AND WHITE MINSTRELS			
Spotlight on the Black and White Minstrels			
(UK) *HMV*	12 10 64	6	3
Magic of the Minstrels			
(UK) *HMV*	12 2 65	9	2
[see also: **GEORGE MITCHELL**]			
BLACK SABBATH			
Black Sabbath			
(UK) *Vertigo*	4 4 70	8	7
Paranoid			
(UK) *Vertigo*	10 3 70	1	9
(US) Warner Brothers	2 27 71	12	–
Master of Reality			
(UK) *Vertigo*	8 21 71	3	4
(US) Warner Brothers	9 11 71	8	5
Black Sabbath, Vol. 4			
(UK) *Vertigo*	8 30 72	8	5
(US) Warner Brothers	11 25 72	14	–
Sabbath Bloody Sabbath			
(UK) *WWA*	12 8 73	4	2
BLIND FAITH			
Blind Faith			
(US) Atlantic	8 23 69	1	4
(UK) *Polydor*	9 20 69	1	5
BLODWYN PIG			
Ahead Rings Out			
(UK) *Island*	8 16 69	9	1
Getting to This			
(UK) *Island*	5 2 70	8	1
BLOOD, SWEAT AND TEARS			
Blood, Sweat and Tears			
(US) Columbia	2 8 69	1	50
(UK) *CBS*	4 9 69	15	–
Blood, Sweat and Tears III			
(US) Columbia	7 18 70	1	11
(UK) *CBS*	8 15 70	14	–
Blood, Sweat and Tears IV			
(US) Columbia	7 17 71	10	2
Blood, Sweat and Tears Greatest Hits			
(US) Columbia	4 8 72	19	–
BLOOMFIELD, MIKE (see **AL KOOPER**)			

LABEL	DATE OF ENTRY TO TOP 20	HIGHEST POSITION REACHED	NUMBER OF WEEKS IN TOP 10
BLUE CHEER			
Vincebus Eruptum			
(US) *Philips*	4 6 68	11	–
BOOKER T AND THE MG'S			
Green Onions			
(UK) London	*7 23 64*	*11*	–
BOSKOVSKY (Vienna Philharmonic Orchestra)			
World of Johann Strauss			
(UK) Decca†	*3 5 69*	*7*	*1*
BOSTON POPS (see **AL HIRT**)			
BOWIE, DAVID			
The Rise and Fall of Ziggy Stardust			
(UK) RCA	*7 1 72*	*5*	*20*
Space Oddity			
(UK) RCA (reissue)	*2 10 73*	*17*	–
(US) RCA (reissue)	3 31 73	16	–
Aladdin Sane			
(UK) RCA	*5 5 73*	*1*	*27*
(US) RCA	6 9 73	17	–
Hunky Dory			
(UK) RCA	*7 7 73*	*3*	*12*
Pin Ups			
(UK) RCA	*11 3 73*	*1*	*12*
BREAD			
On the Water			
(US) Elektra	8 22 70	12	–
Baby I'm-a Want You			
(US) Elektra	2 19 72	3	10
(UK) Elektra	*3 25 72*	*9*	*1*
Guitar Man			
(US) Elektra	12 16 72	19	–
Best of Bread			
(UK) Elektra	*10 28 72*	*7*	*3*
(US) Elektra	4 14 73	2	8
BROUGHTON, EDGAR			
Sing Brothers Sing			
(UK) Harvest	*6 27 70*	*18*	–
BROWN, ARTHUR			
Crazy World of Arthur Brown			
(UK) Track	*7 17 68*	*2*	*8*
(US) Track-Atlantic	10 12 68	7	7
BROWN, JAMES			
Pure Dynamite			
(US) King	4 4 64	10	1
I Can't Stand Myself When You Touch Me			
(US) King	4 27 68	17	–

| :--- | :---: | :---: | :---: |

BRUCE, JACK
Songs for a Tailor
  (UK) Polydor   *10 4 69*   *6*   *2*
[see also: **CREAM**]

BURDON, ERIC, AND WAR
Eric Burdon Declares War
  (US) MGM   8 22 70   18   –
[see also: **WAR; ANIMALS**]

BYGRAVES, MAX
World of Max Bygraves
  (UK) Decca†   *3 5 69*   *6*   *1*
Sing Along with Max Bygraves
  (UK) Pye   *9 30 72*   *4*   *6*
Sing Along with Max Bygraves, Vol. 2
  (UK) Pye   *12 9 72*   *12*   –
Singalongamax
  (UK) Pye   *5 5 73*   *5*   *1*
Singalongamax, Vol. 4
  (UK) Pye   *9 29 73*   *7*   *3*
Singalongapartysong
  (UK) Pye   *12 15 73*   *15*   –

BYRDS
Mr. Tambourine Man
  (US) Columbia   7 31 65   6   3
  (UK) CBS   8 26 65   7   5
Turn Turn Turn
  (US) Columbia   2 26 66   17   –
  (UK) CBS   *4 7 66*   *11*   –
Byrds' Greatest Hits
  (US) Columbia   9 23 67   6   5
Notorious Byrd Brothers
  (UK) CBS   *5 8 68*   *12*   –
Dr. Byrds and Mr. Hyde
  (UK) CBS   *5 21 69*   *15*   –
Untitled (DLP)
  (UK) CBS   *11 28 70*   *11*   –
Byrds
  (US) Asylum   5 12 73   20   –

CAMPBELL, GLEN
By the Time I Get to Phoenix
  (US) Capitol   7 13 68   15   –
Gentle on My Mind
  (US) Capitol   9 14 68   5   14
Wichita Lineman
  (US) Capitol   12 7 68   1   22
Galveston
  (US) Capitol   4 19 69   2   10
Glen Campbell Live

LABEL	DATE OF ENTRY TO TOP 20	HIGHEST POSITION REACHED	NUMBER OF WEEKS IN TOP 10
(US) Capitol	10 11 69	13	–
(UK) Capitol	2 7 70	16	–
Try a Little Kindness			
(US) Capitol	2 28 70	12	–
Glen Campbell Album			
(UK) Capitol	1 2 71	16	–
Glen Campbell's Greatest Hits			
(UK) Capitol	12 4 71	8	2
[see also: **BOBBIE GENTRY**]			
CANNED HEAT			
Boogie with Canned Heat			
(UK) Liberty	7 24 68	5	6
(US) Liberty	10 19 68	16	–
Livin' the Blues			
(US) Liberty	1 25 69	18	–
Cookbook			
(UK) Liberty	2 14 70	8	3
'70 Concert			
(UK) Liberty	7 11 70	15	–
CAPTAIN BEEFHEART			
Lick My Decals Off Baby			
(UK) Straight	1 30 71	20	–
CARLIN, GEORGE			
FM-AM			
(US) Little David	3 25 72	13	–
CARLOS, WALTER; and FOLKMAN, BENJAMIN			
Switched-On Bach			
(US) Columbia	3 22 69	10	1
CARPENTERS			
Close to You			
(US) A&M	10 10 70	2	15
(UK) A&M	11 27 71	18	–
Carpenters			
(US) A&M	6 5 71	2	24
(UK) A&M	10 30 71	10	2
Ticket to Ride			
(UK) A&M	4 15 72	20	–
A Song for You			
(US) A&M	7 15 72	4	5
(UK) A&M	10 28 72	13	–
Now and Then			
(US) A&M	6 23 73	2	8
(UK) A&M	7 7 73	2	21
The Singles			
(UK) A&M	12 15 73	2	3
CARR, VIKKI			
It Must Be Him			

LABEL	DATE OF ENTRY TO TOP 20	HIGHEST POSITION REACHED	NUMBER OF WEEKS IN TOP 10
(*UK*) *Liberty*	8 23 67	*15*	–
(US) Liberty	12 9 67	12	–
CASH, JOHNNY			
At Folsom Prison			
(US) Columbia	8 17 68	13	–
(*UK*) *CBS*	*9 4 68*	*7*	*3*
At San Quentin			
(US) Columbia	7 26 69	1	20
(*UK*) *CBS*	*8 23 69*	*2*	*27*
Hello, I'm Johnny Cash			
(US) Columbia	2 28 70	6	4
(*UK*) *CBS*	*3 7 70*	*6*	*3*
World of Johnny Cash			
(*UK*) *CBS*	*8 22 70*	*5*	*5*
Johnny Cash's Greatest Hits			
(*UK*) *CBS*	*11 21 70*	*19*	–
Johnny Cash Show			
(*UK*) *CBS*	*12 19 70*	*18*	–
Man in Black			
(*UK*) *CBS*	*9 18 71*	*11*	–
A Thing Called Love			
(*UK*) *CBS*	*5 27 72*	*8*	*1*
Star Portrait (DLP)			
(*UK*) *CBS*	*10 21 72*	*16*	–
CASSIDY, DAVID			
Cherish			
(US) Bell	2 26 67	15	–
(*UK*) *Bell*	*5 20 72*	*2*	*10*
Rock Me Baby			
(*UK*) *Bell*	*2 24 73*	*2*	*8*
Dreams Are Nothin' More than Wishes			
(*UK*) *Bell*	*11 24 73*	*1*	*6*
[see also: **PARTRIDGE FAMILY**]			
CHACKSFIELD, FRANK			
World of Frank Chacksfield			
(*UK*) *Decca*†	*3 5 69*	*10*	–
CHAMBERS BROTHERS			
Time Has Come			
(US) Columbia	9 21 68	4	10
A New Time—A New Day			
(US) Columbia	11 30 68	16	–
CHARLES, RAY			
Ingredients in a Recipe for Soul			
(US) ABC-Paramount	1 4 64	14	–
Sweet and Sour Tears			
(US) ABC-Paramount	4 4 64	9	2
Crying Time			
(US) ABC	7 2 66	15	–

LABEL	DATE OF ENTRY TO TOP 20	HIGHEST POSITION REACHED	NUMBER OF WEEKS IN TOP 10
CHARLES, RAY, SINGERS			
Something Special for Young Lovers			
(US) Command	6 13 64	11	–
CHEECH AND CHONG			
Big Bambu			
(US) Ode	7 22 72	2	12
Los Cochinos			
(US) Ode	9 15 73	2	12
CHER			
All I Really Want to Do			
(UK) Liberty	*9 30 65*	*7*	*3*
(US) Imperial	10 30 65	16	–
Sonny Side of Cher			
(UK) Liberty	*5 19 66*	*11*	–
Cher			
(US) Kapp	11 20 71	16	–
CHICAGO			
Chicago Transit Authority			
(US) Columbia	7 5 69	17	–
Chicago (DLP)			
(UK) CBS	*1 24 70*	*6*	*7*
(US) Columbia	2 21 70	4	33
Columbia 3 (DLP)			
(UK) CBS	*8 29 70*	*14*	–
(US) Columbia	2 6 71	2	10
Chicago at Carnegie Hall			
(US) Columbia	11 20 71	3	13
Chicago 5			
(US) Columbia	8 5 73	1	13
Chicago 6			
(US) Columbia	7 21 73	1	10
CHICKEN SHACK			
40 Blue Fingers Freshly Packed			
(UK) Blue Horizon	*6 26 68*	*12*	–
OK Ken?			
(UK) Blue Horizon	*2 12 69*	*9*	*1*
CHI-LITES			
Give More Power to the People			
(US) Brunswick	10 16 71	12	–
Lonely Man			
(US) Brunswick	5 20 72	5	6
CHIPMUNKS			
Chipmunks Sing the Beatles' Hits			
(US) Liberty	10 3 64	14	–
CHRISTIE, TONY			
With Loving Feeling			
(UK) MCA	*2 17 73*	*19*	–

LABEL	DATE OF ENTRY TO TOP 20	HIGHEST POSITION REACHED	NUMBER OF WEEKS IN TOP 10
CHURCHILL, SIR WINSTON			
The Voice of Sir Winston Churchill			
(*UK*) *Decca*	*2 11 65*	*6*	*6*
CLAPTON, ERIC			
Eric Clapton			
(US) Atco	8 15 70	13	–
(*UK*) *Polydor*	*9 5 70*	*14*	–
History of Eric Clapton (DLP)			
(US) Atco	9 16 72	20	–
Eric Clapton's Rainbow Concert			
(US) RSO	10 20 73	18	–
(*UK*) *RSO*	*11 10 73*	*19*	–
[see also: **JOHN MAYALL; CREAM; BLIND FAITH; DEREK & THE DOMINOS**]			
CLARK, DAVE, FIVE			
Session with Dave Clark Five			
(*UK*) *Columbia*	*4 16 64*	*3*	*11*
Glad All Over			
(US) Epic	4 25 64	3	10
Dave Clark Five Return			
(US) Epic	7 4 64	5	7
American Tour			
(US) Epic	9 12 64	11	–
Coast to Coast			
(US) Epic	1 23 65	6	6
Catch Us If You Can			
(*UK*) *Columbia*	*8 12 65*	*8*	*3*
Having a Wild Weekend			
(US) Epic	10 9 65	15	–
Dave Clark Five's Greatest Hits			
(US) Epic	4 9 66	9	4
CLARK, PETULA			
I Couldn't Live Without Your Love			
(*UK*) *Pye*	*8 4 66*	*11*	–
Color My World			
(*UK*) *Pye*	*2 23 67*	*16*	–
Hit Parade			
(*UK*) *Pye*	*3 2 67*	*18*	–
CLEVELAND, JAMES (see **ARETHA FRANKLIN**)			
COCKER, JOE			
Joe Cocker			
(US) A&M	12 20 69	11	–
Mad Dogs and Englishmen (DLP)			
(US) A&M	9 5 70	2	8
(*UK*) *A&M*	*10 10 70*	*16*	–
COHEN, LEONARD			
Songs of Leonard Cohen			
(*UK*) *CBS*	*10 30 68*	*13*	–

LABEL	DATE OF ENTRY TO TOP 20	HIGHEST POSITION REACHED	NUMBER OF WEEKS IN TOP 10
Songs from a Room			
(UK) CBS	*4 30 69*	*2*	*6*
Songs of Love and Hate			
(UK) CBS	*4 24 71*	*4*	*6*
COLE, NAT "KING"			
I Don't Want to Be Hurt Any More			
(US) Capitol	8 22 64	18	–
L-O-V-E			
(US) Capitol	3 13 65	4	5
Unforgettable Nat "King" Cole			
(UK) Capitol	*3 25 65*	*11*	–
Ramblin' Rose			
(US) Capitol	4 17 65	7	2
Best of Nat "King" Cole			
(UK) Capitol	*12 23 68*	*12*	–
COLLINS, JUDY			
Wild Flowers			
(US) Elektra	12 21 68	5	6
Whales and Nightingales			
(US) Elektra	1 9 71	17	–
COLOSSEUM			
Colosseum			
(UK) Fontana	*5 14 69*	*15*	–
Valentine Suite			
(UK) Vertigo	*11 22 69*	*15*	–
Colosseum Live			
(UK) Bronze	*6 26 71*	*17*	–
COMO, PERRY			
It's Impossible			
(UK) RCA	*4 17 71*	*13*	–
And I Love You So			
(UK) RCA	*7 7 73*	*1*	*39*
CONNIFF, RAY			
Somewhere My Love			
(US) Columbia	7 30 66	3	17
His Orchestra, His Chorus, His Singers, His Sound			
(UK) CBS	*6 18 69*	*1*	*16*
I'd Like to Teach the World to Sing			
(UK) CBS	*2 19 72*	*17*	–
CORBETT, HARRY; and BRAMBLE, WILFRED			
More Junk			
(UK) Pye	*3 12 64*	*20*	–
COSBY, BILL			
Wonderfulness			
(US) Warner Brothers	6 25 66	7	5
Why Is There Air?			
(US) Warner Brothers	8 13 66	19	–

LABEL	DATE OF ENTRY TO TOP 20	HIGHEST POSITION REACHED	NUMBER OF WEEKS IN TOP 10
Revenge			
(US) Warner Brothers	5 20 67	2	12
Silver Throat			
(US) Warner Brothers	11 4 67	18	–
To Russell My Brother Whom I Slept With			
(US) Warner Brothers	4 20 68	7	4
200 MPH			
(US) Warner Brothers	12 14 68	16	–
COWSILLS			
In Concert			
(US) MGM	5 31 69	16	–
CREAM			
Fresh Cream			
(UK) Reaction	*1 12 67*	*6*	*6*
Disraeli Gears			
(UK) Reaction	*11 22 67*	*5*	*8*
(US) Atco	12 30 67	4	30
Wheels of Fire (DLP)			
(US) Atco	7 27 68	1	20
(UK) Polydor	*8 14 68*	*3*	*9*
Wheels of Fire (Studio)			
(UK) Polydor	*8 21 68*	*7*	*2*
Goodbye			
(US) Atco	2 22 69	2	8
(UK) Polydor	*3 12 69*	*1*	*13*
Best of Cream			
(US) Atco	8 2 69	3	13
(UK) Polydor	*11 8 69*	*6*	*5*
Live			
(US) Atco	5 16 70	11	–
(UK) Polydor	*7 4 70*	*4*	*3*
Live, Vol. 2			
(UK) Polydor	*7 8 72*	*15*	–
CREEDENCE CLEARWATER REVIVAL			
Bayou Country			
(US) Fantasy	3 8 69	7	13
Green River			
(US) Fantasy	9 20 69	1	15
(UK) Liberty	*1 24 70*	*20*	–
Willie and the Poor Boys			
(US) Fantasy	12 20 69	3	16
(UK) Liberty	*4 4 70*	*10*	*2*
Cosmo's Factory			
(US) Fantasy	7 25 70	1	19
(UK) Liberty	*9 12 70*	*1*	*9*
Pendulum			
(US) Fantasy	12 26 70	5	11
Mardi Gras			
(US) Fantasy	5 6 72	12	–

LABEL	DATE OF ENTRY TO TOP 20	HIGHEST POSITION REACHED	NUMBER OF WEEKS IN TOP 10
Creedence Gold			
(US) Fantasy	2 3 73	15	–
CROCE, JIM			
Life and Times			
(US) ABC	10 27 73	7	8
Don't Mess Around with Jim			
(US) ABC	11 3 73	5	7
I Got a Name			
(US) ABC	12 29 73	12	–
CROSBY, DAVID			
If I Could Only Remember My Name			
(UK) Atlantic	*3 27 71*	*12*	–
[see also: **CROSBY, STILLS & NASH; CROSBY, STILLS, NASH & YOUNG; GRAHAM NASH; BYRDS**]			
CROSBY, STILLS & NASH			
Crosby, Stills & Nash			
(US) Atlantic	7 12 69	6	17
CROSBY, STILLS, NASH & YOUNG			
Déjà Vu			
(US) Atlantic	4 4 70	1	23
(UK) Atlantic	*5 30 70*	*5*	*5*
4 Way Street			
(US) Atlantic	4 24 71	1	13
(UK) Atlantic	*5 22 71*	*5*	*2*
CRUSH, BOBBY			
Piano			
(UK) Philips	*11 25 72*	*15*	–
CURVED AIR			
Air Conditionaing			
(UK) Warner Brothers	*12 5 70*	*8*	*1**
Curved Air			
(UK) Warner Brothers	*10 9 71*	*9*	*1*
Phantasmagoria			
(UK) Warner Brothers	*5 20 72*	*20*	–
DALTREY, ROGER			
Daltrey			
(UK) Track	*5 26 73*	*6*	*2*
DANA, VIC			
Red Roses for a Blue Lady			
(US) Dolton	5 8 65	13	–
DAVIDSON, JOHN			
Time of My Life			
(US) Columbia	12 10 66	19	–
DAVIS, MAC			
Baby, Don't Get Hooked on Me			
(US) Columbia	10 14 72	11	–

LABEL	DATE OF ENTRY TO TOP 20	HIGHEST POSITION REACHED	NUMBER OF WEEKS IN TOP 10
DAVIS, JR., SAMMY			
Now			
(US) MGM	6 24 72	11	–
DAVIS, SPENCER, GROUP			
Their First LP			
(*UK*) *Fontana*	*1 6 66*	*6*	*5*
The 2nd Album			
(*UK*) *Fontana*	*1 20 66*	*3*	*13*
Autumn			
(*UK*) *Fontana*	*9 8 66*	*4*	*8*
DAVE DEE, DOZY, BEAKY, MICK and TITCH			
Dave Dee, Dozy, Beaky, Mick and Titch			
(*UK*) *Fontana*	*7 7 66*	*11*	–
DEEP PURPLE			
In Rock			
(*UK*) *Harvest*	*6 27 70*	*4*	*26**
Fireball			
(*UK*) *Harvest*	*9 18 71*	*1*	*7*
Machine Head			
(*UK*) *Purple*	*4 15 72*	*1*	*8*
(US) Warner Brothers	7 7 73	7	6
Made in Japan			
(*UK*) *Purple*	*1 6 73*	*16*	–
(US) Warner Brothers	5 26 73	6	10
Who Do We Think We Are			
(*UK*) *Purple*	*2 17 73*	*4*	*2*
(US) Warner Brothers	2 17 73	15	–
DENNY, SANDY			
North Star Grassman			
(*UK*) *Island*	*10 2 71*	*19*	–
[see also: **FAIRPORT CONVENTION; FOTHERINGAY**]			
DENVER, JOHN			
Poems, Prayers and Promises			
(US) RCA	7 17 71	15	–
(*UK*) *RCA*	*6 23 73*	*19*	–
Rocky Mountain High			
(US) RCA	12 9 72	4	9
(*UK*) *RCA*	*6 2 73*	*11*	–
Farewell Andromeda			
(US) RCA	7 28 73	16	–
DEODATO			
Prelude/Deodato			
(US) CTI	3 3 73	3	5
Deodato 2			
(US) CTI	9 22 73	19	–
DEREK AND THE DOMINOS			
Layla (DLP)			

LABEL	DATE OF ENTRY TO TOP 20	HIGHEST POSITION REACHED	NUMBER OF WEEKS IN TOP 10
(US) Atco	12 5 72	16	–
(US) Atco (re-entry)	7 22 72	17	–
In Concert			
(US) RSO (DLP)	3 24 73	20	–

DIAMOND, NEIL
Gold

(US) UNI	9 5 70	10	2
Tap Root Manuscript			
(US) UNI	12 5 70	13	–
(UK) UNI	*4 3 71*	*18*	*–*
Stones			
(US) UNI	11 27 71	11	–
(UK) UNI	*12 11 71*	*17*	*–*
Moods			
(US) UNI	7 29 72	5	11
(UK) UNI	*8 5 72*	*7*	*5*
Hot August Night			
(US) MCA (DLP)	12 23 72	5	9
Jonathan Livingstone Seagull			
(US) Columbia	11 17 73	2	6

DIDDLEY, BO
Bo Diddley's Beach Party

(UK) Pye	*2 13 64*	*13*	*–*

DIMBLEBY, RICHARD
Voice of Richard Dimbleby

(UK) MFP†	*6 2 66*	*14*	*–*

DIRKSON, SENATOR EVERETT MCKINLEY
Gallant Men

(US) Capitol	2 4 67	16	–

DODD, KEN
Tears of Happiness

(UK) Columbia	*12 23 65*	*6*	*3*
Hits for Now and Always			
(UK) Columbia	*7 28 66*	*14*	*–*

DONOVAN
What's Been Did and What's Been Hid

(UK) Pye	*6 3 65*	*3*	*9*
Sunshine Superman			
(US) Epic	10 22 65	11	–
Fairy Tale			
(UK) Pye	*11 4 65*	*20*	*–*
Mellow Yellow			
(US) Epic	3 25 67	14	–
Universal Soldier			
(UK) Marble Arch†	*10 18 67*	*5*	*9*
Gift from a Flower to a Garden			
(US) Epic	2 17 68	19	–
(UK) Pye	*5 29 68*	*13*	*–*

LABEL	DATE OF ENTRY TO TOP 20	HIGHEST POSITION REACHED	NUMBER OF WEEKS IN TOP 10
In Concert			
(US) Epic	9 7 68	18	–
Hurdy Gurdy Man			
(US) Epic	12 21 68	20	–
Donovan's Greatest Hits			
(US) Epic	3 1 69	4	14
Open Road			
(US) Epic	7 25 70	16	–
Cosmic Wheels			
(UK) Epic	3 24 73	15	–
DOOBIE BROTHERS			
Captain and Me			
(US) Warner Brothers	5 19 73	7	3
DOONICAN, VAL			
Lucky 13 Shades of Val Doonican			
(UK) Decca	12 10 64	2	20
Gentle Shades of Val			
(UK) Decca	12 8 66	5	9
Val Doonican Rocks but Gently			
(UK) Pye	12 13 67	1	13
Val			
(UK) Pye	12 4 68	6	4
World of Val Doonican			
(UK) Decca†	3 5 69	2	18
DOORS			
Doors			
(US) Elektra	6 24 67	2	22
Strange Days			
(US) Elektra	11 11 67	3	9
Waiting for the Sun			
(US) Elektra	8 24 68	1	9
(UK) Elektra	10 9 68	16	–
Soft Parade			
(US) Elektra	8 16 69	6	9
Morrison Hotel			
(US) Elektra	3 14 70	4	6
(UK) Elektra	4 11 70	12	–
Absolutely Live			
(US) Elektra	8 15 70	8	2
L.A. Woman			
(US) Elektra	5 22 71	9	3
DRAMATICS			
Whatcha See Is Whatcha Get			
(US) Volt	3 25 72	20	–
DRISCOLL, JULIE, with **BRIAN AUGER TRINITY**			
Open			
(UK) Marmalade	6 26 68	12	–

LABEL	DATE OF ENTRY TO TOP 20	HIGHEST POSITION REACHED	NUMBER OF WEEKS IN TOP 10
DUBLINERS			
A Drop of the Hard Stuff			
(*UK*) *Major-Minor*	5 18 67	5	10
More of the Hard Stuff			
(*UK*) *Major-Minor*	10 18 67	8	1
DYLAN, BOB			
Times They Are A'Changin'			
(US) Columbia	4 18 64	20	–
(*UK*) *CBS*	7 9 64	4	9
Freewheelin'			
(*UK*) *CBS*	5 21 64	1	22
Bob Dylan			
(*UK*) *CBS*	7 16 64	13	–
Another Side of Bob Dylan			
(*UK*) *CBS*	11 19 64	8	1
Bringing It All Back Home			
(*UK*) *CBS*	5 13 65	1	23
(US) Columbia	5 15 65	6	14
Highway 61 Revisited			
(*UK*) *CBS*	10 7 65	4	12
(US) Columbia	10 16 65	3	8
Blonde on Blonde (DLP)			
(*UK*) *CBS*	8 18 66	3	8
(US) Columbia	8 20 66	9	2
Bob Dylan's Greatest Hits			
(*UK*) *CBS*	1 26 67	6	6
(US) Columbia	5 27 67	10	1
John Wesley Harding			
(US) Columbia	2 10 68	2	10
(*UK*) *CBS*	3 6 68	1	21
Nashville Skyline			
(US) Columbia	5 10 69	3	13
(*UK*) *CBS*	5 14 69	1	18
Self-Portrait (DLP)			
(US) Columbia	7 11 70	4	6
(*UK*) *CBS*	7 11 70	1	6
New Morning			
(US) Columbia	11 21 70	7	3
(*UK*) *CBS*	11 28 70	1	3
Bob Dylan's Greatest Hits, Vol. 2			
(US) Columbia	12 18 71	14	–
(*UK*) *CBS* (*DLP*)	1 8 72	12	–

[see also: sound tracks; **PAT GARRET AND BILLY THE KID;** various artists: **CONCERT FOR BANGLADESH**]

LABEL	DATE OF ENTRY TO TOP 20	HIGHEST POSITION REACHED	NUMBER OF WEEKS IN TOP 10
EMERSON, LAKE AND PALMER			
Emerson, Lake and Palmer			
(*UK*) *Island*	12 5 70	4	7
(US) Cotillion	4 3 71	18	–

LABEL	DATE OF ENTRY TO TOP 20	HIGHEST POSITION REACHED	NUMBER OF WEEKS IN TOP 10
Tarkus			
(UK) Island	6 19 71	1	10
(US) Cotillion	7 10 71	9	2
Pictures at an Exhibition			
(UK) Island†	12 4 71	2	4
(US) Cotillion	2 5 72	10	2
Trilogy			
(UK) Island	7 15 72	2	5
(US) Cotillion	8 5 72	5	7
Brain Salad Surgery			
(UK) Manticore	12 22 73	2	3
ENGLAND FOOTBALL SQUAD			
Worldbeaters Sing the Worldbeaters			
(UK) Pye	5 16 70	4	6
EQUALS			
Unequalled			
(UK) President	11 29 67	10	1
ESSEX, DAVID			
Rock On			
(UK) CBS	12 8 73	7	4
EVERLY BROTHERS			
Original Hits (DLP)			
(UK) CBS	9 19 70	7	4
FACES			
A Nod's As Good As A Wink			
(UK) Warner Brothers	1 1 72	2	11
(US) Warner Brothers	1 22 72	6	6
Ooh-La-La			
(UK) Warner Brothers	4 21 73	1	4
FAIRPORT CONVENTION			
Unhalfbricking			
(UK) Island	7 30 69	13	–
Liege and Lief			
(UK) Island	1 31 70	17	–
Full House			
(UK) Island	7 25 70	13	–
Angel Delight			
(UK) Island	7 3 71	8	1
FAITH, ADAM			
Faith Alive			
(UK) Parlophone	9 23 65	14	–
FAITHFULL, MARIANNE			
Come My Way			
(UK) Decca	6 3 65	12	–
Marianne Faithfull			
(UK) Decca	6 3 65	15	–
(US) London	8 28 65	12	–

LABEL	DATE OF ENTRY TO TOP 20	HIGHEST POSITION REACHED	NUMBER OF WEEKS IN TOP 10
FAME, GEORGIE			
Fame at Last			
(*UK*) *Columbia*	10 15 64	15	–
Sweet Things			
(*UK*) *Columbia*	5 12 66	6	10
Sound Venture			
(*UK*) *Columbia*	10 13 66	9	1
Hall of Fame			
(*UK*) *Columbia*	3 23 67	12	–
FAMILY			
Family Entertainment			
(*UK*) *Reprise*	3 19 69	6	1
A Song for Me			
(*UK*) *Reprise*	2 7 70	4	4
Anyway			
(*UK*) *Reprise*	11 28 70	7	1
Fearless			
(*UK*) *Reprise*	11 20 71	10	1
Bandstand			
(*UK*) *Reprise*	10 7 72	15	–
FARLOWE, CHRIS			
14 Things to Think About			
(*UK*) *Immediate*	3 31 66	19	–
FELICIANO, JOSE			
Feliciano			
(US) RCA	8 24 68	2	19
(*UK*) *RCA*	11 6 68	6	4
10 to 23			
(US) RCA	7 19 69	16	–
FERRY, BRYAN			
These Foolish Things			
(*UK*) *Island*	11 3 73	5	4
[see also: **ROXY MUSIC**]			
FIFTH DIMENSION			
Up Up and Away			
(US) Soul City	7 22 67	8	3
Age of Aquarius			
(US) Soul City	6 7 69	2	9
Greatest Hits			
(US) Soul City	5 30 70	5	5
Portrait			
(US) Bell	1 30 71	20	–
Love's Lines Angles and Rhymes			
(US) Bell	4 17 71	17	–
Greatest Hits on Earth			
(US) Bell	10 28 72	14	–
FLACK, ROBERTA			
Quiet Fire			
(US) Atlantic	1 1 72	18	–

LABEL	DATE OF ENTRY TO TOP 20	HIGHEST POSITION REACHED	NUMBER OF WEEKS IN TOP 10
First Take			
(US) Atlantic	4 8 72	1	14
Roberta Flack and Donny Hathaway			
(US) Atlantic	5 27 72	3	8
Killing Me Softly			
(US) Atlantic	9 8 73	3	7
FLEETWOOD MAC			
Peter Green's Fleetwood Mac			
(*UK*) *Blue Horizon*	*3 13 68*	*4*	*17*
Mr. Wonderful			
(*UK*) *Blue Horizon*	*9 11 68*	*10*	*1*
Pious Bird of Good Omen			
(*UK*) *Blue Horizon*	*8 30 69*	*18*	–
Then Play On			
(*UK*) *Reprise*	*10 4 69*	*6*	*5*
FOCUS			
Moving Waves			
(*UK*) *Polydor*	*1 27 73*	*2*	*6*
(US) Sire	3 24 73	8	4
Focus 3			
(*UK*) *Polydor*	*2 10 73*	*6*	*5*
FOLKMAN, BENJAMIN (see **WALTER CARLOS**)			
FONTANA, WAYNE, AND THE MINDBENDERS			
Wayne Fontana and the Mindbenders			
(*UK*) *Philips*	*2 18 65*	*18*	–
FOTHERINGAY			
Fotheringay			
(*UK*) *Island*	*7 11 70*	*18*	–
FOUR PENNIES			
2 Sides of Four Pennies			
(*UK*) *Philips*	*11 5 64*	*13*	–
FOUR SEASONS			
Dawn (Go Away) and 11 Other Great Songs			
(US) Philips	4 4 64	6	5
Rag Doll			
(US) Philips	8 15 64	7	5
Four Seasons Gold Vault of Hits			
(US) Philips	2 5 66	10	2
Edizione d'Oro			
(*UK*) *Philips* (*DLP*)	*4 10 71*	*11*	–
FOUR TOPS			
Four Tops 2nd Album			
(US) Motown	1 29 66	20	–
Four Tops on Top			
(*UK*) *Tamla Motown*	*11 24 66*	*9*	*1*
Four Tops Live!			
(*UK*) *Tamla Motown*	*2 16 67*	*5*	*12*
(US) Motown	2 18 67	17	–

LABEL	DATE OF ENTRY TO TOP 20	HIGHEST POSITION REACHED	NUMBER OF WEEKS IN TOP 10
Reach Out			
(US) Motown	8 26 67	11	–
(UK) Tamla Motown	11 29 67	9	12
Four Tops' Greatest Hits			
(US) Motown	10 14 67	4	7
(UK) Tamla Motown	1 24 68	1	18
Four Tops' Greatest Hits, Vol. 2			
(UK) Tamla Motown	11 27 71	16	–
[see also: **SUPREMES**]			
FRANKLIN, ARETHA			
I Never Loved a Man the Way I Love You			
(US) Atlantic	5 6 67	2	17
Aretha Arrives			
(US) Atlantic	9 2 67	5	10
Lady Soul			
(US) Atlantic	3 2 68	2	16
Aretha Now			
(US) Atlantic	7 27 68	3	8
(UK) Atlantic	9 18 68	6	3
Aretha in Paris			
(US) Atlantic	12 14 68	13	–
Soul '69			
(US) Atlantic	3 1 69	15	–
Aretha's Gold			
(US) Atlantic	8 2 69	18	–
This Girl's in Love with You			
(US) Atlantic	4 4 70	17	–
Live at Fillmore West			
(US) Atlantic	6 12 71	7	4
Aretha's Greatest Hits			
(US) Atlantic	10 23 71	19	–
Young, Gifted and Black			
(US) Atlantic	3 11 72	11	–
Amazing Grace (with **JAMES CLEVELAND**)			
(US) Atlantic	7 8 72	7	3
FREDDIE & THE DREAMERS			
Freddie & the Dreamers			
(UK) Columbia	1 2 64	4	15
(US) Mercury	6 19 65	19	–
FREE			
Fire and Water			
(UK) Island	7 11 70	2	7
(US) A&M	10 10 70	17	–
Live			
(UK) Island	6 26 71	4	6
Free at Last			
(UK) Island	6 25 72	9	1
Heartbreaker			
(UK) Island	2 3 73	9	3

LABEL	DATE OF ENTRY TO TOP 20	HIGHEST POSITION REACHED	NUMBER OF WEEKS IN TOP 10
FRIJID PINK			
Frijid Pink			
(US) Parrot	3 21 70	11	–
FRYE, DAVID			
I Am the President			
(US) Elektra	2 7 70	19	–
GALLAGHER, RORY			
Live in Europe			
(UK) Polydor	*5 20 72*	*12*	–
Blueprint			
(UK) Polydor	*3 3 73*	*12*	–
[see also: **TASTE**]			
GARFUNKEL, ART			
Angel Clare			
(US) Columbia	10 6 73	5	5
(UK) CBS	*10 13 73*	*14*	–
[see also: **SIMON AND GARFUNKEL**]			
GARY, JOHN			
Catch a Rising Star			
(US) RCA	1 4 64	19	–
Encore			
(US) RCA	3 21 64	16	–
Little Bit of Heaven			
(US) RCA	4 10 65	17	–
Nearness of You			
(US) RCA	8 28 65	11	–
GAYE, MARVIN			
What's Going On			
(US) Tamla	7 3 71	6	10
Trouble Man (sound track)			
(US) Tamla	2 3 73	14	–
Let's Get It On			
(US) Tamla	9 22 73	2	8
GEILS J., BAND			
Bloodshot			
(US) Atlantic	5 26 73	10	1
GENESIS			
Foxtrot			
(UK) Charisma	*10 14 72*	*12*	–
Genesis Live			
(UK) Charisma	*8 11 73*	*13*	–
Selling England by the Pound			
(UK) Charisma	*10 20 73*	*3*	*4*
GENTRY, BOBBIE			
Ode to Billy Joe			
(US) Capitol	9 23 67	1	10
Bobbie Gentry and Glen Campbell			
(US) Capitol	11 16 68	11	–

LABEL	DATE OF ENTRY TO TOP 20	HIGHEST POSITION REACHED	NUMBER OF WEEKS IN TOP 10
GERRY & THE PACEMAKERS			
How Do You Like It			
(UK) Columbia	1 2 64	3	17
Ferry 'Cross the Mersey			
(UK) Columbia	2 4 65	19	–
(US) United Artists	4 17 65	13	–
GETZ, STAN; and GILBERTO, JOAO			
Stan Getz and João Gilberto			
(US) Verve	6 27 64	2	16
GLITTER, GARY			
Glitter			
(UK) Bell	10 28 72	8	2
Touch Me			
(UK) Bell	6 16 73	2	6
GOLDSBORO, BOBBY			
Honey			
(US) United Artists	5 18 68	5	9
GOONS			
Last Goon Show of All			
(UK) BBC	11 18 72	8	1
GOULET, ROBERT			
My Love Forgive Me			
(US) Columbia	1 30 65	5	8
GRAND FUNK RAILROAD			
Grand Funk Railroad			
(US) Capitol	2 7 70	11	–
Closer to Home			
(US) Capitol	7 11 70	6	12
Live			
(US) Capitol	12 5 70	5	8
Survival			
(US) Capitol	5 8 71	6	6
E Pluribus Funk			
(US) Capitol	12 11 71	5	5
Mark, Don and Mel			
(US) Capitol	6 10 72	17	–
Phoenix			
(US) Capitol	11 4 72	7	3
We're an American Band			
(US) Capitol	8 25 73	2	8
GRATEFUL DEAD			
Wake of the Flood			
(US) Grateful Dead	12 8 73	18	–
GREEN, AL			
Let's Stay Together			
(US) Hi	3 4 72	8	6
I'm Still in Love with You			
(US) Hi	11 18 72	4	6

LABEL	DATE OF ENTRY TO TOP 20	HIGHEST POSITION REACHED	NUMBER OF WEEKS IN TOP 10
Green Is Blues			
(US) Hi	3 3 73	19	–
Call Me			
(US) Hi	6 9 73	10	2
GROUNDHOGS			
Thank Christ for the Bomb			
(*UK*) *Liberty*	6 13 70	9	*1*
Split			
(*UK*) *Liberty*	4 3 71	5	*9*
Who Will Save the World			
(*UK*) *United Artists*	3 18 72	10	*1*
GUESS WHO			
American Woman			
(US) RCA	4 18 70	9	7
Share the Land			
(US) RCA	11 7 70	14	–
Best of the Guess Who			
(US) RCA	5 15 71	12	–
GUTHRIE, ARLO			
Alice's Restaurant			
(US) Reprise	11 8 69	17	–
HARRIS, RICHARD			
A Tramp Shining			
(US) Dunhill	6 15 68	4	*5*
HARRISON, GEORGE			
All Things Must Pass			
(US) Apple } (TLP)	12 19 70	1	14
(*UK*) *Apple* } (TLP)	*12 26 70*	*5*	*4**
Living in the Material World			
(US) Apple	6 16 73	1	7
(*UK*) *Apple*	*7 7 73*	*2*	*5*
[see also: **BEATLES**; various artists: **CONCERT FOR BANGLADESH**]			
HATHAWAY, DONNY			
Donny Hathaway Live			
(US) Atco	7 8 72	18	–
[see also: **ROBERTA FLACK**]			
HAWKINS, EDWIN, SINGERS			
Let Us Go into the House of the Lord			
(US) Pavilion	5 31 69	15	–
HAWKWIND			
In Search of Space			
(*UK*) *United Artists*	*8 19 72*	*18*	–
Dore Mefaso Latido			
(*UK*) *United Artists*	*12 23 72*	*14*	–
Space Ritual Alive			
(*UK*) *United Artists*	*6 9 73*	*9*	*1*

LABEL	DATE OF ENTRY TO TOP 20	HIGHEST POSITION REACHED	NUMBER OF WEEKS IN TOP 10
HAYES, ISAAC			
Hot Buttered Soul			
(US) Enterprise	9 6 69	8	4
Isaac Hayes Movement			
(US) Enterprise	5 9 70	8	6
To Be Continued			
(US) Enterprise	12 12 70	11	—
Shaft (sound track)			
(US) Enterprise	9 4 71	1	15
(UK) *Stax*	*12 18 71*	*12*	—
Black Moses			
(US) Enterprise	12 25 71	10	2
Isaac Hayes Live at the Sahara Tahoe			
(US) Enterprise	12 8 73	16	—
Joy			
(US) Enterprise	12 8 73	16	—
HAZLEWOOD, LEE (see **NANCY SINATRA**)			
HENDRIX, JIMI, EXPERIENCE			
Are You Experienced			
(UK) *Track*	*6 1 67*	*2*	*19*
(US) Reprise	9 23 67	5	32
Axis: Bold As Love			
(UK) *Track*	*12 20 67*	*8*	*5*
(US) Reprise	2 24 68	3	8
Smash Hits			
(UK) *Track*	*5 8 68*	*4*	*10*
(US) Reprise	8 16 69	6	6
Electric Ladyland			
(US) Reprise }(DLP)	11 2 68	1	10
(UK) *Track* }(DLP)	*11 20 68*	*18*	—
Band of Gypsies (with **BUDDY MILES, BILLY COX**)			
(US) Capitol	5 2 70	5	7
(UK) *Track*	*7 4 70*	*6*	*2*
Jimi Hendrix Experience/Otis Redding, at Monterey			
(US) Reprise	10 10 70	16	—
Cry of Love			
(US) Reprise	3 6 71	3	7
(UK) *Track*	*4 3 71*	*2*	*7***
Isle of Wight			
(UK) *Track*	*11 20 71*	*12*	—
Rainbow Bridge			
(US) Reprise	10 23 71	15	—
(UK) *Reprise*	*12 4 71*	*10*	*1*
In the West			
(UK) *Polydor*	*2 12 72*	*7*	*4*
(US) Reprise	3 18 72	12	—
HERMAN'S HERMITS			
Introducing Herman's Hermits			
(US) MGM	4 3 65	2	17

LABEL	DATE OF ENTRY TO TOP 20	HIGHEST POSITION REACHED	NUMBER OF WEEKS IN TOP 10
Herman's Hermits on Tour			
(US) MGM	7 3 65	2	18
Herman's Hermits			
(UK) Columbia	9 16 65	16	–
Best of Herman's Hermits			
(US) MGM	11 27 65	5	16
Hold On!			
(US) MGM	4 14 66	14	–
Best of Herman's Hermits, Vol. 2			
(US) MGM	2 4 67	20	–
There's a Kind of a Hush All over the World			
(US) MGM	4 8 67	13	–
HILL, BENNY			
Words and Music			
(UK) Columbia	12 11 71	9	1
HILTON, RONNIE			
Chitty Chitty Bang Bang			
(UK) MFP†	3 5 69	17	–
HIRT, AL			
Honey in the Horn			
(US) RCA	2 8 64	3	24
Cotton Candy			
(US) RCA	6 13 64	6	11
Sugar Lips			
(US) RCA	9 19 64	9	3
"Pops" Goes the Trumpet (with the **BOSTON POPS**)			
(US) RCA	11 28 64	18	–
Best of Al Hirt			
(US) RCA	2 27 65	13	–
HO, DON			
Tiny Bubbles			
(US) Reprise	3 25 67	15	–
HOLLIES			
Stay with the Hollies			
(UK) Parlophone	2 13 64	2	18
The Hollies			
(UK) Parlophone	9 30 65	8	8
Would You Believe			
(UK) Parlophone	7 14 66	16	–
Evolution			
(UK) Parlophone	6 22 67	13	–
Hollies' Greatest Hits			
(US) Imperial	7 22 67	11	–
(UK) Parlophone	8 14 68	1	22
Hollies Sing Dylan			
(UK) Parlophone	5 14 69	3	3

LABEL	DATE OF ENTRY TO TOP 20	HIGHEST POSITION REACHED	NUMBER OF WEEKS IN TOP 10
HOLLY, BUDDY			
Buddy Holly Showcase			
(*UK*) *Coral*	*6 11 64*	*3*	*9*
Holly in the Hills			
(*UK*) *Coral*	*6 24 65*	*13*	—
Buddy Holly's Greatest Hits			
(*UK*) *Ace of Hearts*†	*7 26 67*	*9*	*2*
Giant			
(*UK*) *MCA*	*4 9 69*	*13*	—
HOLLYRIDGE STRINGS			
Beatles Songbook			
(US) Capitol	*8 1 64*	*15*	—
HOPKIN, MARY			
Postcard			
(*UK*) *Apple*	*2 26 69*	*3*	*4*
HUMBLE PIE			
Smokin'			
(US) A&M	*4 15 72*	*6*	*4*
(*UK*) *A&M*	*4 22 72*	*20*	—
Eat It			
(US) A&M	*4 28 73*	*13*	—
HUMPERDINCK, ENGELBERT			
Release Me			
(*UK*) *Decca*	*6 1 67*	*6*	*15*
(US) Parrot	7 22 67	7	7
Last Waltz			
(*UK*) *Decca*	*11 29 67*	*3*	*10*
(US) Parrot	1 20 68	10	2
A Man Without Love			
(*UK*) *Decca*	*8 7 68*	*3*	*13*
(US) Parrot	10 26 68	12	—
Engelbert			
(*UK*) *Decca*	*2 26 69*	*3*	*5*
(US) Parrot	4 19 69	12	—
Engelbert Humperdinck			
(*UK*) *Decca*	*12 6 69*	*6*	*5*
(US) Parrot	1 10 70	5	9
We Made It Happen			
(*UK*) *Decca*	*7 18 70*	*17*	—
(US) Parrot	8 1 70	19	—
IFIELD, FRANK			
Born Free			
(*UK*) *Columbia*	*1 2 64*	*5*	*13*
Blue Skies			
(*UK*) *Columbia*	*3 26 64*	*10*	*1*
Greatest Hits			
(*UK*) *Columbia*	*12 17 64*	*9*	*1*

LABEL	DATE OF ENTRY TO TOP 20	HIGHEST POSITION REACHED	NUMBER OF WEEKS IN TOP 10
IMPRESSIONS			
Keep on Pushing			
(US) ABC-Paramount	9 26 64	8	6
INCREDIBLE STRING BAND			
The Hangman's Beautiful Daughter			
(UK) Elektra	*4 10 68*	*5*	*10*
INDIOS TABAJARAS, LOS			
Maria Elena			
(US) RCA	1 4 64	7	2
IRON BUTTERFLY			
In-a-Gadda-da-Vida			
(US) Atco	9 21 68	4	49
Ball			
(US) Atco	2 22 69	3	8
Live			
(US) Atco	6 6 70	20	—
Metamorphosis			
(US) Atco	9 26 70	16	—
ISLEY BROTHERS			
3+3			
(US) T-Neck	10 13 73	8	3
JACKSON, MICHAEL			
Got to Be There			
(US) Motown	3 4 72	14	—
Ben			
(US) Motown	10 14 72	5	6
(UK) Tamla Motown	*1 13 73*	*17*	—
[see also: **JACKSON FIVE**]			
JACKSON FIVE			
I Want You Back			
(US) Motown	2 7 70	5	11
ABC			
(US) Motown	6 13 70	4	9
Third Album			
(US) Motown	10 3 70	4	11
Maybe Tomorrow			
(US) Motown	5 8 71	11	—
Going Back to Indiana			
(US) Motown	11 6 71	16	—
Greatest Hits			
(US) Motown	1 15 72	12	—
Looking Through the Windows			
(US) Motown	6 24 72	7	5
(UK) Tamla Motown	*11 25 72*	*16*	—
JAMES, TOMMY, AND THE SHONDELLS			
Crimson and Clover			
(US) Roulette	2 15 69	8	5

LABEL	DATE OF ENTRY TO TOP 20	HIGHEST POSITION REACHED	NUMBER OF WEEKS IN TOP 10
JAMES GANG			
James Gang Rides Again			
(US) ABC	10 31 70	20	–
JANKOWSKI, HORST			
The Genius of Jankowski			
(US) Mercury	8 7 65	18	–
JEFFERSON AIRPLANE			
Surrealistic Pillow			
(US) RCA	5 13 67	3	20
After Bathing at Baxters			
(US) RCA	1 27 68	17	–
Crown of Creation			
(US) RCA	9 28 68	6	5
Bless Its Pointed Little Head			
(US) RCA	3 15 69	17	–
Volunteers			
(US) RCA	12 6 69	13	–
Worst of the Jefferson Airplane			
(US) RCA	1 2 71	12	–
Bark			
(US) RCA	9 25 71	11	–
Long John Silver			
(US) Grunt	9 30 72	20	–
JETHRO TULL			
This Was			
(*UK*) *Island*	*11 6 68*	*10*	*2*
Stand Up			
(*UK*) *Island*	*8 9 69*	*1*	*8*
(US) Reprise	11 15 69	20	–
Benefit			
(*UK*) *Island*	*2 9 70*	*3*	*4*
(US) Reprise	5 30 70	11	–
Aqualung			
(*UK*) *Island*	*4 3 71*	*4*	*8***
(US) Reprise	5 22 71	7	16
Thick As a Brick			
(*UK*) *Chrysalis*	*3 18 72*	*5*	*4*
(US) Reprise	5 20 72	1	10
Living in the Past			
(*UK*) *Chrysalis* } (DLP)	*7 15 72*	*8*	*2*
(US) Chrysalis }	12 2 72	3	10
A Passion Play			
(*UK*) *Chrysalis*	*8 4 73*	*16*	–
(US) Chrysalis	8 4 73	1	6
JOBIM, ANTONIO CARLOS (see **FRANK SINATRA**)			
JOHN, ELTON			
Elton John			
(US) UNI	12 26 70	4	6

LABEL	DATE OF ENTRY TO TOP 20	HIGHEST POSITION REACHED	NUMBER OF WEEKS IN TOP 10
Tumbleweed Connection			
(UK) DJM	1 23 71	6	3***
(US) UNI	1 30 71	5	9
Elton John			
(UK) DJM	4 3 71	11	—
(US) UNI	6 5 71	11	—
The Live Album			
(UK) DJM	5 1 71	20	—
Madman Across the Water			
(US) UNI	12 11 71	8	4
Honky Chateau			
(UK) DJM	6 4 72	2	7
(US) UNI	7 1 72	1	18
Don't Shoot Me I'm Only the Piano Player			
(UK) DJM	2 10 73	1	11
(US) MCA	2 27 73	1	9
Goodbye Yellow Brick Road			
(US) MCA ⎫ (DLP)	10 20 73	1	10
(UK) DJM ⎭	11 3 73	1	24

JONES, JACK

LABEL	DATE OF ENTRY	HIGHEST POSITION	NUMBER OF WEEKS
Wives and Lovers			
(US) Kapp	4 25 64	19	—
Dear Heart and Other Great Songs of Love			
(US) Kapp	2 13 65	11	—
Impossible Dream			
(US) Kapp	9 24 66	9	2
A Song for You			
(UK) RCA	5 6 72	16	—
Breadwinners			
(UK) RCA	6 4 72	7	4
Together			
(UK) RCA	4 14 73	8	1

JONES, TOM

LABEL	DATE OF ENTRY	HIGHEST POSITION	NUMBER OF WEEKS
Along Came Jones			
(UK) Decca	6 3 65	11	—
Green, Green Grass of Home			
(UK) Decca	4 13 67	3	11
Live at the Talk of the Town			
(UK) Decca	7 12 67	6	22
13 Smash Hits			
(UK) Decca	12 27 67	5	14
Delilah			
(UK) Decca	7 31 68	1	16
Help Yourself			
(UK) Decca	12 18 68	4	4
(US) Parrot	3 1 69	5	13
Fever Zone			
(US) Parrot	4 26 69	14	—

LABEL	DATE OF ENTRY TO TOP 20	HIGHEST POSITION REACHED	NUMBER OF WEEKS IN TOP 10
Live			
(US) Parrot	5 10 69	13	–
This Is Tom Jones			
(UK) Decca	6 25 69	2	9
(US) Parrot	6 28 69	4	11
Live in Las Vegas			
(UK) Decca	11 15 69	2	16
(US) Parrot	11 22 69	3	18
Tom			
(UK) Decca	4 25 70	4	5
(US) Parrot	5 16 70	6	2
I Who Have Nothing			
(UK) Decca	11 21 70	10	1
She's a Lady			
(UK) Decca	5 29 71	9	2
(US) Parrot	6 12 71	17	–
Live at Caesar's Palace			
(UK) Decca	11 27 71	18	–
Close Up			
(UK) Decca	7 1 72	17	–
JOPLIN, JANIS			
I've Got Dem Ol' Kozmic Blues Again			
(US) Columbia	10 25 69	5	5
Pearl			
(US) Columbia	2 6 71	1	15
Joplin in Concert			
(US) Columbia	5 20 72	4	8
[see also: **BIG BROTHER AND THE HOLDING COMPANY**]			
KAEMPFERT, BERT			
Blue Midnight			
(US) Decca	3 6 65	5	5
Bye Bye Blues			
(UK) Polydor	3 3 66	4	10
Swinging Safari			
(UK) Polydor	6 9 66	20	–
Strangers in the Night			
(UK) Polydor	8 4 66	13	–
KANTNER, PAUL, AND THE JEFFERSON STARSHIP			
Blows Against the Empire			
(US) RCA	1 9 71	20	–
[see also: **JEFFERSON AIRPLANE**]			
KEATING, JOHN			
Top TV Themes			
(UK) Studio 2	3 18 72	13	–
KENDRICKS, EDDIE			
Eddie Kendricks			
(US) Tamla	10 20 73	18	–

LABEL	DATE OF ENTRY TO TOP 20	HIGHEST POSITION REACHED	NUMBER OF WEEKS IN TOP 10
KERR, ANITA (see **ROD MCKUEN**)			
KHATCHATURIAN, ARAM			
Spartacus			
(*UK*) *Decca*	*2 19 72*	*16*	–
KING, CAROLE			
Tapestry			
(US) Ode	5 1 71	1	46
(*UK*) *A&M*	*8 7 71*	*3*	*21*
Music			
(US) Ode	12 18 71	1	16
(*UK*) *A&M/Ode*	*1 22 72*	*18*	–
Rhymes and Reasons			
(US) Ode	11 11 72	2	16
Fantasy			
(US) Ode	6 30 73	6	5
KING CRIMSON			
In the Court of the Crimson King			
(*UK*) *Island*	*11 1 69*	*5*	*4*
In the Wake of Poseidon			
(*UK*) *Island*	*5 30 70*	*4*	*3*
Larks' Tongues in Aspic			
(*UK*) *Island*	*4 14 73*	*20*	–
KINGSMEN			
Louie Louie			
(US) Wand	6 6 64	20	–
Kingsmen, Vol. 2			
(US) Wand	11 21 64	15	–
KINGSTON TRIO			
Time to Think			
(US) Capitol	3 7 64	18	–
KINKS			
Kinks			
(*UK*) *Pye*	*10 15 64*	*3*	*22*
Kinda Kinks			
(*UK*) *Pye*	*3 11 65*	*3*	*9*
Kinks Size			
(US) Reprise	5 8 65	13	–
The Kink Kontroversy			
(*UK*) *Pye*	*12 2 65*	*9*	*1*
Well-Respected Kinks			
(*UK*) *Marble Arch†*	*9 15 66*	*5*	*9*
Kinks' Greatest Hits			
(US) Reprise	10 1 66	9	3
Face to Face			
(*UK*) *Pye*	*11 10 66*	*12*	–
Sunny Afternoon			
(*UK*) *Marble Arch†*	*12 6 67*	*9*	*1*

412

LABEL	DATE OF ENTRY TO TOP 20	HIGHEST POSITION REACHED	NUMBER OF WEEKS IN TOP 10

KIRBY, KATHY
16 Hits from Stars and Garters
   (*UK*) *Decca*   1 2 64   11   –

KNIGHT, GLADYS, AND THE PIPS
Neither One of Us
   (US) Soul   4 14 73   9   4
Imagination
   (US) Buddah   11 24 73   9   2

KOOPER, AL; and BLOOMFIELD, MIKE (*and STILLS, STEPHEN)
Supersession*
   (US) Columbia   10 19 68   12   –
Live Adventures of Al Kooper and Mike Bloomfield
   (US) Columbia   3 8 69   18   –

KRAMER, BILLY J.
Listen to . . .
   (*UK*) *Parlophone*   1 2 64   11   –

KUNZ, CHARLIE
World of Charlie Kunz
   (*UK*) *Decca*†   6 11 69   9   2

LAINE, FRANKIE
I'll Take Care of Your Cares
   (US) ABC   7 1 67   16   –

LAST, JAMES
This is James Last
   (*UK*) *Polydor*†   5 4 67   6   6
Trumpet a go go, Vol. 3
   (*UK*) *Polydor*   5 28 69   13   –
James Last in Concert
   (*UK*) *Polydor*   4 29 72   13   –
Music of James Last
   (*UK*) *Polydor*   1 27 73   19   –
James Last in Russia
   (*UK*) *Polydor*   2 24 73   13   –

LAWRENCE, SYD
More Miller and Other Big Band Magic
   (*UK*) *RCA*   8 8 70   14   –
Syd Lawrence with the Glen Miller Sound
   (*UK*) *Fontana*   1 1 72   17   –

LED ZEPPELIN
Led Zeppelin
   (US) Atlantic   3 8 69   10   1
   (*UK*) *Atlantic*   4 9 69   6   5
Led Zeppelin II
   (*UK*) *Atlantic*   11 8 69   1   53***
   (US) Atlantic   11 15 69   1   24
Led Zeppelin III
   (US) Atlantic   10 24 70   1   14
   (*UK*) *Atlantic*   11 7 70   1   13*

LABEL	DATE OF ENTRY TO TOP 20	HIGHEST POSITION REACHED	NUMBER OF WEEKS IN TOP 10
Runes			
(UK) *Atlantic*	11 27 71	1	12
(US) Atlantic	12 4 71	2	14
Houses of the Holy			
(UK) *Atlantic*	3 14 73	1	5
(US) Atlantic	4 21 73	1	14
LEFEVRE, RAYMOND			
Raymond Lefevre			
(UK) *Major-Minor*	10 4 67	10	1
LEHRER, TOM			
That Was the Year That Was			
(US) Reprise	12 25 65	18	–
LENNON, JOHN			
John Lennon and the Plastic Ono Band			
(US) Apple	12 26 70	6	4
(UK) *Apple*	1 16 71	11	–
Imagine			
(US) Apple	10 2 71	1	12
(UK) *Apple*	10 30 71	1	18
Sometime in New York City (with **YOKO ONO**)			
(UK) *Apple* (*DLP*)	10 14 72	11	–
Mind Games			
(US) Apple	11 24 73	9	4
(UK) *Apple*	12 15 73	13	–
[see also: **BEATLES; PLASTIC ONO BAND**]			
LETTERMEN			
Hit Sounds of the Lettermen			
(US) Capitol	9 25 65	13	–
Best of the Lettermen			
(US) Capitol	1 7 67	17	–
And Live!			
(US) Capitol	2 17 68	10	5
Goin' out of My Head			
(US) Capitol	4 27 68	13	–
Hurt So Bad			
(US) Capitol	10 4 69	17	–
LEWIS, GARY, AND THE PLAYBOYS			
Session with Gary Lewis and the Playboys			
(US) Liberty	11 13 65	18	–
Golden Greats			
(US) Liberty	11 26 66	10	4
LEWIS, RAMSEY, TRIO			
The "In" Crowd			
(US) Argo	9 11 65	2	15
Hang On Ramsey			
(US) Cadet	4 2 66	15	–
(UK) *Chess*	6 2 66	20	–

LABEL	DATE OF ENTRY TO TOP 20	HIGHEST POSITION REACHED	NUMBER OF WEEKS IN TOP 10
Wade in the Water			
(US) Cadet	10 15 66	16	0
LIGHTFOOT, GORDON			
If You Could Read My Mind			
(US) Reprise	2 13 71	12	–
LINDISFARNE			
Fog on the Tyne			
(UK) Charisma	*10 30 71*	*1*	*23*
Nicely out of Tune			
(UK) Charisma	*4 1 72*	*8*	*2*
Dingly Dell			
(UK) Charisma	*9 30 72*	*5*	*5*
LOGGINS, KENNY; and MESSINA, JIM			
Loggins and Messina			
(US) Columbia	1 13 73	16	–
Full Sail			
(US) Columbia	12 8 73	11	–
LONDON SYMPHONY ORCHESTRA			
Tommy			
(US) Ode (TLP)	1 6 73	5	6
The Strauss Family			
(UK) Polydor	*1 20 73*	*2*	*7*
LONGET, CLAUDINE			
Claudine			
(US) A&M	7 1 67	11	–
LOPEZ, TRINI			
At P.J.'s			
(UK) Reprise	*1 2 64*	*10*	*1*
(US) Reprise	1 4 64	5	1
More Trini Lopez at P.J.'s			
(US) Reprise	1 4 64	11	–
Latin Album			
(US) Reprise	10 24 64	18	–
Folk Album			
(US) Reprise	3 27 65	18	–
Trini Lopez in London			
(UK) Reprise	*3 30 67*	*6*	*3*
LOVIN' SPOONFUL			
Daydream			
(UK) Pye	*5 12 66*	*8*	*2*
(US) Kama Sutra	5 14 66	10	1
Hums of the Lovin' Spoonful			
(US) Kama Sutra	2 11 67	14	–
Best of the Lovin' Spoonful			
(US) Kama Sutra	4 8 67	3	9
MAHAVISHNU ORCHESTRA			
Birds of Fire			

LABEL	DATE OF ENTRY TO TOP 20	HIGHEST POSITION REACHED	NUMBER OF WEEKS IN TOP 10
(*UK*) *CBS*	*3 31 73*	*20*	–
(US) Columbia	3 31 73	15	–
[see also: **JOHN MCLAUGHLIN**]			
MALO			
Malo			
(US) Warner Brothers	4 22 72	14	–
MAMAS AND PAPAS			
If You Can Believe Your Eyes and Ears			
(US) Dunhill	4 30 66	1	20
The Mamas and Papas			
(*UK*) *RCA*	*6 23 66*	*3*	*11*
(US) Dunhill	10 15 66	4	13
The Mamas and Papas Deliver			
(US) Dunhill	3 25 67	2	15
(*UK*) *RCA*	*6 29 67*	*4*	*9*
Farewell to the First Golden Era			
(US) Dunhill	12 2 67	5	11
Papas and Mamas			
(US) Dunhill	7 6 68	15	–
Hits of Gold			
(*UK*) *Stateside*	*4 23 69*	*7*	*1*
MANCINI, HENRY			
Charade			
(US) RCA	2 15 64	6	8
Pink Panther			
(US) RCA	5 2 64	8	2
Concert Sound of Henry Mancini			
(US) RCA	9 5 64	15	–
Dear Heart and Other Songs About Love			
(US) RCA	3 13 65	11	–
Warm Shade of Ivory			
(US) RCA	6 21 69	5	6
MANN, HERBIE			
Memphis Underground			
(US) Atlantic	7 19 69	20	–
MANN, MANFRED			
The Five Faces of Manfred Mann			
(*UK*) *HMV*	*9 17 64*	*3*	*13*
Mann Made			
(*UK*) *HMV*	*10 21 65*	*7*	*7*
Mann Made Hits			
(*UK*) *HMV*	*9 22 66*	*11*	–
MANN, ROBERTO			
Great Waltzes			
(*UK*) *Deram*	*12 27 67*	*19*	–
MANTOVANI			
Mantovani Magic			
(*UK*) *Decca*	*4 14 66*	*3*	*7*

LABEL	DATE OF ENTRY TO TOP 20	HIGHEST POSITION REACHED	NUMBER OF WEEKS IN TOP 10
Mantovani's Golden Hits			
(UK) Decca	2 9 67	10	1
World of Mantovani			
(UK) Decca†	3 5 69	6	11
World of Mantovani, Vol. 2			
(UK) Decca†	10 4 69	4	3
Mantovani Today			
(UK) Decca	5 23 70	17	–
MARK AND ANN			
Music for a Royal Wedding			
(UK) BBC	12 8 73	7	1
MARTIN, DEAN			
Everybody Loves Somebody			
(US) Reprise	8 29 64	2	16
Dream with Dean			
(US) Reprise	11 7 64	15	–
The Door Is Still Open to My Heart			
(US) Reprise	12 12 64	9	3
Dean Martin Hits Again			
(US) Reprise	4 3 65	13	–
I'm the One Who Loves You			
(US) Reprise	10 23 65	12	–
Houston			
(US) Reprise	12 11 65	11	–
Welcome to My World			
(US) Reprise	11 25 67	20	–
Gentle on My Mind			
(US) Reprise	2 8 69	14	–
(UK) Reprise	2 19 69	7	3
Best of Dean Martin			
(UK) Capitol	2 19 69	9	1
MARTIN, GEORGE (see **BEATLES**)			
MARTINO, AL			
Living a Lie			
(US) Capitol	3 7 64	13	–
My Cherie			
(US) Capitol	3 12 66	19	–
Spanish Eyes			
(US) Capitol	3 19 66	8	2
MARVIN, HANK			
Hank Marvin			
(UK) Columbia	11 22 69	14	–
[see also: **SHADOWS**]			
MASEKELA, HUGH			
Promise of a Future			
(US) UNI	8 10 68	17	–
MASSED WELSH CHOIRS			
Cymansa Gann			
(UK) BBC Ent.	8 9 69	5	3

MATHIS, JOHNNY
Tender Is the Night
  (US) Mercury · 3 7 64 · 13 · –
Shadow of Your Smile
  (US) Mercury · 6 4 66 · 9 · 2

MAURIAT, PAUL
Blooming Hits
  (US) Philips · 2 17 68 · 1 · 14

MAXWELL, ROBERT, HIS HARP AND HIS ORCHESTRA
Shangri-La
  (US) Decca · 6 6 64 · 17 · –

MAYFIELD, CURTIS
Curtis
  (US) Curtom · 11 28 70 · 19 · –
Back to the World
  (US) Curtom · 7 21 73 · 16 · –
Superfly
  (US) Curtom · 9 23 72 · 1 · 11
[see also: **IMPRESSIONS**]

MAYALL, JOHN
Blues Breakers (with **ERIC CLAPTON**)
  (UK) Decca · 8 11 66 · 6 · 7
A Hard Road (with the **BLUES BREAKERS**)
  (UK) Decca · 3 16 67 · 10 · 1
Crusade
  (UK) Decca · 9 27 67 · 9 · 1
Bare Wires (with the **BLUES BREAKERS**)
  (UK) Decca · 7 17 68 · 3 · 7
Looking Back
  (UK) Decca · 8 23 69 · 14 · –
The Turning Point
  (UK) Polydor · 11 15 69 · 11 · –
Empty Rooms
  (UK) Polydor · 4 11 70 · 9 · 1

MCCARTNEY, PAUL
Paul McCartney
  (UK) Apple · 5 1 70 · 2 · 18
  (US) Apple · 5 9 70 · 1 · 13
Ram (and **LINDA MCCARTNEY**)
  (UK) Apple · 6 5 71 · 1 · 18
  (US) Apple · 6 5 71 · 2 · 24
Red Rose Speedway (and **WINGS**)
  (UK) Apple · 5 19 73 · 5 · 6
  (US) Apple · 5 26 73 · 1 · 9
Band on the Run (and **WINGS**)
  (UK) Apple · 12 22 73 · 1 · 45
[see also: **BEATLES**; **WINGS**; sound track: *Live and Let Die*]

LABEL	DATE OF ENTRY TO TOP 20	HIGHEST POSITION REACHED	NUMBER OF WEEKS IN TOP 10
MCGUINNESS FLINT			
McGuinness Flint			
(UK) Capitol	*1 30 71*	9	*1**
MCKUEN, ROD			
Home to the Sea (with **ANITA KERR** and the **SAN SEBASTIAN STRINGS)**			
(US) Warner Brothers	2 15 69	20	–
MCLAUGHLIN, JOHN			
Love, Devotion and Surrender (with **CARLOS SANTANA)**			
(US) Columbia	7 28 73	14	–
(UK) CBS	*7 28 73*	*7*	*2*
[see also: **MAHAVISHNU ORCHESTRA**]			
MCLEAN, DON			
American Pie			
(US) United Artists	12 18 71	1	17
(UK) United Artists	*3 11 72*	*2*	*16*
Tapestry			
(UK) United Artists	*6 25 72*	*16*	*–*
MELANIE			
Candles in the Rain			
(US) Buddah	6 20 70	17	–
(UK) Buddah	*10 3 70*	*5*	*10*
Good Book			
(UK) Buddah	*5 29 71*	*9*	*1*
Gather Me			
(US) Buddah	12 25 71	15	–
(UK) Buddah	*1 22 72*	*14*	*–*
Garden in the City			
(UK) Buddah	*4 8 72*	*19*	*–*
MENDES, SERGIO, AND BRASIL '66			
Sergio Mendes and Brasil '66			
(US) A&M	10 29 66	7	3
Look Around			
(US) A&M	4 13 68	5	9
Fool on the Hill			
(US) A&M	12 21 68	3	5
MERSEYBEATS			
The Merseybeats			
(UK) Fontana	*6 18 64*	*12*	*–*
MICHAELS, LEE			
5th			
(US) A&M	9 25 71	16	–
MIDLER, BETTE			
The Divine Miss M			
(US) Atlantic	2 10 73	9	2
Bette Midler			
(US) Atlantic	12 29 73	16	–

LABEL	DATE OF ENTRY TO TOP 20	HIGHEST POSITION REACHED	NUMBER OF WEEKS IN TOP 10
MIDNIGHT STRING QUARTET			
Rhapsodies for Young Lovers			
(US) Viva	3 18 67	17	–
MILLER, GLEN			
Best of Glen Miller			
(*UK*) *RCA International*†	7 9 69	5	4
Glen Miller Memorial, 1944–46			
(*UK*) *RCA*	4 25 70	18	–
MILLER, MRS.			
Mrs. Miller's Greatest Hits			
(US) Capitol	6 18 66	15	–
MILLER, ROGER			
Return of Roger Miller			
(US) Smash	4 3 65	4	7
3rd Time Around			
(US) Smash	8 14 65	13	–
Golden Hits			
(US) Smash	12 25 65	6	10
MILLER, STEVE			
The Joker			
(US) Capitol	11 10 73	2	6
MILLIGAN, SPIKE (see **HARRY SECOMBE; GOONS**)			
MILLS, MRS.			
Come to My Party			
(*UK*) *Parlophone*	12 22 66	17	–
MINELLI, LIZA			
Liza with a "Z"			
(US) Columbia	11 18 72	19	–
(*UK*) *CBS*	4 21 73	9	2
MIRACLES (see **SMOKEY ROBINSON**)			
MITCHELL, GEORGE			
Black & White Minstrel Show			
(*UK*) *HMV*	1 2 64	15	–
Black & White Minstrels on Tour			
(*UK*) *HMV*	1 2 64	6	3
Here Come the Minstrels			
(*UK*) *HMV*	12 1 66	11	–
[see also: **BLACK AND WHITE MINSTRELS**]			
MITCHELL, JONI			
Ladies of the Canyon			
(*UK*) *Reprise*	6 13 70	8	2
Blue			
(US) Reprise	7 17 71	15	–
(*UK*) *Reprise*	7 31 71	3	6
For the Roses			
(US) Asylum	1 13 73	11	–

LABEL	DATE OF ENTRY TO TOP 20	HIGHEST POSITION REACHED	NUMBER OF WEEKS IN TOP 10
MOBY GRAPE			
Wow			
(US) Columbia	6 15 68	20	–
MONKEES			
Monkees			
(US) Colgems	10 22 66	1	32
(UK) RCA	*1 26 67*	*1*	*26*
More of the Monkees			
(US) Colgems	2 11 67	1	25
(UK) RCA	*4 13 67*	*1*	*19*
Headquarters			
(US) Colgems	6 17 67	1	21
(UK) RCA	*7 5 67*	*2*	*12*
Pisces, Aquarius, Capricorn and Jones Ltd.			
(US) Colgems	12 2 67	1	12
(UK) RCA	*1 17 68*	*5*	*8*
The Birds, the Bees and the Monkees			
(US) Colgems	5 18 68	3	9
MONRO, MATT			
I Have Dreamed			
(UK) Parlophone	*8 5 65*	*20*	–
MONTENEGRO, HUGO			
Music from the Good, the Bad and the Ugly, for a Few Dollars More			
(US) RCA	5 4 68	9	6
MONTGOMERY, WES			
A Day in the Life			
(US) A&M	12 16 67	13	–
MONTY PYTHON'S FLYING CIRCUS			
Another Record			
(UK) Charisma	*11 6 71*	*17*	–
MOODY BLUES			
In Search of the Lost Chord			
(UK) Deram	*8 7 68*	*5*	*8*
On the Threshold of a Dream			
(UK) Deram	*4 30 69*	*1*	*11*
(US) Deram	7 26 69	20	–
To Our Children's Children's Children			
(UK) Threshold	*12 6 69*	*2*	*6*
(US) Threshold	1 31 70	14	–
Question of Balance			
(UK) Threshold	*8 15 70*	*1*	*10*
(US) Threshold	9 19 70	3	4
Every Good Boy Deserves Favor			
(UK) Threshold	*8 7 71*	*1*	*9*
(US) Threshold	10 7 72	3	6
Days of Future Passed			
(US) Threshold	10 7 72	3	6

LABEL	DATE OF ENTRY TO TOP 20	HIGHEST POSITION REACHED	NUMBER OF WEEKS IN TOP 10
Seventh Sojourn			
(US) Threshold	11 25 72	1	12
(UK) Threshold	12 2 72	5	3
MOORE, DUDLEY			
The Other Side of Dudley Moore			
(UK) Decca	12 2 65	13	—
Genuine Dud (with the **DUDLEY MOORE TRIO)**			
(UK) Decca	6 16 66	13	—
MORRISON, VAN			
Saint Dominic's Preview			
(US) Warner Brothers	9 9 72	15	—
MOTT THE HOOPLE			
Mott			
(UK) CBS	8 11 73	7	2
MOUNTAIN			
Mountain Climbing			
(US) Windfall	5 2 70	17	—
Nantucket Slayride			
(US) Windfall	2 13 71	16	—
MOUSKOURI, NANA			
Over and Over			
(UK) Fontana	6 4 69	10	1
The Exquisite Nana Mouskouri			
(UK) Fontana	4 4 70	10	1
Turn On the Sun			
(UK) Fontana	5 8 71	16	—
MOVE			
Move			
(UK) Regal Zonophone	4 17 68	15	—
MUNGO JERRY			
Mungo Jerry			
(UK) Dawn	8 15 70	13	—
Electronically Tested			
(UK) Dawn	4 17 71	14	—
NASH, GRAHAM			
Songs for Beginners			
(UK) Atlantic	6 26 71	13	—
(US) Atlantic	7 3 71	15	—
Graham Nash and David Crosby (with **DAVID CROSBY)**			
(US) Atlantic	4 29 72	4	7
(UK) Atlantic	5 20 72	13	—
[see also: **CROSBY, STILLS & NASH; HOLLIES)**			
NAZARETH			
Razamanaz			
(UK) Mooncrest	8 18 73	11	—
Loud 'n' Proud			
(UK) Mooncrest	11 24 73	10	1

LABEL	DATE OF ENTRY TO TOP 20	HIGHEST POSITION REACHED	NUMBER OF WEEKS IN TOP 10
NELSON, RICK			
Rick Nelson Sings for You			
(US) Decca	2 15 64	14	–
NEW CHRISTY MINSTRELS			
Today			
(US) Columbia	5 23 64	9	2
NEW SEEKERS			
We'd Like to Teach the World to Sing			
(UK) Polydor	4 1 72	2	7
NEWTON, WAYNE			
Red Roses for a Blue Lady			
(US) Capitol	6 12 65	17	–
NEW VAUDEVILLE BAND			
Winchester Cathedral			
(US) Fontana	12 24 66	5	7
NICE			
Nice			
(UK) Immediate	9 13 69	3	2
Five Bridges			
(UK) Charisma	7 4 70	2	3
Elegy			
(UK) Charisma	4 17 71	5	2
NILSSON			
Nilsson Schmilsson			
(US) RCA	2 12 72	3	12
(UK) RCA	2 19 72	4	12
Son of Schmilsson			
(US) RCA	8 19 72	12	–
A Little Touch of Schmilsson in the Night			
(UK) RCA	8 11 73	20	–
O'CONNOR, DES			
I Pretend			
(UK) Columbia	1 1 69	8	3
OFARIM, ESTHER AND ABI			
2 in 3			
(UK) Philips	3 6 68	6	5
O'JAYS			
Back Stabbers			
(US) Philadelphia International	10 21 72	10	2
OLDFIELD, MIKE			
Tubular Bells			
(UK) Virgin	7 21 73	1	42
OLIVER			
Good Morning Starshine			
(US) Crewe	9 27 69	19	–
ORBISON, ROY			
In Dreams			
(UK) London	1 2 64	6	17

LABEL	DATE OF ENTRY TO TOP 20	HIGHEST POSITION REACHED	NUMBER OF WEEKS IN TOP 10
Exciting Sounds of Roy Orbison			
(UK) Ember	7 23 64	17	–
More of Roy Orbison's Greatest Hits			
(US) Monument	10 24 64	19	–
Oh Pretty Woman			
(UK) London	12 3 64	5	10
There Is Only One Roy Orbison			
(UK) London	9 23 65	10	1
The Orbison Way			
(UK) London	2 24 66	11	–
The Classic Roy Orbison			
(UK) London	9 29 66	12	–
OSIBISA			
Osibisa			
(UK) MCA	6 12 71	11	–
Woyoya			
(UK) MCA	2 12 72	11	–
OSMOND, DONNY			
Donny Osmond			
(US) MGM	8 28 71	13	–
To You with Love			
(US) MGM	11 20 71	12	–
Portrait of Donny			
(US) MGM	6 17 72	6	4
(UK) MGM	9 30 72	5	11
Too Young			
(US) MGM	8 19 72	11	–
(UK) MGM	12 16 72	7	9
Alone Together			
(UK) MGM	5 26 73	6	4
A Time for Us			
(UK) MGM	12 15 73	5	4
[see also: **OSMONDS**]			
OSMOND, LITTLE JIMMY			
Killer Joe			
(UK) MGM	3 24 73	20	–
OSMONDS			
Osmonds			
(US) MGM	2 20 71	14	–
Phase III			
(US) MGM	2 12 72	10	1
Live			
(US) MGM	7 15 72	13	–
(UK) MGM	1 6 73	13	–
Crazy Horses			
(US) MGM	12 2 72	15	–
(UK) MGM	12 16 72	9	4
The Plan			
(UK) MGM	8 25 73	6	5

LABEL	DATE OF ENTRY TO TOP 20	HIGHEST POSITION REACHED	NUMBER OF WEEKS IN TOP 10
O'SULLIVAN, GILBERT			
Gilbert O'Sullivan Himself			
(*UK*) *MAM*	*1 15 72*	*5*	*8*
(US) MAM	8 26 72	9	4
Back to Front			
(*UK*) *MAM*	*11 18 72*	*1*	*22*
I'm a Writer Not a Fighter			
(*UK*) *MAM*	*10 13 73*	*2*	*15*
PARTRIDGE FAMILY			
Partridge Family			
(US) Bell	11 7 70	4	8
Up to Date			
(US) Bell	4 10 71	3	12
Sound Magazine			
(US) Bell	9 4 71	9	3
(*UK*) *Bell*	*4 29 72*	*14*	–
Shopping Bag			
(US) Bell	4 22 72	18	–
PAUL, BILLY			
360 Degrees of Billy Paul			
(US) Philadelphia International	1 20 73	17	–
PAXTON, TOM			
The Compleat Tom Paxton			
(*UK*) *Elektra*	*4 10 71*	*18*	–
PEDDLERS			
Birthday			
(*UK*) *CBS*	*2 14 70*	*16*	–
PENTANGLE			
Basket of Light			
(*UK*) *Transatlantic*	*11 1 69*	*5*	*4*
PETER AND GORDON			
Peter and Gordon			
(*UK*) *Columbia*	*6 18 64*	*18*	–
PETER, PAUL AND MARY			
Peter, Paul and Mary			
(*UK*) *Warner Brothers*	*1 2 64*	*18*	–
(US) Warner Brothers	1 4 64	4	10
In the Wind			
(US) Warner Brothers	1 4 64	4	10
(*UK*) *Warner Brothers*	*3 19 64*	*11*	–
Moving			
(US) Warner Brothers	1 4 64	7	5
In Concert			
(US) Warner Brothers	8 29 64	4	8
(*UK*) *Warner Brothers*	*2 11 65*	*20*	–
A Song Will Rise			
(US) Warner Brothers	4 31 65	8	5
See What Tomorrow Brings			
(US) Warner Brothers	12 4 65	11	–

LABEL	DATE OF ENTRY TO TOP 20	HIGHEST POSITION REACHED	NUMBER OF WEEKS IN TOP 10
Album 1700			
(US) Warner Brothers	9 23 67	15	–
Late Again			
(US) Warner Brothers	11 9 68	14	–
Peter, Paul and Mommy			
(US) Warner Brothers	6 28 69	12	–
Ten Years Together			
(US) Warner Brothers	6 27 70	15	–
PETERS AND LEE			
We Can Make It			
(UK) Philips	*6 30 73*	*1*	*15*
PINK FLOYD			
Piper at the Gates of Dawn			
(UK) Columbia	*8 16 67*	*6*	*7*
Saucerful of Secrets			
(US) Columbia	7 17 68	9	1
More			
(UK) Columbia	*6 25 69*	*9*	*2*
Ummagumma			
(UK) Harvest (DLP)	*11 15 69*	*5*	*2*
Atom Heart Mother			
(UK) Harvest	*10 24 70*	*1*	*5*
Meddle			
(UK) Harvest	*6 18 72*	*2*	*2*
Obscured by Clouds			
(UK) Harvest	*6 18 72*	*6*	*4*
Dark Side of the Moon			
(UK) Harvest	*3 31 73*	*2*	*32*
(US) Harvest	4 7 73	1	27
PINKY AND PERKY			
Christmas with Pinky and Perky			
(UK) MFP†	*1 3 70*	*15*	–
PITNEY, GENE			
Blue Gene			
(UK) United Artists	*4 9 64*	*7*	*6*
Gene Pitney's Big 16			
(UK) Stateside	*2 4 65*	*12*	–
I'm Gonna Be Strong			
(UK) Stateside	*3 18 65*	*15*	–
Looking thru the Eyes of Love			
(UK) Stateside	*11 18 65*	*15*	–
Nobody Needs Your Love			
(UK) Stateside	*9 15 66*	*13*	–
Best of Gene Pitney			
(UK) Stateside	*9 20 69*	*8*	*1*
PLASTIC ONO BAND			
Live Peace in Toronto			
(US) Apple	1 24 70	10	2

LABEL	DATE OF ENTRY TO TOP 20	HIGHEST POSITION REACHED	NUMBER OF WEEKS IN TOP 10
POINTER SISTERS			
Pointer Sisters			
(US) Blue Thumb	9 29 73	13	–
PRESLEY, ELVIS			
Elvis' Golden Records, Vol. 3			
(US) RCA	1 4 64	4	1
(*UK*) *RCA*	4 9 64	6	8
Fun in Acapulco			
(US) RCA	1 4 64	3	7
(*UK*) *RCA*	1 9 64	9	5
Kissin' Cousins			
(US) RCA	4 25 64	6	5
(*UK*) *RCA*	7 2 64	5	16
Elvis' Golden Hits, Vol. 1			
(*UK*) *RCA*	5 7 64	16	–
Roustabout			
(US) RCA	11 28 64	1	12
(*UK*) *RCA*	1 7 65	12	–
Girl Happy			
(*UK*) *RCA*	4 29 65	7	8
(US) RCA	5 15 65	8	6
Flaming Star and Summer Kisses			
(*UK*) *RCA*	9 23 65	16	–
Elvis for Everyone			
(US) RCA	10 9 65	10	1
(*UK*) *RCA*	12 2 65	8	3
Harem Scarum			
(US) RCA	12 4 65	8	4
(*UK*) *RCA* (*as Harem Holiday*)	1 13 66	11	–
Frankie and Johnny			
(*UK*) *RCA*	5 15 66	11	–
(US) RCA	5 28 66	20	–
Paradise Hawaiian Style			
(*UK*) *RCA*	8 4 66	7	2
(US) RCA	8 27 66	15	–
California Holiday			
(*UK*) *RCA*	12 1 66	17	–
Spinout			
(US) RCA	12 17 66	18	–
How Great Thou Art			
(*UK*) *RCA*	4 20 67	11	–
(US) RCA	5 13 67	18	–
Elvis			
(US) RCA	2 1 69	8	3
(*UK*) *RCA*	4 30 69	2	6
From Elvis in Memphis			
(US) RCA	6 21 69	13	–
(*UK*) *RCA*	8 23 69	1	5

LABEL	DATE OF ENTRY TO TOP 20	HIGHEST POSITION REACHED	NUMBER OF WEEKS IN TOP 10
Flaming Star			
(*UK*) *RCA International*†	7 2 69	*2*	*10*
From Memphis to Vegas/From Vegas to Memphis			
(US) RCA ⎱ (DLP)	12 6 69	12	–
(*UK*) *RCA* ⎰	*3 14 70*	*3*	*4*
Elvis-NBC TV Special			
(*UK*) *RCA* (*DLP*)	*2 21 70*	*18*	–
On Stage			
(US) RCA	7 4 70	13	–
(*UK*) *RCA*	*8 1 70*	*2*	*8*
That's the Way It is			
(*UK*) *RCA*	*1 30 71*	*12*	–
Elvis Country			
(US) RCA	2 6 71	12	–
I'm 10,000 Years Old			
(*UK*) *RCA*	*4 10 71*	*6*	*3*
Love Letters from Elvis			
(*UK*) *RCA*	*7 24 71*	*7*	*2*
Elvis Now			
(*UK*) *RCA*	*5 27 72*	*12*	
Elvis at Madison Square Garden			
(*UK*) *RCA* ⎱ (DLP)	*7 15 72*	*3*	*3*
(US) RCA ⎰	7 29 72	11	–
Aloha from Hawaii via Satellite			
(*UK*) *RCA*	*2 24 73*	*11*	–
(US) RCA	3 17 73	1	7
Elvis			
(*UK*) *RCA*	*9 15 73*	*16*	–
PRETTY THINGS			
Pretty Things			
(*UK*) *Fontana*	*3 25 65*	*6*	*5*
PROBY, P. J.			
I'm P. J. Proby			
(*UK*) *Liberty*	*2 25 65*	*16*	–
PROCOL HARUM			
Procol Harum in Concert with the Edmonton Symphony Orchestra			
(US) A&M	6 3 72	5	5
PUCKETT, GARY, AND THE UNION GAP			
Incredible			
(US) Columbia	1 4 69	20	–
RARE EARTH			
Get Ready			
(US) Rare Earth	4 18 70	12	–
Ecology			
(US) Rare Earth	7 25 70	15	–
RAWLS, LOU			
Live			
(US) Capitol	6 18 66	4	6

LABEL	DATE OF ENTRY TO TOP 20	HIGHEST POSITION REACHED	NUMBER OF WEEKS IN TOP 10
Soulin'			
(US) Capitol	10 15 66	7	6
Carryin' On			
(US) Capitol	4 1 67	20	—
Too Much			
(US) Capitol	6 17 67	18	—
REDDING, OTIS			
Otis Blue			
(UK) *Atlantic*	*2 17 66*	*6*	*14*
King and Queen (with **CARLA THOMAS)**			
(UK) *Stax*	*10 18 67*	*18*	—
History of Otis Redding			
(US) Volt	2 17 **68**	9	3
(UK) *Volt*	*2 28 68*	*2*	*16*
Dock of the Bay			
(US) Volt	3 30 68	4	7
(UK) *Stax*	*6 5 68*	*1*	*7*
Otis Redding in Europe			
(UK) *Stax*	*4 3 68*	*14*	—
Immortal Otis Redding			
(UK) *Atlantic*	*10 30 68*	*19*	—
[see also: **JIMI HENDRIX**]			
REDDY, HELEN			
I Am Woman			
(US) Capitol	1 27 73	14	—
Long Hard Climb			
(US) Capitol	9 1 73	8	4
REED, LOU			
Transformer			
(UK) *RCA*	*5 19 73*	*13*	—
Berlin			
(UK) *RCA*	*10 27 73*	*7*	*1*
REED, NEIL			
Neil Reed			
(UK) *Decca*	*2 5 72*	*1*	*10*
REEVES, JIM			
God 'n' Country			
(UK) *RCA Camden†*	*3 26 64*	*10*	*1*
Gentleman Jim			
(UK) *RCA*	*5 7 64*	*3*	*14*
A Touch of Velvet			
(UK) *RCA*	*8 13 64*	*8*	*3*
International Jim			
(UK) *RCA*	*8 13 64*	*11*	—
He'll Have to Go			
(UK) *RCA*	*8 20 64*	*16*	—
God Be with You			
(UK) *RCA*	*8 27 64*	*10*	*1*

LABEL	DATE OF ENTRY TO TOP 20	HIGHEST POSITION REACHED	NUMBER OF WEEKS IN TOP 10
The Intimate Jim Reeves			
(*UK*) *RCA*	8 27 64	*12*	–
Moonlight and Roses			
(*UK*) *RCA*	9 3 64	*2*	*16*
The Country Side of Jim Reeves			
(*UK*) *RCA Camden†*	9 17 64	*12*	–
We Thank Thee			
(*UK*) *RCA*	9 24 64	*17*	–
Best of Jim Reeves			
(US) RCA	10 10 64	*9*	*3*
(*UK*) *RCA*	1 28 65	*3*	*16*
12 Songs of Christmas			
(*UK*) *RCA*	11 20 64	*4*	*5*
Have I Told You Lately That I Love You			
(*UK*) *RCA Camden†*	4 8 65	*14*	–
The Jim Reeves Way			
(*UK*) *RCA*	5 20 65	*16*	–
Distant Drums			
(*UK*) *RCA*	11 3 66	*2*	*13*
Touch of Sadness			
(*UK*) *RCA*	2 26 69	*15*	–
According to My Heart			
(*UK*) *RCA International†*	7 2 69	*1*	*13*
On Stage			
(*UK*) *RCA*	11 29 69	*13*	–
Songs of Christmas			
(*UK*) *RCA*	12 27 69	*15*	–
REVERE, PAUL, AND THE RAIDERS			
Just Like Us			
(US) Columbia	3 19 66	*5*	*4*
Midnight Ride			
(US) Columbia	7 2 66	*9*	*4*
Spirit of '67			
(US) Columbia	1 28 67	*15*	–
Greatest Hits			
(US) Columbia	6 3 67	*9*	*2*
Indian Reservation			
(US) Columbia	7 31 71	*19*	–
RICH, CHARLIE			
Behind Closed Doors			
(US) Epic	12 22 73	*13*	–
RICHARD, CLIFF (and the **SHADOWS**)			
Wonderful Life			
(*UK*) *Columbia*	7 9 64	*2*	*19*
Aladdin			
(*UK*) *Columbia*	1 7 65	*13*	–
Cliff Richard			
(*UK*) *Columbia*	4 15 65	*11*	–

LABEL	DATE OF ENTRY TO TOP 20	HIGHEST POSITION REACHED	NUMBER OF WEEKS IN TOP 10
More Hits by Cliff			
(UK) Columbia	*8 12 65*	*20*	–
Love Is Forever			
(UK) Columbia	*1 6 66*	*19*	–
Kinda Latin			
(UK) Columbia	*5 26 66*	*9*	*1*
Finders Keepers			
(UK) Columbia	*1 5 67*	*6*	*5*
Best of Cliff			
(UK) Columbia	*7 16 69*	*5*	*2*
RIGHTEOUS BROTHERS			
You've Lost That Lovin' Feeling			
(US) Philles	2 6 65	4	10
Right Now			
(US) Moonglow	2 13 65	11	–
Some Blue-Eyed Soul			
(US) Moonglow	2 20 65	14	–
Just Once in My Life			
(US) Philles	7 31 65	9	3
Back to Back			
(US) Philles	2 19 66	16	–
Soul and Inspiration			
(US) Verve	5 7 66	7	5
RILEY, JEANNIE C.			
Harper Valley PTA			
(US) Plantation	11 9 68	12	–
RIOS, WALDO DE LOS			
Symphonies for the Seventies			
(US) A&M	5 1 71	6	9
RIVERS, JOHNNY			
Johnny Rivers at the Whiskey a Go Go			
(US) Imperial	7 18 64	12	–
Unwind			
(US) Imperial	7 22 67	14	–
Realization			
(US) Imperial	8 3 68	5	9
ROBINSON, SMOKEY, AND THE MIRACLES			
Going to a Go Go			
(US) Tamla	1 15 66	8	4
Greatest Hits			
(US) Tamla	3 16 68	7	2
ROCKIN' BERRIES			
In Town			
(UK) Pye	*6 17 65*	*15*	–
ROLLING STONES			
Rolling Stones			
(UK) Decca	*4 23 64*	*1*	*41*
(US) London	8 1 64	11	–

LABEL	DATE OF ENTRY TO TOP 20	HIGHEST POSITION REACHED	NUMBER OF WEEKS IN TOP 10
12×5			
(US) London	11 28 64	3	8
Rolling Stones, Vol. 2			
(UK) Decca	*1 21 65*	*1*	*23*
Rolling Stones Now			
(US) London	4 10 65	5	9
Out of Our Heads			
(US) London	8 14 65	1	16
(UK) Decca	*9 30 65*	*2*	*16*
December's Children			
(US) London	12 18 65	4	8
Aftermath			
(UK) Decca	*4 21 66*	*1*	*22*
(US) London	7 16 66	2	11
Big Hits (High Tides and Green Grass)			
(US) London	4 30 66	3	9
(UK) Decca	*11 10 66*	*4*	*10*
Got Life If You Want It			
(US) London	1 7 67	6	5
Between the Buttons			
(UK) Decca	*1 26 67*	*3*	*12*
(US) London	3 4 67	2	10
Flowers			
(US) London	7 29 67	3	10
Their Satanic Majesties Request			
(UK) Decca	*12 27 67*	*3*	*5*
(US) London	12 30 67	2	10
Beggar's Banquet			
(UK) Decca	*12 18 68*	*3*	*8*
(US) London	1 4 69	5	4
Through the Past Darkly			
(US) London	9 20 69	2	9
(UK) Decca	*9 27 69*	*2*	*12*
Let It Bleed			
(UK) Decca	*12 20 69*	*1*	*9*
(US) London	12 20 69	3	10
Get Yer Ya Ya's Out			
(UK) Decca	*9 19 70*	*1*	*7*
(US) London	10 17 70	6	7
Stone Age			
(UK) Decca	*4 3 71*	*4*	*2*****
Sticky Fingers			
(UK) Rolling Stones	*5 8 71*	*1*	*18*
(US) Rolling Stones	5 15 71	1	15
Gimme Shelter			
(UK) Decca	*9 25 71*	*12*	—
Hot Rocks			
(US) London (DLP)	1 22 72	4	7
Milestones			
(UK) Decca	*3 11 72*	*14*	—

	LABEL	DATE OF ENTRY TO TOP 20	HIGHEST POSITION REACHED	NUMBER OF WEEKS IN TOP 10

Exile on Main Street
- (US) Rolling Stones } (DLP) — 6 10 72 — 1 — 11
- *(UK) Rolling Stones* } (DLP) — *6 11 72* — *1* — *5*

More Hot Rocks (Big Hits and Fazed Cookies)
- (US) London — 1 27 73 — 9 — 5

Goat's Head Soup
- *(UK) Rolling Stones* — *9 22 73* — *1* — *6*
- (US) Rolling Stones — 10 6 73 — 1 — 11

ROSS, DIANA
Diana Ross
- (US) Motown — 9 19 70 — 19 — –
- *(UK) Tamla Motown* — *10 24 70* — *14* — –

Everything Is Everything
- *(UK) Tamla Motown* — *9 25 71* — *17* — –

I'm Still Waiting
- *(UK) Tamla Motown* — *10 9 71* — *9* — *3*

Lady Sings the Blues (sound track)
- (US) Motown — 12 23 72 — 1 — 13

Touch Me in the Morning
- (US) Motown — 8 4 73 — 5 — 6
- *(UK) Tamla Motown* — *9 1 73* — *7* — *2*

[see also: **SUPREMES**]

ROSS, DIANA, AND THE SUPREMES
Greatest Hits
- (US) Motown — 10 7 67 — 1 — 24
- *(UK) Tamala Motown* — *1 24 68* — *1* — *24*

Live at the Talk of the Town
- *(UK) Tamla Motown* — *4 3 68* — *6* — *6*

Reflections
- (US) Motown — 6 1 68 — 18 — –

Diana Ross and the Supremes Join the Temptations (with the TEMPTATIONS)
- (US) Motown — 12 28 68 — 2 — 8
- *(UK) Tamla Motown* — *2 5 69* — *1* — *11*

Love Child
- (US) Motown — 12 28 68 — 14 — –
- *(UK) Tamla Motown* — *2 19 69* — *13* — –

TCB (with the TEMPTATIONS)
- (US) Motown — 1 11 69 — 1 — 11
- *(UK) Tamla Motown* — *7 2 69* — *11* — –

ROXY MUSIC
Roxy Music
- *(UK) Island* — *9 2 72* — *10* — *1*

For Your Pleasure
- *(UK) Island* — *4 7 73* — *4* — *6*

Stranded
- *(UK) Island* — *12 1 73* — *1* — *7*

LABEL	DATE OF ENTRY TO TOP 20	HIGHEST POSITION REACHED	NUMBER OF WEEKS IN TOP 10
RUDY, ART; AND RADIO PULSE-BEAT NEWS			
Beatles' American Tour			
(US) News Documentary	7 25 64	20	—
RUSSELL, LEON			
Leon Russell/Shelter People			
(US) Shelter	7 3 71	17	—
Carney			
(US) Shelter	8 12 72	2	10
Leon Live			
(US) Shelter	7 21 73	9	4
[see also: various artists; **CONCERT FOR BANGLADESH; JOE COCKER**]			
SADLER BARRY			
Ballad of the Green Berets			
(US) RCA	3 12 66	1	10
SANDPIPERS			
Guantanamera			
(US) A&M	12 3 66	13	—
SANTANA			
Santana			
(US) Columbia	10 11 69	4	28
Abraxas			
(US) Columbia	10 10 70	1	30
(UK) CBS	*12 5 70*	*7*	*1*
Santana 3			
(US) Columbia	10 16 71	1	11
(UK) CBS	*11 13 71*	*5*	*2*
Caravanserai			
(US) Columbia	11 18 72	8	6
(UK) CBS	*11 25 72*	*6*	*1*
Welcome			
(UK) CBS	*12 15 73*	*8*	*1*
SANTANA, CARLOS; and MILES, BUDDY			
Live			
(US) Columbia	7 29 72	8	8
[see also: **JOHN MCLAUGHLIN; SANTANA**]			
SARSTEDT, PETER			
Peter Sarstedt			
(UK) United Artists	*3 12 69*	*8*	*1*
SEALS AND CROFT			
Summer Breeze			
(US) Warner Brothers	11 4 72	7	5
Diamond Girl			
(US) Warner Brothers	5 19 73	4	12
SEARCHERS			
Sugar and Spice			
(UK) Pye	*1 2 64*	*8*	*2*
Meet the Searchers			
(UK) Pye	*1 9 64*	*5*	*16*

	DATE OF ENTRY TO TOP 20	HIGHEST POSITION REACHED	NUMBER OF WEEKS IN TOP 10
It's the Searchers			
(*UK*) *Pye*	*5 28 64*	*4*	*11*
Sounds Like the Searchers			
(*UK*) *Pye*	*3 25 65*	*8*	*1*
SEBASTIAN, JOHN			
John B. Sebastian			
(*US*) *Reprise*	*4 25 70*	20	–
SECOMBE, HARRY			
How to Win an Election (with **PETER SELLERS** and **SPIKE MILLIGAN**)			
(*UK*) *Philips*	*4 16 64*	20	–
Secombe's Personal Choice			
(*UK*) *Philips*	*5 4 67*	*6*	*5*
[see also: **GOONS**]			
SEDAKA, NEIL			
The Tra-La Days Are Over			
(*UK*) *MGM*	*9 15 73*	*13*	–
SEEKERS			
A World of Our Own			
(*UK*) *Columbia*	*7 1 65*	*5*	*8*
Seekers			
(*UK*) *Decca*	*7 1 65*	*16*	–
Come the Day			
(*UK*) *Columbia*	*11 24 66*	*3*	*23*
Georgy Girl			
(*US*) *Capitol*	*4 1 67*	*10*	*2*
Seekers Seen in Green			
(*UK*) *Columbia*	*12 6 67*	*15*	–
Live at the Talk of the Town			
(*UK*) *Columbia*	*9 18 68*	*2*	*17*
Best of the Seekers			
(*UK*) *Columbia*	*11 20 68*	*1*	*40*
Four and Only			
(*UK*) *MFP‡*	*5 3 69*	*1*	*3*
SELLERS, PETER (see **HARRY SECOMBE; GOONS**)			
SERENDIPITY SINGERS			
Serendipity Singers			
(*US*) *Philips*	*4 25 64*	11	–
SHADOWS			
Greatest Hits			
(*UK*) *Columbia*	*1 2 64*	*5*	*15*
Dance with the Shadows			
(*UK*) *Columbia*	*5 7 64*	*2*	*15*
Sound of the Shadows			
(*UK*) *Columbia*	*7 15 65*	*4*	*11*
Shadow Music			
(*UK*) *Columbia*	*5 26 66*	*5*	*8*
Jigsaw			
(*UK*) *Columbia*	*7 19 67*	*8*	*4*
[see also: **CLIFF RICHARD**]			

LABEL	DATE OF ENTRY TO TOP 20	HIGHEST POSITION REACHED	NUMBER OF WEEKS IN TOP 10
'Nuff Said			
(*UK*) *RCA*	2 12 69	11	–
SINATRA, FRANK			
Sinatra's Sinatra			
(US) Reprise	1 4 64	19	–
(*UK*) *Reprise*	*1 9 64*	*13*	–
Days of Wine and Roses, Moon River and Other Academy Award Winners			
(US) Reprise	4 25 64	10	2
It Might as Well Be Swing (with **COUNT BASIE**)			
(*UK*) *Reprise*	*9 17 64*	*17*	–
(US) Reprise	9 26 64	13	–
Softly As I Leave You			
(US) Reprise	3 6 65	19	–
(*UK*) *Reprise*	*3 18 65*	*20*	–
Sinatra '65			
(US) Reprise	7 31 65	9	3
September of My Years			
(US) Reprise	10 16 65	5	11
A Man and His Music			
(*UK*) *Reprise*	*1 20 66*	*9*	*6*
(US) Reprise	1 29 66	9	3
Moonlight Sinatra			
(*UK*) *Reprise*	*6 9 66*	*18*	–
Strangers in the Night			
(*UK*) *Reprise*	*6 30 66*	*4*	*8*
(US) Reprise	7 2 66	1	14
Sinatra at the Sands			
(US) Reprise	9 17 66	9	2
(*UK*) *Reprise*	*9 29 66*	*7*	*4*
That's Life			
(US) Reprise	1 21 67	6	9
Francis Albert Sinatra/António Carlos Jobim			
(US) Reprise	5 20 67	19	–
Frank Sinatra's Greatest Hits			
(*UK*) *Reprise*	*10 23 68*	*8*	*1*
Best of Frank Sinatra			
(*UK*) *Capitol*	*1 8 69*	*17*	–
Cycles			
(US) Reprise	1 25 69	18	–
My Way			
(US) Reprise	5 24 69	11	–
(*UK*) *Reprise*	*6 4 69*	*2*	*8*
A Man Alone			
(*UK*) *Reprise*	*10 11 69*	*18*	–
Watertown			
(*UK*) *Reprise*	*5 16 70*	*14*	–
Frank Sinatra's Greatest Hits, Vol. 2			
(*UK*) *Reprise*	*12 19 70*	*6*	*6*

LABEL	DATE OF ENTRY TO TOP 20	HIGHEST POSITION REACHED	NUMBER OF WEEKS IN TOP 10
Frank Sinatra and Company			
(UK) *Reprise*	6 5 71	9	2
Ol' Blue Eyes Is Back			
(US) Reprise	12 8 73	13	–
(UK) *Warner Brothers*	12 8 73	18	–
SINATRA, NANCY			
Boots			
(US) Reprise	3 26 66	5	8
(UK) *Reprise*	4 28 66	12	–
How Does That Grab You			
(UK) *Reprise*	6 16 66	17	–
Nancy and Lee (with **LEE HAZLEWOOD**)			
(US) Reprise	6 8 68	13	–
(UK) *Reprise*	7 3 68	19	–
SINGING NUN			
Singing Nun			
(US) Philips	1 4 64	1	12
SLADE			
Slade Alive			
(UK) *Polydor*	4 8 72	2	25
Slayed?			
(UK) *Polydor*	12 9 72	1	16
Sladest			
(UK) *Polydor*	10 6 73	1	13
SLY AND THE FAMILY STONE			
Stand			
(US) Epic	5 24 69	13	–
Greatest Hits			
(US) Epic	11 14 70	2	15
There's a Riot Goin' On			
(US) Epic	11 20 71	1	10
Fresh			
(US) Epic	7 21 73	7	6
SMALL FACES			
Small Faces			
(UK) *Decca*	5 19 66	3	12
From the Beginning			
(UK) *Decca*	6 29 67	17	–
Small Faces			
(UK) *Immediate*	7 5 67	12	–
Ogden's Nut Gone Flake			
(UK) *Immediate*	6 19 68	1	9
SMITH			
A Group Called Smith			
(US) Dunhill	11 22 69	17	–
SMITH, JIMMY			
Who's Afraid of Virginia Woolf?			
(US) Verve	6 13 64	16	–

LABEL	DATE OF ENTRY TO TOP 20	HIGHEST POSITION REACHED	NUMBER OF WEEKS IN TOP 10
The Cat			
(US) Verve	12 5 64	12	–
Organ Grinder Swing			
(US) Verve	11 13 65	15	–
Got My Mojo Working			
(UK) Verve	*6 16 66*	*19*	–
SMITH, KEELEY			
Lennon-McCartney Songbook			
(UK) Reprise	*1 14 65*	*12*	–
SMITH, O. C.			
Hickory Holler Revisited			
(US) Columbia	12 28 68	19	–
SMITH, STEPHEN, AND HIS FATHER			
Great Songs			
(UK) Decca	*5 13 72*	*17*	–
SMOTHERS BROTHERS			
Curb Your Tongue			
(US) Mercury	1 18 64	13	–
SOFT MACHINE			
Third			
(UK) CBS	*7 4 70*	*18*	–
SONNY AND CHER			
Look at Us			
(US) Atco	9 4 65	2	14
(UK) Atlantic	*10 14 65*	*7*	*6*
The Wondrous World of Sonny and Cher			
(UK) Atlantic	*5 26 66*	*15*	–
All I Ever Need Is You			
(US) Kapp	4 1 72	14	–
[see also: **CHER**]			
SOUNDS ORCHESTRAL			
Cast Your Fate to the Wind			
(UK) Piccadilly	*6 10 65*	*17*	–
(US) Parkway	6 26 65	11	–
SPINNERS (Liverpool)			
Singing City			
(UK) Philips	*11 13 71*	*13*	–
SPINNERS (Detroit)			
Spinners			
(US) Atlantic	5 26 73	14	–
SPRINGFIELD, DUSTY			
A Girl Called Dusty			
(UK) Philips	*4 23 64*	*6*	*10*
Everything Is Coming Up Dusty			
(UK) Philips	*10 21 65*	*6*	*8*
Golden Hits			
(UK) Philips	*10 27 66*	*2*	*10*

LABEL	DATE OF ENTRY TO TOP 20	HIGHEST POSITION REACHED	NUMBER OF WEEKS IN TOP 10
STAPLE SINGERS			
Bealtitude/Respect Yourself			
(US) Stax	5 20 72	19	–
STARR, RINGO			
Sentimental Journey			
(*UK*) *Apple*	*4 25 70*	*7*	*1*
Ringo			
(US) Apple	11 17 73	2	6
(*UK*) *Apple*	*12 8 73*	*7*	*2*
[see also: **BEATLES**; various artists; **CONCERT FOR BANGLADESH**]			
STATUS QUO			
Piledriver			
(*UK*) *Vertigo*	*1 27 73*	*5*	*2*
Hello			
(*UK*) *Vertigo*	*10 6 73*	*1*	*9*
STEELY DAN			
Can't Buy a Thrill			
(US) ABC	3 10 73	17	–
STEPPENWOLF			
Steppenwolf			
(US) Dunhill	8 3 68	6	7
Second			
(US) Dunhill	11 2 68	3	14
Birthday Party			
(US) Dunhill	3 29 69	7	2
Monster			
(US) Dunhill	12 27 69	17	–
Live			
(US) Dunhill	4 25 70	7	5
(*UK*) *Stateside*	*7 18 70*	*15*	*–*
(US) ABC-Dunhill	12 5 70	19	–
STEVENS, CAT			
Matthew and Son			
(*UK*) *Deram*	*4 6 67*	*7*	*4*
Teaser and the Firecat			
(*UK*) *Island*	*10 2 71*	*3*	*20*
(US) A&M	10 16 71	2	17
Tea for the Tillerman			
(*UK*) *Island*	*1 29 72*	*20*	*–*
(US) A&M	3 27 71	8	6
Catch Bull at Four			
(*UK*) *Island*	*10 7 72*	*2*	*10*
(US) A&M	11 4 72	1	12
Foreigner			
(*UK*) *Island*	*7 21 73*	*3*	*6*
(US) A&M	8 11 73	3	6
STEWART, ROD			
Every Picture Tells a Story			

	LABEL	DATE OF ENTRY TO TOP 20	HIGHEST POSITION REACHED	NUMBER OF WEEKS IN TOP 10
	(US) Mercury	7 3 71	1	20
	(*UK*) *Mercury*	*7 24 71*	*1*	*29*
Never a Dull Moment				
	(*UK*) *Mercury*	*8 5 72*	*1*	*18*
	(US) Mercury	8 19 72	2	15
Sing It Again Rod				
	(*UK*) *Mercury*	*8 25 73*	*1*	*9*
[see also: **FACES; JEFF BECK GROUP**]				
STILLS, STEPHEN				
Stephen Stills				
	(US) Atlantic	12 5 70	3	10
Stephen Stills II				
	(US) Atlantic	7 24 71	8	3
	(*UK*) *Atlantic*	*8 21 71*	*14*	–
Manassas				
	(US) Atlantic	5 6 72	4	7
[see also: **CROSBY, STILLS, NASH & YOUNG; AL KOOPER**]				
STRAWBERRY ALARM CLOCK				
Incense and Peppermint				
	(US) UNI	12 9 67	11	–
STRAWBS				
Grave New World				
	(*UK*) *A&M*	*3 4 72*	*11*	–
Bursting at the Seams				
	(*UK*) *A&M*	*3 3 73*	*2*	*5*
STREISAND, BARBRA				
Barbra Streisand Album				
	(US) Columbia	1 4 64	14	–
Second Barbra Streisand Album				
	(US) Columbia	1 4 64	3	7
The Third Album				
	(US) Columbia	3 14 64	5	22
People				
	(US) Columbia	10 10 64	1	21
My Name Is Barbra				
	(US) Columbia	6 5 65	2	17
My Name is Barbra, Two				
	(US) Columbia	11 20 65	2	19
	(*UK*) *Columbia*	*1 20 66*	*6*	*11*
Color Me Barbra				
	(US) Columbia	4 23 66	3	9
Je M'Appelle Barbra				
	(US) Columbia	12 10 66	5	6
Simply Streisand				
	(US) Columbia	12 23 67	12	–
Stoney End				
	(US) Columbia	2 27 71	10	4
Barbra Joan Streisand				
	(US) Columbia	10 2 71	11	–

LABEL	DATE OF ENTRY TO TOP 20	HIGHEST POSITION REACHED	NUMBER OF WEEKS IN TOP 10
Live in Concert at the Forum			
(US) Columbia	12 30 72	19	—
SUPREMES			
Where Did Our Love Go			
(US) Motown	11 21 64	2	19
Meet the Supremes			
(UK) Stateside	*12 3 64*	*13*	—
More Hits by the Supremes			
(US) Motown	10 2 65	6	4
Supremes Live at the Copa			
(US) Motown	12 18 65	11	—
I Hear a Symphony			
(US) Motown	4 2 66	8	6
Supremes à Go Go			
(US) Motown	10 8 66	1	15
(UK) Tamla Motown	*1 5 67*	*15*	—
Supremes Sing Holland-Dozier-Holland			
(US) Motown	3 4 67	6	5
Supremes Sing Motown			
(UK) Tamla Motown	*6 8 67*	*15*	—
Supremes Sing Rodgers and Hart			
(US) Motown	7 22 67	20	—
Magnificent 7 (with the **FOUR TOPS**)			
(UK) Tamla Motown	*6 12 71*	*6*	*3*
[see also: **DIANA ROSS AND THE SUPREMES**]			
SWINGLE SINGERS			
Bach's Greatest Hits			
(US) Philips	1 4 64	15	—
Jazz Sebastian Bach			
(UK) Philips	*1 30 64*	*14*	—
TASTE			
On the Boards			
(UK) Polydor	*2 14 70*	*18*	—
TAYLOR, JAMES			
Sweet Baby James			
(US) Warner Brothers	9 5 70	3	12
(UK) Warner Brothers	*12 12 70*	*7*	*7*
Mudslide Slim and the Blue Horizon			
(US) Warner Brothers	5 15 71	2	20
(UK) Warner Brothers	*5 29 71*	*3*	*18*
One Man Dog			
(US) Warner Brothers	12 16 72	4	6
TEMPTATIONS			
Temptin' Temptations			
(US) Gordy	1 15 66	11	—
Gettin' Ready			
(US) Gordy	9 10 66	12	—

LABEL	DATE OF ENTRY TO TOP 20	HIGHEST POSITION REACHED	NUMBER OF WEEKS IN TOP 10
Greatest Hits			
(US) Gordy	1 21 67	5	11
(UK) Tamla Motown	*2 14 68*	*17*	–
Temptations Live			
(US) Gordy	5 6 67	10	1
(UK) Tamla Motown	*8 9 67*	*20*	–
Temptations with a Lot o' Soul			
(US) Gordy	8 26 67	7	5
(UK) Tamla Motown	*12 13 67*	*19*	–
In a Mellow Mood			
(US) Gordy	2 10 68	13	–
I Wish It Would Rain			
(US) Gordy	8 3 68	13	–
Live at the Copa			
(US) Gordy	2 8 69	15	–
Cloud Nine			
(US) Gordy	3 29 69	4	9
Puzzle People			
(US) Gordy	10 25 69	5	11
(UK) Tamla Motown	*2 21 70*	*20*	–
Psychedelic Shack			
(US) Gordy	4 11 70	9	4
Greatest Hits, Vol. 3			
(US) Gordy	10 24 70	15	–
Sky's the Limit			
(US) Gordy	5 29 71	16	–
All Directions			
(US) Gordy	10 7 72	2	11
(UK) Tamla Motown	*2 3 73*	*19*	–
Masterpiece			
(US) Gordy	3 31 73	7	5
[see also: **DIANA ROSS AND THE SUPREMES**]			
TEN YEARS AFTER			
Stonehenge			
(UK) Deram	*2 19 69*	*6*	*3*
Ssssh			
(UK) Deram	*10 4 69*	*4*	*4*
(US) Deram	10 4 69	20	–
Cricklewood Green			
(UK) Deram	*5 2 70*	*4*	*5*
(US) Deram	5 16 70	14	–
Watt			
(UK) Deram	*1 2 71*	*5*	*2*
A Space in Time			
(US) Columbia	9 18 71	17	–
TEX, JOE			
I Gotcha			
(US) Dial	6 24 72	17	–

LABEL	DATE OF ENTRY TO TOP 20	HIGHEST POSITION REACHED	NUMBER OF WEEKS IN TOP 10
THOMAS, B. J.			
Raindrops Keep Falling on My Head			
(US) Scepter	2 14 70	12	—
THOMAS, CARLA (see **OTIS REDDING**)			
THREE DOG NIGHT			
Three Dog Night			
(US) Dunhill	5 3 69	11	—
Suitable for Framing			
(US) Dunhill	8 2 69	16	—
Three Dog Night Captured Live at the Forum			
(US) Dunhill	12 13 69	6	11
It Ain't Easy			
(US) Dunhill	5 9 70	8	5
Naturally			
(US) Dunhill	12 26 70	16	—
(US) Dunhill (re-entry)	5 29 71	14	—
Golden Biscuits			
(US) Dunhill	3 20 71	5	9
Harmony			
(US) Dunhill	11 6 71	8	4
Seven Separate Fools			
(US) ABC-Dunhill	8 19 72	6	6
Recorded Live in Concert Around the World			
(US) Dunhill (DLP)	5 5 73	18	—
TIJUANA-STYLE TORERO BAND			
Tijuana-Style Torero Band Play Lennon-McCartney			
(UK) MFP†	*1 3 70*	*16*	—
TINY TIM			
God Bless			
(US) Reprise	6 29 68	7	2
TOMLIN, LILY			
This Is a Recording			
(US) Polydor	4 17 71	15	—
TOWER OF POWER			
Tower of Power			
(US) Warner Brothers	8 18 73	15	—
TRAFFIC			
Mr. Fantasy			
(UK) Island	*1 10 68*	*16*	—
Traffic			
(UK) Island	*10 30 68*	*9*	*1*
(US) United Artists	1 11 69	17	—
Last Exit			
(US) United Artists	6 7 69	19	—
John Barleycorn Must Die			
(US) United Artists	8 1 70	5	5
(UK) Island	*8 15 70*	*11*	—
Low Spark of the High-Heeled Boys			
(US) Island	1 15 72	7	2

LABEL	DATE OF ENTRY TO TOP 20	HIGHEST POSITION REACHED	NUMBER OF WEEKS IN TOP 10
Shoot-Out at the Fantasy Factory			
(US) Island	2 24 73	6	6
TREMELOES			
Here Come the Tremeloes			
(*UK*) *CBS*	6 22 67	15	–
T. REX			
T. Rex			
(*UK*) *Fly*	4 3 71	13	–
Electric Warrior			
(*UK*) *Fly*	10 9 71	1	28
Bolan Boogie			
(*UK*) *Fly*	5 20 72	1	9
The Slider			
(*UK*) *EMI*	8 5 72	4	7
(US) Reprise	10 28 72	17	–
Tanx			
(*UK*) *EMI*	3 31 73	4	4
TROGGS			
From Nowhere			
(*UK*) *Fontana*	8 4 66	6	6
Trogglodynamite			
(*UK*) *Page One*	2 23 67	10	2
TURTLES			
Happy Together			
(*UK*) *London*	8 9 67	18	–
Golden Hits			
(US) White Whale	1 6 68	7	6
TYRANNOSAURUS REX			
My People Were Fair			
(*UK*) *Regal Zonophone*	7 24 68	15	–
Unicorn			
(*UK*) *Regal Zonophone*	6 4 69	12	–
Doubleback			
(*UK*) *Fly (DLP)*	4 29 72	1	5
[see also: **T. REX**]			
URIAH HEEP			
Demons and Wizards			
(*UK*) *Island*	6 11 72	20	–
Sweet Freedom			
(*UK*) *Bronze*	10 6 73	18	–
VANILLA FUDGE			
Vanilla Fudge			
(US) Atco	9 30 67	6	11
Beat Goes On			
(US) Atco	3 30 68	17	–
Renaissance			
(US) Atco	9 14 68	20	–

LABEL	DATE OF ENTRY TO TOP 20	HIGHEST POSITION REACHED	NUMBER OF WEEKS IN TOP 10
Near the Beginning			
(US) Atco	3 22 69	16	–
VAUGHN, BILLY			
Pearly Shells			
(US) Dot	4 10 65	18	–
VENTURES			
Walk Don't Run			
(US) Dolton	12 12 64	17	–
Ventures à Go Go			
(US) Dolton	11 20 65	16	–
Hawaii Five-O			
(US) Liberty	6 14 69	11	–
VILLAGE STOMPERS			
Washington Square			
(US) Epic	1 4 64	12	–
VINTON, BOBBY			
There, I've Said It Again			
(US) Epic	2 22 64	8	5
Bobby Vinton's Greatest Hits			
(US) Epic	1 2 65	12	–
Mr. Lonely			
(US) Epic	2 13 65	18	–
WAKEMAN, RICK			
The Six Wives of Henry VIII			
(UK) A&M	2 24 73	7	2
[see also: **YES**]			
WALKER, SCOTT			
Scott			
(UK) Philips	9 20 67	3	8
Scott 2			
(UK) Philips	5 1 68	1	12
Scott 3			
(UK) Philips	4 2 69	3	3
Songs from His TV Series			
(UK) Philips	7 9 69	7	1
[see also: **WALKER BROTHERS**]			
WALKER BROTHERS			
Take It Easy			
(UK) Philips	12 16 65	8	24
Portrait			
(UK) Fontana	9 8 66	3	11
Images			
(UK) Philips	3 23 67	6	6
Walker Brothers Story			
(UK) Philips	9 20 67	10	4
WALSH, JOE			
The Smoker You Drink the Player You Get			
(US) Dunhill	9 8 73	6	6

AMERICAN AND BRITISH TOP TWENTY ALBUMS, 1964–73   447

LABEL	DATE OF ENTRY TO TOP 20	HIGHEST POSITION REACHED	NUMBER OF WEEKS IN TOP 10
Live at Leeds			
(UK) Track	6 6 70	3	5
(US) Decca	6 6 70	4	14
Who's Next			
(US) Decca	8 21 71	4	11
(UK) Track	9 11 71	1	10
Meaty, Beaty, Big and Bouncy			
(US) Decca	11 27 71	11	—
(UK) Track	12 18 71	10	1
Quadrophenia			
(UK) Track } (DLP)	11 17 73	2	5
(US) MCA	11 17 73	2	7
WILLIAMS, ANDY			
Days of Wine and Roses			
(US) Columbia	1 18 64	17	—
Wonderful World of Andy Williams			
(US) Columbia	2 22 64	9	4
Call Me Irresponsible and Other Hit Songs			
(US) Columbia	5 30 64	5	8
Great Songs from My Fair Lady and other Broadway Hits			
(US) Columbia	10 17 64	5	8
Dear Heart			
(US) Columbia	4 24 65	4	15
Almost There			
(UK) CBS	6 24 65	2	24
Can't Get Used to Losing You			
(UK) CBS	8 5 65	16	—
May Each Day			
(UK) CBS	3 17 66	11	—
Shadow of Your Smile			
(US) Columbia	6 11 66	6	4
Born Free			
(US) Columbia	6 3 67	5	12
Love Andy			
(US) Columbia	12 23 67	8	4
(UK) CBS	5 15 68	1	9
Honey			
(UK) CBS	6 10 68	4	2
(US) Columbia	7 13 68	9	5
Happy Heart			
(US) Columbia	5 31 69	9	3
Get Together with Andy Williams			
(UK) CBS	12 27 69	13	—
Andy Williams' Greatest Hits			
(UK) CBS	4 11 70	1	58***
Can't Help Fallin' in Love			
(UK) CBS	6 20 70	7	7***
Andy Williams Show			
(UK) CBS	12 5 70	10	1

LABEL	DATE OF ENTRY TO TOP 20	HIGHEST POSITION REACHED	NUMBER OF WEEKS IN TOP 10
Love Story			
(US) Columbia	3 6 71	3	9
(UK) CBS	8 7 71	8	2
Home-Lovin' Man			
(UK) CBS	4 3 71	1	15**
Love Theme from *The Godfather*			
(UK) CBS	7 29 72	11	–
WILLIAMS, MASON			
Phonograph Record			
(US) Warner Brothers	8 31 68	14	–
WILLIAMS, ROGER			
Born Free			
(US) Kapp	12 24 66	7	4
WILLIAMSON, SONNY BOY			
Down and Out Blues			
(UK) Pye	6 18 64	20	–
WILSON, FLIP			
The Devil Made Me Buy This Dress			
(US) Little David	6 20 70	17	–
WILSON, NANCY			
Yesterday's Love Songs, Today's Blues			
(US) Capitol	2 15 64	4	6
Today, Tomorrow, Forever			
(US) Capitol	6 13 64	10	3
How Glad I Am			
(US) Capitol	9 26 64	4	10
Today—My Way			
(US) Capitol	7 3 65	7	2
Gentle Is My Love			
(US) Capitol	10 30 65	17	–
Touch of Today			
(US) Capitol	7 23 66	15	–
WINGS			
Wild Life			
(UK) Apple	12 18 71	8	2
(US) Apple	1 1 72	10	2
[see also: **PAUL MCCARTNEY**]			
WINTER, EDGAR, GROUP			
They Only Come Out at Night			
(US) Epic	4 14 73	3	9
WINTER, JOHNNY			
Johnny Winter Live			
(UK) CBS	5 22 71	20	–
WISHBONE ASH			
Pilgrimage			
(UK) MCA	10 9 71	11	–

LABEL	DATE OF ENTRY TO TOP 20	HIGHEST POSITION REACHED	NUMBER OF WEEKS IN TOP 10
Argus			
(UK) MCA	5 13 72	3	4
Wishbone Four			
(UK) MCA	5 26 73	12	—
WITHERS, BILL			
Still Bill			
(US) Sussex	7 1 72	4	4
WONDER, STEVIE			
My Cherie Amour			
(UK) Tamla Motown	12 13 69	17	—
Talking Book			
(US) Tamla	12 23 72	3	9
(UK) Tamla Motown	2 10 73	16	—
Innervisions			
(US) Tamla	9 1 73	4	10
(UK) Tamla Motown	9 1 73	10	1
WOOD, ROY			
Boulders			
(UK) Harvest	9 1 73	15	—
[see also: **MOVE**]			
WOODWARD, EDWARD			
Edward Woodward Album			
(UK) Jam	8 19 72	20	—
YARDBIRDS			
Yardbirds			
(UK) Columbia	8 11 66	20	—
YES			
The Yes Album			
(UK) Atlantic	4 3 71	7	5**
Fragile			
(UK) Atlantic	12 4 71	6	2
(US) Atlantic	2 5 72	4	15
Close to the Edge			
(UK) Atlantic	9 23 72	4	4
(US) Atlantic	10 28 72	3	6
Yessongs			
(UK) Atlantic	5 26 73	7	1
(US) Atlantic	6 9 73	12	—
Tales from Topographic Oceans			
(UK) Atlantic (DLP)	10 22 73	1	4
YOUNG, NEIL			
After the Gold Rush			
(US) Reprise	9 26 70	8	9
(UK) Reprise	10 31 70	7	1
Harvest			
(US) Reprise	3 4 72	1	16
(UK) Reprise	3 4 72	1	12

LABEL	DATE OF ENTRY TO TOP 20	HIGHEST POSITION REACHED	NUMBER OF WEEKS IN TOP 10
Time Fades Away			
(*UK*) *Warner Brothers*	*10 27 73*	*20*	–
YOUNG-HOLT UNLIMITED			
Soulful Strut			
(US) Brunswick	2 8 69	9	2
YOUNG RASCALS			
Young Rascals			
(US) Atlantic	6 25 66	15	–
Collections			
(US) Atlantic	4 15 67	14	–
Groovin'			
(US) Atlantic	8 26 67	5	13
Once upon a Dream			
(US) Atlantic	3 9 68	9	3
Time Peace/Greatest Hits			
(US) Atlantic	7 27 68	1	24
Freedom Suite			
(US) Atlantic	4 5 69	17	–
ZAPPA, FRANK			
Hot Rats			
(*UK*) *Reprise*	*3 7 70*	*11*	–

SOUND-TRACK ALBUMS

SOUND-TRACK ALBUMS

	DATE OF ENTRY ON CHARTS	HIGHEST POSITION REACHED	NUMBER OF WEEKS ON CHARTS
American Graffiti			
(US) MCA	11 10 73	17	–
Bonnie and Clyde			
(US) Warner Brothers	4 20 68	12	–
Butch Cassidy and the Sundance Kid			
(US) A & M	1 31 70	16	–
By Bye Birdie			
(US) RCA	1 11 64	11	–
Cabaret			
(UK) Probe	5 19 73	13	–
Camelot			
(US) Warner Brothers	1 13 68	11	–
Chitty Chitty Bang Bang			
(UK) United Artists	2 26 69	10	1
Clockwork Orange			
(UK) Warner Brothers	2 17 73	4	5
Deliverance			
(US) Warner Brothers	2 24 73	1	9
Dr. Zhivago			
(US) MGM	6 4 66	1	71
(UK) MGM	10 13 66	3	14
Easy Rider (see various artists) (see Gerry and the Pacemakers)			
Funny Girl			
(UK) Capitol	5 5 66	11	–
(US) Capitol	11 23 68	12	–
Goldfinger			
(UK) United Artists	10 29 64	14	–
(US) United Artists	2 6 65	1	22

	DATE OF ENTRY ON CHARTS	HIGHEST POSITION REACHED	NUMBER OF WEEKS ON CHARTS
The Good, the Bad and the Ugly			
(US) United Artists	4 6 68	4	10
(UK) United Artists	*10 30 68*	*2*	*12*
The Graduate			
(US) Columbia	3 23 68	1	26
(UK) CBS	*10 30 68*	*3*	*11*
Jungle Book			
(US) Disney	3 16 68	19	–
(UK) Disney	*5 1 68*	*5*	*18*
Lady Sings the Blues			
(see Diana Ross)			
Live and Let Die			
(UK) United Artists	*8 25 73*	*17*	*–*
Love Story			
(US) Paramount	1 30 71	2	13
(UK) Paramount	*7 10 71*	*8*	*3*
A Man and a Woman			
(US)	3 18 67	10	2
Mary Poppins			
(US) Vista	12 12 64	1	48
(UK) HMV	*1 14 65*	*2*	*55*
Midnight Cowboy			
(US) United Artists	10 11 69	19	
My Fair Lady			
(UK) CBS	*10 29 64*	*9*	*7*
(US) Columbia	11 21 64	4	30
Oliver			
(UK) RCA	*2 12 69*	*4*	*25*
(US) Colgems	5 24 69	20	–
Paint Your Wagon			
(UK) Paramount	*2 14 70*	*2*	*25*
Pat Garrett and Billy the Kid			
(US) Columbia	10 20 73	16	–
Presley, Elvis, albums			
(see Log of American and British Top Twenty Albums, 1964–73)			

	DATE OF ENTRY ON CHARTS	HIGHEST POSITION REACHED	NUMBER OF WEEKS ON CHARTS
Romeo and Juliet			
(US) Capitol	5 10 69	2	17
Sound of Music			
(UK) RCA	*4 8 65*	*1*	*232*
(US) RCA	4 17 65	1	109
South Pacific			
(UK) RCA	*1 2 64*	*8*	*9*
Superfly (see Curtis Mayfield)			
Thoroughly Modern Millie			
(US) Decca	5 13 67	16	–
(UK) Brunswick	*11 8 67*	*9*	*1*
To Sir, with Love			
(US) Fontana	12 2 67	16	–
Trouble Man			
(see Marvin Gaye)			
2001—A Space Odyssey			
(UK) MGM	*6 11 69*	*3*	*4*
Unsinkable Molly Brown			
(US) MGM	8 22 64	11	–
Valley of the Dolls			
(US) 20th Century Fox	3 9 68	11	–
West Side Story			
(UK) CBS	*1 2 64*	*2*	*61*
What's New Pussycat?			
(US) United Artists	9 11 65	14	–
Wild Angels			
(US) Tower	1 7 67	17	–
Wild in the Streets			
(US) Tower	10 5 68	12	–
Yellow Submarine			
(see Beatles)			
Your Cheatin' Heart			
(US) MGM	4 10 65	16	–

ORIGINAL-CAST RECORDINGS

ORIGINAL-CAST RECORDINGS

	DATE OF ENTRY ON CHARTS	HIGHEST POSITION REACHED	NUMBER OF WEEKS ON CHARTS
All in the Family (US) Atlantic	12 4 71	8	3
At the Drop of a Hat (*UK*) *Parlophone*	*3 24 64*	*9*	*1*
At the Drop of Another Hat (*UK*) *Parlophone*	*2 20 64*	*12*	–
Camelot (Broadway) (*UK*) *CBS*	*10 1 64*	*11*	–
Camelot (London) (*UK*) *HMV*	*1 14 65*	*19*	–
Dark Shadows (US) Philips	9 13 69	18	–
Fiddler on the Roof (London) (*UK*) *CBS*	*3 30 67*	*4*	*20*
Fiddler on the Roof (New York) (US) RCA	1 2 65	7	3
Funny Girl (US) Capitol	5 9 64	2	22
Godspell (London) (*UK*) *Bell*	*4 22 72*	*11*	–
Hair (London) (*UK*) *Polydor*	*1 8 69*	*3*	*14*
Hair (Broadway) (US) RCA	3 22 69	1	28
(*UK*) *Polydor*	*2 14 70*	*20*	–

	DATE OF ENTRY ON CHARTS	HIGHEST POSITION REACHED	NUMBER OF WEEKS ON CHARTS
Hello Dolly (US) RCA	3 7 64	1	36
My Fair Lady (Broadway) (*UK*) *Philips*	*1 2 64*	*19*	–

VARIOUS ARTISTS
COMPILATIONS

VARIOUS ARTISTS COMPILATIONS

	DATE OF ENTRY ON CHARTS	HIGHEST POSITION REACHED	NUMBER OF WEEKS ON CHARTS
BBC 1922–1972			
(*UK*) *BBC*	*11 18 72*	*16*	–
Beatlemania			
(*UK*) *Topsix*	*2 27 64*	*19*	–
Believe in Music			
(*UK*) *K-Tel*	*4 28 73*	*2*	*4*
The Blues, Vol. 1			
(*UK*) *Pye*	*1 2 64*	*15*	–
The Blues, Vol. 2			
(*UK*) *Pye*	*5 28 64*	*16*	–
Breakthrough			
(*UK*) *Studio 2*	*10 25 67*	*2*	*15*
British Motown Chartbusters			
(*UK*) *Tamla Motown*	*10 25 67*	*2*	*23*
Christmas from Guilford Cathedral			
(*UK*) *MFP†*	*1 3 70*	*17*	–
Collection of Tamla Motown Hits			
(*UK*) *Tamla Motown*	*4 1 65*	*16*	–
Concert for Bangladesh			
(US) Apple } (TLP)	*1 8 72*	*2*	*10*
(*UK*) *Apple*	*1 22 72*	*1*	*5*
Easy Rider			
(US) Dunhill	*11 1 69*	*6*	*6*
(*UK*) *Stateside*	*12 20 69*	*2*	*33*
Folk Festival of the Blues			
(*UK*) *Pye*	*2 20 64*	*16*	–

	DATE OF ENTRY ON CHARTS	HIGHEST POSITION REACHED	NUMBER OF WEEKS ON CHARTS
Forty Fantastic Hits from the '50s and '60s			
(UK) Arcade	4 7 73	2	7
Hit the Road Stax			
(UK) Stax	5 11 67	10	1
Hot Hits			
(UK) MFP†	3 5 69	13	—
Impact			
(UK) EMI	3 5 69	15	—
Jesus Christ Superstar			
(US) Decca	12 5 70	1	41
(UK) MCA	1 8 72	6	3
JFK—The Presidential Years			
(US) 20th Century	1 18 64	11	—
JFK Memorial Album			
(US) Premier	2 1 64	18	—
Living Presence Stereo			
(UK) SFXL	3 5 69	17	—
Motown Chartbusters, Vol. 2			
(UK) Tamla Motown	12 18 68	8	3
Motown Chartbusters, Vol. 3			
(UK) Tamla Motown	10 25 69	1	36
Motown Chartbusters, Vol. 4			
(UK) Tamla Motown	10 24 70	1	5*
Motown Chartbusters, Vol. 5			
(UK) Tamla Motown	4 17 71	1	21
Motown Chartbusters, Vol. 6			
(UK) Tamla Motown	10 23 71	2	13
Motown Chartbusters, Vol. 7			
(UK) Tamla Motown	12 2 72	9	1

	DATE OF ENTRY ON CHARTS	HIGHEST POSITION REACHED	NUMBER OF WEEKS ON CHARTS
Motown Chartbusters, Vol. 8			
(UK) Tamla Motown	11 3 73	9	3
The Music People			
(UK) CBS (DLP)	5 27 72	10	1
Nice Enough to Eat			
(UK) Island‡	1 10 70	10	1
Out Came the Blues			
(UK) Ace of Hearts†	5 14 64	19	—
Pure Gold			
(UK) EMI†	6 2 73	1	5
Ready Steady Go			
(UK) Decca	2 6 64	20	—
Rock Machine I Love You			
(UK) CBS†	7 23 69	15	—
Rock Machine Turns You On			
(UK) CBS†	7 9 69	18	—
Shut Down			
(US) Capitol	1 18 64	14	—
Solid Gold Soul			
(UK) Atlantic	3 31 66	12	—
Stars Charity Fantasia			
(UK) SCF	9 15 66	6	5
Stars from Stars and Garters			
(UK) Golden Guinea†	3 26 64	17	—
Super Hits			
(US) Atlantic	9 16 67	12	—
Tamla Motown Hits, Vol. 5			
(UK) Tamla Motown	7 12 67	11	—
That'll Be the Day			
(UK) Ronco‡ (DLP)	6 23 73	1	8
That Was the Week That Was			
(US) Decca	1 25 64	5	2

	DATE OF ENTRY ON CHARTS	HIGHEST POSITION REACHED	NUMBER OF WEEKS ON CHARTS
This Is Soul (UK) Atlantic†	6 11 69	16	–
Thrill to the Sensational Super Stereo (UK) CBS	7 12 67	20	–
Tighten Up, Vol. 2 (UK) Trojan‡	1 3 70	2	3
Tijuana Christmas (UK) MFP‡	1 3 70	10	1
Twenty All-Time Hits of the '50s (UK) K-Tel†	10 7 72	1	15
Twenty Dynamic Hits (UK) K-Tel†	6 11 72	1	15
Twenty Fantastic Hits (UK) Arcade†	7 29 72	1	15
Twenty Fantastic Hits, Vol. 2 (UK) Arcade†	11 25 72	2	10
Twenty Fantastic Hits, Vol. 3 (UK) Arcade†	5 26 73	3	5
Twenty Flashback Greats of the '60s (UK) K-Tel†	3 31 73	1	6
Twenty Original Chart Hits (UK) Philips†	6 9 73	9	3
Twenty Star Tracks (UK) Ronco†	10 21 72	2	9
Twenty-five Rockin' and Rollin' Greats (UK) K-Tel†	12 2 72	1	10
Twenty-two Dynamic Hits, Vol. 2 (UK) K-Tel†	11 25 72	2	9

	DATE OF ENTRY ON CHARTS	HIGHEST POSITION REACHED	NUMBER OF WEEKS ON CHARTS
Ultimate Stereo Presentation			
(UK) EMI	1 3 70	14	–
Welcome to the LBJ Ranch			
(US) Capitol	12 4 65	3	6
Woodstock			
(US) Cotillion (TLP)	6 6 70	1	24
Woodstock 2			
(US) Cotillion (DLP)	4 17 71	7	2
World of Brass Bands			
(UK) Decca†	7 16 69	13	–
World of Hits			
(UK) Decca†	3 5 69	5	1
World of Hits, Vol. 2			
(UK) Decca†	9 6 69	7	2
World of Progressive Music (Wowie Zowie)			
(UK) Decca†	9 20 69	17	–
You Can All Join In			
(UK) Island†	6 11 69	18	–
You Don't Have to Be Jewish			
(US) Kapp	11 6 65	9	2

CHART TOPPERS
ALBUMS 1964–73

CHART TOPPERS

U. S. ALBUMS 1964–73

					WEEKS AT NO. 1
1964					
Jan.	4	Singing Nun	Singing Nun	Philips	6
Feb.	15	Beatles	Meet the Beatles	Capitol	11
May	2	Beatles	The Beatles' Second	Capitol	5
June	6	Original-cast	*Hello Dolly*	RCA	1
June	13	Louis Armstrong	*Hello Dolly*	Kapp	6
July	25	Beatles	*A Hard Day's Night*	United Artists	14
Oct.	31	Barbra Streisand	People	Columbia	5
Dec.	5	Beach Boys	Beach Boys' Concert	Capitol	4
1965					
Jan.	2	Elvis Presley	*Roustabout*	RCA	1
Jan.	9	Beatles	Beatles '65	Capitol	9
Mar.	13	Sound track	*Mary Poppins*	Vista	1
Mar.	20	Sound track	*Goldfinger*	United Artists	3
Apr.	10	Sound track	*Mary Poppins*	Vista	13
July	10	Beatles	Beatles VI	Capitol	6
Aug.	21	Rolling Stones	Out of Our Heads	London	3
Sept.	11	Beatles	*Help*	Capitol	9
Nov.	13	Sound track	*Sound of Music*	RCA	2
Nov.	27	Herb Alpert and the Tijuana Brass	Whipped Cream and Other Delights	A & M	6
1966					
Jan.	8	Beatles	Rubber Soul	Capitol	6

468

Feb.	19	Herb Alpert and the Tijuana Brass	Whipped Cream and Other Delights	A & M	2
Mar.	5	Herb Alpert and the Tijuana Brass	Going Places	A & M	1
Mar.	12	Barry Sadler	Ballad of the Green Berets	RCA	5
Apr.	16	Herb Alpert and the Tijuana Brass	Going Places	A & M	5
May	21	Mamas and Papas	If You Can Believe Your Eyes and Ears	Dunhill	1
May	28	Herb Alpert and the Tijuana Brass	What Now My Love	A & M	8
July	23	Frank Sinatra	Strangers in the Night	Reprise	1
July	30	Beatles	Yesterday and Today	Capitol	5
Sept.	3	Herb Alpert and the Tijuana Brass	What Now My Love	A & M	8
Sept.	10	Beatles	Revolver	Capitol	6
Oct.	22	Supremes	Supremes a Go Go	Motown	2
Nov.	5	Sound track	*Dr. Zhivago*	MGM	1
Nov.	12	Monkees	Monkees	Colgems	13

1967

Feb.	11	Monkees	More of the Monkees	Colgems	18
June	17	Herb Alpert and the Tijuana Brass	Sounds Like Herb Alpert	A & M	1
June	24	Monkees	Headquarters	Colgems	1
July	1	Beatles	Sgt. Pepper's Lonely Hearts Club Band	Capitol	15
Oct.	14	Bobbie Gentry	Ode to Billy Joe	Capitol	2
Oct.	28	Diana Ross and the Supremes	Greatest Hits	Motown	5
Dec.	2	Monkees	Pisces, Aquarius, Capricorn and Jones	Colgems	5

1968

Jan.	6	Beatles	Magical Mystery Tour	Capitol	8
Mar.	2	Paul Mauriat and Orchestra	Blooming Hits	Philips	5
Apr.	6	Sound track	*The Graduate*	Columbia	7
May	25	Simon and Garfunkel	Bookends	Columbia	3
June	15	Sound track	*The Graduate*	Columbia	2
June	29	Simon and Garfunkel	Bookends	Columbia	4
July	27	Herb Alpert and the Tijuana Brass	Beat of the Brass	A & M	2
Aug.	10	Cream	Wheels of Fire (DLP)	Atco	4
Sept.	7	Doors	Waiting for the Sun	Elektra	3
Sept.	28	Rascals	Time Peace/ Greatest Hits	Atlantic	1
Oct.	5	Doors	Waiting for the Sun	Elektra	1
Oct.	12	Big Brother and the Holding Company	Cheap Thrills	Columbia	5
Nov.	16	Jimi Hendrix Experience	Electric Ladyland (DLP)	Reprise	2
Nov.	30	Big Brother and the Holding Company	Cheap Thrills	Columbia	3
Dec.	21	Glen Campbell	Wichita Lineman	Capitol	1
Dec.	28	Beatles	Beatles (DLP)	Apple	3

1969

Feb.	8	Diana Ross and the Supremes with the Temptations	TCB	Motown	1
Feb.	15	Beatles	Beatles (DLP)	Apple	3
Mar.	8	Glen Campbell	Wichita Lineman	Capitol	1
Mar.	29	Blood, Sweat and Tears	Blood, Sweat and Tears	Columbia	1
Apr.	5	Glen Campbell	Wichita Lineman	Capitol	1
Apr.	12	Blood, Sweat and Tears	Blood, Sweat and Tears	Columbia	2

Apr.	26	Original-cast	*Hair*	RCA	13
July	26	Blood, Sweat and Tears	Blood, Sweat and Tears	Columbia	4
Aug.	23	Johnny Cash	At San Quentin	Columbia	4
Sept.	20	Blind Faith	Blind Faith	Atlantic	2
Oct.	4	Creedence Clearwater Revival	Green River	Fantasy	4
Nov.	1	Beatles	Abbey Road	Apple	8
Dec.	27	Led Zeppelin	Led Zeppelin II	Atlantic	1

1970

Jan.	3	Beatles	Abbey Road	Apple	2
Jan.	17	Led Zeppelin	Led Zeppelin II	Atlantic	1
Jan.	24	Beatles	Abbey Road	Apple	1
Jan.	31	Led Zeppelin	Led Zeppelin II	Atlantic	5
Mar.	7	Simon and Garfunkel	Bridge over Troubled Water	Columbia	10
May	16	Crosby, Stills, Nash and Young	Déjà Vu	Atlantic	1
May	23	Paul McCartney	McCartney	Apple	3
June	13	Beatles	Let It Be	Apple	4
July	11	Various artists	*Woodstock* (TLP)	Cotillion	4
Aug.	8	Blood, Sweat and Tears	Blood Sweat and Tears III	Columbia	2
Aug.	22	Creedence Clearwater Revival	Cosmo's Factory	Fantasy	9
Oct.	24	Santana	Abraxas	Columbia	1
Oct.	31	Led Zeppelin	Led Zeppelin III	Atlantic	4
Nov.	28	Santana	Abraxas	Columbia	5

1971

Jan.	2	George Harrison	All Things Must Pass (TLP)	Apple	7
Feb.	20	Various artists	*Jesus Christ Superstar*	Decca	1
Feb.	27	Janis Joplin	Pearl	Columbia	9
May	1	Various artists	*Jesus Christ Superstar*	Decca	2

May	15	Crosby, Stills, Nash and Young	4 Way Street (DLP)	Atlantic	1
May	22	Rolling Stones	Sticky Fingers	Rolling Stones	4
June	19	Carole King	Tapestry	Ode	15
Oct.	2	Rod Stewart	Every Picture Tells a Story	Mercury	4
Oct.	30	John Lennon	Imagine	Apple	1
Nov.	6	Sound track	*Shaft*	Enterprise	1
Nov.	13	Santana	Santana	Columbia	5
Dec.	18	Sly and the Family Stone	There's a Riot Goin' On	Epic	2

1972

Jan.	1	Carole King	Music	Ode	3
Jan.	22	Don McLean	American Pie	United Artists	7
Mar.	11	Neil Young	Harvest	Reprise	2
Mar.	25	America	America	Warner Brothers	5
Apr.	29	Roberta Flack	First Time Ever I Saw Your Face	Atlantic	5
June	3	Jethro Tull	Thick As a Brick	Reprise	2
June	17	Rolling Stones	Exiles on Main Street (DLP)	Rolling Stones	4
July	15	Elton John	Honky Chateau	UNI	5
Aug.	19	Chicago	Chicago V (DLP)	Columbia	9
Oct.	21	Curtis Mayfield	*Superfly*	Curtom	4
Nov.	18	Cat Stevens	Catch Bull at Four	A & M	3
Dec.	9	Moody Blues	Seventh Sojourn	Threshold	5

1973

Jan.	13	Carly Simon	No Secrets	Elektra	5
Feb.	17	War	The World Is a Ghetto	United Artists	2
Mar.	3	Elton John	Don't Shoot Me I'm Only the Piano Player	MCA	2
Mar.	17	Sound track	*Deliverance*	Warner Brothers	3

Apr.	7	Diana Ross	*Lady Sings the Blues* (DLP)	Motown	2
Apr.	21	Alice Cooper	Billion Dollar Babies	Warner Brothers	1
Apr.	28	Pink Floyd	Dark Side of the Moon	Harvest	1
May	5	Elvis Presley	Aloha from Hawaii via Satellite	RCA	1
May	12	Led Zeppelin	Houses of the Holy	Atlantic	2
May	26	Beatles	1967–70 (DLP)	Apple	1
June	2	Paul McCartney and Wings	Red Rose Speedway	Apple	3
June	23	George Harrison	Living in the Material World	Apple	5
July	28	Chicago	Chicago VI (DLP)	Columbia	3
Aug.	18	Jethro Tull	Passion Play	Chrysalis	1
Aug.	25	Chicago	Chicago VI (DLP)	Columbia	2
Sept.	8	Allman Brothers Band	Brothers and Sisters	Capricorn	5
Oct.	13	Rolling Stones	Goat's Head Soup	Rolling Stones	4
Nov.	30	Elton John	Goodbye Yellow Brick Road (DLP)	MCA	8

CHART TOPPERS
U.K. ALBUMS 1964–73

					WEEKS AT NO. 1
1964					
Jan.	2	Beatles	With the Beatles	Parlophone	17
Apr.	30	Rolling Stones	Rolling Stones	Decca	12
July	23	Beatles	A Hard Day's Night	Parlophone	21
Dec.	17	Beatles	Beatles for Sale	Parlophone	3
1965					
Jan.	7	Beatles	Beatles for Sale	Parlophone	4
Feb.	4	Rolling Stones	Rolling Stones, Vol. 2	Decca	3
Feb.	25	Beatles	Beatles for Sale	Parlophone	1
Mar.	4	Rolling Stones	Rolling Stones, Vol. 2	Decca	6
Apr.	15	Bob Dylan	Freewheelin'	CBS	1
Apr.	22	Rolling Stones	Rolling Stones, Vol. 2	Decca	1
Apr.	29	Beatles	Beatles for Sale	Parlophone	3
May	20	Bob Dylan	Freewheelin'	CBS	1
May	27	Bob Dylan	Bringing It All Back Home	CBS	1
June	3	Sound track	*Sound of Music*	RCA	10
Aug.	12	Beatles	Help	Parlophone	9
Oct.	14	Sound track	*Sound of Music*	RCA	10
Dec.	23	Beatles	Rubber Soul	Parlophone	2
1966					
Jan.	6	Beatles	Rubber Soul	Parlophone	6
Feb.	17	Sound track	*Sound of Music*	RCA	10
Apr.	28	Rolling Stones	Aftermath	Decca	8
June	23	Sound track	*Sound of Music*	RCA	7

Aug.	11	Beatles	Revolver	Parlophone	7
Sept.	29	Sound track	*Sound of Music*	RCA	14

1967

Jan.	5	Sound track	*Sound of Music*	RCA	4
Feb.	2	Monkees	The Monkees	RCA	7
Mar.	23	Sound track	*Sound of Music*	RCA	7
May	11	Monkees	More of the Monkees	RCA	1
May	18	Sound track	*Sound of Music*	RCA	1
May	25	Monkees	More of the Monkees	RCA	1
June	1	Sound track	*Sound of Music*	RCA	1
June	8	Beatles	Sgt. Pepper	Parlophone	23
Nov.	15	Sound track	*Sound of Music*	RCA	1
Nov.	22	Beatles	Sgt. Pepper	Parlophone	1
Nov.	29	Sound track	*Sound of Music*	RCA	2
Dec.	20	Beatles	Sgt. Pepper	Parlophone	2

1968

Jan.	3	Val Doonican	Val Doonican Rocks but Gently	Pye	3
Jan.	24	Sound track	*Sound of Music*	RCA	1
Jan.	31	Beatles	Sgt. Pepper	Parlophone	1
Feb.	7	Four Tops	Four Tops Greatest Hits	Tamla Motown	1
Feb.	14	Diana Ross and the Supremes	Diana Ross and the Supremes Greatest Hits	Tamla Motown	3
Mar.	6	Bob Dylan	John Wesley Harding	CBS	10
May	15	Scott Walker	Scott II	Philips	1
May	22	Bob Dylan	John Wesley Harding	CBS	3
June	12	Andy Williams	Love Andy	CBS	1
June	19	Otis Redding	Dock of the Bay	Stax	1
June	26	Small Faces	Ogden's Nut Gone Flake	Immediate	6
Aug.	7	Tom Jones	Delilah	Decca	1

Aug.	14	Simon and Garfunkel	Bookends	CBS	5
Sept.	18	Tom Jones	Delilah	Decca	1
Sept.	25	Simon and Garfunkel	Bookends	CBS	2
Oct.	9	Hollies	Hollies Greatest Hits	Parlophone	6
Nov.	20	Sound track	*Sound of Music*	RCA	1
Nov.	27	Hollies	Hollies Greatest Hits	Parlophone	1
Dec.	9	Beatles	Beatles (DLP)	Apple	4

1969

Jan.	1	Beatles	Beatles (DLP)	Apple	3
Jan.	22	Seekers	Best of the Seekers	Columbia	1
Jan.	29	Beatles	Beatles (DLP)	Apple	1
Feb.	5	Seekers	Best of the Seekers	Columbia	1
Feb.	12	Diana Ross and the Supremes	Join the Temptations	Tamla Motown	3
Mar.	5	Seekers	Four and Only Seekers	MFP	2
Mar.	19	Cream	Goodbye	Polydor	2
Mar.	26	Seekers	Best of the Seekers	Columbia	2
Apr.	9	Cream	Goodbye	Polydor	1
Apr.	16	Seekers	Best of the Seekers	Columbia	1
Apr.	23	Cream	Goodbye	Polydor	1
Apr.	30	Seekers	Best of the Seekers	Columbia	1
May	7	Moody Blues	On the Threshold of a Dream	Deram	2
May	21	Bob Dylan	Nashville Skyline	CBS	4
June	18	Ray Conniff	His Orchestra, His Chorus, His Singers, His Sounds	CBS	3
July	9	Jim Reeves	According to My Heart	RCA	4
Aug.	2	Jethro Tull	Stand Up	Island	3
Aug.	30	Elvis Presley	From Elvis in Memphis	RCA	1

Sept. 6	Jethro Tull	Stand Up	Island	2
Sept. 20	Blind Faith	Blind Faith	Polydor	2
Oct. 4	Beatles	Abbey Road	Apple	11
Dec. 20	Rolling Stones	Let It Bleed	Decca	1
Dec. 27	Beatles	Abbey Road	Apple	1

1970

Jan. 3	Beatles	Abbey Road	Apple	5
Feb. 7	Led Zeppelin	Led Zeppelin II	Atlantic	1
Feb. 14	Various Artists	Motown Chartbusters, Vol. 3	Tamla Motown	1
Feb. 21	Simon and Garfunkel	Bridge over Troubled Water	CBS	12
May 23	Beatles	Let It Be	Apple	3
June 13	Simon and Garfunkel	Bridge over Troubled Water	CBS	4
July 11	Bob Dylan	Self Portrait (DLP)	CBS	1
July 18	Simon and Garfunkel	Bridge over Troubled Water	CBS	5
Aug. 22	Moody Blues	A Question of Balance	Threshold	3
Sept. 12	Creedence Clearwater Revival	Cosmos Factory	Liberty	1
Sept. 19	Rolling Stones	Get Yer Ya Ya's Out	Decca	2
Oct. 3	Simon and Garfunkel	Bridge over Troubled Water	CBS	1
Oct. 10	Black Sabbath	Paranoid	Vertigo	1
Oct. 17	Simon and Garfunkel	Bridge over Troubled Water	CBS	1
Oct. 24	Pink Floyd	Atom Heart Mother	Harvest	1
Oct. 31	Various artists	Motown Chartbusters, Vol. 4	Tamla Motown	1
Nov. 7	Led Zeppelin	Led Zeppelin III	Atlantic	3
Nov. 28	Bob Dylan	New Morning	CBS	1

Dec.	5	Andy Williams	Andy Williams Greatest Hits	CBS	1
Dec.	12	Led Zeppelin	Led Zeppelin III	Atlantic	2
Dec.	19	Andy Williams	Andy Williams Greatest Hits	CBS	2

1971

Jan.	2	Andy Williams	Andy Williams Greatest Hits	CBS	1
Jan.	9	Simon and Garfunkel	Bridge over Troubled Water	CBS	4
Feb.	6	Print strike			
Apr.	3	Andy Williams	Home-Loving Man	CBS	2
Apr.	17	Various artists	Motown Chartbusters, Vol. 5	Tamla Motown	3
May	8	Rolling Stones	Sticky Fingers	Rolling Stones	4
June	5	Paul and Linda McCartney	Ram	Apple	3
June	26	Emerson, Lake and Palmer	Tarkus	Island	1
July	3	Simon and Garfunkel	Bridge over Troubled Water	CBS	5
Aug.	7	Moody Blues	Every Good Boy Deserves Favor	Threshold	4
Sept.	4	Simon and Garfunkel	Bridge over Troubled Water	CBS	2
Sept.	18	Who	Who's Next	Track	1
Sept.	25	Deep Purple	Fireball	Harvest	1
Oct.	2	Rod Stewart†	Every Picture Tells a Story	Parlophone	4
Oct.	30	John Lennon	Imagine	Apple	2
Nov.	13	Rod Stewart	Every Picture Tells a Story	Parlophone	3
Dec.	4	Led Zeppelin	Runes	Atlantic	2
Dec.	18	T Rex	Electric Warrior	Fly	2

1972

| Jan. | 1 | T Rex | Electric Warrior | Fly | 4 |

				WEEKS AT NO. 1
Jan.	29	Various artists	Concert for Bangladesh (TLP)	Apple	1
Feb.	5	T Rex	Electric Warrior	Fly	2
Feb.	19	Neil Reed	Neil Reed	Decca	3
Mar.	11	Neil Young	Harvest	Reprise	1
Mar.	18	Paul Simon	Paul Simon	CBS	1
Mar.	25	Lindisfarne	Fog on the Tyne	Charisma	4
Apr.	22	Deep Purple	Machine Head	Purple	2
May	6	Tyrannosaurus Rex	Doubleback (DLP)	Fly	1
May	13	Deep Purple	Machine Head	Purple	1
May	20	T Rex	Bolan Boogie	Fly	3
June	11	Rolling Stones	Exiles on Main Street (DLP)	Rolling Stones	1
June	18	Various artists	20 Dynamite Hits	K-Tel	8
Aug.	12	Various artists	20 Fantastic Hits	Arcade	5
Sept.	16	Rod Stewart	Never a Dull Moment	Mercury	2
Sept.	30	Various artists	20 Fantastic Hits	Arcade	1
Oct.	7	Various artists	20 All Time Hits of the 50's	K-Tel	8
Dec.	2	Various artists	25 Rockin' and Rollin' Greats	K-Tel	3
Dec.	23	Various artists	20 All Time Hits of the 50's	K-Tel	2

1973

Jan.	6	Various artists	Twenty All Time Hits	K-Tel	1
Jan.	13	Slade	Slayed?	Polydor	1
Jan.	20	Gilbert O'Sullivan	Back to Front	MAM	1
Jan.	27	Slade	Slayed?	Polydor	2
Feb.	10	Elton John	Don't Shoot Me I'm Only the Piano Player	DJM	6
Mar.	24	Alice Cooper	Billion Dollar Babies	Warner Brothers	1
Mar.	31	Various artists	Twenty Flash-Back Greats of the '60s	K-Tel	2

Apr.	14	Led Zeppelin	Houses of the Holy	Atlantic	2
Apr.	28	Faces	Ooh-La-La	Warner Brothers	1
May	5	David Bowie	Aladdin Sane	RCA	5
June	2	Various artists	Pure Gold	EMI	3
June	30	Various artists	*That'll Be the Day* (DLP)	Ronco	7
Aug.	18	Peters and Lee	We Can Make It	Philips	2
Sept.	1	Rod Stewart	Sing It Again Rod	Mercury	3
Sept.	22	Rolling Stones	Goat's Head Soup	Rolling Stones	2
Oct.	6	Slade	Sladest	Polydor	3
Oct.	27	Status Quo	Hello	Vertigo	1
Nov.	3	David Bowie	Pin-Ups	RCA	5
Dec.	8	Roxy Music	Stranded	Island	1
Dec.	15	David Cassidy	Dreams Are Nothin' More Than Wishes	Bell	1
Dec.	22	Elton John	Goodbye Yellow Brick Road (DLP)	DJM	1

ROLL CALL
OF HIT MAKERS
ALBUMS, 1964–73

ROLL CALL OF HIT MAKERS—ALBUMS, 1964–73

TOTAL NUMBER OF HITS	ARTIST	NUMBER OF HITS IN USA	NUMBER OF HITS IN UK
28	Elvis Presley	18	26
25	Beatles	21	15
24	Rolling Stones	20	17
21	Frank Sinatra	14	15
20	Beach Boys	10	16
	Diana Ross/& Supremes	15	12
	Andy Williams	11	12
19	Jim Reeves	1	19
17	Temptations	17	7
15	Tom Jones	7	13
13	Herb Alpert & the Tijuana Brass	10	7
	Bob Dylan	10	13
12	Aretha Franklin	12	1
	Barbra Streisand	12	1
11	Donovan	7	5
10	Jimi Hendrix	9	9
	Peter, Paul & Mary	10	3
	Supremes	7	4
9	Glen Campbell	7	3
	Johnny Cash	3	9
	Dean Martin	8	2
	Three Dog Night	9	–
8	Joan Baez	5	7
	Dave Clark Five	6	2
	Cream	5	8

TOTAL NUMBER OF HITS	ARTIST	NUMBER OF HITS	
		IN USA	IN UK
	Grand Funk Railroad	8	–
	Jefferson Airplane	8	–
	Elton John	7	6
	Kinks	2	6
	Pink Floyd	1	8
	Cliff Richard	–	8
	Seekers	1	7
	Who	5	8
7	Byrds	4	5
	David Cassidy/Partridge Family	5	4
	Creedence Clearwater Revival	7	3
	Doors	7	2
	Four Tops	4	6
	Isaac Hayes	7	1
	Herman's Hermits	6	1
	Jackson Five	7	1
	Jethro Tull	6	7
	John Mayall	–	7
	Moody Blues	6	6
	Roy Orbison	1	6
	Otis Redding	3	6
	Dionne Warwick	5	3
6	Animals	3	4
	Bachelors	–	6
	Max Bygraves	–	6
	Carpenters	5	5
	Chicago	6	2
	Bill Cosby	6	–
	Neil Diamond	6	3
	Fifth Dimension	6	–
	Hollies	1	6
	Engelbert Humperdinck	6	6
	Jack Jones	3	3
	Mamas & Papas	5	3
	Donny Osmond	4	4
	Gene Pitney	–	6
	Righteous Brothers	6	–
	Steppenwolf	6	1
	Traffic	5	3

ROLL CALL OF HIT MAKERS—ALBUMS, 1964–73   483

TOTAL NUMBER OF HITS	ARTIST	NUMBER OF HITS IN USA	IN UK
	Nancy Wilson	6	–
	Young Rascals	6	–
5	Shirley Bassey	–	5
	Bee Gees	5	5
	George Mitchell/Black & White Minstrels	–	5
	Black Sabbath	3	5
	David Bowie	2	5
	Nat "King" Cole	3	2
	Eric Clapton/Derek & the Dominos	5	2
	Deep Purple	3	5
	Val Doonican	–	5
	Emerson, Lake & Palmer	4	5
	Family	–	5
	Al Hirt	5	–
	James Last	–	5
	Led Zeppelin	5	5
	John Lennon/Plastic Ono Band	4	4
	Lettermen	5	–
	Trini Lopez	4	2
	Henry Mancini	5	–
	Mantovani	–	5
	Paul McCartney/Wings	4	5
	Monkees	5	4
	Osmonds	4	3
	Paul Revere & the Raiders	5	–
	Santana	4	4
	Shadows	–	5
	Simon and Garfunkel	4	5
	Cat Stevens	4	5
	Rod Stewart/Faces	3	5
	Ten Years After	3	4
	T. Rex	1	5
	Yes	3	5
4	28 artists		
3	53 artists		
2	58 artists		
1	202 artists		

CUMULATIVE STATISTICS

	NUMBER OF ARTISTS		
NUMBER OF HITS	ALL TOGETHER	IN U.S.A.	IN U.K.
one or more	438	292	266
only one	202	136	116
more than one	236	156	160
ten or more	18	13	10

44